WE ARE ALL LIVING WITH
AIDS

 Silence = Death    Action = Life

WE ARE ALL LIVING WITH
AIDS

How You Can Set
Policies and Guidelines
for the Workplace

Earl C. Pike

Deaconess Press

Minneapolis

Library of Congress Cataloging-in-Publication Data

Pike, Earl C. (Earl Claude), 1956—
    We are all living with AIDS : how you can set policies and
guidelines for the workplace / Earl C. Pike
             p.   cm.
    Includes bibliographical references.
    ISBN 0-925190-68-3 (pbk.)
    1. AIDS (Disease)   2. Industrial hygiene.   3. Personnel
management.   I. Title.
RA644.A25P52   1993
362.1'969892--dc20   93-26894
                                                                                                                                                  CIP

    We Are All Living With AIDS © 1993 by Earl C. Pike
    All Rights reserved. No part of this publication may be used or reproduced in any manner whatsoever without written permission, except in the case of brief quotations embodied in critical articles and reviews. For further information, please contact the publisher.

    Published by Deaconess Press (a service of Fairview Riverside Medical Center, a division of Fairview Hospital and Healthcare Services, 2450 Riverside Avenue South, Minneapolis, MN 55454).

    Cover design by Tabor Harlow.
    Cover art by Kathy Rogers.

    First Printing: September 1993
    Printed in the United States of America

96 95 94 93   7 6 5 4 3 2 1

    Publisher's Note: Deaconess Press publishes books and other materials related to the subjects of physical health, mental health, and chemical dependency. Its publications, including *We Are All Living With AIDS*, do not necessarily reflect the philosophy of Fairview Hospital and Healthcare Services or their treatment programs.

    For a current catalog of Deaconess Press titles,
    please call this Toll-Free number: 1-800-544-8207.

Dedication

It is perhaps uncustomary to provide a dedication for a book of this kind. But the fight against HIV and AIDS has challenged, and rightfully so, much that is "customary," and one more challenge cannot hurt. I therefore dedicate this book to Perry Tilleraas, Eric Lerner, and "Wee-zee" Hoeschler, whose passions and loves in the fight against AIDS helped many of us remember what it was all about: that our lives are tempestuous, sometimes heavy with pain and sometimes wild with joy, and ultimately, always, precious and sacred.

About the Symbols

The origins of the red ribbon (depicted on the cover of this book) as a symbol for concern about AIDS are murky, but it is commonly believed to be a creation of the group "Visual AIDS" which introduced it in 1991.

Wearing a red ribbon has become popular, even somewhat trendy in a few circles. Some AIDS activists even contend that it has lost its meaning through overuse. Others still consider the ribbon a source of both financial assistance (since it is sometimes used to raise funds) and moral support for people living with HIV or AIDS.

I say wear the ribbon. As a symbol, it's important. But remember: it should never be a hollow gesture. Wear it as a commitment to do something about AIDS, as a promise to remember, as a dedication to work for an end to discrimination, an end to isolation and rejection, an end to hate. Wear it; make it mean something.

On the title page, the symbol "Silence = Death" first began appearing in New York City in the early 1980s, serving as a call to activism among people with HIV/AIDS and the people who cared about them. It is often credited to ACT-UP (the AIDS Coalition To Unleash Power).

The corollary symbol, "Action = Life," began appearing in more recent years.

I've always supported the proposition that silence—or apathy or inertia or lethargy or passivity—in the face of this epidemic is ultimately an acquiescence, either physical or metaphorical. But I've sometimes thought that "Silence = Death" is, alone, insufficient. So when its companion symbol surfaced—"Action = Life"—it seemed to me that the two equations together epitomize much of the essence of the current struggle against HIV and AIDS...and for life.

Acknowledgements

There are at least three groups of people I need to acknowledge for their generous assistance and support in the development of this book.

First of all, I want to thank the Minnesota AIDS Funding Consortium and my project liaison, Mary Hunter. They provided me with a grant that gave me the time, freedom, and economic resources to write the book, and were patient with my requests for help (and extensions of deadlines).

When I first started on *We Are All Living With AIDS,* I realized that it would be a good idea to assemble a sort of personal advisory committee—a group that could guide me, and perhaps, as needed, tell me I was off-base. I gathered together a small team of people whose thinking about HIV and related issues I trusted a great deal, who I respected personally, politically, and intellectually. They were fantastic. The committee was composed of the following people, the second group to which I owe my heartfelt appreciation:

Jolynn Blaeser	Sharon Day	Janet Flood
Leo Guzman	Jonathan Hanft	Mary Hunter
Elizabeth Klein	Fraser Nelson	Tim Reardon
Jennifer Reinhart	Sally Swallen	Kim Sundet
Stella West	Cindy Zegers	

And the following people reviewed various drafts of the book, and provided incisive feedback and advice. Their comments and viewpoints were invaluable (organizational affiliations are listed for purposes of identification only).

Cordelia Anderson, Sensibilities, Inc.
Julia Ashley, Minnesota AIDS Project
Terry Backhaus, West Central Community Service Center (Willmar, MN)
Sara Baron, St. Paul Red Cross
Lori Beaulieu, Minnesota Indian Women's Resource Center
Linda Brandt, Rural AIDS Action Network
Dan Capouch, Hennepin County (MN) Social Services
Kevin Cwayna, M.D., Hemophilia Treatment Center
Lori Dablow, Developmental Disabilities Division, MN Dept. of Human Services
Norma Denbrook, Corrections AIDS Prevention Program, Hennepin County (MN) Community Health
Nancy Devitt, Hennepin County (MN) Planning
Gayle Dixon, Minnesota AIDS Project Legal Program
Vern Drilling, LaMancha Corporation
Linda Ernst, Minneapolis Red Cross
Dorothy Flynn, Hazelden Institute

Tom Flynn, private consultant
Dan Ford, Minnesota AIDS Project
Karen Helfand, Chicanos Latinos Unidos en Servicios
Carlton Hogan, Community Programs for Clinical Research on AIDS (Statistical Centers)
Mariann Johnson, Arts Over AIDS
Sara Judson, private consultant
Kara Korach, St. Paul Jewish Community Center
Pat Lamb, Employee Assistance Program, Cargill Corporation
Frank Lamendola, Journeywell
Susan Langston, Hennepin County (MN) Social Services
Al Mayotte, Austin Community College
Beth O'Neill, Chicago AIDS Foundation
Carolyn Patierno, Sex Education and Information Council of the U. S. (New York)
Barb Perrin, Abbott Northwestern Chemical Dependency Treatment Program
Frank Rhame, M.D., University of Minnesota Hospitals
Jim Rothenberger, University of Minnesota School of Public Health
Steven Schaefer, Ramsey Hospital HIV Program
Sandra Schwartzer, New Beginnings at Waverly
Tom Soles, Crisis Connection
Patsy Stinchfield, Children's Hospital
Scott Strickland, M.D., Park-Nicollet Medical Center
Edward Wedman, Deaconess Press, Fairview Hospital and Healthcare Services
Taylor Wilcox, Youth and AIDS Program

For their assistance and support, thanks also go to: Mike Moen, Minnesota Department of Health; Ruth Ellen Luehr, Minnesota Department of Education; and Carol Falkowski, Minnesota Department of Human Services.

Finally, I would be remiss if I failed to extend my ongoing thanks to Jay Johnson, my editor at Deaconess Press, whose unfailing commitment to this project (as well as some appropriate nagging) helped shepherd its completion.

And, as always, my immeasurable thanks to EDK.

TABLE OF CONTENTS

Introduction xiii
A Note on National and International Resources xv
Before You Start xvii

Section One: Policy Areas 1

Chapter 1: The Ethical Basis for Policy 3
Chapter 2: Discrimination and Access to Services/Benefits 7
Chapter 3: Infection Control/Universal Precautions 17
Chapter 4: Client and Staff Education 25
Chapter 5: HIV Antibody Testing 35
Chapter 6: Confidentiality 45
Chapter 7: Clinical Care of HIV-Infected Clients 61
Chapter 8: HIV-Related Issues—Nurturing Diversity 79
Chapter 9: Shaping Policy for Business Settings 89
    Assessing Workplace Readiness materials 102
    Survey Instruments: 108
    Coming to Terms with AIDS: Organizational Stages 109
    AIDS and the Organization 122
    AIDS and the Organization: Scoring 123
    HIV/AIDS Questionnaire 124
    HIV/AIDS Questionnaire: Scoring 129
    Beliefs and Attitudes about Bisexuality/Homosexuality 135
    Beliefs and Attitudes about Bisexuality/Homosexuality: Scoring 138

Section Two: Policy from Beginning to End 141

Chapter 10: Taking Action: Policy from Beginning to End 143
    Step One: Deciding 145
    Step Two: Researching 149
    Step Three: Surveying/Assessing 157
    Step Four: Planning 161
    Step Five: Implementing 171

Step Six: Evaluating	177
Chapter 11: Sample Policies	179
ABC Agency HIV/AIDS Policy Statement	180
Oak Manors, Inc. AIDS Policy/Procedures	182
A Caring Agency, Inc. HIV/AIDS Policy	184
Memo: Administration of AIDS Questionnaire	187
Memo: Confidentiality of A Caring Agency, Inc. Clients and HIV	188
Memo: Education for Clients with HIV	189
Anytown Municipal Hospital Approved Policy on HIV/AIDS	190
Care of the Patient with Human Immunodeficiency Virus (HIV)	196
Form: Patient Authorization Human Immunodeficiency Virus (HIV) Testing	200
Guidelines for Obtaining Consent for HIV Testing (Non-Healthcare Worker Exposure)	201
Form: Consent for Communicable Disease Blood Testing	203
Careplace HIV/AIDS Policy Statement	204
About the HIV Antibody Test ("the AIDS Test")	207
Program Statement About HIV/AIDS	208
Statement: Client HIV Status	209
Turnaround House, Inc. HIV Virus Guideline	210
Human Immunodeficiency Virus (HIV) Policy and Procedure Manual	211
County Policy Statement Regarding AIDS in the Workplace	216
HIV Antibody Testing Policy, Yellowstone Treatment Center	219
Crisis Concern Services, HIV/AIDS Policy	221
Memo: Brown Printing Company, Corporate Policy	222
Cedarwood Community College, Policy on AIDS and HIV	224
State College Coordinating Board Policies and Regulations: Requirements for All Colleges Regarding AIDS	228
Affiliated Arts Alliance HIV/AIDS Policy	230
Minnesota Dept. of Human Services Policy Statement: Infection Control/Universal Precautions	233
Recommendations for Prevention of HIV Transmission in Healthcare Settings	238
OSHA Compliance Assistance Guideline for Enforcement Procedures for Occupational Exposure to HBV and HIV	257

Section Three: Special Policy Considerations for Particular Populations   265

HIV, Children, and Family Law: Legal and Policy Issues for Care Providers	268
Agencies Serving the Severely and Persistently Mentally Ill	273
Employee Assistance Programs	276
Arts Organizations: Arts Over AIDS—Education and Initiatives	278
Substance Abuse Treatment and Care Programs	281
Primary Healthcare Settings	282

Special Note for Healthcare Workers 286
Community Mental Health Centers 288
Homeless Populations/Homelessness and HIV: Problems and Recommendations 291
Cultural Communities 299
Native American Communities 300
HIV/AIDS and Correctional Facilities 302
Agencies Serving People with Developmental Disabilities 309
Agencies Serving Adolescents 312
Disability in the Workplace 314
Religious Institutions/The Atlanta Declaration 321
School/Educational Settings 325
Women's Programs 330

Section Four: Support Materials 333

Resource Sheets for Staff Training and Education:
    About HIV and AIDS 335
    Evaluating AIDS Data and Media Reporting 339
    How HIV is Transmitted 341
    Safer Sex and Risk Reduction 343
    HIV Antibody Testing 345
    Discrimination 347
    Confidentiality 348
    Infection Control 349
    Pre/Post-Test for HIV/AIDS Training 350
    Taking Care of Yourself in the Face of HIV/AIDS 354
    When a Friend Has AIDS 355
    Educational Materials 357
    HIV/AIDS Terminology 366
    Commonly Used HIV (and General Medical) Terms 371
    Common HIV (and Medical) Abbreviations 373
    Common HIV Medications in Use 375

Section Five: Appendices 377

Informational Bulletin No. 89-53A (The Minnesota Health Threat Procedures Act) 379
Daily Care of the Child with AIDS, HIV Infection, and Related Conditions 383
Resources: 388
    National HIV/AIDS Referral Lines and Hotlines 388
    National Organizations, Foundations, and Coalitions 388
    Federal Government Agencies 394
    Policy Research Groups and Clearinghouses 396

INTRODUCTION

I wanted to write *We Are All Living With AIDS* because I was frustrated, and because I suspect that you may be frustrated as well.

We are now in the second decade of the HIV/AIDS epidemic. Friends of mine have died from this disease, and I will probably see more people, people I love, die before the whole thing is over. You, the reader, may have had the same experience.

For far too long far too little was done to recognize, face, and address HIV and its effects on millions of people. Many individuals—and agencies and businesses and governments—were too frightened, too appalled, too angry, too repulsed, too occupied, too *whatever* to respond. Even some of the best-intentioned people were sometimes hoping that the whole terrifying, confusing disease would just go away.

It didn't, and it won't anytime soon.

And consulting with workplaces of almost every stripe, serving a wide variety of clients and customers, I have come to recognize how critical the organization's role is, and will be, in fighting this epidemic—both in terms of treating clients and employees with HIV or AIDS well, and in terms of providing education and support for behavior change to reduce the transmission of HIV.

Still, many workplaces haven't yet developed HIV policy or provided education about HIV. And I don't think it's merely that workplaces have been resistant to dealing with HIV and HIV-related issues—though, certainly, HIV has evoked a lot of strong emotional reactions. As often as not, I think workplaces haven't developed needed policy because they don't know *how*— and sometimes, they don't even know where to start. It's not for lack of intelligence or sophistication or, most of the time, caring. It's just that when you combine what seems like the complicated information about HIV, along with the range of feelings that usually attend the issue, it's no wonder that individuals and workplaces as a whole feel overwhelmed, incapacitated, stuck.

This book doesn't try to convince you that there is a need for HIV policy in workplaces and human service organizations and private businesses. I'm assuming that if you've picked up this book, it's because you already see that need. Rather, *We Are All Living With AIDS* is designed to help individuals and workplaces get *unstuck*. It's geared toward workplaces of every variety, and can be employed by boards, managers, or line staff from those organizations. It discusses not only the specifics of HIV/AIDS policy, but also the particular and sometimes unique obstacles that individuals may encounter in the policy development process. It will help you and your organization get ready for HIV/AIDS.

The book is separated into four sections:

- *The first section,* Policy Areas, *provides background information on eight different HIV/AIDS policy subtopics that the workplace will want to address in order to create a comprehensive HIV/AIDS policy. Survey instruments to gauge the worksite's knowledge and attitudes about HIV are also included.*

- Policy from Beginning to End *outlines the process of HIV/AIDS policy development. It provides you with everything you need to initiate, guide, and conclude HIV/AIDS policy development—including sample agendas for a policy planning group.*

- Special Policy Considerations for Particular Populations *was written by experts in each identified area. Although the core of policy remains the same across many workplace populations, the details may vary. With the inclusion of this section, you won't have to translate a body of policy knowledge for your setting.*

- Support Materials *consists of a series of Resource Sheets on HIV/AIDS and HIV/AIDS-related topics. They'll provide you with the training and staff education materials you'll need to effectively implement policy.* Feel free to reproduce these materials.

The scope and architecture of this book is designed so that you will find most everything you need herein and be able to use it, practically and effectively, to develop policy.

I should note that when the book was first drafted, its target audience was almost exclusively human service agencies in the state of Minnesota. Since then, it has undergone considerable revision to reach audiences in all states, and across national borders. Its focus has also shifted to embrace workplaces, both for-profit and non-profit, without jettisoning the discussions of particular "client-service" topics that will be of concern primarily to human service agencies. In its present form it should be of use to any workplace, in nearly any locale.

One more comment needs to be made by way of introduction. In the time during which this book was developed, some important debates about certain aspects of HIV/AIDS were still being aired. The awareness of an HIV-infected doctor in Minnesota, for example, in addition to news of the HIV-infected dentist in Florida, renewed discussion about the possibility of mandating HIV antibody testing for healthcare workers.

The general public often views such discussions from a distance and shakes its collective head—it's all too confusing, the facts keep changing, there's nothing you can count on. Policymakers, in turn, may he hesitant to develop policy when some discussions are not yet fully resolved, believing it better to wait.

Nothing could be further from the truth. Although debate continues in some arenas, the vast body of knowledge, and the mass of policy that has derived from it, is constant. Administrators need not avoid policy development for fear that "things will change." If anything, workplaces should be concerned about the *absence* of policy and the legal vulnerability that such absence creates. If you don't have policy, there's no reason to wait: the epidemic is here, and the time is now.

A NOTE ON NATIONAL AND INTERATIONAL RESOURCES

Most of what is found in *We Are All Living With AIDS* will prove appropriate for nearly any locale. The policy development process, for example, does not depend on geography. Neither do the sections on *Client Education, Infection Control, Clinical Care of HIV-Infected Clients,* and *Diversity.* But in some areas—antibody testing, confidentiality, and discrimination—there are minor variations among different states and provinces, both in terms of the details of law and procedural questions.

Workplaces in states other than Minnesota, as well as other countries, will want to base their HIV/AIDS policies on the regulations in their area. Therefore, they will need to supplement this book with additional information.

It's not as laborious as it may seem. In fact, a handful of resources should be able to provide you with most of the information you need.

The first, the **AIDS Policy Project,** will be of special assistance to most states and territories within the U. S. Established in 1987 by the Intergovernmental Health Policy Project at Georgetown University, the AIDS Policy Project monitors and reports on HIV/AIDS law and policy on a state-by-state and federal basis. They publish summaries of that research, which detail each state's laws and regulations about confidentiality, discrimination, HIV antibody testing, and a host of other HIV-related concerns. The summaries are comprehensive and very accessible. Used as an adjunct to *We Are All Living With AIDS,* social service and business professionals in any locale should be able to develop the comprehensive HIV/AIDS policy outlined in this book.

It would be convenient to some to reproduce state-by-state laws and regulations in this volume, but it would automatically double its size and constitute an unnecessary redundancy. You are encouraged to contact the AIDS Policy Project directly at:

> AIDS Policy Project
> Intergovernmental Health Policy Project
> 2011 I Street, N.W.
> Suite 200
> Washington, D.C. 20006
> (202) 872-1445

The second resource is a fairly exhaustive paperback called ***How to Find Information about AIDS*** (Huber, J. T., ed. Binghampton, NY: Harrington Park Press, 1992. Second edition. $14.95). Huber's book lists just about every organizational resource in the United States and provides information on their services. Listed are both community-based organizations and governmental offices, including research institutions, health departments, hotlines, print and electronic information sources, and audiovisual producers. Some of those resources are included in this book, of course, but *How to Find Information About AIDS* stands as one of the most comprehensive catalogs.

A third resource will be of particular use to readers outside the United States. ***AIDS in the World: A Global Report*** (Mann, J., Tarantola, D.J.M., & Netter, T.W., eds. Cambridge, MA: Harvard University Press, 1992) is a massive 1,037-page book, a rich and phenomenally wide-ranging work that surveys AIDS and AIDS-related issues in every country of the world where information could be obtained. It includes essential information on policies and programs in many parts of the world, and even reviews current political and policy debates of an international character.

A significant portion of the data in *AIDS in the World: A Global Report* originates, in one way or another, from the work of the **World Health Organization's Global Programme on AIDS** (WHO/GPA). International readers unfamiliar with policy activities and directives in their region will want to begin by researching local resources; WHO/GPA can help point you in the right direction. They can be contacted at:

>World Health Organization
>Global Programme on AIDS
>1121 Geneva 27
>Switzerland

Canadian readers can contact their national AIDS office directly at:

>Federal Centre for AIDS
>301 Elgin Street
>Ottawa, Canada K1A 0L2
>(613) 957-1772

I want to take one more opportunity to reassure the reader, wherever she or he may live, that the implementation of comprehensive HIV/AIDS policy need not be overly-intimidating. It can be done—but I would be misleading if I proposed that it was effortless. That it may demand hard work is somewhat arguable. That it is necessary work is incontestable.

Before You Start

"I never thought we'd have to deal with it. We're in a small town. Our clients aren't promiscuous and don't shoot up drugs. And when Jim came, it caught us all completely off guard."
—Director of a mental health facility, speaking about
a new HIV seropositive client

"When Leslie [a co-worker] told me her husband had AIDS, I was blown away. I didn't know what to say. I still don't."
—Advertising executive

"I wouldn't create a new service. I would just make what is current more efficient to the client. There's massive amounts of red tape. The guy's half-dead as it is and has to run around getting papers."
—A person with AIDS

As the HIV/AIDS epidemic enters its second decade, workplaces around the world are beginning to realize that they need to prepare for the possible consequences that HIV/AIDS brings. For many, that's a frightening prospect. In the beginning it seemed that only certain social service agencies, like substance abuse treatment programs, needed to seriously address HIV/AIDS and its attendant issues. But one by one other social service programs and private sector businesses are being impacted—community mental health centers, daycare sites, group homes, schools, primary healthcare clinics, disability services, and many, many others. The program or business that has yet to face HIV/AIDS, in some form or another, is rapidly becoming the exception, not the norm.

This book is designed to help you get ready.

That process may appear overwhelming. But "getting ready" for HIV/AIDS comes down to three simple things:

- *Appropriate policy;*

- *Trained, sensitive staff; and*
- *On-going mechanisms for policy implementation and staff training.*

"Appropriate policy" means that the workplace has, in writing, guidelines and rules to address the critical legal, administrative, and clinical aspects of HIV/AIDS. Some of those areas are relatively simple and straightforward; others are a little more complicated. But a significant number of organizations have already tackled the task successfully. It can be done.

"Trained, sensitive staff" implies that employees understand at least the basics about HIV/AIDS and can respond to dilemmas and challenges in a knowledgeable and clinically appropriate manner. The facts about HIV/AIDS may be cast in complex language, beyond the reach of the non-medical layperson, but in reality they are entirely accessible to most everybody. Of course, the more staff know the better equipped they will be to handle a variety of situations, but it is not necessary that everyone become an "expert." Programs need only ensure that all staff meet a minimum standard of awareness.

And "on-going mechanisms" indicates that policy and training are not stagnant, time-limited activities. There are two reasons this is true, especially in the case of HIV/AIDS. First, as everyone who has worked in a social service agency or private sector business knows, the existence of policy that is not consistently implemented renders that policy useless. The program that states, "sure, we have a policy about that here somewhere—but we're not sure what it says" may as well not have policy at all. Policy needs to be an animated thing, something that guides and shapes the daily work of employees. Second, the legal and clinical environment of HIV/AIDS does shift, and even well-designed policy requires occasional review, and perhaps revision. For example, there are now treatments available to people who are infected with HIV but who do not show any symptoms; some of those treatments can slow down the rate at which the virus reproduces in the body. The fact that early medical intervention is possible has meant that HIV antibody testing (one of the policy areas addressed in this book) is a much more viable option for many people.

"Getting ready," then, is fairly elementary. What often makes it *feel* daunting is the fact that it is difficult to discuss HIV and AIDS without broaching some fairly difficult and sometimes delicate topics: human sexuality and sexual behavior, homosexuality, drug use, sickness and death, and more. This book will help guide you through the process of change on both levels—outlining the objective steps that workplaces need to take to prepare for HIV/AIDS, and navigating the subjective realities that can sabotage effective change.

Policy Development, Personal Awareness, and Organizational Change

Ultimately, getting ready for HIV/AIDS implies that your organization will change. Organizational change, in this instance, is driven by the twin engines of policy and awareness. Policy without a staff sufficiently knowledgeable to carry out its dictates is empty; awareness, without the guidance of policy, means that workplace and social service professionals are constantly reinventing the wheel.

The task of policy development and implementation intimidates a lot of people. It is often viewed as a specialized, almost mystical skill that few can claim. It is not. Policy development follows a logical series of steps that many people, supplied with the right information and proper direction, can follow. Perhaps the most basic way to characterize policy is that *it is a statement of organizational beliefs or values, about what is right and wrong, about what is desirable, and what should be avoided.* It is a contract that the organization makes with itself, to uphold certain values that have been deemed important. The details of policy development are merely elaborations on that central definition, and this book assumes that the reader is fully capable of researching, writing, and executing comprehensive and workable policy about HIV/AIDS. If the job seems, at any point, overwhelming, keep in mind the goal of policy related to HIV/AIDS: *to ensure that all people, HIV-infected or not, are treated with respect, dignity, sensitivity, and concern for their continued emotional, physical, and spiritual well-being.* In the end, for each workplace and social service professional, that's what the job is all about.

Section One:
POLICY AREAS

Chapter One:
THE ETHICAL BASIS FOR POLICY

"We want to create hope for the person and acceptance in the hearts of people. We must give hope, always hope, and remove the bitterness that is harming them when they are avoided by everyone."
—Mother Teresa on AIDS

"Unless you have looked into the tortured face of a person with AIDS and seen the terror, not only at the thought of dying, but at the thought of being tossed out of their homes because they haven't the money to pay the rent, or of having their phone service, electricity, or heat terminated because they cannot work and therefore have no income with which to pay these bills, you cannot fully appreciate the tremendous need that exists...."
—Tony Ferrara, a person with AIDS, before U.S. Congress, April, 1984

"When AIDS is over we're going to look back and say that, because of AIDS, we learned how to love ourselves and each other."
—Louie Nassaney, a person with AIDS

Before we begin an overview of HIV/AIDS policy, we should discuss the ethical foundations that support that policy. Those foundations are critical and should be brought out into the open, for they allow us to state clearly the *values* and *beliefs* that lead us to propagate HIV/AIDS policy in the first place.

The following ideas form the ethical basis for all that comes after:

• Our goal is to affirm life and hope over death and despair. *In the face of life-threatening illness, we want to help people* live *with HIV,* not *die from it.*

- We need to respect the rights and dignity of all people. *People with HIV deserve the same consideration and support as any other client or employee. And they may have a lot to teach us about ourselves, each other, and being alive.*

- We need to affirm the individual's right to choose. *A lot of choices face us all in relation to HIV: strategies to reduce risk, whether or not to get tested, what medical protocols to choose, which doctor would be most effective, and so on. Everyone has the right to all the information they need to make a wise choice, and to make the choices that are uniquely appropriate for them.*

- We should recognize and affirm the diversity of individuals and communities. *HIV has had a disproportionate effect on gay men, people of color, drug users, and other "marginalized" people. Because of this, the epidemic calls upon us to treat those differences as something to be celebrated, rather than rejected.*

- Our policies and programs should be based on solid epidemiological and virological fact. *Some of the information presented about HIV can feel confusing or contradictory. And sometimes the information is just plain inaccurate. In such cases we should search out the truth as the only basis for our actions.*

- Our policies and programs should be based on a positive view of human sexuality. *Many people experience so much condemnation in relation to their sexuality that they are not likely to respond to further rejection. Even despite differences of view about specific matters related to sexuality, most of us can agree that human sexuality itself is a positive and healing force.*

- Our policies and programs should take a long-term perspective. *Myopic views will no longer suffice; reliable indicators tell us that HIV is going to be around for a while. That indicates that we will need to develop policies and programs that will last, not just something that will get us through the next few months.*

- We need to recognize that the crisis of HIV/AIDS is not merely medical. *Responding to HIV as only a medical crisis will neglect some of the most important features of the epidemic: sexuality and homophobia, drug use and how we feel about it, illness and death, and many others.*

- We need to remember that HIV tends to affect most those who have already suffered oppression for other reasons. *It's not just that people with HIV are mistreated because of their illness, they're just as often mistreated because they're, for example, Hispanic, gay, and HIV-infected. We need to take all of those realities into account.*

- We need to be careful not to "blame the victim." *People with HIV have heard all too often, both overtly and subtly, that they're "at fault" for their illness, that they're "dirty," that they're "sinners" or "corrupt," and much more in a similar vein. Social service agencies cannot allow themselves to add to the negative messages people with HIV are already getting.*

The Ethical Basis for Policy

• We need to affirm the right of people with HIV to accurate information and good care. *Practice and policy should aim for the best service that can be provided, rather than mere adequacy.*

• *And finally, if for whatever reason we cannot serve people with HIV well, we have a responsibility to* facilitate *good service. If personal or organizational limitations prevent the provision of good service and information, we need to make sure that it happens, even if it means, as it often will, that referrals are made.*

Chapter Two:
DISCRIMINATION AND ACCESS TO SERVICES/BENEFITS

Sarah is a very popular client who has been coming to the county social service agency, for a variety of services, over the past three years. Three weeks ago she gave birth prematurely to a very sick baby. Two days later the baby died and the autopsy revealed HIV infection. Sarah's counselor at the social service agency took it hard—he asked for vacation time, and hasn't come in since.

Another counselor approached the director privately and requested she not be assigned "any AIDS cases," because her religious views conflict with discussions about "safer sex" and she doesn't think she could work with "someone like that." The director promised to think it over.

Since then a new client has applied for counseling services. The client openly disclosed on his application that he is HIV seropositive. The director, aware of the stress and pain that AIDS has already caused the agency, believes that the agency can't handle any more right now, even though there is room on some caseloads. He considers referring the client elsewhere—maybe an AIDS agency, where "they specialize in that sort of thing."

Introduction

Do people living with HIV infection or a diagnosis of AIDS face discrimination? The facts are stark and disheartening. In a recent survey of 339 Minnesotans affected by HIV infection, participants reported case after case of discrimination in housing, health and medical services, social services, employment, and all other areas of life (*Meeting the Needs of Minnesotans with HIV Disease: The Report from the HIV Services, Planning Project*. Minnesota Department of Health, 1991). People with HIV reported having difficulty finding a dentist who would treat them, a treatment program that would admit them, or a place to call home.

"When I first moved into my building the residents started a petition against persons with AIDS living there."

In another report, the National Association of People with AIDS (NAPWA) surveyed thousands of Americans living with HIV infection (*HIV in America: A Report by the National Association of People with AIDS*. September, 1992. Available from NAPWA for $15.00 at 1413 K Street, Washington, D.C. 20005). Some of the results were startling—even to AIDS activists who had been cataloging countless cases of HIV discrimination over the years.

"The survey explored the possibility that 'being HIV+ has caused violence towards me' and responses to those questions demonstrate a stark and very present reality for a surprising number of people with HIV infection and AIDS. Of all respondents, 12.3% have experienced violence towards them in the home, 21.5% have experienced violence towards them in the community, and an additional 12.7% have experienced violence elsewhere in their lives as a result of HIV infection. In addition, 15% are worried about future violence at home, and a full 30% are worried about future violence in the community...." An additional question in the NAPWA survey asked respondents if they had experienced discrimination in various life situations, with the following results:

Being HIV+ has caused discrimination toward me:

when receiving health care.	36.5%
in my job.	26.1%
in my neighborhood.	19.2%
in getting housing.	17.2%
in keeping my housing.	16.3%
in going to school.	9.0%
in keeping my children.	5.5%

For many people with HIV, the discrimination is compounded because of sexual orientation, race, or perceived drug-use history. Living with HIV or AIDS means facing discrimination as a *daily* fact of life.

Background

Legal rulings and regulations about discrimination and access to services in relation to HIV are based on a number of scientific facts and clinical observations. They form the basis for our thinking about working with people who are infected or who have AIDS.

First, HIV is *not* transmitted through casual contact. There is no scientific basis for segregation, isolation, discrimination, or substandard provision of services. The rationale for discrimination or enforced isolation is fear, not fact.

Second, there is no *clinical* or *psychosocial* advantage to be achieved, either by people with HIV/AIDS or by those around them, by enforced discrimination or isolation. In fact, only psychosocial damage, in the long term, will result.

Third, it is incorrect to believe that people with HIV/AIDS do not need the same social services available to the uninfected. In some areas the need for access may be more compelling. While people with HIV/AIDS may require specialized services or supports at various times, those requirements do not negate the need for mainstream services.

Finally, from a legal point of view AIDS and HIV seropositivity are *disabilities,* the same as blindness or mobility impairment. Our political, legal, and moral tradition asserts firmly that people with disabilities should not be mistreated or separated from the mainstream of life.

General Disclaimer:

Legal matters are inherently complex, and rarely lend themselves to absolute solutions for all conditions. When agencies and businesses are faced with legal questions or concerns, especially those that do not "fit neatly" into standard interpretations, it is a profound mistake to attempt resolution without competent legal advice. Trying to resolve legal problems simply by reading an article, or on the basis of mass media information, can be shortsighted and yield unforeseen consequences. And it stands to reason that all policy proposed about HIV/AIDS and HIV/AIDS-related matters should be reviewed and approved by legal counsel knowledgeable about HIV/AIDS.

The Federal Rehabilitation Act of 1973

The Rehabilitation Act of 1973 (commonly referred to simply as "504") was enacted as U. S. federal law to protect the civil rights of individuals with handicaps. It is a major legal foundation on the federal level for non-discrimination against people with HIV/AIDS.

The Act applies to all U. S. federal agencies, as well as any "program or activity" that receives federal financial assistance. For the vast number of human service agencies which receive federal money directly or indirectly, 504 applies. It protects three groups of people broadly defined as "individuals with handicaps":

1. People who have a current "physical or mental" impairment that substantially limits one or more of their major life activities;

2. People who have a history or record of such impairment; and

3. People who are regarded or perceived as having such an impairment.

Only those persons with handicaps who are "otherwise qualified" are protected by U. S. law. (This point will be explained further below.)

In 1988, the U. S. Congress amended 504 in a manner that makes it clear that the "handicaps" it covers include AIDS. The U. S. Department of Health and Human Services has also formally ruled that AIDS is covered by the Act. Because 504 applies to past and perceived handicaps as well as current ones, its protections also extend to persons who have a history or record of AIDS-related conditions, as well as people who are HIV seropositive or perceived, even incorrectly, to be HIV seropositive.

The intent of 504, and its application to HIV/AIDS, is clear. *It is against federal law to discriminate against people with AIDS or HIV infection, or people perceived as such, in employment or access to services* that derive part of their program support, directly or indirectly, from federal monies—as long as the person in question is "otherwise qualified."

"Otherwise Qualified" and "Reasonable Accommodations"

What does "otherwise qualified" mean? Simply, that the person in question meets other conditions or prerequisites for access to services or employment. If you are the facilitator of a support group for *women,* for instance, and an HIV-infected *man* wants to join, he is not "otherwise qualified," and you would not be guilty of discrimination against people with handicaps to reject his admission request. If the person does not "meet the essential eligibility requirements" either for employment or services, the program is not required to change its rules.

One agency, acting out of unrestrained fear, attempted to circumvent the law by rewriting their eligibility requirements so that they stated explicitly, "this program does not serve people with HIV infection or AIDS." That, too, is illegal; an agency cannot encode discrimination that is prohibited by local, state, or federal government.

Recognizing that the "otherwise qualified" clause carries with it the potential for arbitrary application, and to ensure that handicapped persons have meaningful access to services, 504 also specifies that "reasonable accommodations" may have to be made, provided they do not cause the program undue financial hardship or change the basic nature of the program. If every human service program in the state were housed on the *third* floor of buildings that had no elevators or electric stairs, human services would be effectively barred to all persons using wheelchairs for mobility. But if a third floor human service agency could use space on the *first* floor for client services, and the first floor were otherwise accessible, then the program has made a "reasonable accommodation" that allows for the participation of a wheelchair-using client. On the same note, if first floor space were completely unavailable, and the only solution was the installation of an elevator, many (though not all) programs would properly experience the cost as "undue financial hardship." (This example should not be construed as official legal interpretation; it is meant to highlight some way of viewing provisions of the law.)

What does this mean for clients who are infected with HIV or who have AIDS? *It means that clients must be admitted as long as they are "otherwise qualified."*

Applications for Hiring and Employment

All of the preceding apply in employment cases as well. As long as someone is "otherwise qualified" they must be considered equally for employment. If "reasonable accommodations" need to be made in order to hire the person, they must be implemented. Of course, no employer is required to hire someone for a job that she or he is unable to perform. The focus here is *performance,* not *condition.* While one person with a diagnosis of AIDS may in fact become too sick to perform adequately in a position, or even show up for work, another may be quite capable of executing her or his job responsibilities. Likewise, employers are allowed in a hiring interview to make *job-related* physical inquiries—to ask about a prospective employee's ability to do certain tasks required of any person in that position. The employer, however, carries the legal burden to show that an individual cannot meet job-related performance requirements. Courts have ruled that employers cannot justify discriminatory actions on the basis of possible future sickness or impairment, higher absenteeism risks, or higher insurance cost risks that may be associated with HIV or AIDS.

Employee Benefits and Insurance

In 1992 the U. S. Supreme Court ruled on a case that may have a significant impact on some insurance claims submitted by people with AIDS or other chronic (and therefore, commonly, expensive) diseases.

John McGann was an employee at the H & H Music Company in Houston, Texas. As their employee he was protected by a company insurance policy that allowed for a maximum benefit of $1 million. In 1988 McGann submitted his first claim for an AIDS-related illness. Worried about keeping their company health plan financially sound, H & H quickly rewrote its coverage. McGann's new coverage allowed for a $5,000 maximum in benefits—an amount that could be quickly eaten up in AIDS care by a single drug or treatment.

McGann sued his employer and lost, even when the case was appealed all the way to the Supreme Court. According to the courts, his employer had acted legally and claims of "fairness" were not germane. To escape higher premiums from the AIDS claim, H & H had "self-insured"—that is, instead of paying premiums to an insurance company as it had done before McGann became ill, H & H had assumed the risk of its employees and financed healthcare costs directly. Self-insurance plans are not subject to state insurance regulations, under which a claim of fairness might have been productively introduced. McGann only received financial assistance for his medical bills after he spent himself into poverty, and Medicaid kicked in. McGann died in 1991.

Many employees are not aware that they are covered by self-insurance plans, but up to 60% of U. S. workers are. While other insurance plans cannot discriminate against covered individuals in setting caps on coverage, the 1992 decisions indicate that self-insurers may be able to do just that.

All of this indicates that people living with HIV disease or other chronic illness (or for that matter, all of us who could face such illness) should be thoroughly familiar with our insurance coverage, its exclusions, and its limitations.

A Step Further: The Americans with Disabilities Act

In 1990 Congress passed the federal Americans with Disabilities Act (ADA), a landmark piece of legislation that has been compared to the Civil Rights Act of 1964. While Section 504 limits its jurisdiction to programs receiving federal money, directly or indirectly, ADA goes much further. Affecting employment, public and private transportation, public accommodations and telecommunications, it covers an estimated 43 million Americans living with disabilities—including people with HIV or AIDS and people recovering from substance abuse. Since the law is so sweeping, various sections of the law go into effect on a staggered basis. The law's employment provisions went into effect in July of 1992; for two years from that date, the law exempts employers with twenty-five or fewer employees. Beginning in July 1994, only employers with fewer than fifteen employees will be exempt, and it remains as such thereafter. (Senator Jesse Helms was able to attach an amendment to the ADA allowing special provisions to deny employment in food-handling to those who have an infectious or communicable disease. It directs the U.S. Department of Health and Human Services to determine which diseases can be transmitted through food handling, and to update such a list of diseases annually.)

For many human service and non-profit agencies, the practical effect of ADA will be negligible, since they have been operating under the provisions of Section 504 since 1973. The Americans with Disabilities Act essentially replicates Section 504; the difference—and it is significant—is scope. It means that much of society, not merely those settings receiving federal funds, will have to become accessible. And it underscores, once again, what has already been stated in a number of local, state, and federal laws and regulations: *discrimination against people with disabilities, including people with HIV or AIDS, is illegal.*

State Statutes and City Ordinances

In addition to federal law, many state governments in the U. S. and provincial governments in Canada have their own regulations with respect to discrimination and disability. Such is the case in Minnesota. Minnesota Statutes, Chapter 363, explicitly prohibit discrimination based on disability. That prohibition applies both to employment and access to services. One cannot refuse admission or employment to a disabled person who is otherwise qualified. The Minnesota Department of Human Rights interprets the Minnesota statute to prohibit discrimination against all persons infected with HIV, and has already acted successfully on that interpretation in a number of cases. Similar statutes exist in other states.

Since HIV has had a disproportionate effect on gay men, it should also be noted here that both the cities of Minneapolis and St. Paul have ordinances prohibiting discrimination against people on the basis of sexual orientation, and Minnesota is one of fewer than ten states that have passed anti-discrimination statutes. A handful of other cities and municipalities have enacted similar legislation over the past several decades, but it remains true that the overwhelming majority of Americans are still *not* protected by civil rights legislation that incorporates sexual orientation as a protected category. And in recent years some cities have overturned existing gay rights laws through voter referenda that have been fueled by heavy doses of fear and homophobia.

Minnesota Department of Health Rules for Supervised Living Facilities

Many freestanding residential human service programs are licensed under the

What Would HIV/AIDS-Based Discrimination Look Like?

• Upon receiving the client file for a prospective new admission, staff notes that she is documented as being HIV positive. Until that point, her admission seemed logical and warranted. As they review the file, however, staff decides not to admit because "we aren't really set up for that sort of thing yet."

Is that discrimination? Probably. If the client is "otherwise qualified"—and it sounds like she is—then the only remaining concern is whether accommodations need to be made, and should that prove to be the case, whether they can be made reasonably (that is, without disrupting the nature of the program or causing undue financial hardship). In this case, an HIV+ client who is not evidencing symptoms would require little in the way of accommodations at all. Therefore, it would be difficult for the program to justify admission refusal.

• A group home admits an HIV+ client. The program accommodates 20; each client shares a room with several other clients. Worried about room assignments for the new HIV+ client, program staff have decided to move one of the beds out of a room that accommodates two, so that the HIV+ client can be assigned a room by himself.

Is this discrimination? It is difficult to see how it couldn't be. Since we know HIV is not transmitted through casual contact, there is no danger to a client's potential roommate, and hence no valid scientific cause for isolation. The only probable cause is ungrounded fear, and it is precisely fear-based action that non-discrimination legislation is designed to prohibit.

• A community mental health center is interviewing candidates for a new group supervisor position. The top three candidates all look very good, and it seems like a difficult decision. One of the three notes on his resume that he has done a significant amount of volunteer work for a local AIDS service organization, leading support groups for people newly tested seropositive. Worried that people in the community and significant others of those in the treatment program might react negatively if they believed there was an infected person on staff, one of the interviewers asks this candidate, "Are you positive for the virus? I mean, is that part of what motivated you to get involved in AIDS?"

Is that discrimination? Given that the candidate is "otherwise qualified," and there is no reason to fear casual transmission of HIV through the performance of job duties, the interviewer's question is irrelevant and inherently discriminatory. Further, basing a hiring decision on the *perception* that the candidate is HIV+ is equally discriminatory. That doesn't make it easy. It may very well be that the program is situated in a very conservative, fearful community, and it may be that there will be undesirable consequences, such as other staff fears and reluctance to give referrals to the program if others found out. It is important to note that the only way others will be aware of the candidate's HIV status is if you tell them—and that disclosure is also illegal. Accordingly, asking a job applicant if she or he is disabled in some way is, itself, an illegal act; the employer can only inquire about the applicant's ability to perform specific job-related tasks.

• A staff member in a Rule 36 facility (a group home for persons with chronic mental illness), upon finding out that one of the clients is seropositive, states, "Well, it's fine with me if she's here—I just don't want her on my caseload."

Is this discrimination? The example is more subtle than one in which a program refuses admission, and depends to a certain degree on existing personnel policies within the agency. After all, the client cannot claim a denial of access to program services if another staff person takes on the responsibilities that the staff member mentioned above refused to perform. As long as the service is the same as it would be for any other client, it is difficult to make an absolute determination of discrimination. But what if the second staff member, who took over the case, is less qualified in terms of training or experience? Then the client might successfully argue that the services received were "less than" she might have otherwise received.

The real issues in a case such as this may be broader than a strict interpretation of anti-discrimination law allows. Is it appropriate for *any* counselor to decide that she or he doesn't want to work with someone, if that decision is based on misinformation and unfounded fear? Is it appropriate for counselors to decide who they want to work with, and who they want to avoid, solely on the basis of personal comfort? Probably not. And if it *is* inappropriate, harder questions follow. Is it professionally competent for the supervisor of that counselor to pander to her or his fears, ignorance, and personal prejudices by allowing them to refuse direct service? No. In fact, permitting the continuation of such beliefs and attitudes will, eventually, put the program in serious legal jeopardy. Sooner or later that counselor will be in a position to actively and directly discriminate against a person with HIV.

Minnesota Department of Health Rules for Supervised Living Facilities (SLFs). Minnesota Rule 4665.0900 for supervised living facilities prohibits SLFs from accepting residents having or suspected of having a communicable disease. Until recently HIV qualified as such, indicating that strict interpretation of the rule would prohibit SLFs from admitting clients known to be HIV+. That interpretation was in obvious conflict with federal and state laws that prohibit refusal of HIV+ clients who are otherwise qualified. Therefore agencies had to comply with both state and federal laws prohibiting discrimination and the conflicting SLF rule by securing a waiver to the SLF rule. Programs were required to contact the Minnesota Department of Health in order to acquire a waiver that would allow for the admission of an HIV+ client.

Given what seemed an inherent contradiction, the 1989 Minnesota Legislature amended the law to specify that SLFs must admit, as a resident, a person infected with HIV, unless the facility cannot meet the care needs of the individual. The statutory language supersedes the provision in the rules. The amendment means that *the need to secure a waiver for admission of HIV+ clients in an SLF has been eliminated.*

Programs that have been operating on the basis of the need to secure an HIV+ waiver no longer need to do so. They can simply admit HIV+ clients from now on without contacting the Minnesota Department of Health and without being in violation of the rule.

Some Additional Points

- *In the U. S., employees terminated for reasons associated with HIV or AIDS may have a claim to wrongful discharge. Employees who suffer intentional or negligent HIV-related actions by employers may also have personal injury claims.*

- *U. S. federal law bars employers from taking adverse actions (such as suspension or discharge) against participants in an employee benefit plan for the purpose of interfering with rights provided in those plans. For example, employers may not take such actions in order to reduce health insurance or pension costs.*

- *Employers may be held liable for the actions of managers which violate the Minnesota Human Rights Act. And in some cases, management employees may be held personally liable for their illegal acts, including failure to take appropriate corrective measures.*

- *The Minnesota Human Rights Act forbids, by implication, requiring or requesting HIV antibody testing unless it is explicitly job-related, and unless all applicants for the position are subject to the same medical requirement.*

- *You are encouraged to check with your state, provincial, municipal, or other territorial governing body for additional laws and regulations that will affect your worksite and specific situations. Check out all the facts and align your organization with good, well-informed legal counsel so that your AIDS/HIV policies and guidelines conform to local requirements.*

Policy Recommendations

Organizational policy in this area speaks to several key issues. First, it asserts that discrimination is wrong, and will not be permitted in the organizational environment. Second, it contends that the injunction is operative at every level of organizational functioning, under all conditions, and for both staff and clients. And third, it outlines the measures by which that injunction will be enforced, both proactively (e.g., training of staff and clients, as appropriate, on discrimination and disability law) and reactively (e.g., spelling out grievance mechanisms and disciplinary actions to be taken when discrimination occurs).

Why encode policy strictures that are, in many settings, already legally binding, even in the absence of explicit policy? Because it allows the organization to *take a public stand,* to openly assert organizational values. Apart from the legal considerations, the organization should state firmly what it considers right and what it considers wrong—and communicate clearly to all staff and clients that discrimination will not be tolerated.

The fundamental assertion of the preceding is that *no one* should be discriminated against simply because of a medical diagnosis—whether the disease in questions is AIDS, cancer, diabetes, or any number of other conditions. *What matters is behavior or performance, not diagnosis.*

In the following chapter we will look at HIV infection from a different angle by contending that we ought to treat *everyone* as if they are already infected with HIV and hepatitis B. Such an approach will help reduce cases of HIV discrimination because it removes some of the need for "separate treatment." It also goes a long way to reducing the potential fears of clients and co-workers who are concerned about occupational risk. That's a legitimate concern, to be sure, but when ill-informed and unchecked, it has all too often helped keep discriminatory practices alive.

Important Legal Cases Related to HIV/AIDS

ACLU v. District of Columbia, 645 F.Supp. 84 (D.C. Cir. 1986): The court upheld the constitutionality of a D.C. statute prohibiting discrimination in the provision of insurance.

Wiedmon v. Rogers (U.S.D.C., E.D., N. Carolina, #C-85-116-G): This suit sought mass screening of prison inmates and an end to sharing of kitchen, toilet, linen, and clothing with HIV+ inmates. Case dismissed.

Chalk v. U.S. Dist. Ct. Cent. Dist. of California, 840 F.2d 701 (9th Cir. 1988): A teacher diagnosed with AIDS was granted a temporary injunction authorizing his return to class. The court held that there was no threat of harm to the students and an injunction was justified based on the irreparable emotional harm to Chalk from not being able to teach.

District 27 Community School Board v. Board of Education, 502 N.Y.S.12d 325 (Sup. 1986): A New York school board unsuccessfully attempted to exclude two HIV positive children from school. The court held that automatic exclusion of children with HIV would not serve the interests of public health, safety and welfare, and constituted discrimination under Section 504 of the Federal Rehabilitation Act of 1973.

Doe v. Centinela Hospital, D.C. Calif., No. CV 87-2514 PAR (PX), 6/30/88: An asymptomatic HIV positive person, excluded from a federally-funded program because of fear of HIV contagion, was regarded as handicapped within the meaning of Section 504, and was ruled entitled to protection.

Glover v. Eastern Nebraska Community Office of Retardation, CN 87-0-83056, L.W. 2560 (4/12/88): In this case mandatory testing of employees for HIV and Hepatitis B was found to be unconstitutional. The court found testing to protect clients unnecessary, given the "zero risk" of transmission.

Thomas v. Atascadero Unified School District, 662 F.Supp. 376 (C.D. Cal. 1987): Ryan Thomas, a child with AIDS, was granted a permanent injunction to attend kindergarten. The court stated, "any theoretical risk of transmission...is so remote that it cannot form the basis for any exclusionary action."

Raytheon v. Fair Employment and Housing Commission, No. 167995 (Cal. App. Super. Ct., 1988): The court upheld the decision of the Fair Employment and Housing Commission finding Raytheon had discriminated against an employee denied reinstatement after the employee was diagnosed with AIDS. The court found no evidence that HIV would be transmitted in the workplace.

School Board of Nassau County, Fla. v. Arline, 107 S.Ct. 1123 (1987): The court ruled that the Rehabilitation Act of 1973 applies to persons with communicable diseases (here tuberculosis).

Robertson v. Granite City Community Unit School District No. 9, 684 F. Supp. 1002 (S.D. Ill., 1988): The court granted a preliminary injunction brought by the parents of a student diagnosed with ARC who had been placed in a separate "modular" classroom after diagnosis. The court ruled that the student would suffer irreparable harm if the school continued to exclude him from a normal classroom setting, and that the public interest would be best served by granting the injunction.

New York Association of Retarded Citizens v. Carey, 612 F.2d. 644 (2d Cir. 1979): Efforts to exclude mentally retarded children who were carriers of Hepatitis B were ruled invalid under Section 504, since no evidence indicated that the supposed health hazard was any more than a remote possibility.

Chapter Three:
INFECTION CONTROL/UNIVERSAL PRECAUTIONS

"At the program I was at, all the staff, before they came in my room, would put on two pair of gloves. Of course, they did the same thing when they went into other patients' rooms—but it didn't start until I was diagnosed as HIV positive."
—Recovering addict with HIV infection

"After Willie went on disability, they cleaned out his office. They actually took up the carpet and had it fumigated."
—Secretary in a large corporate office

Introduction

If HIV discrimination finds little legal or moral justification, it follows that people with HIV will be living, working, and receiving services in all sectors of our society. That means that many workplaces and social service facilities will be concerned with infection control.

Infection control refers to those procedures designed to stem the spread of any number of infectious diseases or conditions in a particular setting. The practice of infection control pre-dates HIV/AIDS, but HIV has underlined its importance. Many settings which should have been following infection control procedures long ago have only now begun to maintain rigorous adherence to its procedures.

In the vast majority of workplaces, the possibility of HIV infection from accidental exposure is nearly non-existent. But everyone who has worked in a close-knit job setting is well aware that other infectious diseases which, unlike HIV, *can* be spread by casual contact, often spread quickly among staff and clients. Colds, flus, and other maladies usually affect more than one person in a worksite before they begin to dissipate. Adoption of infection control policies will, in non-medical settings, have very little impact on overall transmission of HIV. *They just make sense,* and staff and clients will be healthier for the effort. It may have taken the fear of HIV to get many programs to pay attention to infectious disease; if so, it is an opportunity, not a threat.

Basic Terms and Principles

Understanding infection control requires familiarity with a few basic terms and concepts.

"Exposure"

The term is imperfect, because it is too broad and vague, but it is in common use, and will be employed here. *Exposure* refers to any activity or event wherein HIV can get inside the body of an uninfected person and cause infection. Touching HIV-infected blood when one's skin is unbroken is *not* exposure, because the virus cannot pass through the skin. Touching someone with HIV is *not* exposure, because there is no way the virus can pass on to the uninfected person. Contact with saliva, as through coughing or sneezing, is *not* exposure, because saliva cannot transmit HIV. But cleaning up HIV-infected blood spills with bare hands *could* be exposure if one has small cuts or lesions on the skin—and sometimes we scarcely notice or pay attention to such things.

Exposure then has a very specific meaning and ought not be used casually or generally. It requires direct contact with bodily fluids known to be infectious for HIV, and a means for those fluids to get inside the body.

"Bodily fluids"

This is another imprecise term in the context of HIV/AIDS, since not all bodily fluids are capable of transmitting HIV. For all practical purposes, staff and clients in non-medical human service settings need only concern themselves with *blood, semen, or vaginal secretions*. (There have been a few documented cases of HIV infection in infants as a result of exposure to the breast milk of an HIV-infected woman. Therefore, daycare workers who use bottled breast milk with babies should take precautions.) While other bodily fluids, such as cerebrospinal fluid or synovial fluid, are believed to be potentially infectious for HIV, it is difficult to conceive how any non-medical personnel would ever come into direct contact with them. And it has already been noted that saliva, sweat, tears, urine, feces, and other bodily fluids into which people come into common contact cannot transmit HIV.

"Universal Precautions"

Finally, the idea of universal precautions refers to the proposition that since one cannot know for certain whether someone is infected with HIV or hepatitis B, we ought to treat *all* blood, semen, vaginal secretions, and other bodily fluids containing *visible* blood as potentially infectious for the two diseases. The recommendation is literal and stringent. In the absence of such an approach we will naturally fall back on unreliable assumptions, like treating a blood spill from a gay IV drug user with great caution, but responding to a similar blood spill from an elderly patient in a nursing home with considerably less deliberation and care.

Infection control indicates the implementation of *universal precautions* designed to prevent inadvertent *exposure* to potentially infectious *bodily fluids*.

Infection Control/Universal Precautions

Hepatitis B and HIV: Facts, Similarities, and Differences

Since you are probably familiar with essential facts about HIV, this section will discuss basic facts about hepatitis B.

Hepatitis B is a disease affecting primarily the liver, caused by the hepatitis B virus (HBV). The severity of the disease can range widely, from a relative lack of symptoms to (less commonly) severe and sometimes fatal effects. About 25% of HBV-infected individuals develop acute hepatitis, and of infected individuals, 5–10% will become HBV carriers. Carriers (people who have been infected with HBV for six months or more) are at risk of developing chronic liver disease, including active hepatitis, cirrhosis, and primary liver cancer. It is estimated that there are 300,000 cases of HBV infection a year in the United States. From 5,000–7,500 people die each year in the United States from diseases associated with HBV; HIV, by contrast, is much more likely to cause serious illness or death.

HBV and HIV are often grouped together because their routes of transmission are similar—they are both blood-borne pathogens ("causes of disease"). Of the two, HBV is much more easily transmitted and does, in fact, pose a significant risk to healthcare workers upon accidental exposure. About 12,000 healthcare workers whose job-related duties require exposure to blood become infected with HBV every year. But as with HIV, most transmission takes place through unprotected intercourse (vaginal or anal) and the sharing of drug injection equipment.

HIV and HBV: Similarities and Differences

	HBV	HIV
Mode of Transmission:		
Blood	Yes	Yes
Semen	Yes	Yes
Vaginal Secretions	Yes	Yes
Saliva (From a Bite)	Uncertain	No
Target in the Body	Liver	Immunity
Risk of Infection After Needlestick Exposure to Infected Blood (Hypothetical Model) *	6–30%	0.5%
Fatality	Rare	High, But Not Certain
Vaccine Available	Yes	No
Cure	No	No

* The hypothetical model for exposure to infected blood has been taken from *Guidelines for Prevention of Transmission of Human Immunodeficiency Virus and Hepatitis B Virus to Health-Care and Public-Safety Workers* (U.S. Department of Health and Human Services, Public Health Service, Centers for Disease Control, Atlanta: February, 1989; updated November, 1991).

One very important difference between HIV and HBV is that, although there is *no* vaccine available against HIV, there *are* effective vaccines against HBV. They provide over 70% protection against hepatitis B for seven years or more. In addition, a combination of hepatitis B immune globulin (HBIG) and the vaccine, administered shortly after exposure to

19

HBV, will prove over 90% effective in preventing hepatitis B. Because the routes of transmission are quite alike, HBV and HIV are often grouped together in infection control policies addressing the issue. This means that existing policies detailing infection control procedures against the spread of HBV will be entirely satisfactory in controlling the spread of HIV. The difference, in terms of policy, has to do with recommendations about the appropriateness of vaccination and post-exposure procedures.

After the Fact: Accidental Exposure

More and more workplaces are finding it desirable to have policy and procedure which outlines individual and organizational response should accidental exposure to HIV or HBV take place. While a cause for concern, it should be noted again that *exposure* does not mean *infection* (especially in the case of HIV); it only means that an opportunity for infection, however slight, has taken place.

Occupational Infection and Agency Liability

Can a human services agency or its staff be found liable if a client or staff person becomes infected while in the program, allegedly because of exposure through a client or staff person? The agency that may need to seriously concern itself with such a prospect is that which has failed to implement appropriate policy. For as long as the agency has instituted, and made reasonable efforts to enforce, rules and regulations designed to avoid the risk of transmission and has provided staff and clients with effective education about HIV and risk reduction, it is unlikely that any court would hold the agency liable. By taking such steps agencies can generally fulfill their legal obligation to protect the health and safety of clients and staff. Since many court decisions have ruled that segregation is not necessary to implement transmission control, and would in fact prove illegal, protection of staff/client safety does not require such drastic measures.

In any event, as a practical matter it would be difficult for a staff person or client to prove that she or he became infected as a result of occupational exposure, rather than in some other area of their personal life. Even among healthcare workers who became HIV-infected, the self-reported cause, in the vast majority of cases, was personal sexual or IV drug-using behavior.

In the case of HBV, the discussion is a little less complicated because of the availability of a vaccine and HBIG. Standard protocol recommends administration of a combination of the vaccine and HBIG after exposure, and medical monitoring thereafter.

Some have speculated that immediate administration of zidovine (commonly known by the trade name AZT) after significant exposure to HIV may stop replication of the virus. Those speculations cannot be conclusively supported or negated by research to date. While it may be reassuring to believe that "taking something" after exposure will keep a person safe, it may actually be "magical thinking." Based on the evidence to date,

Infection Control/Universal Precautions

prophylactic administration of AZT after HIV exposure seems unnecessary and is not recommended by the vast consensus of medical and public health authorities.

Standard protocol for post-exposure management in the case of both HIV and HBV is similar. In summary, it includes:

- *Documentation of all facts and conditions related to the exposure;*
- *Seeking consent for HIV and HBV serostatus disclosure and/or testing of the source individual (see sample consent form following);*
- *Strict maintenance of confidentiality of both the source patient and the worker; and*
- *On-going provision of counseling, diagnostics, and medical management for both the source patient and the worker.*

In the points above, the "source individual" is the person from whom exposure occurred. Minnesota law [Chapter 154, Section 5 (144.7605) 1989] states that if consent cannot be obtained, a test cannot be compelled against the individual, or obtained by subterfuge, such as drawing blood for another purpose and then testing it for HIV/HBV. The only exception is in the case of prisoners in custody or under the jurisdiction of the commissioner of corrections. Check with your local, state, or provincial government for specific requirements that may differ from the Minnesota law. Specific recommendations about procedure and policy are discussed below.

Infection Control Approaches

Infection control procedures extend from a handful of commonsense practices. In one way or another, most infection control policies are merely an elaboration of these practices.

First, individuals should avoid direct contact with blood and other relevant bodily fluids. When contact is required, a barrier—preferably latex gloves—must be employed.

Second, any surface which may be contaminated with infectious bodily fluids should be cleaned. Common household bleach kills HIV. (A bleach-to-water mixture of 1:10 is perfectly adequate.)

Third, staff and clients will want to take care with sharp objects, such as knives, broken glass, or needles. Cuts, sores, or other wounds should be thoroughly bandaged to prevent leakage, and needles should always be properly disposed without recapping.

And fourth, all staff and clients should practice good personal hygiene, such as regular handwashing. While this will have no bearing on the control of HIV, it *will* help minimize the diseases that are spread by casual contact.

A business or program's *specific* approach to infection control will depend entirely on the nature and scope of the program. Four broad kinds of service arrays can be outlined, each of which will require a progressively more detailed set of procedures. These involve the following.

- Non-residential programs in which the primary concern will be accidental blood spills;

- Non-residential programs, such as daycare centers, which may at times involve exposure to other fluids such as urine, or which may include other services such as on-site food preparation;

- Residential programs; and

- Primary healthcare settings.

Childcare providers are encouraged to consider, as a procedural attachment to infection control policy, *Daily Care of the Infant and Child with Acquired Immunodeficiency Syndrome (AIDS), Human Immunodeficiency Virus (HIV) and Related Conditions* (reprinted in the Appendices section of this book). It will also prove instructive for anyone, whether working in a personal or professional capacity, caring for people with HIV or AIDS in home/residential settings. Infection control procedures, and the policy statements which incorporate them, have become fairly standardized over time. There is no reason for your organization to spend a great deal of time researching and developing policy from the ground up. It only remains to locate an existing policy statement that responds to your individual program's service configuration, and adopt it as your own.

Policy addressing the management of potential workplace exposure to HIV and HBV will be the same for all four types of care settings—though of course, exposure in a non-residential, non-medical setting is extremely remote. Of the four groupings, primary healthcare settings are likely to be the most concerned about establishing policy and protocol. They are encouraged to consider adopting, on a formal basis, the guidelines established by the Centers for Disease Control; they are reprinted, in full, elsewhere in this book.

Policy Recommendations

There are very few human service settings that do not need to address infection control as an organizational issue. True, for some the need for policy will prove more critical, but *everybody ought to pose the question* and consider the need for policy.

You will find, in Section Two of this book, some policy statements which correspond to the four "kinds" of programs outlined earlier. An additional set of guidelines addresses the infection control needs of public safety workers, including fire and emergency medical services, law enforcement, and correctional facility officers. In adopting one of those policies, however, a few questions still need to be posed.

- Who is responsible *for research, selection, and (if necessary) adaptation of an infection control policy?*

- How will the policy be disseminated and implemented *among staff and clients? Is there a need for training to ensure that all are aware of the details of the policy?*

Infection Control/Universal Precautions

• How will compliance with policy be ensured *among both staff and clients? When policy is not followed, how will non-compliance be addressed?*

Effective infection control presumes that staff and clients are already knowledgeable about the basics of HIV, its transmission, and personal risk reduction strategies. The following chapter will explore the need for, and the parameters of, HIV education in human service settings.

23

WE ARE ALL LIVING WITH AIDS

Source Patient Consent for HIV [hepatitis B] Testing

An emergency medical service (EMS) [or other healthcare] worker accidentally came into contact with your blood. We are asking you to give us information about your medical history so that we can determine if you have been exposed to Human Immunodeficiency Virus (HIV) [hepatitis B], the virus believed to cause AIDS. We want to determine whether you are infected with HIV [hepatitis B] so that we can inform you of this infection and counsel you about what it means to you and others. Any information you may give us will be recorded in your hospital medical record and may be disclosed to the EMS [healthcare] worker, and/or a representative of the EMS [healthcare] agency, and/or to healthcare workers caring for the EMS [healthcare] worker.

We also ask that you provide us with a sample of your blood to test for the presence of antibodies to HIV [hepatitis B]. The results of your test will also be entered in your hospital record. Please be advised that although medical records are protected as private data under the law, they can be accessed by insurance carriers. While insurance companies cannot drop coverage for people who test positive for HIV [hepatitis B], it may, in some cases, affect your ability to apply for new, different coverage in the future.

If you are infected with HIV [hepatitis B], your test result will be given to the EMS [healthcare] worker, but your name will not be disclosed to him or her. However, we are required by law to inform the Minnesota Department of Health (MDH) * of your test results and your name. The law maintains the privacy of that information, but it is likely that an MDH disease control specialist will contact you, in a manner that assures your confidentiality, to inquire about your sexual partners, or others who may have been exposed to your infection. This is done so that those people can be notified, in a manner that protects your anonymity, that they may have been exposed to HIV [hepatitis B].

You will not need to pay for the testing if you choose to be tested, or counseling if it is needed.

You are not required to give the blood sample or information. It is a decision you should weigh carefully, taking into account your personal situation, as well as the well-being of the EMS [healthcare] worker who may have been exposed. If you do refuse, we are required by law to notify the EMS [healthcare] worker and her or his employer that you have refused. In such a case, again, your name will not be disclosed.

By signing below, you are consenting to being tested for the presence of HIV [hepatitis B] antibodies.

_____   _____
Date   Patient's Signature

                                                            _____
                                                            (legal guardian, patient representative)

* Substitute your own state or regional health department in this form; be certain to check with them for appropriate guidelines and laws pertaining to testing for HIV and hepatitis B.

Chapter Four:
CLIENT AND STAFF EDUCATION

Janet is the clinical director of a facility for persons with chronic mental illness. About 6 months ago she began to bring up concerns about HIV/AIDS education in staff meetings. She tried very hard to keep staff abreast of current information by circulating pamphlets, news clippings, and brochures. She did all this out of simple concern—she wasn't touched personally by HIV/AIDS, and to date, the facility (to its knowledge) had no clients with HIV.

But Janet has become increasingly discouraged because it seems that staff has sabotaged all her efforts to provide client HIV education. She asked the intake counselor months ago to pass out HIV brochures to clients at admission, and to discuss risk and risk reduction as part of the admission interview. But Janet discovered that the brochures ran out a month ago—and she's not sure what, if anything, is being discussed verbally with clients.

Even more, Janet discovered that primary counselors—who were supposed to follow up with clients by discussing safer sex—were doing little, if anything. The only reason she found out was by asking at this morning's staff meeting, quite directly, what people were doing. She was met with unease, then hostility. Staff asserted that "after all, we have yet to see even one AIDS case—and probably won't see one, either." Janet was exasperated. She never thought there was a need for policy in this area, believing that staff would be naturally concerned and proactive.

Introduction

Human service programs have a pivotal role to play in the on-going provision of accurate education about HIV to their clients and staff. That role is inherent in the missions of most agencies: the health and well-being of clients and staff is a paramount concern. Public and private service institutions—from daycare centers to secondary schools, from job service programs to arts programs—can exercise indispensable leadership by seizing the opportunity to effectively educate clients and staff about HIV/AIDS. Private sector businesses can also follow their lead, enhancing the workplace for staff and customers.

Background: What Works

Some have assumed that if individuals were given all the facts about HIV and AIDS they would summarily change whatever behavior was putting them at risk of infection. Some did. Most did not.

It would be a mistake to think of HIV education as a merely cognitive process. It is in fact an enormously intricate task, in that it must address individual and societal beliefs, attitudes, experiences, histories, and desires about a wide range of issues, including (most evidently) sexuality and health. The true evaluation of HIV education, therefore, lies not in what individuals come to *know*, but rather what they *do* with that knowledge. In other words, HIV education is about *behavior change*.

What behaviors should HIV education target? There are at least three:

* *Behavior that puts people at risk of infection or reinfection, such as unprotected intercourse and sharing of drug injection equipment.*

* *Negative behavior toward people with HIV, or individuals or groups of people commonly assumed to be HIV-infected, such as gay men, sex workers ("prostitutes"), or people of color.*

* *Health behavior that will boost immunity and increase long-term survival chances (e.g., smoking, diet, stress reduction)—most obviously for people known to be living with HIV, but also as a general strategy for health promotion for all people.*

Risk Reduction versus Risk Elimination

There are two main schools of thought about the approach that should be taken in the provision of HIV/AIDS education. The first is Risk Elimination. It says that in the face of HIV/AIDS, one should take whatever measures are necessary to eliminate, entirely, the risk of HIV infection. Some countries have adopted this philosophy; Cuba, for example, requires mandatory testing of all citizens and segregates, in special camps, those who test positive for the HIV antibody. The second approach is Risk Reduction. It contends that there are many risks in life, and no realistic way to eradicate danger to individuals. It focuses on those behaviors that are most likely to cause HIV infection—sharing contaminated needles, for example—and directs its resources on a "most urgent" basis. This is the philosophy adopted by most public health officials in the United States, including federal, state, local, and community organizations.

Changing behavior is not easy. Witness the years of effort and dollars spent on getting people to quit smoking (a clearly irrational, dangerous behavior) or wearing seat belts. It seems senseless, on the surface, that anyone would refuse to use their seat belt, when such a simple act has been clearly demonstrated to save lives. But millions still leave them unbuckled every time they drive. Education for behavior change in the age of HIV/AIDS demands, first of all, a solemn respect for the complexity of the task.

Research and experience offer some clues, however, about what constitutes effec-

Client and Staff Education

tive behaviorally-based education about HIV/AIDS.

First, a knowledge of the basics is essential in order to construct a foundation for behavior change. It may be tempting to presume that nearly everyone now understands the basics, but the fact is that most people's understanding of HIV/AIDS is sketchy and incomplete.

What are the basics? A comprehensive agenda for client education would incorporate the following information:

- *The fundamentals of HIV/AIDS;*
- *Strategies for personal risk reduction;*
- *Relevant organization policy regarding HIV/AIDS that affects clients;*
- *HIV antibody testing;*
- *Confidentiality rules and expectations; and*
- *An overview of HIV resources in your community, state, or province.*

The facts should be presented clearly, without avoiding sensitive areas, in a style and language that is appropriate to the listener. And respect for your audience insists that education speak explicitly of the sexual behaviors (like unprotected anal intercourse) that can result in infection, rather than clothing those behaviors in comfortable, but often misleading, euphemisms.

Second, evidence indicates that one of the most powerful motivators for behavior change to reduce the chance of infection is *actually knowing someone with HIV or AIDS.* It stands to reason, then, that educators need to *personalize* education as much as possible, to give it meaning in the reality of individuals' lives.

Third, the context for education should be culture-, gender-, and age-appropriate. The language women and men employ to talk about human sexuality is, for example, sometimes dramatically different, sometimes subtly so. Individuals will respond much more readily to behavior change attempts if those programs honor and respect their identity.

Fourth, most people need immediate and real consequences, of both a positive and negative nature, if they are going to change their behavior. The effects of today's behavior, such as unprotected intercourse, may not reveal themselves for many years, should individuals get sick from HIV infection. For most people such a consequence is too abstract, too remote.

Fifth, in any behavior-changing process, individuals will need to manage the change one step at a time. It is simply unrealistic to expect that anyone will suddenly alter a set of behaviors that has been deeply inculcated over a long period of time. This is particularly true when approaching the sexual behaviors that may put people at risk of HIV infection. Aside from abstinence, the truly cautious person would: (1) use condoms every time they engage in anal or vaginal intercourse, or fellatio; (2) use dental dams, or latex squares, whenever they engage in cunnilingus or analingus; (3) use latex gloves for digital exploration of the vagina or anus; (4) avoid any rough sex that may cause cuts or bleeding; (5) avoid any sexual activity that involves sharing of urine or feces; and (6) avoid deep kissing if there is a possibility of a cut or opening inside the mouth. It is unlikely that even a highly motivated person would be capable of changing such a range of behaviors overnight. And it is really quite unnecessary; the list moves down a hierarchy of behaviors from the riskiest (unprotected anal intercourse) to theoretical (deep kissing).

Effective education for behavior change will identify the riskiest behavior an individual is engaging in, and then the next riskiest, and then the next—and for each behavior will help the individual develop a realistic set of goals and strategies that will help them consistently accomplish that behavior change.

Sixth, behavior change education requires that individuals are given opportunities to practice new behavior, to internalize and regularize new ways of doing things. If a young man has never used a condom before, he can be advised to practice alone at first, so that he can become adept and comfortable with what may feel like a somewhat clumsy procedure.

"You're Encouraging Them to Have Sex"

Some critics have charged that explicit education about safer sex encourages people to engage in behavior they would not engage in otherwise. They contend that educators ought to be teaching sexual and drug-taking abstinence as the only viable, and the only completely effective, responses to HIV risk.

However, "...as with much of the language surrounding AIDS, the meaning of 'abstinence' is not always clear. For many people, abstinence means not engaging in vaginal sexual intercourse. Does abstinence also include the avoidance of mutual masturbation, or keep kissing, or petting, or even oral sex?" (Hochhauser and Rothenberger, *AIDS Education.* Dubuque, IA: William C. Brown Publishers, 1992.)

Research indicates that explicit sexual education does not tend to heighten sexual activity. In fact, all other things being equal, teenagers who do receive detailed information about human sexuality, including data about birth control and sexually-transmitted diseases, tend to delay the age of first intercourse, and make safer choices about sexual behavior thereafter. The aforementioned critics are presenting what is essentially a religious argument as though it were a public health argument.

It is essentially dishonest to withhold information about the range of choices—safer sex, monogamous sex with a non-infected partner, and abstinence—each individual can make in relation to HIV risk reduction. Of course, educators will have their own biases about which choice is preferable, and they ought to be honest about those biases and their sources.

And *seventh,* HIV/AIDS education will be more effective if it is constructed as a dialogue rather than a pedantic exercise. Educators should actively solicit individuals' feelings, reactions, perceptions, and obstacles. The subject of HIV/AIDS generates a wide range of sometimes strong feelings, and individuals will want to feel heard and understood.

Implications for Human Service Agencies

There are two implications that arise out of the preceding discussion:

• *Human service organizations ought to embrace their leadership role in HIV/AIDS by providing HIV/AIDS education—even if, because of limited resources, it is minimal—to all staff and clients.*

• *That education ought to have a behavioral focus in line with the earlier discussion.*

One additional point should be added here:

- *The content of HIV/AIDS education should be roughly the same for both staff and clients.* Unfortunately, human service agencies will sometimes compartmentalize education according to inaccurate assumptions. They may, for example, provide training on infection control for staff, and a session on safer sex for clients. However, staff need to know about safer sex, and clients need to know the basics of infection control—the division is based on a false premise. Or they may provide education based on an untenable risk assessment provided for clients, which may lead to inaccurate conclusions about risk behavior.

Integrating HIV/AIDS Education into Programs: Clients

There are a variety of strategies programs can employ to provide effective education to clients. An obvious approach is to offer regularly scheduled workshops or lectures led by local experts. Since many human service programs already have, as a matter of course, educational programs on an array of topics, there is a preexisting structure into which HIV/AIDS education can be smoothly added.

But HIV/AIDS education ought not be limited to traditional settings; programs can find creative ways to seize other educational opportunities. For example:

- *Brochures can be made available in waiting areas, or distributed to all clients when they come into the program for services;*

- *Educational posters can be placed around the facility;*

- *The topic can be broached in individual or group counseling settings, especially if clients are discussing sexuality, relationship, or health concerns;*

- *Programs can provide condoms to clients, making them freely available in the waiting room or other areas;*

- *Staff can make resources (books or videos) available to clients for check-out;*

- *People living with HIV or AIDS can be invited to share their experience with clients; or*

- *Clients can be encouraged to attend HIV-related events, such as benefit walks or displays of the Names Quilt. Or, the agency can publicize opportunities for volunteer work with AIDS service organizations. (The Names Project AIDS Memorial Quilt is a tapestry of 3'x 6' panels, each memorializing the life of someone who has died of AIDS. The cloth panels are made by surviving friends, families, and/or lovers of the person who has died, so each is unique. The Quilt travels from city to city for public viewing; already over 2,000,000 people have seen the Quilt or part of it during one of its displays. When it first started in 1987, the Quilt consisted of 1,920 panels; in the middle of 1992, there were over 15,000.)*

Client HIV Education:
A Sample Presentation Agenda

1. Brainstorm: What Thoughts/Feelings Come Up for You When You Think about HIV/AIDS?

2. Presentation: About HIV/AIDS
    - What HIV/AIDS Is and How It Works
    - How HIV Is Transmitted
    - How HIV Is Not Transmitted
    - The HIV Antibody Test

3. Presentation and Discussion: Sexuality
    - Myths and Facts
    - Values and Beliefs

4. Risk Reduction
    - Presentation: Strategies and Choices (Advantages/Disadvantages of Each)
        - Abstinence
        - Monogamy
        - Safer Sex
    - Safer Sex
        - Brainstorm: Low-Risk Ways of Being Sexual
        - Condoms: How to Use Them (Demonstration)
    - Needles
        - Discussion: Getting High and HIV
        - Cleaning Your Works: Demonstration

5. Living with HIV
    - Video or Sharing from Person with HIV

6. Resources
    - Local/Regional AIDSline
    - Other Resources

Client and Staff Education

[One drug rehab program developed its own handout about HIV, which is distributed to all clients at intake.]

Program Statement
About HIV/AIDS

AIDS, and the virus that can cause AIDS (HIV), is very hard to detect. Someone can look fine—perfectly healthy—and be carrying the HIV virus or have AIDS. In fact, most people carrying the virus don't even know they have it. And even if someone tells you, "I had the test and I'm safe," they might not be telling the truth. That's an important point, since you don't actually have to have AIDS to pass HIV on to other people. You only have to be carrying the virus.

Because it's hard to tell, doctors recommend that we assume that everyone we come into contact with is carrying the virus. That means friends, people you know, other residents here at the halfway house. And it certainly means everyone you have sex with, or share needles with.

And it means you. We're not saying this to make you scared; you are probably not carrying the virus. But it makes sense to assume that you are. That's why this program assumes that everybody—all the staff, all the residents—is carrying the HIV virus. We make that assumption in the education about AIDS that we do, in how we talk about the disease. We make that assumption in infection control (stopping the spread of diseases and germs). So if you were to accidentally cut yourself and bleed on a surface, we would assume that your blood has the HIV virus in it, and we would put on rubber gloves before cleaning it up (as we would for any other resident or staff person). And likewise we advise you not to share razors, toothbrushes, or anything else that might have blood, semen, or vaginal fluids (the bodily liquids that contain HIV) in it.

Again, we don't want to scare you. It's just that this is the only way to be safe.

We should also say that we believe that people with AIDS, or who are carrying the HIV virus, should be treated in a loving and caring way. If someone tells you they are carrying the virus, or that they have AIDS, remember that what they told you is private: if you start telling other people, without that person's permission, some really hurtful things could happen to that person. So keep it to yourself, unless you have permission; if you need to talk to someone about how it feels to know, talk to your counselor.

If you have AIDS or are HIV-infected, feel free to talk to your counselor about your concerns and feelings. We will try to help you however we can, and won't tell other people without your permission. And you should know that it's against the law, and just plain wrong, to discriminate against people with HIV or AIDS.

If you have any questions about HIV or AIDS, ask your counselor. He or she would be glad to help. Or you can call the Minnesota AIDSline, without having to tell them who you are, at 870-0700.

Integrating HIV/AIDS Education into Programs: Staff

If you haven't yet worked with clients around HIV issues, you probably will in the near future. It is difficult to imagine the human service professional that doesn't need to know at least *a minimum set of data* about HIV.

- *Clients may be HIV-infected themselves and require support and sensitivity;*
- *Clients may be directly affected by HIV because of a family member or loved one who is HIV-infected; and/or*

• *Clients may be at risk of infection because of sexual or drug-taking behavior.*

At the least, staff training about HIV should cover the following:

• *Basic facts about HIV/AIDS, to include information about personal and occupational risk reduction and the HIV antibody test;*
• *A review of the psychosocial issues of people with HIV and AIDS;*
• *A thorough outline of agency policy about HIV/AIDS; and*
• *Community resources for education, support, and care.*

But what if a human services agency aimed for the *best* they could achieve in staff training about HIV and AIDS? They would provide *skill-based* training, dealing with emotions, on a number of critical topics related to HIV:

• *The information mentioned above, provided in detail;*
• *Strategies for teaching clients about HIV (and role-play practice in doing so);*
• *Working with HIV-infected and HIV-affected clients to include role-playing, case studies, and treatment or case management planning;*
• *Illness, death, and dying;*
• *Human sexuality and homophobia;*
• *Chemical abuse; and*
• *Diversity issues such as race, class, and gender.*

Such an agenda may be a difficult one for some human service agencies to tackle, but its mere consideration points to the fact that *dealing effectively with HIV is not merely learning about a virus.*

The agenda on page 34, provided as an example, is a good place for agencies to *start*—and I urge agencies to embrace the best, rather than the least of what they can achieve in preparing staff for HIV/AIDS.

Policy Recommendations

Policy addressing HIV/AIDS education for clients and staff should address, at the least, the following questions.

• *Should we provide any education at all? The need for education should not be lightly dismissed, and it will be a rare setting that is unable, for whatever reason, to provide at least some information about HIV to its staff, clients, or service users.*

- *If we do, what form should it take? Do we provide lectures or pamphlets? films or videos? referral resources?* You should consider that form of education which is most likely to be impactful and comprehensive, while recognizing the realistic constraints of organizational resources.

- *If it includes presentations or staff trainings, who will do them, and how often?* Should we train one or more of our existing staff to carry out the task, or use existing community resource people?

- *To what source will we refer clients for additional information?* Most states or provinces, for example, have a hotline about HIV, and there are national, toll-free numbers to call for more information.

- *Who is responsible for implementation of this policy?* Once a policy is adopted, implementation should be assigned to one or more people. It will be their task to procure materials, arrange schedules and speakers, and document compliance. This should not be viewed as an extracurricular job that someone takes on simply because they are curious or interested. It should be assigned to a person as a job-related function, and evaluated accordingly.

Part of HIV education includes information on HIV antibody testing: facts, options, advantages, and disadvantages. The subject is so significant in AIDS—it encompasses the three previous chapters on discrimination, infection control, and education—that it deserves a chapter of its own. It is to that topic that we turn to next.

Agenda for Day-Long Training Workshop

[This is one possible approach to more intensive staff training about HIV—and a beginning, not a conclusion. It is from a day-long workshop for mental health, chemical dependency, and education professionals.]

1. Introductions

2. Presentation:
    A. "Why Talking about HIV is Difficult"
    B. "Fundamental Assumptions about Working with AIDS"

3. Psychosocial Issues of HIV/AIDS
    A. Presentation by Panel of people with AIDS (PWAs) and/or people with HIV (PWHIVs)
    B. Small Group Discussion
    C. Presentation: "Psychosocial Issues"
    D. Role Plays
    E. Presentation: "Clinical Tasks, Treatment Planning, and Case Management"
    F. Case Studies

4. Teaching Clients about HIV/AIDS
    A. Presentation: "Behavior Change and Principles of HIV Education"
    B. "What HIV/AIDS Is"
        a. Facts
        b. Group Exercise
        c. Role Plays
    C. "Transmission"
        a. Facts
        b. Small Group Brainstorms
        c. Role Plays
    D. "HIV Antibody Testing"
        a. Facts
        b. Role Plays
    E. "Risk Reduction Strategies"
    F. "Condoms and Other Barriers"
        a. Presentation/Demonstration
        b. Role Plays
    G. Needles and Pregnancy: Demonstration and Discussion
    H. Case Studies
        a. Developing Education Plans for Individuals
        b. Developing Education Plans for Agencies
    I. Presentation Skills

5. Policy: A Review of Considerations for Human Service Agencies

6. National, State, and Community HIV Resources and Services

7. Evaluation

Chapter Five:
HIV Antibody Testing

Leonard was the director of a halfway house for adolescent males who were getting out of prison. It was a highly structured facility, with clear rules about behavior and firm expectations for "graduating."

Leonard was concerned about HIV and decided that the best way to address those concerns was to emphasize testing. He drew up a policy statement directing the facility nurse to begin making referrals for testing, though the nurse had little training in risk assessment. When the nurse decided a client should be tested, there was no choice: clients who refused the test could be expelled from the program. When clients came back from the clinic they were expected to inform the nurse of their test results or, again, face expulsion if they declined to so disclose.

When Leonard was told that his policy statement was uninformed and may be subject to legal challenge, he became angry. He felt it was his right, as the director, to know and to take the steps necessary to protect residents and staff from HIV.

Introduction

Although the HIV antibody testing process itself is relatively simple and straightforward, there are a number of procedural questions that make the reality of testing somewhat more complex. It is an area that is potentially hazardous for those with insufficient information about the testing process, options and consequences, and one about which laws and regulations are more likely to change than, say, discrimination. Even further, the management of antibody testing varies from state to state or other legal jurisdictions. All of this makes it essential that human service programs and other businesses address testing in the form of policy in order to protect the rights and well-being of staff and clients.

Basic Principles

There are a few essential principles that should govern our approach to, and conclusions about, HIV antibody testing.

First, no one should be forced to take the test against her or his will without incontestable cause and consent. Of course, such a clause can be widely interpreted, but the basic ethic is preeminent. Mandatory testing, without consent, is an invasion of a person's very being, and cannot be required unless there is some other value, more compelling, that overrules it.

Workplace Testing

One question that has been raised in business settings is this: Why is drug testing allowed for many occupations, but HIV antibody testing is generally not allowable? The differences between the two are significant. The mere presence of certain chemicals in the body indicates impairment likely to affect performance, while the mere presence of HIV tells the employer nothing about the individual's capacity to do a particular job. And there is no corollary to the "window period" of HIV antibody testing in drug testing; the HIV antibody test is not a reliable, fixed-point indicator of HIV serostatus. Employers should note that in almost every case where a private employer has implemented routine mandatory HIV screening and testing, it has been delimited by the courts.

There is at least one U. S. employer, however, that can and does test all new employees: the military. Arguments for and against that policy are numerous and well-reasoned on both sides; but either way, if you join the U. S. armed services, you will receive the HIV antibody test.

Second, no one should be tested unless true, informed consent has first taken place. The *legal* requirement for informed consent is easily satisfied; a signature, on a long form that few may take the time to read carefully, is all it takes. But *true* informed consent insists that individuals getting tested know what the test is, how it works, what it does and does not do, testing options, and the personal and legal consequences of positive and negative test results.

Third, testing should not be used as a screening device for employment or services. Not only is it an inaccurate predictor of who is in fact seropositive at any one time, it serves no purpose, since discrimination is illegal and unethical.

Fourth, individuals have the right to all available information about testing, including the range of opinions about the advantages and disadvantages of testing, as a part of their decision-making process. The implication for human service providers and enlightened business leaders in relation to clients is clear: we are to provide, or assist in the provision of, all the facts and viewpoints we have at our disposal, perhaps even those that run counter to our personal views.

Fifth, the decision about whether or not to get tested rests with the individual, without any coercion—including emotional coercion—from others. It follows that when clients ask their care providers (as they will), "should I get tested?", the provider will not decide for the client. Rather, the professional will help the client by providing information and access to information, so that the client can decide what is uniquely appropriate for her or him.

HIV Antibody Testing

> ### *If You're Thinking about Getting Tested, Ask Yourself First...*
>
> - Do I know what the test is, and what it does and does not do?
> - Are my reasons for getting tested logical and well-reasoned?
> - Have I considered what I will do if the test turns up positive? negative?
> - Am I aware that no matter how the test turns out, the real focus is behavior change?
> - Am I aware of the difference between getting tested privately versus getting tested at one of the Counseling and Testing Sites?
> - Do I need to get tested immediately, do I need to get more information, or do I need to wait a while?
> - If I do decide to get tested, is there a "support person" who can help me through the process?

Background: The HIV Antibody Test

When health officials speak of the HIV antibody test, they are generally referring to two specific test procedures which determine the presence or absence of the HIV antibody. The first is the ELISA, or the Enzyme-linked Immunosorbent Assay. The second is the Western Blot, which is more exacting and expensive than the ELISA. The Western Blot is generally used to confirm a positive ELISA test result. The tests require only that a healthcare professional draw a small sample of blood from the patient.

The HIV antibody test is often referred to as "the AIDS test," especially among the general public. However, it is *not* a test that tells the patient whether she or he has AIDS. Nor can it indicate at what point in the past the person may have become infected. Nor can it predict whether, or when, or to what degree the individual may experience symptoms related to AIDS. *All the test does is indicate, with considerable reliability, whether or not the person is currently producing the HIV antibody.* Individuals should therefore avoid referring to it as "the AIDS test" because it muddles public perceptions.

When an individual has unprotected sex or shares drug injection equipment with someone who is infected, HIV may pass into the bloodstream. At that point the body begins manufacturing an antibody in an attempt to counteract the infection. In the case of HIV, the antibody the body generates is ineffective; it is incapable of destroying the virus.

The infected person's body doesn't manufacture the HIV antibody immediately after infection. The antibody is produced over time. Some individuals produce detectable levels of the antibody within a few weeks after infection; others may take up to six months (and in rare cases, even longer) to produce a detectable amount.

It is because of the preceding that some difficulties arise in relation to the HIV antibody test.

First, as mentioned, the ELISA and Western Blot both detect the antibody to HIV, not the actual presence of the virus itself. The tests and those who interpret their results *assume* that the virus is present because a specific antibody that is trying to counteract HIV is present at sufficient levels to be noted by the test.

Second, since infected individuals manufacture the HIV antibody at a variable rate, the test results cannot be said to be reliable unless the individual has waited six months after engaging in any high-risk behavior that may have resulted in exposure to HIV. This is one of the primary *technical* reasons why mandatory testing is ineffective as a means of determining universally who currently carries HIV. The "window period" of six months, during which time most bodies develop an antibody in sufficient quantity to be discovered by the ELISA and Western Blot, would mean that at least some of the results of that mandatory testing would be erroneous.

Getting Tested: Pros and Cons

On the one hand...

- While there is yet no cure for AIDS in sight, early determination of seropositivity can lead to medical interventions that may aid in stemming replication of the virus.
- Early detection of HIV seropositivity can lead to lifestyle and behavior changes that will additionally support the maintenance of long-term health and well-being.
- For some, experiencing the testing process and determining one's HIV status may help raise awareness about the importance of behavior change that will reduce the risk of infecting others or getting infected.
- For others, there is considerable anxiety surrounding the possibility of HIV infection, and the only way that anxiety is relieved is by getting tested.
- The results of the HIV antibody test can assist individuals in their personal decision-making about childbearing, family planning, relationships, and other matters.
- Finally, early detection of HIV seropositivity can enable early notification of the person's sexual or IV drug partners who may be at risk of HIV infection.

On the other hand...

- Some people have heard a lot about the test, but actually know very little about it. Some have come to believe that the test "does something" that will protect them from infection. In fact, the only thing the test "does" is indicate the presence of the antibody to HIV.
- Some have used the test as a way to give themselves a "clean bill of health," so that they can return to previous behaviors without concern.
- Some people may not be emotionally ready to hear that their test results indicate seropositivity. Unprepared, individuals are vulnerable to a wide variety of emotional responses, ranging from denial to utter despair.
- Some people might choose the test because they have heard repeated recommendations from others to do so. But unless getting tested is *personally and uniquely sensible,* such blanket recommendations are not germane to the individual and his or her situation.
- Some new couples are getting tested simultaneously so that they don't have to use condoms or other barriers when having sex. But to be truly effective, such a strategy has to take into account the six-month window period, and place considerable trust in on-going sexual and needle-sharing monogamy.

State Approaches to HIV Antibody Testing

The design and procedure for HIV antibody testing varies from state to state, but in general there are two main protocols: confidential testing and anonymous testing. Anonymous testing is just that—names and other identifiers are not linked to test results. Confidential testing means that certain public health authorities are permitted to discover who has tested HIV positive, but those authorities are required to keep that information confidential, and it cannot be released to others. Anonymous testing is easy to understand; confidential testing is a little more complicated. Minnesota, as a state that offers confidential (but not anonymous) testing, serves as a helpful illustration.

In Minnesota there are two main avenues for the HIV antibody test. The first is testing conducted by a private physician or healthcare professional—an avenue that would include any clinic, hospital, or healthcare setting. The second is testing conducted at one of Minnesota's established Counseling and Testing Sites (CTS).

There are a number of persuasive reasons many people choose to be tested at a CTS rather than in other possible settings:

• All Minnesota CTSs provide, as standard protocol, pre- and post-test counseling. Such counseling is critical if the testing process is to become an educational, rather than a merely diagnostic, experience. Pre-test counseling allows the technician to probe the patient's understanding of the test, his or her risk history, strategize in advance possible self-care plans should the test turn up positive, and much more. The nature of post-test counseling depends on the test results. If positive, the technician can provide immediate emotional support and referrals for medical and social services. If negative, the technician can reinforce the on-going importance of risk reduction, so that a future test does not turn up positive. While private healthcare professionals are certainly capable of providing pre- and post-test counseling, they are not required to, and many do not.

• Test results at a CTS are always reported in person. Such is not always the case in other settings.

• When a patient gets a positive test result in a private setting, that result is recorded on the patient's permanent medical record. By itself that is of no consequence; however, when the patient applies for insurance thereafter, he or she can be denied coverage by many carriers. Positive test results in a CTS setting are not entered on the patient's medical record.

• For individuals with little or no money, CTSs offer testing on a donation-only basis. If the patient cannot afford anything, she or he will still get the test. Individuals will be billed for such procedures in other settings; the cost varies widely.

One program took the initiative to develop and print up copies of the information sheet reproduced on the following page. It's distributed to all clients upon admission to the program, and is a good example of client-sensitive, proactive education.

About the HIV Antibody Test ("the AIDS Test")

There are some important things you should know about the HIV Antibody Test (what a lot of people call "the AIDS Test") as a client here at XYZ agency. First of all, you deserve to know where we stand. XYZ agency believes that:

1. It's up to the individual to decide whether they want to get tested. It's not our place to tell you what you should do, because there are many things to think about, and so many things about your life or situation that make it unique. XYZ staff can help, by giving facts and counseling, but we won't tell you what to do.

2. If you have been tested, you don't have to tell us the results. If you choose to get tested during treatment, you still don't have to tell us. That's private information, and you decide what you want to do with it.

3. If you have questions or concerns about testing, ask your counselor; she or he will be glad to help, and will keep it confidential. And you can always call the Minnesota AIDSline at 870-0700. You don't have to give your name when you call, and trained volunteers will answer your questions or talk to you about your concerns.

Secondly, there are a few things about the test itself, and the testing process, that you should know about:

1. The test itself is a blood test. That is, a nurse or a doctor will draw a blood sample for lab work. It takes a while (7–10 days) before the results come back.

2. The test doesn't tell you if you have AIDS. If the test comes back "positive," that means you are probably carrying the virus, or germ, that can lead to AIDS. You can carry the virus (called HIV) without being or feeling at all sick, just like you can be carrying cold germs without actually having a cold.

3. If the test comes back positive, it won't tell you when the HIV—the virus— got inside your body. It could have been six months ago, or six years ago.

4. Having a positive test result doesn't mean you're going to die of AIDS. It means there are some medical matters that you will need to pay attention to.

5. And having a "negative" test result doesn't necessarily mean that you don't have the virus inside your body. There are some problems connected with the test that don't always make the results 100% correct.

6. There are a number of different places to get tested, each of which has advantages and disadvantages. Depending on where you go, there are differences in how much you will have to pay, whether you will get counseling, and what happens to the results of your test. Because of that, if you do decide to get tested, it's really important to talk over the options with someone who knows, beforehand.

7. Whether or not you get tested, you should know that the most important thing any of us can do is to avoid getting the virus inside our bodies in the first place. That means never sharing needles, and practicing safer sex. Getting tested, without changing some of the things that might put us at risk, is the wrong way to go about it. That's why XYZ agency offers educational programs on AIDS for all clients while they are in treatment.

HIV Antibody Testing in Minnesota:
Comparing "Private" and "CTS" Options

	CTS	**PRIVATE**
Trained Test Technicians	Yes	Uncertain
Pre-Test Counseling	Yes	Uncertain
Post-Test Counseling	Yes	Uncertain
Cost	By Donation	Yes: Varies
In-Person Reporting of Test Results	Yes	Uncertain
Results Recorded on Medical Record	No	Yes
Reported to Health Dept. (If HIV+)	Yes*	Yes
Anonymous	No	No

* In the case of the CTS, the name of the seropositive person actually reported to the Minnesota Department of Health is the name given by the patient when he or she gets tested. It may, in fact, be a pseudonym; a number of people choose not to use their real name.

In both cases, either testing by a private physician or healthcare professional or being tested at a CTS, the names of patients testing HIV seropositive is reported to the Minnesota Department of Health for purposes of partner notification. "Partner notification" refers to the process by which sexual or IV drug partners of HIV-infected persons are informed of their possible exposure to the virus. Names so forwarded are kept confidential by the Department; in fact, they are even exempt from a court order demanding release.

At that point a staff person in the Disease Investigation Unit will contact the HIV+ individual and request his or her assistance in developing a plan to notify the individual's sexual or IV drug partners that they may have been exposed to HIV. Compliance with that request is completely voluntary, and the contact is always made in a manner that will not disclose the HIV-infected individual's identity to third parties.

And if the HIV+ person is uncomfortable, for whatever reason, informing past sexual or IV partners of their possible exposure, Disease Investigation staff can inform those partners in a manner that will not disclose the identity of the person who is HIV+. Partner notification is one of a series of public health interventions designed to fight the HIV epidemic. It is designed to be a supportive, non-coercive approach to containment of further HIV transmission, as well as a method for early intervention and care. It is not without critics, however, who have raised some valid concerns about privacy, confidentiality of records should laws change, and the possibility of third-party disclosure.

HIV Antibody Testing and Early Intervention

Even as recently as 1989, some people saw little reason to be tested. After all, there was little that medicine could do to treat HIV asymptomatic seropositivity; patients were told, in essence, to "wait and see; watch for symptoms," before healthcare professionals could offer much hope.

The prospect of early intervention and the possible prevention of symptoms has changed the way a number of people view testing. A significant number of people who had earlier rejected testing, are now seeking it. This has resurfaced a problem, that of maintaining confidentiality. For in order to take advantage of the benefits of early intervention, HIV+ individuals will need to, at some point, see a doctor or healthcare professional.

Why is this problematic? Currently, confidential *testing* is available through the Counseling and Testing Sites. Let us assume that an individual gets tested at a CTS, and the results are HIV positive. At that point, her or his serostatus is still confidential—while the name is reported to the state or provincial department of health, no medical record is established, which means that there is no documentation of seropositivity which can be accessed by insurance companies.

But at that point the patient will want to visit his or her primary healthcare physician, who will perform various diagnostic tests and make an assessment of possible early intervention. *At that point, HIV will be entered on one's medical record.*

HIV Antibody Testing and Informed Consent

In discussions about the issue of HIV antibody testing, concerns about informed consent for testing need to be raised. It is vital that anyone who gets the test understand all of its possible meanings, limitations, and ramifications. Otherwise, consent is not truly *informed.*

There are a number of factors that may undermine the intent of informed consent. Many people, for example, sign a consent form in a healthcare setting without really reading and analyzing the document; they have come to associate the signing of such forms as a bothersome, but necessary obligation in the care process. The language of the document may be beyond the reader's comprehension; millions of people, for example, are functionally illiterate, but would be embarrassed or ashamed to admit that fact to a stranger. Or, the language may be indirect; the patient may sign an authorization that consents for "testing for diseases of the immune system," unaware that the HIV antibody test is implied.

True consent for HIV antibody testing means that the patient knows in advance the nature of the test, its process and limitations, and what possible consequences she or he may face if the results are negative or positive. Consent also means that the individual is not subject to coercion of any kind. Only then can consent be freely given, and accepted.

The American Bar Association's Policy and Report on AIDS (*University of Toledo Law Review,* Vol. 21, No. 1) supports these contentions fully, and further recommends that HIV antibody testing be performed only after consent specific to the test (rather than general, broad consent) has been properly secured.

Confidential testing affords the individual a period of time, after testing positive and before seeing a doctor, to research her or his current insurance coverage and alterna-

HIV Antibody Testing

tives. Sooner or later, it seems, seropositive individuals will lose confidentiality in terms of medical documentation. This way they can still exercise control over *when* that takes place.

The Changing Picture: Testing of Healthcare Workers

At this writing, a number of events have pushed the idea of mandatory HIV testing for healthcare workers to the fore of public and political discussion. The revelation that an HIV-infected doctor in Minnesota—on top of the earlier disclosure of an HIV-infected dentist in Florida—generated widespread alarm and concern about individual safety in the healthcare setting. While there are now a number of proposals at both the state and federal level mandating HIV testing of healthcare workers, it seems unlikely at this point that such proposals will be adopted as law at any point in the near future. Instead, state and federal agencies are likely to follow the Centers for Disease Control guidelines recently promulgated in response to such concerns. The *Recommendations for Preventing Transmission of Human Immunodeficiency Virus and Hepatitis B Virus to Patients During Exposure-Prone Invasive Procedures* emphasizes an intensive education of healthcare workers, scrupulous monitoring of infection control procedures, and states, in part:

> *"Mandatory testing of healthcare workers for HIV antibody [or hepatitis] is not recommended. The current assessment of the risk that infected healthcare workers will transmit HIV or HBV to patients during exposure-prone procedures does not support the diversion of resources that would be required to implement mandatory testing programs. Compliance by healthcare workers with recommendations can be increased through education, training, and appropriate confidentiality safeguards."*

While there is a slim possibility that this stance will change in the future, most analysts do not believe so. Providers should monitor any changes in the law that come out of upcoming legislative sessions. At any rate, despite the possibility of new developments, no one should forgo the development of HIV antibody testing policy because some matters may be in flux. There is still a considerable volume of facts and approaches about testing that is *not* changing, and the issue, and its implications for staff and clients, is too important to ignore.

Policy Recommendations

Organizational policy about HIV antibody testing needs to answer a number of critical questions:

> • *Does the agency or business require or request an HIV antibody test as a prerequisite for services or employment? As has been said, mandatory testing is strongly discouraged. The question, however, still needs to be posed.*

- *Will the agency or business provide for voluntary HIV antibody testing as part of the services it offers to either staff or clients? If on-site testing is conducted, what safeguards will be enacted to protect confidentiality, pre- and post-test counseling support, and informed consent? The vast majority of human service agencies and general businesses will logically avoid on-site testing for two reasons. First, it is beyond the resources of most organizations to provide such a service with all the necessary counseling and confidentiality supports. Second, such services already exist, as noted, through centers like the Counseling and Testing Sites.*

- *If the agency or business does not provide on-site testing, where will clients and staff who seek testing be referred?*

- *What information, if any, will be provided to staff and clients about HIV antibody testing and testing options?*

- *What is the program stance on HIV antibody testing? In other words, when clients ask, "should I get tested?", how will staff respond?*

HIV antibody testing raises a number of questions about confidentiality that were not answered in this chapter. The most basic, obviously, has to do with the privacy of test results. But there are many more dilemmas related to confidentiality, and they have received considerable ongoing discussion and debate in many circles. The following chapter outlines those questions, details some possible responses, and suggests feasible policy alternatives.

Chapter Six:
CONFIDENTIALITY

Jackson was a counselor in an alcohol detox program. One Friday evening he admitted a young woman, Leslie, who had been picked up by the police because she was wandering the streets, yelling and very drunk.

Jackson knew of Leslie—that she was a sex worker who worked the streets, that she was chronically drunk, that she had a young daughter. But Jackson didn't know, at least until that day when he read it in her medical chart, that Leslie was HIV-infected.

And when he read those words, his stomach dropped.

It seemed that Jackson's best friend was a married man named Manuel. And just a few weeks before, Manuel had regaled Jackson with tales of picking up Leslie on the street, paying her $150, and having anal intercourse with her. When Manuel told Jackson of the incident Jackson had responded with anger, telling his friend "you're crazy," and wincing when Manuel referred to Leslie as "a sloppy lay."

Jackson knew that Leslie was HIV-infected because of confidential, legally-protected medical information to which he had legitimate access as a detox technician. And he also knew that his best friend could be at risk of HIV infection because he had sex with Leslie. Should he tell Manuel and break the law? Or should he adhere to the requirements of law, and hope that his friend didn't acquire HIV? Or was there a third choice?

Introduction

Imagine testing HIV antibody positive in most any small town in America. Once home from the clinic, bursting with feelings and reactions, you realize that you really need to talk to somebody.

But who do you tell? How do you know if a friend will keep a confidence, if a family member will respect your wish for personal privacy? Can you trust your doctor, your dentist, your therapist? Who might they tell—and is there anyone they *have* to tell? And if word gets out—in your neighborhood, among local merchants, at your job—how will it affect your life, including specific matters like insurance coverage, job security and satisfaction, parenting, and health care?

Generally, the American system of law has held that personal privacy ought not be violated for cavalier reasons; we hold privacy as a near-sacred thing. Without protections, gross abuses of personal safety and liberty would be possible—publishing the names of incest victims, broadcasting the personal utterances of the psychologist's office or priest's confessional, and much worse.

In the case of HIV/AIDS, an unwarranted fear and lingering hatred of some groups (gay men, for example) can combine to produce very real harm or danger to people with HIV or AIDS when their identities are inadvertently or deliberately revealed. In this country and in many others, people with HIV infection or AIDS, and sometimes people erroneously *believed* to be HIV infected, have been:

- *refused employment and terminated from current employment, despite qualifications;*
- *refused mental health services, and ejected from programs they were already in;*
- *denied medical care, including emergency services;*
- *evicted from their apartments and homes;*
- *placed in unnecessary isolation or segregation in care settings, schools, and even court rooms;*
- *denied entrance to schools and other public institutions;*
- *refused entry into the country, even for the purposes of research and study;*
- *victimized by taunting, threats, and verbal harassment; and*
- *the targets of violence.*

The responsibility to protect the confidentiality of people living with HIV or AIDS, then, is not merely a legal obligation, but an ethical one as well. Human service programs and most business settings have a particularly compelling duty in that regard. There are exceptions, of course, and they will be discussed later. But we begin with the assertion that confidentiality is cardinal, and deviate from that principle for only the most convincing of reasons.

In the U. S., the Relationship Between Federal and State Law

A variety of federal and state laws speak to a host of confidentiality concerns in the United States, and it is important at the outset to understand the relationship between such laws.

Federal law essentially puts a floor, not a ceiling, on the extent of confidentiality required. If state law *requires* data disclosure in a specific case, but federal law *forbids* it, disclosure cannot be made. On the other side, states can pass laws mandating a *greater* degree of confidentiality in a specific instance than federal law mandates; in such a case, state law prevails. Federal law determines a minimum standard that states can exceed, but cannot violate. This distinction will be important in a few of the cases that follow.

Federal Confidentiality Laws

While there is as yet no federal statute that specifically protects the confidentiality of individuals who are HIV seropositive, there are a number of statutes and regulations that have a direct bearing on such matters.

The *Privacy Act of 1974* requires federal agencies to protect the confidentiality of the records they maintain about any individual, including HIV/AIDS-related medical records. Generally, the law prohibits disclosure of protected records without the person's consent, but there are a few exceptions:

> *• Records can be disclosed to other federal agencies for civil or criminal law enforcement purposes;*
>
> *• Records may be released upon court order authorizing disclosure; and*
>
> *• Records may be released to anyone upon a showing of "compelling circumstances affecting the health or safety of an individual." (We have already seen that Minnesota state law forbids involuntary source patient HIV or HBV testing in cases of accidental exposure.)*

Congress also passed legislation in the early 1970s protecting the confidentiality of anyone receiving drug and alcohol treatment services. *42 Code of Federal Regulations, Part 2,* provides strict guidelines for data protection and disclosure in such cases (see the guidelines given on the following page).

The U. S. Public Health Services Act has confidentiality provisions that apply to certain federal agencies conducting health-related research. The Centers for Disease Control, for example, must comply with the Act in its AIDS surveillance activities. While this does not pertain to human service agencies, it is another federal law that encodes a philosophy of data protection.

Finally, under a clause of the Public Health Service Act, public and private agencies receiving federal money to establish HIV/AIDS education and surveillance programs must keep confidential all individually identifying information they obtain unless: (1) the subject of the information consents or (2) state or local law requires the disclosure.

42 Code and Drug/Alcohol Programs

The U. S. federal government enacted legislation in the early 1970s to guarantee strict confidentiality of persons receiving alcohol or drug abuse treatment (42 U.S.C. & 240dd-3 and 290ee-3). The Department of Health and Human Services issued revised regulations implementing these laws in June of 1987; they are published in 42 Code of Federal Regulations, Part 2.

In enacting regulations, the U. S. Congress reasoned that because of the *stigma* attached to alcohol and drug abuse, a firm assurance of confidentiality would be required, so that substance abusers would continue to seek treatment.

The law and regulations govern when and how drug and alcohol programs may make any disclosures about clients, including HIV/AIDS-related information. In general, such information cannot be revealed in a manner that would directly or indirectly identify the client as a substance abuser. There are a few very limited and specific exceptions:

- Programs can disclose information if the client so consents on a written form, but the form must meet certain criteria.
- Disclosures can be made without client consent to other staff within the program or to an "entity having direct administrative control over that program" if the disclosure is needed in order to provide drug or alcohol services.

Disclosures can also be made without client consent:

- if the disclosure will not identify the individual as a drug or alcohol abuser;
- to "qualified service organizations" when the information is needed by that organization to provide services to that program;
- to qualified medical personnel in a medical emergency;
- for scientific research, audits or evaluations, if certain safeguards against redisclosure are followed;
- by a court order obtained through procedures outlined in the federal regulations;
- to law enforcement authorities when a client commits or threatens to commit a crime on program premises or against program personnel;
- to comply with state laws mandating reporting of suspected child abuse and neglect.

HIV/AIDS data must adhere to the same rule and exceptions; that is, agencies covered by the federal confidentiality laws and regulations may disclose information relating to AIDS or HIV infection only if that disclosure would be permitted, according to the guidelines above, by federal rules.

One Example: Minnesota State Confidentiality Laws

There is at present no single statute in Minnesota that specifically governs confidentiality protections of HIV-infected persons. There are, however, a number of statutory and case law sources that may have a direct or indirect bearing on HIV data confidentiality.

The Minnesota Government Data Practices Act (1987) classifies government health data on individuals as "private data," that is, it can be accessed by the subject of the data but *not* by the public. This act would also apply to agencies receiving state funds, but does not apply to privately-funded agencies. The statute *does* allow the government to disclose data to the subject's physician for certain purposes, or with the approval of the Commissioner of Health, for a variety of public health purposes, such as location of a carrier or prevention of the spread of disease. But health data on an individual "collected by public health officials conducting an epidemiological investigation to reduce morbidity or mortality is not subject to discovery in a legal action" (i.e., the Minnesota Department of Health cannot be legally commanded to release data gathered on an individual's HIV status).

Another section of the Act defines medical data as "private" with a very few, specific exceptions. Medical data is defined as "data collected because an individual is or was a patient or client of a hospital, nursing home, medical center, clinic, health or nursing agency operated by a state agency" (or receiving state funds for operation). Again, this means that only the subject has the right to access that information. Adjudicated violation of the Act by an agency is subject to civil action and potential damages of $10,000; violation by an individual is a misdemeanor and subjects him or her to job suspension or termination.

Another statute (144.651, subd.16:1986) addresses confidentiality of medical records under the "Patients and Residents of Health Care Facilities Bill of Rights." The statute covers persons in acute care inpatient facilities for longer than twenty-four hours, persons in long-term care, and persons receiving mental health treatment on an outpatient basis. It states, in part, that patients and residents "shall be assured confidential treatment of their personal and medical records," and may approve or refuse their release to any individual outside the agency.

What these statutes indicate is that, as with federal law, data accumulated about individuals by health and human service professionals, in many different areas, is to be regarded as private, with very few, specific, generally uncommon exceptions.

Is HIV Data Different Than Other Data?

Anyone familiar with the management of human service programs and many private sector businesses already has more than a passing acquaintance with federal and state laws governing confidentiality of records. The question is, does HIV data qualify as an exception to current law? The answer, clearly, is no.

What is different about HIV data is that:

- *The need for data confidentiality is heightened, not in a legal sense, but because public fear about HIV is still very high;*
- *There are sometimes strong feelings among staff about "right to know" versus "privacy rights"; and*
- *Measures to assure the confidentiality of HIV information are still evolving.*

Specific HIV Data Confidentiality Concerns

Numerous questions concerning HIV data confidentiality have already arisen and human service programs and businesses have begun struggling with the answers. Crucial decisions need to be made on such issues as:

1. Admission/Hiring: *Does the program request information on client or candidate HIV status as part of the admission or job application process?*

2. Internal Disclosure: *When clients or staff are known to be HIV seropositive, who "needs to know" that information? Who has no claim to that knowledge? What guidelines govern those decisions?*

3. In-program Client Disclosure: *Does the program expect, implicitly or explicitly, clients who are tested during the course of their involvement with the agency to reveal test results to program staff? to other clients?*

4. Disclosure Liability: *What agency or business responsibilities and/or liabilities emerge if a client voluntarily reveals positive test results? What if those results are revealed without the client's permission, either by another client or a staff member?*

5. Charting: *Should the results of an HIV antibody test be charted? What about the fact that a client took the test, or requested it, apart from the results? What if the client simply discloses to staff that she or he is HIV seropositive? If information is charted, where, by whom, and how does that take place?*

6. Client Transfer: *If the agency maintains files that identify client HIV status, and the client's records are transferred to another agency, does the HIV status data get transferred as well?*

7. Test Confirmation: *If a client self-reports a positive HIV status, should the agency seek confirmation, either through the M. D. who ordered the test or through a confirmatory test?*

8. Duty to Warn: *What third party disclosure might be and might not be warranted according to "Duty To Warn"?*

9. Consent for Release of Information: *When clients sign a consent for release of information to a third party, are they aware that charted HIV data may be included? How can the agency ensure that such consent is informed?*

General Principles

There are a few general principles which precede a discussion of specific issues and inform possible resolutions of confidentiality problems.

1. Agencies and businesses should actively safeguard and protect the HIV sta-

tus confidentiality of all clients and staff.

2. When the HIV seropositivity of a client is shared, either through charts or verbally with other staff, incontestable "need to know" is the criterion for disclosure. What constitutes such need should be determined beforehand through clear standards and rules.

3. Agencies should not pressure any client to reveal his or her HIV status. The truth is that many human service providers will not need to know client HIV status in order to provide the service they make available.

4. Agencies and businesses ought to assume that all staff and all clients are already and currently HIV and HBV seropositive.

5. Agencies and businesses should provide education to all staff, and as appropriate, to clients, about basic issues and policy relating to confidentiality, so that inadvertent violation of data privacy can be avoided.

Policy Questions and Recommendations

1. Should HIV status be requested at intake?

If the basic operating assumption is that all staff and clients are already currently infected, then requesting of clients that they reveal (if known) their HIV antibody status seems counterproductive. Further, it raises again the thorny question of how to record or manage the data acquired through such a question. Finally, it may only encourage clients to lie, especially when they are new to the agency and have not yet developed a level of trust that makes honesty possible. Generally, questions about whether the client has taken the HIV antibody test, or what the client's (known) HIV antibody status might be, need not be asked at all during the admissions process.

2. Who needs to know a client's HIV status?

When a client reveals to agency staff his or her seropositivity, it is logical to assume that other staff members may need to know. But "need to know" has always been an uncertain principle, open to varying interpretation. The Minnesota Employee Right to Know Act, for example, requires employers to provide basic training and information on hazardous substances and harmful physical agents to which employees are routinely exposed at work. Some employee groups have brought legal actions claiming that the Act compels their employers to notify them of the known presence of HIV-infected co-workers or service users. The judicial response has been clear in stating that the Act, because it requires the condition of "repeated exposure," generally applies to hospitals, clinics, and blood banks. Therefore, social service agency employees would not qualify under the provision of the act. *Any* care should assume all clients and staff are HIV seropositive as a matter of course.

The first answer is that *anytime* professionals intend to reveal a client's HIV status to other staff, they should inform the client and obtain their consent *beforehand*, letting him or her know who is being informed and why. Not only is that a courtesy, it is also sound clinical management.

Beyond that, no definitive answer is possible. However, agencies and businesses should consider the following when determining who among staff (both on-site and adjunct) "needs to know":

- *The client's right to privacy;*
- *Program liability;*
- *The continuity of care, especially medical care;*
- *The potential for discrimination against the client, both within and outside the agency; and*
- *The extent to which agency staff are trained and knowledgeable about HIV issues.*

Such guidelines ought to be established *before* questions of "need to know" arise in actual practice.

3. Should clients be expected to reveal results if they are tested during the course of treatment?

The client should not be expected to disclose to everybody; good mental health and clear personal boundaries indicate that most people should carefully consider who needs to know and who does not, who is "safe" to tell and who is not (including program staff), and make self-disclosure decisions accordingly. As for the professional, there may be considerable clinical benefit in letting the client know that "it's up to you, but if you want to disclose your results, we may be of some help."

4. What program liabilities or responsibilities are incurred if a client self-reports seropositivity?

If a client voluntarily reveals his or her seropositive status, the agency is ethically and legally bound to keep confidential that self-report according to the requirements of the law. The agency that intentionally or unintentionally violates that confidentiality is subject to civil damages of up to $10,000 under Minnesota state law; the individual who made the illegal disclosure is also subject to criminal charges (conditions will vary in other jurisdictions).

There is *no* law or statute that compels the human service professional to report a client *self*-disclosure of HIV seropositivity to the Minnesota Department of Health or any other agency. The only person so obligated in human service agencies would be the healthcare professional, a doctor or nurse attached to the agency, who actually orders the HIV antibody test. And unless one is a physician who will be providing HIV medical care, there is no reason to seek independent confirmation of client-disclosed HIV infection.

5. What is the program liability if another dient breaks HIV seropositivity confidentiality?

Human service providers are well aware that even when staff uphold confidentiality obligations, clients will often disclose personal information to each other, sometimes with unfortunate consequences. There have been more than a few cases, for example, of clients disclosing HIV seropositivity to another client, in strict confidence, only to find the vow of secrecy broken. What is the agency's liability, particularly if harm—harassment, for example—comes to the client as a result? There is a growing indication that courts may hold managers responsible when an employee is harassed by peers, even when the manager did nothing directly to cause or incite the harassment, if it can be shown that the manager failed to take preventative steps or to intervene effectively after the fact. The legal application to clients in human service settings has not been fully established, but the principle is clear: administrators are responsible for the safety and well-being of all clients, inasmuch as they are capable of taking reasonable steps to ensure it.

As a practical matter, agencies should take two steps to address legal liabilities as well as the service needs of clients. First, when a client self-reports HIV seropositivity to a staff member, that client should receive specific counseling and supportive guidance about who to inform and who it might be best not to inform. Clients should be assisted in thinking through, with a careful consideration of possible consequences, their own self-disclosure plan or strategy. Secondly, all clients and all staff should receive, as part of their comprehensive HIV/AIDS education, specific information on HIV confidentiality. In addition, clients should be advised of the importance of honoring the HIV-related confidence of a friend or peer.

6. Should the agency chart client HIV status? If so, how?

Human service agencies or professionals are generally under no legal obligation either to chart client HIV data or to report the positive HIV status of clients to the Minnesota Department of Health. Different jurisdictions may have different requirements, however. If a client self-discloses to the professional that she or he is HIV seropositive, no law compels a non-medical human service professional or administrator (except for some exceptions) to document that information.

Why chart HIV status, then? Before answering that question, there are a number of questions that should first be asked and answered:

> • *What liabilities may be incurred for failing to chart client HIV status? For example, physicians may invite malpractice lawsuits by failing to chart such information, and primary healthcare settings may find themselves in non-compliance with the Joint Commission on Accreditation of Health Care Organizations (JCAHCO) standards for either dual charting or failure to chart.*
>
> • *Who has internal (agency) access to client charts? If all staff have access to client charts, then it is certainly conceivable that staff who have no "need to know" will come to know anyway.*
>
> • *How will charted HIV data be protected from confidentiality violations after client discharge? If, for example, HIV seropositivity information is contained in a client's chart, and at some point in the future your agency receives a*

"request for release" from another agency, a client's HIV status may be disclosed. Of course, the client will have signed a "Consent for Release" form, but may be unaware, or have forgotten, that the chart includes information on her or his HIV status.

• Is staff professionally competent to deliver human services that address the broad range of psychosocial issues relating to HIV, such as death, separation, etc.? If not, there is dubious value in making available through the medium of a client chart information that staff are not qualified to address.

• What is the real value of charting HIV status? The implicit value is, of course, that better knowledge of the client and her or his situation will lead to better care. Yet at the same time, the program may be incapable of providing better care because staff are insufficiently trained and support services will be more appropriately delivered by professionals who specialize in such matters. Secondly, it could be argued from a therapeutic treatment point of view that the disclosure is best left up to the client, thus empowering the client to take direct responsibility for her or his needs, concerns, and wishes.

In light of the preceding, the following recommendations can be made. Agencies under the accreditation jurisdiction of the JCAHCO ("Joint Commission") should follow the advice of accreditation officials. This pertains to primary healthcare organizations; most human service organizations and general businesses will not need to concern themselves with JCAHCO rules.

Clinics and other healthcare settings not bound by JCAHCO rules ought to follow standard medical data reporting practice. But in either case, whenever a medical recording of HIV seropositivity is made in any healthcare setting, the patient ought to be informed of that fact, as well as the ramifications of such recording (e.g., effect on future insurability).

Other, non-healthcare human service agencies have four options, any of which is satisfactory:

• When a client self-discloses HIV seropositivity, the program can choose not to record anything. One program took the innovative approach of attaching an opening page to every client file that said, in part, "this agency, based on the epidemiological evidence, assumes that every staff person and every client, including the one mentioned herein, is seropositive for HIV and HBV; therefore, there is no reason to record a self-disclosure of either." (See exarnple on the following page.)

• Agencies can chart client self-disclosure of HIV seropositivity in the most general, euphemistic terms, e.g., "client talked about sexuality concerns," "we talked about client health issues," and so on. For the purposes of internal documentation, that serves as sufficient reminder to the counselor involved that HIV issues may have been discussed. But to the outsider and to the staff member who doesn't "need to know," it is adequately vague so as to disallow HIV carrier identification.

Confidentiality

> [For one organization, this statement is found at the beginning of every client's file.]
>
> ## *Program Statement on Client HIV Status*
>
> The best medical and epidemiological evidence about HIV infection and AIDS suggests that, since it is extremely difficult to know with certainty who is HIV infected and who is not, individuals and medical/human service providers should assume that everyone with whom they come in contact is, in fact, HIV seropositive (carrying the Human Immunodeficiency Virus). Therefore, this agency acts as if every client, including the person identified in this case file, is HIV positive. This assumption is made in the context of infection control, risk reduction education, maintenance of confidentiality, prevention of discrimination, and all other areas of programming. This does not imply that this agency has definite knowledge of the HIV seropositivity of the client identified herein, or any other client. It only indicates the wisdom of assuming HIV seropositivity. This statement will be found in the file of every client of the agency, and all new clients are instructed as to its content.

- Agencies can maintain a client medical file that is separate from the client's "clinical progress" file. The medical file is accessed only by an agency nurse or physician, and is not available to general staff without compelling "need to know." HIV seropositivity data is then recorded in the medical file, which is typically not requested or released in a standard Request for Release. By maintaining a separate file, healthcare professionals who need to know will know and others will be barred from such data.

- Or, agencies could record self-reported HIV seropositivity in a general clinical progress file, but maintain scrupulous control over file access by both internal and external parties who have no need to know client HIV status.

The choice a program makes will vary, but it should be that which maintains maximum confidentiality, empowers clients to self-disclose HIV status as appropriate, and simultaneously meets any clinical or accreditation standards.

7. If the agency maintains files that identify client HIV antibody status and the client is transferred to another agency, does the HIVstatus identifying data get transferred as well?

The most clinically appropriate and ethically sound strategy is to allow the client to reveal her or his own HIV antibody status to others as she or he deems fitting and useful. File transfer of such information may undermine that approach. It will be preferable to keep such information out of client files in the first place, or to record it euphemistically. That way programs can avoid the dilemma of transfer of sensitive data and serve the client's best interests at the same time.

8. What third party disclosure might and might not be warranted according to "Duty to Warn"?

Tarasoff v. Regents of the University of California, 17 Cal. 3rd 425, 551 p.2d 334 (Cal. 1976), and related decisions impose a common law duty upon mental health professionals to take reasonable steps to protect identifiable third party victims of patients believed to pose a serious threat of violence. Such "duty to warn" is seen as superseding obligations of confidentiality.

Does Duty to Warn apply in some HIV cases? Perhaps. The law in this area is uncertain; no volume could give absolute advice. Again, programs are urged to consult competent legal counsel as specific cases arise. It does appear that in cases where a specific threat can be identified against a specific individual, a duty to warn is implied. If a client, for example, tests HIV seropositive and refuses to disclose that fact to his sexual partner and the client continues to engage in unprotected sexual intercourse with his partner, then a duty to warn that partner may prevail. It should be noted, however, that the intent of such common law is not to circumvent necessary therapeutic intervention. When faced with a client as resistant as the one just mentioned, the clinician should attempt every available therapeutic strategy before resorting to the duty to warn. The best advice—which should be encoded in policy—is that in those rare instances that may enjoin a duty to warn of HIV exposure, staff should consult with legal counsel, as well as their state Department of Health or other appropriate jurisdictional body, before acting. No one should ever make that decision without thorough consultation.

Though technically not a function of "Duty to Warn" case law, human service providers should be aware that in 1987 Minnesota law established a civil judicial procedure by which Minnesota health authorities can compel education, counseling, medical testing, treatment and confinement upon individuals who are, or who are suspected of being, carriers of serious infectious disease (including HIV) and who behave in a manner which subjects other people to a risk of contracting the disease. The law, the Minnesota Health Threat Procedures Act, is most decidedly not intended to apply to the overwhelming majority of HIV-infected persons, but rather intended to provide intervention measures in those extreme cases where HIV-infected clients continue to willfully and knowingly place others at risk, or in those cases where an incapacity to function at a reasonable level renders the person functionally unable to practice risk reduction measures. If human service agencies do encounter such clients, and if all therapeutic avenues have been exhausted to no avail, the Minnesota Department of Health (or your appropriate local authorities) should be contacted, as a matter of policy, for legal and procedural clarification. A copy of DHS Informational Bulletin No. 89-53A, which explains the Act in more detail, is included in the Appendices section. It outlines the specific steps that must be taken in order to have an individual deemed a "non-compliant carrier" and subject to the legal provisions of the Act. If you are not a Minnesota resident, you will need to check if your area of jurisdiction has similar provisions.

9. Do Consent for Release of Information forms protect client HIV confidentiality?

Agencies should ask themselves whether the "Consent for Release of Information" forms they use adequately address HIV confidentiality concerns. Of course, no one can control the language of such forms used by other agencies; in that regard, the previous comments about charting are germane. But agencies can ensure that their forms provide the necessary protections. The sample form at the end of this chapter affords such protections, and can be freely expropriated by human service agencies.

A Final Disclaimer

The importance of securing legal counsel on specific agency situations involving confidentiality and the laws and regulations by which it is governed cannot be overstated. While there is much about which agencies can be assured, and many areas around which policy and protocol can be confidently designed, confidentiality issues surrounding HIV can precipitate new and complicated agency dilemmas and represent an area about which program administrators often feel most uneasy. It is essential, however, that human service agencies respond to such dilemmas proactively, through the implementation of good policy and education, rather than wait for a crisis to occur.

Policy Recommendations

Confidentiality policy in relation to HIV, as we have seen, addresses a wide array of concerns and practical dilemmas. Because of their complexity, those concerns and recommended policy responses are best summarized in the chart on the following page.

Confidentiality Policy

Topic	Policy Question	Recommended Policy Response
Admission/Hiring	Request HIV Status at Client Intake or Staff Hiring?	"Will not be requested"
Internal Disclosure	When client discloses HIV+ to staff, who needs to know?	Adopt clear procedures and guidelines
In-program Client Disclosure	Should a client be required to disclose results if tested while a client?	"Will not be required"
Disclosure Liability: Obligations	What legal obligations do staff have when a client self-reports HIV seropositivity?	Spell out confidentiality laws and their application (no obligation to report to health authorities)
Disclosure Liability: Client Breaches	What program liability is there if another client breaks the confidentiality of an HIV+ client?	Liability unclear; but must protect clients from harassment; "we will educate clients about importance of confidentiality"
Charting HIV Data	If a client self-discloses as HIV+, should that be charted? If so, how?	Varies with kind of program/policy; should specify whether and how
Client Data External Transfer	If client HIV seropositivity is charted, and client information is transferred to another agency, is HIV data transferred as well?	Depends on consent for release
Test Confirmation	If client self-discloses as HIV+, should staff seek independent confirmation?	"Will not (no need to) seek confirmation"
Duty to Warn	If client self-discloses as HIV+, and a third party may be at risk of infection, is there a duty to warn?	Policy should spell out legal and clinical responses and safeguards
Consent for Release	Do consent for release forms make it clear whether HIV data is included?	Forms should be clear

Consent for Release of Confidential Information

I, _____, authorize
      (Name of patient/client)

_____
(Name or general designation of program making disclosure)

to disclose to _____
     (Name of person/organization to which disclosure is to be made)

the following information:

_____
_____
_____
_____
_____
_____

(Nature of the information, as limited as possible)

The purpose of the disclosure authorized herein is to:

_____
(Purpose of disclosure, as specific as possible)

I understand that my records are protected by state and federal law, and cannot be released without my consent except as provided for by law. I understand that I can specify which information will be released and which will not, and understand fully the nature of the information, specified above, that will be released. I also understand that I may revoke this consent at any time except to the extent that action has been taken in reliance on it, and that in any event this consent expires automatically as follows:

_____
(Specification of the date, event, or condition upon which this consent expires)

I have read and understanding this consent fully; or, as necessary, it has been read and explained fully to me.

Date: _____ Signature of above: _____

Signature of parent/guardian/authorized representative, when required:

_____

Chapter Seven:
CLINICAL CARE OF HIV-INFECTED CLIENTS

Vincent was Sharon's new case manager. When Vincent reviewed Sharon's chart, he noted, to his surprise, that she had been diagnosed with AIDS. Vincent had worked with a lot of people with developmental disabilities and had been an effective advocate, but a client with AIDS was a new experience for him.

Vincent brought up the subject with his supervisor, but didn't get much support or guidance. It seemed he was on his own.

Vincent got to know Sharon, and soon the number of crises and difficulties in her life—many of them related to AIDS—multiplied. Sharon was sick a lot, and Vincent tried, often frustrated, to hook her up with other services. Sharon's family was having a rough time, and he sometimes took calls, punctuated with heavy sobs, from her mother. Sharon was being evicted from her apartment, and when they found out she had AIDS in the fast food restaurant where she worked, her boss panicked and suggested she take an indefinite leave of absence. Every day, the problems seemed to multiply. Concerned as he was, Vincent began to realize that providing effective case management for Sharon could be an overwhelming task—and that he needed help. Not just practically, but emotionally as well.

Introduction

So far we have surveyed HIV policy issues that are largely legal or administrative in nature; though, of course, all of the previous issues have profound impact on individual well-being. But in order for an HIV policy statement to be comprehensive, it must address concerns that are more explicitly clinical in nature, or that speak to matters of organizational culture, behavior, and safety. This chapter and the next (which discusses larger issues of diversity and cultural competence) will round out the HIV policy package.

While working with HIV-infected clients does not require vastly new and refined expertise on the part of most human service professionals, it does demand sensitivity, a working knowledge of HIV/AIDS, and some skill in addressing HIV/AIDS-specific issues. Some specialized services do exist—medical case management programs, dedicated clinics, legal advocacy, and more—but people with HIV and AIDS will also need to utilize existing social services for a wide array of needs. Coordinated care, and a sensitization of the social service system, will be the key.

Unlike other areas of policy which may set absolutes for behavior, such as infection control, policy about the care and treatment of HIV-infected clients paints broad guidelines to aid the professional in clinical decision-making.

Clinical/Psychosocial Issues of People with AIDS

In some ways, AIDS is very much like a host of other life-threatening diseases. It seriously alters the quality of life. It can produce pain, discomfort. It often generates intense emotion, both for the person with AIDS and for those close to her or him. It causes financial stress. It can devastate self-esteem.

But in other ways, AIDS is different. People with AIDS commonly experience a unique and complex set of psychological and social realities and reactions. While many of these realities also hold true for people with so-called ARC (AIDS-Related-Complex) and those who are asymptomatic-infected, there may be some differences. It is absolutely essential that clinicians relate to the individual's *reality*, not merely their *diagnosis*.

Social Isolation

People with AIDS often suffer from an acute *withdrawal of usual social supports,* from friends, family, and acquaintances.

> *"You really find out who your friends are when you have AIDS. Some of the people I thought I could count on, through thick and thin, abandoned me."*

There are a variety of reasons for such withdrawal, some of which are logical psychological reactions, and some of which are based on an inadequate understanding of the disease.

1. Being around or close to people with AIDS often triggers one's own fears of mortality and death. Developmentally, most people do not begin to examine the issue of mortality until they are in their fifties and beyond, when friends their own age begin to die. But AIDS is killing people in their twenties and thirties; suddenly, friends and family members of the same age are forced to confront the possibility of their own deaths. And sometimes they just don't want to, or aren't ready yet. So rather than face mortality, it may be psychologically easier to "push away" the person with a life-threatening illness.

> *"I got tired of everyone around me getting sick and dying. I don't want to think about it. So when I hear now that someone has gotten it, I just cross them out of my address book."*

2. Being around or close to people with AIDS can also trigger a sense of helplessness based on the inability to change the illness. Often, there is very little—if anything—we

can do to "make the patient feel better."

> "When Todd was really sick we would go to the hospital and sit at his bedside. But there wasn't a damn thing we could do; we just sat there. It seemed hopeless. I stopped going."

3. It is sometimes quite easy for friends and family members to "overidentify" with the patient. Gay men who get AIDS, for example, are likely to have a number of gay friends of similar age, background, experience, beliefs, and values. It is easy for such a friend to look at the person with AIDS and "see too much of me." Again, there are times when one would just as soon not "see" such realities, and one will turn away instead.

4. Fear of contagion also plays a significant part in the withdrawal of common social supports.

> "When my brother came to live with us after he was diagnosed, I was afraid. I worried about my own children—could they get infected? It wasn't terribly rational, I know, but the fear was there."

Amidst conflicting and occasionally unreliable media reports, it's difficult for the layperson to sort through the facts about HIV transmission. AIDS can be so frightening that, even when one knows the facts, it's difficult to align emotions and intellect. It's one thing to think in the abstract, Yes, I know you can't get infected from casual contact. It's another thing entirely, and an emotional dilemma, to sit on the edge of a hospital bed when a friend has AIDS, holding their hand.

People with AIDS also suffer *isolation in hospital and other primary healthcare settings.* though in the nineties this experience is changing due to massive education and policy in the healthcare profession. At times this has taken the form of actual quarantine of people with AIDS, separating them from other patients and limiting contact between patients. More often this has expressed itself in the form of severe infection control precautions.

> "I remember when the night nurse came into my room the first time. He was wearing a mask, a plastic gown, gloves—the whole bit. He just came in to check my IV drip. He didn't even touch me."

In addition, care professionals are no less likely to exhibit homophobic and other judgmental attitudes as any other group of people. Such attitudes will only reinforce isolation in healthcare settings. Staff may be uncomfortable, for example, when significant others visit the patient with AIDS, or perhaps concerned with the image the hospital is presenting to other patients.

> "Everyone around here seems squeamish when my lover visits. They keep politely closing the door to my room if Bill is in here with me. They don't even think of doing that with the straight patients."

Alteration in Quality of Life

People with AIDS are often subjected to *crisis, disruption, and disorganization in thinking and daily habits*. In a sense, everything has become unpredictable and unreliable; even the day-to-day routines that keep most people grounded—going to work or school, playing and socializing with friends, sleeping, eating, and so on—are completely unstable. One doesn't know, from one day to the next, how sick she or he will be. One can't predict who will "be there for me," and who won't.

> *"It's hard for me even to say to a friend, 'Sure, I'll come over for dinner Friday night,' because maybe I'll be sick then, and maybe I won't. And I hate to let people down—it feels like I always do that because of AIDS, that I'm always canceling out on things because I don't feel up to it physically or emotionally."*

Many people do not realize the extent to which they base their lives on daily habits and predictable experiences. When those roots are taken away, the effect can be devastating. Because of this disruptive pattern, people with AIDS may live with *intense boredom, isolation, and social withdrawal*. There are several ways in which this presents itself.

1. People with AIDS often report feeling "too sick to work, too well to stay at home." The result is a general malaise in which people do not feel productive or active; they just feel "under the weather" much of the time.

2. AIDS also imposes medical restrictions, both because of the nature of the disease and because of the requirements of some treatment regimens. People may need to make regular clinic visits; again, they may be too sick to drive to the clinic, but not sick enough to be in the hospital. Some medications, such as AZT, must be taken regularly, a number of times a day, and these can have intense side effects. And some AIDS-related infections, such as cytomegalovirus or CMV (which can cause loss of vision or blindness), herpes zoster or shingles (which may be accompanied by severe pain), and candidiasis or oral thrush, can be debilitating and restricting in and of themselves.

3. AIDS often brings about internally-imposed or externally-normed restrictions of sexual outlets. Expressions of sexuality are normal and natural; prohibitions or radical curtailments of those expressions are, for many people, isolating and destructive.

> *"I have AIDS. But I also feel fine right now, and have a normal sex drive. I want to feel close to someone, to touch and be touched. But there's too much in the way. I tried, for a while, meeting people—like other people who were HIV-infected—but when they found out I have AIDS, they didn't want to have anything to do with me. So I don't even try much any more."*

Even when people with AIDS are sexually active with other people, they need to be careful about specific sexual practices, so that infection or reinfection does not occur. Many people, both seropositive and seronegative, have experienced safer sex practices as inhibiting and restrictive. We all must observe safe sex practices, of course, because it's unwise to assume our partner's seronegativity in the absence of some "proof." But people with AIDS are often much more acutely aware of the need to practice safer sex. Some people have suggested that, for excample, two people who are both seropositive do not need to worry about safer sex; after all, "they're both already infected." That is a myth. People who are infected can become "reinfected" with other mutations of the virus, leading to a heightened viral virility. (There are mutations; there is, however, only one Human Immunodeficiency Virus for all practical purposes.)

4. Because of the massive stigma and shame still attached to AIDS, many people with AIDS have internalized an image of themselves as "leprous" or infectious in a generalized sense. This may lead to further isolation from others.

> "Right after my diagnosis I went up to my parents' cabin. And the second morning I was there, family friends stopped by for breakfast. All of a sudden, during breakfast, I started panicklng—we were using the same sugar bowl, taking pancakes and bacon off the same plate, and so on. And I thought, Oh my God, what if I infect them? Of course, I knew it wasn't possible. But that didn't matter. The point was, I was afraid. I thought I should lock myself in my room."

Diminished or Declining Self-Esteem

AIDS can dramatically affect self-esteem; it has the potential to decimate an individual's sense of self-worth. People who, at one point, may have been confident, poised, sure of themselves and the directions they were taking in life, may, after diagnosis, feel little sense of value or purpose at all. Such a reaction is understandable. There is a significant *stigma attached to AIDS*—constant, sometimes intense and hateful. Wherever one goes, the message can be heard: on some level, "only bad people get AIDS." It is very diffIcult not to internalize at least some of those messages, and it becomes very easy to feel "dirty," or to be overcome with a sense of guilt. Internally, people with AIDS may struggle with unending dialogues, asking themselves over and over again, *"What did I do to deserve this?"* Unfortunately, the voices of blame will often surface in response:

> "It's all because I'm gay: if that weren't true, it wouldn't have happened."

> "It was just like that movie, Fatal Attraction. I had a few affairs. And something bad always happens. I got infected. It was stupid; it was my own damn fault."

Some people may take it one step further by "bargaining." A gay man may tell himself, "I'll go straight, if only I'm cured"; a straight women may tell herself, "I won"t ever have sex—not even masturbate—if I get rid of this thing." The bargaining, of course, is useless, but more importantly, it furthers the process of self-blame.

Two key points should be made about the processes of stigma and blame that often accompany AIDS:

1. First of all, blame is psychologically counterproductive. It does not help people with AIDS in any way whatsoever; it can only hurt both emotional and physical well-being.

2. Secondly, no one ever "deserves" AIDS or HIV infection, for any conceivable reason. In other words, the belief is damaging to health, and it is simply wrong.

Intensity of Emotion

It stands to reason that in the face of a life-threatening illness, many people will react with intense emotion and sometimes unclear patterns of thinking. AIDS is no different in that respect, though there are a few factors that may heighten the intensity.

One of the ways that intensity can present itself is through an *obsessive cognitive style*. Overwhelmed by the prospect of disabling sickness or death, people with AIDS can sometimes obsess about day-to-day details over which they have little, if any, control. For example, people may worry endlessly about whether their Social Security disability check will come on time; they may be excessively anxious about losing their jobs; or they may, to use another kind of example, spend all their time making sure their diet or regimen of exercise is "perfect" for maintaining a healthy immune system. Obviously, any of these things by themselves are serious, and deserving of planning and consideration. But the hallmark of obsession is any pattern of repetitive, non-productive thinking that prevents or inhibits meaningful planning and action for change or accommodation.

Again, the response—basically a defense against the feeling of being helpless or overwhelmed—makes sense. Since for many people with AIDS, being sick has come to mean the absence of customary diversions, distractions and daily habits, something needs to fill the void. Obsessive thinking is one of the possible activities that can fill that void, and at least temporarily provide some relief from the pain attached to larger considerations.

> "After I got diagnosed I called Jane [the caseworker] four or five times a day, about everything. None of it was really important; I mean, I couldn't do anything about it and neither could she. Finally, one day she put it to me; she said, 'You've called five times already today about the same thing, and it doesn't help.' And I just broke down and sobbed over the phone, because there was all this fear and pain beneath the constant questions about surface things."

This is *not* to suggest, of course, that the professional should treat concerns, anxieties, and worries with anything less than seriousness and respect. It is only to point out that patterns of downwardly cyclical thinking may be a common reaction among some people with AIDS; if that pattern is severe and persistent, it can be inimical to overall wellness.

People with AIDS can often undergo *profound emotional vacillation* as well. Intense feelings of guilt, rage, depression and fear are possible, and the person may be prone to easy tears or quick anger.

> "At first, I just had all these emotional reactions. I've never been a 'touchy-feely' type; I pretty much kept my feelings to myself. And all of a sudden, I felt like I was being consumed by my emotions."

Feelings may not only be intense, they can also change rapidly, sometimes fluctuating even within the course of a day from, say, rage to depression. The net effect of intensity and fluctuation is easily summarized:

> "I felt like I was on a roller coaster for months and months. Happy one day, rageful the next. I'd react to what my doctor said, what the media said, what friends

Clinical Care of HIV-Infected Clients

said, what my family said. It was all I could do just to hang on and persevere."

Perhaps one of the most difficult, and powerful, emotions that may present with AIDS is anger—or to be more accurate, *a kind of rage.* For there are many legitimate reasons to be angry:

1. At the general lack of justice, fairness in life.

"This disease is so unfair! I'm twenty-five years old, and I was full of dreams and ambitions—now all that has been robbed, just taken away."

2. At the lack of effective governmental response.

"They're still fighting over pennies for AIDS research in Congress. They have been all along. In the meantime more and more people are getting sick, and those of us who are already diagnosed are struggling just to 'make it.'"

3. At victimization by human service professionals and the medical system.

"I went to see a new doctor, just for a checkup. He had me get on the table and disrobe. I told him then that I had AIDS—I thought he should know. He panicked. He virtually ran from the room and started scrubbing down with soap and bleach. And he hadn't even touched me yet."

4. At the continuing hysteria in the media.

"I am so sick of these so-called special media reports, like where they follow some prostitute who is supposedly infecting other people 'on purpose.' And the news people all shake their heads, and say what a horrible person she is. And the implication is that we're all doing that: intentionally infecting others."

5. At the abandomnent of friends and family.

"My father has still refused to visit me since I've been in the hospital. For the first couple days I tried to be understanding; now I just think, 'You bastard, can't you get through your crap about this?' I mean, I'm close to death and he won't come."

6. At the inability to retain control over one's health, one's body, one's life.

"I can't walk so well now. I have to use a cane. It makes me feel like an old man. Sometimes I just get so pissed at that, I want to throw the cane through a window or something."

7. At the "lack of answers," effective treatments, and workable remedies for pain or discomfort.

"Every time I see my doctor I get the same answer: 'Well, we could try this, but it probably won't do all that much for you.' It's not her fault, I know...then she put me on AZT. And it helps some folks, but it just made me so sick I couldn't

take it any more. So here's the thing that's supposed to be the best thing going—that's what they say about AZT—and it makes me sick. What the hell am I supposed to do?"

Once added and accumulated, the justifications for rage are, at times, entirely reasonable. But once again, if *anyone* finds themselves consumed by any powerful emotion, it can block the individual's growth toward wellness and emotional stability.

Loss of "Control"

Often in the human services, "control" is used in a negative sense, as in a "controlling person." But it also has a positive and psychologically important aspect as well: people need to feel some sense of control over their lives, their destinies, and their day-to-day activities. They need to feel that they can have an effect on their own lives, that they can accomplish meaningful goals and take action against pain, discomfort, or uncertainty. In other words, people need to be "in charge" of their own lives.

AIDS often takes that sense of control away from the person. Particularly since AIDS often strikes people between the ages of 20 and 40, the time in one's life when one is most likely to be productive and accomplish new things, the results of loss of control can be devastating. Suddenly one is not an "achiever" any more; one is made into a "victim," a role that is sometimes reinforced by the medical system when it inadvertently "makes" people into passive, helpless patients.

It is difficult for people who are healthy, who are working in jobs that are satisfying, who are building relationships and families, to really comprehend the despair that can result when control over ordinary life is taken away. Imagine, for example, losing effective influence over:

1. One's body.

"I used to be very active. I loved sports, the outdoors. I ran a marathon. Now, that's down to almost nothing. I can't count on my body any more to do the things I want it to do. I might feel fine one day and make plans to do something, only to get sick the next day. And that's very painful to me."

2. One's treatment.

"I'm in an experimental trial for new drugs. But I don't know if I'm getting a placebo or not. I just go in, they take blood and urine, and they give me a pill. I feel like I don't have any say in the whole thing any more."

3. One's occupational and avocational life.

"I'm working now but I've also been out sick a lot. My boss has been very understanding, but I know she can go only so far. So one of these days I probably won't be able to work any more. The problem is, I don't know if that's going to be tomorrow or a year from now."

Clinical Care of HIV-Infected Clients

4. One's thinking (especially in the context of AIDS-related dementia, which can cause forgetfulness, etc.) and emotions.

"I was driving to my support group at the Project one day. And I got to the building, and suddenly I couldn't remember where I was or what I was doing there. It was a complete blank; it took a while, just driving around the block again and again, before I could remember. And I've been there a hundred times. It's a terrifying feeling. Whenever that happens I feel like I'm literally losing my mind."

**For more detailed information on the
neurological complications of HIV, see the following:**

Boccellari, A., and Dilley, J. W. "Caring for Patients with AIDS Dementia." *In:* Face to Face: A Guide to AIDS Counseling, *edited by J. W. Dilley, C. Pies, and M. Helquist, pp. 186–198. AIDS Health Project, San Francisco (1989).*

Bridge, T. P. "AIDS and HIV CNS Disease: A Neuropsychiatric Disorder." *In:* Psychological, Neuropsychiatric, and Substance Abuse Aspects of AIDS, *edited by T. P. Bridge, A. F. Mirsky, and F. K. Goodwin. Raven Press, New York (1988).*

Elder, G. A., and Sever, J. L. "AIDS and Neurological Disorders: An Overview." *Annals of Neurology (1988); 23 (suppl): S4-S6.*

Navia, B. A., Jordon, B. D., and Price, R. W. "The AIDS Dementia Cornplex: Clinical Features." *Annals of Neurology (1986); 19: 517-524.*

Price, R. W., Sidtis, J., and Rosenblum, M. "The AIDS Dementia Complex: Some Current Questions." *Annals of Neurology (1988); 23 (suppl): S24-S33.*

Ragan, M. R. "AIDS Dementia Complex, Competency to Informed Consent, Risk Assessment, and the ADC Defense." *AIDS and Public Policy Journal (1989); 4:183-192.*

---

5. The reactions of friends, family, and others.

"As people found out [about the diagnosis] I was amazed that nobody reacted the way I thought they would. People that I thought would run like crazy, they stuck by me. People I thought I could count on disappeared. There was no rhyme or reason to any of it. It got to the point where I didn't even bother trying to guess, trying to predict any more."

In the midst of such uncertainty, it's no wonder that people with AIDS may, at times, struggle to regain control—even when it's not possible. After diagnosis, for example, people may see another doctor, and then another (and so on), hoping for a reversal of the diagnosis.

> *"I went to see five doctors before it began to sink in that I have AIDS. I kept thinking that they must be wrong, that somebody else will tell me something different."*

People may feel a sense of absolute urgency about figuring out some treatment plan. Or they may jump from one treatment protocol to another, without giving any of them a chance, or despite the fact that a particular treatment may be medically unsound, even dangerous. Control, and its erosion, is a central reality for many people with AIDS; its impact cannot be underestimated.

Denial

Staring at the possibility of severe sickness and death, denial is a common and logical reaction. Any person with a life-threatening illness is likely to react with a certain amount of denial, simply as a coping mechanism. It is important in that sense to recognize that denial in the face of AIDS is not inherently bad; it is a defense that allows people to continue their lives on a day-to-day basis.

Denial in the case of AIDS can take several forms:

1. Refusal to accept the diagnosis.

> *"The doctor told me that I have AIDS but it can't be true. I haven't done anything, really, that would give me AIDS. It's just a freak accident that I have Kaposi's Sarcoma."*

2. Refusal to accept sickness or even the possibility of death due to opportunistic infections associated with AIDS.

> *"I'm going to be the first person to be cured of this disease, mark my words."*

3. Refusal to acknowledge limitations that AIDS places on the individual.

> *"I've always gone to the bars every night, drinking and meeting people. I'll be damned if I'll let AIDS stop me from having my social life."*

4. Belief that one may have already been "cured."

> *"I got on AZT two months ago, and it made a dramatic difference. I feel so good now, I'm not sure I was ever really diagnosed right in the first place. I keep telling my doctor, 'You know, I think I might have licked it completely.'"*

Denial plays an important role in the life of people with AIDS or others with life-threatening illnesses. In fact, a number of the statements above can have a positive effect *if* believing them helps people focus on wellness, stability, and balance. If, for example, the last person above is feeling good, energetic, and broadly "alive," then it matters little whether the diagnosis was true or not. The obverse is certainly true: constant focus on illness, disease, and death will only support the sickness and the feelings of passivity or loss of control.

It should also be noted that individuals can focus on their *abilities,* rather than dwelling on their *disabilities.* Some people with AIDS, and not without some justification, have complained that caregivers "try to make me into a patient"—that is, passive, compliant, and weak. Even when people experience limitations, they can choose to exercise their capacities, and caregivers should never assume that such a stance is unhealthy. It is, in fact, life-affirming.

A good rule of thumb is to *passively support denial unless medical treatment is compromised or unless others are at serious, immediate risk of HIV infection.* Fortunately, that doesn't happen very often; most people with AIDS understand that denial is a coping mechanism, rather than an absolute statement about reality.

Financial Stressors

In addition to all of the above, there is the very real impact of financial stressors. It's not unheard of to see someone working as an investment banker making $75,000 a year, who, within a matter of months, has lost their employment, eaten up their savings, and is now living on Social Security and Medical Assistance. AIDS can wipe people out financially at a time in a person's life when there are many other things to deal with already. And if one is poor to start out with, it can be even worse.

Total medical costs for people with AIDS can easily run between $50,000 and $100,000, sometimes much more. Insurance rarely covers everything, as in this individual's experience:

> *"I was in the hospital for 10 days with pneumocystis [pneumonia]. The total bill for that time was $25,000. Insurance paid for 80% of that, but that still left me with a bill of $5,000. And I have no money—I have maybe $100 in the bank and have always lived from paycheck to paycheck."*

Financial uncertainty is a terrible thing to deal with as well. But to be sick on top of it and facing massive bills—or to have to experience the general humiliation that often comes with applying for public assistance—is devastating.

General Guidelines

The following is a set of overall observations or principles that can guide the professional in her or his work with people with HIV. Much of what is outlined will be equally true whether one is referring to HIV-infected clients or staff.

One of our primary clinical objectives for all clients, whether they are struggling with HIV infection or other difficulties, is to nurture the quality of one's life. This is critical for clients with HIV infection or AIDS, since they are facing more directly the prospect of life-threatening illness.

- *When people have AIDS they are not necessarily dying, they are in fact liv-*

ing, *and need clinical assistance in that process. This holds especially true for people with HIV infection who are asymptomatic.*

• *Professionals should avoid any statements or actions that tend to "blame the victim."*

• *Nearly everybody currently living with AIDS acquired the virus years ago, before public discussion of AIDS was widespread.*

• *Even now individuals may choose to engage in behavior that may put them at risk of HIV infection, however, no one ever chooses to acquire HIV.*

A person with HIV infection or AIDS has the right to accurate information and support about her or his disease.

• *Given that so much of the data about AIDS already appears confusing, and that significant research is ongoing, uninformed comments and opinions are detrimental.*

• *People living with HIV or AIDS deserve to learn as much as they choose to about the infection or the disease, and may need assistance in discovering sources of information.*

A person living with HIV or AIDS, in partnership with care providers, is the final judge on matters relating to her or his health and its management.

• *With AIDS and other potentially life-threatening diseases such as cancer or diabetes, care providers are ultimately teaching people to take care of themselves, to "listen to their bodies," and to seek out sound medical and personal advice and then to weigh it carefully.*

• *People living with HIV or AIDS can form "partnerships" with medical and human service care providers that will cooperatively support their well-being and healing. They can also contest the advice of providers and pursue alternative, non-medical means for dealing with HIV or AIDS.*

The provider should be aware that for people with HIV who are recovering from addiction to chemicals, a rigid insistence on chemical abstinence under every condition can prove harmful to the client with AIDS who requires medically-supervised pharmaceuticals to manage the pain or discomfort of an opportunistic infection.

People living with HIV or AIDS deserve to experience positive sexuality and nurturing relationships.

• *Professionals need not become overly anxious about HIV-infected persons becoming intimately or romantically involved with others, as long as clients adhere to safer sex guidelines. "Safer sex strategies" refers to a range of options, including abstinence, strict monogamy, sexual activities that do not involve the exchange of infected blood, semen or vaginal secretions, and the use of condoms or other latex barriers (such as dental dams). One should always assume one's partner is HIV seropositive, and persons who are seropositive will want to inform prospective partners of their HIV status.*

Clinical Care of HIV-Infected Clients

Professionals working with clients who are HIV-infected or who have AIDS will, at times, confront difficulties as a result of homophobia, racism, sexism, classism, discomfort about human sexuality, grief, loss, and pain.

- *One can expect that work with HIV-infected clients or clients living with AIDS will bring to the surface concerns and anxieties about a host of uncomfortable issues. Such feelings are best viewed as opportunities to expand skills and awareness.*

Professionals can keep in mind that, aside from the commonality of a virus, people with HIV or AIDS are wonderfully diverse.

- *Knowing her or his limitations, and not being afraid to admit them, the effective professional will seek supervisory input, or make appropriate referrals, when faced with clinical dilemmas that cannot be easily resolved.*

We should let people be sick in their own way, and when or if the time comes, die in their own way.

- *How individuals manage their sickness and/or their dying process is the unique result of personal history, experience, and culture. There is no "right way" to approach such realities.*

- *Grief, especially, is an intensely personal affair. While it is likely that most people with HIV disease will experience profound levels of grief and loss, it may not always be evident when viewed from the outside. We should resist the temptation to map out an individual's emotional agenda based on some universally-applied template of human experience.*

If we cannot serve an individual well, for whatever reason, we are obliged to confront our own inabilities and insecurities, and attempt to resolve them in a conscious manner. But sometimes in such cases, "good service" demands that we "get out of the way," and link the client up with providers who can provide good service—but never, ever in a way that leaves the client feeling "dumped" or somehow to blame for the referral.

Finally, care providers are reminded of the most basic care ethic: *"at the very least, do no harm."*

Clinical Tasks

The professional working with HIV-infected clients will be required to pay attention to a number of clinical tasks—most of which, it is worth noting, are not specific to HIV/AIDS, but simply doctrines of good clinical care for *all* clients.

1. We can remain focused on living with AIDS, not on dying. Certainly clients will need, at times, to confront the universal reality of death, and people living with AIDS are often acutely aware of that fact, but if the counselor only views the client as someone who is dying rather than living, the client will tend to behave accordingly. The prospect of death is a reality for all people with life-

threatening illnesses, of course; the topic of death need not be unapproachable. It should be emphasized here that more traditional views of death and dying may not be entirely applicable to people living with HIV or AIDS because of the unique nature of the disease, in that it is often characterized by periods of good health that may alternate with periods of sudden, severe illness.

2. We can nurture client self-esteem *whenever possible. It is likely that people living with HIV or AIDS will suffer a diminution of self-esteem simply because of the internalization of negative societal attitudes about HIV and AIDS.*

3. When a client is feeling overwhelmed or incapacitated by prospects of the future, we can reorient her or his focus to the present. *Obsessive thoughts about the unpredictable are likely to heighten anxiety and helplessness.*

4. At the same time we can help the client regain control over manageable areas of his or her life. *All clients, whether or not they are HIV-infected, need to perceive that their actions and behaviors have some impact on their world and that they are capable of making and implementing decisions. For people living with HIV or AIDS, many additional areas of life (one's health, the reaction of family and friends, one's ability to work or study) are seemingly out of one's control. It is therefore critical that individuals feel that there is* something they can do, *such as change eating habits, practice safer sex, learn about the disease or quit drinking, that will help foster better health.*

5. We can support the client in the development of her or his spirituality *in whatever way is meaningful and sustaining to the client. The client may find it particularly helpful to seek out others on the same "journey"; that is, people living with HIV or AIDS who have built up a strong spiritual base.*

6. We can take care, at the least, not to ridicule alternative strategies for self-care, *and at best, to become informed about such options in order to offer them for client consideration. It is likely that if a client believes strongly that a specific method, such as therapeutic hypnosis, will prove useful, then that method will in fact have some benefit. And there is evidence suggesting that stress management, which may take a variety of forms, can enhance the immune system. The counselor's only concern will be the adoption of methods that are patently dangerous. Above all, no one deserves ridicule for contending that a nontraditional strategy is helpful.*

7. Finally, we should not be overly critical of, or disappointed in clients who, for whatever reason, are unable to feel hope. *One would like to believe that everyone can be brave and strong in the face of AIDS; the task, however, is exceptionally difficult. The counselor cannot allow herself or himself to judge the client who seems incapable of "fighting back"; such a judgement will only heap additional shame on the client's already fragile sense of self-esteem.*

Living with HIV Infection and AIDS: Survivors

George F. Soloman, M.D., Lydia Temoshok, Ph.D., Ann O'Leary, Ph.D. and Jane Zich, Ph.D., reporting from the University of California School of Medicine in San Francisco, have done considerable research in a new field: psychoneuroimmunology. While there is considerable folk wisdom in the idea of "mind over matter" or the belief that a healthy attitude leads to good physical health, psychoneuroimmunology is an emerging branch of scientific study that attempts to provide firmer evidence of the links between belief and being.

In their research, these professionals have worked with people with AIDS to identify a number of factors that seemed significant to long-term survival. They include the following:

• Long-term survivors understand and accept the reality of the AIDS diagnosis, but also refuse to believe that it is an automatic, imminent death sentence.

• They believe that one can cope actively with the disease and refuse to succumb to a helpless/hopeless state.

• They make appropriate, individualized adjustments in personal habits and behaviors to accommodate living with the disease.

• They see the physician as a collaborator, and do not fall into a passive or compliant mode when interacting with their physician. They take an active part in decisions related to treatment.

• They display a belief that the individual patient can influence the outcome of the disease and a sense of personal responsibility for health.

• They have a perceived commitment to life to take care of unfinished business and a sense of unfulfilled goals or dreams.

• Survivors find meaning and purpose in life.

• They identify a sense of meaning in the disease itself.

• They usually have a previous experience with beating a life-threatening illness or overcoming difficult situations and events.

• A program of exercise and physical fitness is a common factor.

• Long-term survivors report the importance of support and information from other people with AIDS, particularly shortly after diagnosis.

• A commitment to helping other people with AIDS seems to have a sustaining quality in and of itself.

• Long-term survivors seem to be generally assertive and have the ability to say no.

• Long-term survivors give themselves permission to withdraw from involvement when they need to take care of themselves.

• They have developed the ability to "read" their bodies and sensitively care for them.

• They seem to have a common ability to communicate openly, including concerns about health issues.

• And interestingly, the authors suggest that gay men who have learned to be comfortable and open about being gay adapt more smoothly to their diagnosis of AIDS than those for whom "coming out" is still an issue.

There are a few additional points to be made that are specific to HIV and AIDS:

* *We need to recognize that discrimination against people living with HIV or AIDS is real and often debilitating.*

* *Perhaps the most powerful role we can play is to model sensitive and respectful care.*

* *We can act as an advocate for and with the client against hurtful attitudes or behaviors. If required, we can identify competent legal counsel and other service providers who are sensitive to HIV.*

* *We should examine our language to determine ways in which it might be unintentionally hurtful toward people with HIV or AIDS, or people who are members of groups at high risk for HIV infection, such as gay men, people of color, and others.*

Policy Recommendations

Policy in this area will not appear as absolute as it may with other topics. But it should be addressed, especially when thinking of policy as a statement of agency/workplace values or beliefs.

One way an agency can accomplish that is by adopting "Principles of Care," like the one that follows (a slightly amended version of the policy wording adopted by the Minnesota AIDS Project), a policy statement that is expanded with language addressing more specific concerns. Those concerns include:

* *Baseline skill/knowledge levels of staff;*
* *Questions of supervision in relation to HIV/AIDS cases;*
* *Interagency referrals and cooperative case management; and*
* *Agency response to violations of the policy.*

Principles of Care for People Living with HIV/AIDS

This agency recognizes and affirms the following rights of all people living with a diagnosis of HIV or AIDS.

- The right to be treated, in all situations, with respect and dignity.

- The right of self-determination.

- The right to be treated as an individual with unique biological, cultural, gender, psychosocial, and spiritual needs.

- The right to receive services from care providers who are sensitive to the client's values, attributes, characteristics, and beliefs.

- The right to obtain comprehensive, appropriate, timely, quality care free from discrimination due to diagnosis, race or ethnicity, gender, age, religion, economic status, or sexual orientation. "Care" is interpreted to mean not only medical care, but nursing services, hospice, social services, emotional support services, homemaker care, and patient advocacy.

- The right to expect that "Quality of Life" will be the central value in the planning and delivery of all services.

- The right, whenever medically feasible and appropriate, to access services in whatever setting she or he chooses.

- The right to uncensored information about her or his disease process and available treatment options.

- The right to make appropriate medical and social service decisions concerning her or his treatment.

- The right to decide, for oneself, the meaning and significance of "family" and "significant other."

- The right of every person to die with dignity.

In addition, we recognize:

- The right of that "family" or "significant other" to be involved in the care of the person with HIV or AIDS as she, he, or they choose.

- The right of the "family" or "significant other" to legal counsel to ensure their voice in medical decision-making, when appropriate.

Chapter Eight:
HIV-Related Issues—Nurturing Diversity

When Captain Williams, the chief of the Royalson police force, issued new policy on HIV and emergency response, he was surprised at the responses that came from the officers. They didn't really have any objection to the policy itself—after all, it just mandated universal precautions and good infection control, and officers were logically interested in protecting themselves. But at the training session to introduce the new policy, officers began asserting that it was the homosexuals and the addicts they really had to watch out for, and that they should take extra precautions in situations involving "those people." Finally, one of the officers said loudly, laughing, but with a degree of seriousness, "We should just put all the faggots on an island, then we can cruise by in our boats and use them for target practice."

It was then that Captain Williams realized that just talking about HIV wasn't going to be enough.

Introduction

Since the beginning of the HIV/AIDS epidemic the disease has been associated with individuals or classes of people who have already suffered rejection, discrimination, and oppression. AIDS has affected gay men more than heterosexuals, people of color more than whites. Rates of HIV infection are proportionately higher among I.V drug users, within prison populations, and among sex workers ("prostitutes") in some areas. People who are poor, in the United States and around the world, are more likely to get HIV-infected than the well-to-do, and when they get sick, they will have less access to health care. These facts have, unfortunately, added fuel to prejudicial attitudes. Faced with the enormity of HIV, it seems some people will look for someone to blame.

One doesn't need to look far to witness the evidence of heightened prejudice. Reports of violence against gay men and lesbians have, since the beginning of the epidemic, climbed at an alarming rate; in one year, from 1985 to 1986, during the height of initial media attention on AIDS, reported cases increased by over 240%.

Human service agencies and businesses in general need to ensure not only that people with HIV are treated well. Those protections ought to extend to people or groups commonly associated with HIV—whether or not, in any individual case, the person is HIV-infected. In the face of oppression, worksites can take a stand, asserting openly that no one deserves, for any reason, to be hurt or devalued because of who they are. In fact, we can maintain the opposite: that the richness of who we are and what we have to offer is in our diversity; that is something to be celebrated, not condemned.

Background: HIV and Homophobia

Much of the animosity that has surfaced around the issue of HIV has been directed at gay/lesbian/bisexual/transgender people. First, a few definitions are in order. A "gay male" refers to a man who experiences the human need for warmth, affection, and love from persons of the same gender; sometimes this includes sexual contact. A "lesbian" is a woman who experiences the same human need for warmth, affection, and love from persons of the same gender; sometimes this includes sexual contact. A "bisexual" is a person who experiences the human need for warmth, affection, and love from persons of either gender; sometimes this includes sexual contact. "Transgender" refers to persons who feel that their gender identity is different than their biological sex. (Some transgender persons wish to change their anatomy to be more congruent with their self-perception; others do not have such a desire. There is no correlation between sexual orientation and transgender issues; transgender persons can be heterosexual, gay, lesbian, or bisexual.) The animosity toward these groups of people is commonly referred to as *homophobia*.

Homophobia is defined as an irrational fear or dread of homosexuality or homosexuals, or an inordinate fear of intimate relationships with others of the same gender. What makes homophobia a societal problem, rather than a merely personal attitude, is that those fears are enforced by law and culture. In most places in the country, it is perfectly legal to discriminate against a gay man or lesbian woman in employment, housing, and many other areas of life. And culture reinforces homophobia in countless day-to-day acts: it is still true that most everywhere in the U. S. two men walking down the street hand-in-hand risk taunts, harassment, assault, and even murder.

It is important to note that those fears, and such behavior, have nothing to do with assessments of people as *individuals*. They are based simply on one aspect of an individual's identity. In that way it is no different than discrimination based on race, gender, religion, class, or age. In fact, studies indicate that if a person is prejudiced against one group of people, she or he is more likely to be prejudiced against other groups.

By its very definition, homophobia hurts everyone. Not only does it generate violence and discrimination against gay/lesbian/bisexual/transgender people, it robs society of their creative talents and contributions. And since homophobia also refers to an inordinate fear of same-gender intimacy, even without a sexual component, it robs heterosexuals of potentially enriching friendships. For many people the fear of being labeled homosexual limits their behavioral options, and even career choices—witness, for example, the widespread belief that all male hair stylists, nurses, decorators, artists, designers, and food service workers are gay.

What Is Homophobia?

Homophobia is sometimes obvious, but often it manifests itself in very subtle ways. The liberal tradition of human service professionals—who care about people—often prohibits blatant displays of homophobia, but its more subtle expressions often continue. In many other workplaces, homophobia is ingrained—from the boardroom to the employee cafeteria. See if any of the following sounds familiar in your organizational setting.

- Assuming that everyone you meet is heterosexual, until you find out otherwise.
- Feeling that homosexuality and discussions about homophobia are unnecessary in human service organizations or other business settings.
- Looking at lesbian women, gay men, bisexuals, or transgenders and automatically thinking about their sexuality, rather than seeing them as whole, complex individuals.
- Thinking you can "spot one."
- Believing that a lesbian is just a woman who couldn't find a man, or that a gay man must have been raped by a male as a child.
- Thinking that if a gay man or lesbian woman touches you, he or she is making sexual advances.
- Wondering which one is "the man" in a lesbian couple, or which one is "the woman" in a gay male couple.
- Changing your seat in a meeting because you believe the person next to you is lesbian, gay, bisexual, or transgender.
- Characterizing lesbian women as "man-haters" or gay men as "woman-haters."
- Feeling repulsed or uncomfortable seeing public displays of affection between lesbian women or gay men, but accepting the same affectional displays between heterosexuals as nice or "sweet."
- Kissing an old friend, but hesitating to shake hands with a gay man or lesbian woman.
- Using the terms "lesbian" or "gay" as accusations or insults.
- Not asking about the lover of a lesbian woman or gay man even though you regularly ask "How is your husband/wife/girlfriend/boyfriend?" when you run into a heterosexual friend.
- Avoiding mentioning to friends that you are involved in a particular organization or that you are friends with a gay/lesbian person, because you're afraid they might think you're gay, lesbian, bisexual, or transgender.
- Failing to be supportive when a lesbian, gay, bisexual, or transgender friend is sad or upset about a quarrel, breakup, or death of a loved one.
- Being outspoken about gay and lesbian rights but making sure that everyone knows that you are heterosexual.
- Worrying about the effect a lesbian, gay, bisexual, or transgender co-worker, volunteer, or client will have on your agency or business.
- Expecting a lesbian woman or gay man to change her or his identity, affectional habits, or mode of dress to work and socialize with you.
- Not confronting a homophobic remark because you're afraid of being labeled gay or lesbian.
- Feeling that many gay men or lesbian women are too outspoken about their rights.

Heterosexual Questionnaire

One of the ways to see how insidious homophobia can be is to "turn it around." Gay men, lesbian women, bisexual people, and some transgender individuals report being asked, at one point or another in their lives, many of the questions below. How would it feel to replace "homosexual" with "heterosexual" in the questions?

1. What caused your heterosexuality?
2. When and how did you first decide that you were heterosexual?
3. Is it possible that your heterosexuality stems from a neurotic fear of the same gender?
4. Is it possible that your heterosexuality is just a phase you could outgrow?
5. Isn't it possible that you just need a good gay/lesbian lover?
6. Heterosexuals usually have histories of failures in gay/lesbian relationships. Do you think you may have turned to heterosexuality out of fear of rejection?
7. If you've never slept with a person of the same gender, how do you know for sure you're heterosexual?
8. If heterosexuality is normal, why are a disproportionate percentage of the mentally ill heterosexual?
9. To whom have you disclosed your heterosexuality?
10. Why do heterosexuals feel compelled to seduce others into their sexual orientation?
11. If you choose to have and nurture children, would you want them to be heterosexual, knowing the problems they would face?
12. The great majority of child molesters are heterosexual. Do you really believe it's safe to expose children to heterosexual teachers?
13. Why do you insist on making a public spectacle of your heterosexuality? Can't you just be what you are and keep it quiet?
14. How can you hope to be a whole person if you limit yourself to an exclusively heterosexual object choice, and remain unwilling to explore and develop your normal, natural, healthy homosexual potential?
15. How can you enjoy a fully satisfying sexual experience or deep emotional rapport with a person of the opposite gender, when the obvious physical, biological, and temperamental differences between you are so vast? How can a man understand what pleases a woman, and vice versa?
16. Heterosexuals are noted for assigning themselves and each other narrow, stereotyped sex-roles. Why do you cling to such unhealthy role-playing?
17. Why do heterosexuals place so much emphasis on sex?
18. With all the societal support marriage receives, the divorce rate is still spiraling. Why are there so few stable relationships among heterosexuals?
19. How could the human race survive if everyone were heterosexual like you, given the menace of overpopulation?
20. There seems to be very few happy heterosexuals. Techniques have been developed that might be able to help you change if you really want to. Have you ever considered aversion therapy?
21. A disproportionate number of criminals, welfare recipients, and other irresponsible or antisocial types are heterosexual. Why would anyone want to hire a heterosexual for a responsible position?
22. Do heterosexuals hate and/or distrust others of the same gender? Is that what makes them heterosexual?
23. Why are heterosexuals so promiscuous?
24. Do you make it a point of attributing heterosexuality to famous people to justify your heterosexuality?
25. Could you really trust a heterosexual therapist or counselor to be unbiased?

Homophobia and what might be termed "AIDSphobia," an irrational fear or hatred of people with HIV, are often intertwined. When individuals contend that HIV is "retribution" for "unnatural acts," homophobia is at the root of the statement. When politicians assert that we can cut down on HIV research because it is a "self-inflicted disease," an assertion rarely heard about cancer or heart disease, homophobia underlies the assertion.

Background: HIV and Racism

No reasonable person would argue that racism is no longer with us, or that it affects all areas of our collective life. Crosses still burn in front yards and protesters hold aloft signs reading "Spear an Indian, Not Walleyes." Leaders in the communities of color get death threats on a regular basis, and some complain that there are "too many Asians" in our colleges. The earning power of African Americans is far below that of European Americans, and many cities experience de facto segregation in housing, education, employment, and political affairs.

Racism is alive and well. It's a hard fact to acknowledge, especially in personal terms. For many of us who see ourselves as concerned and sensitive, the awareness that racism is *inside* us as well as outside is a painful one—and I, as a European American, am certainly one of the "us." Most of us in human services came to our profession, among other reasons, because we care about others. It's not easy to face the fact that we still retain racist attitudes, beliefs, and actions. But in order to move ahead we must admit our prejudices, without excessive self-condemnation or self-pity.

Racism, like homophobia, has also become intertwined with "AIDSphobia." HIV has affected people of color in disproportionate numbers, which has led many in the communities of color to believe that "the government doesn't care, as long and it's people like us who are dying." A lot of HIV educational materials proved to be culturally insensitive. African Americans with AIDS die faster than their European American counterparts because health care isn't as good or accessible in some communities, and people of color with HIV have often felt that the HIV service and care system has not responded well to their cultural realities and needs. As is the case with gay men, African Americans are sometimes automatically viewed as HIV-infected, simply because of their identity.

Tuskeegee, Genocide, and Mistrust

Some leaders in the communities of color have examined the realities of racism and HIV, and have come to the conclusion that a kind of cultural genocide is taking place. It's a potent allegation, and worthy of discussion even if the debaters determine that it is not, indeed, genocide.

Part of the reason for the charge is that American history is replete with examples of racist uses of medicine and public health, many of which are common knowledge within the communities of color, but not outside. They are important to note because they help explain why there is legitimate mistrust of official responses when it comes to HIV and people of color.

One such example is the so-called Tuskeegee Study.

In 1932 Dr. Taliaferro Clark, then Chief of the U. S. Public Health Service's (USPHS) Venereal Disease Control Division, initiated the Tuskeegee Study, intended to study the natural course of untreated, latent syphilis. About 400 African-American men in Macon County, Alabama, known to have syphilis, were chosen for the study. They were told they were ill and were promised free care.

In fact, treatments were *deliberately withheld.* After all, the researchers wanted to study the effects of untreated syphilis. Local doctors and draft boards were approached by USPHS officials, who convinced them to refrain from treating any of the 400 men. Even when penicillin, a known cure for syphilis, became available in the 1950s, it was not administered to any of the men. By the conclusion of the experiment as many as 100 had died directly from advanced syphilitic lesions.

This is not a story of the Old South, an ugly incident from the past that can be dismissed as an unfortunate stain of racism. The experiment did not end until *1972.* As late as 1969, a research review committee recommended that the study be continued.

That committee was at the Centers for Disease Control (CDC).

And the CDC is the front-line federal agency in the fight against HIV.

Of course, the CDC has done a lot of good things in the fight against AIDS, and many honorable and decent men and women work there. But the legacy of Tuskeegee remains. Health professionals have mistreated people of color, and it continues. Even in 1992 it was revealed that American Indian children had been injected with an experimental vaccine, without being fully informed about the possible side effects of that drug. It continues.

So when health officials approach the communities of color and contend that "we want to help you fight AIDS," they shouldn't be surprised if they are met with anger and mistrust. And in the context of the Tuskeegee Study and others like it, the cry of "genocide" is not such an irrational emotion after all.

Background: HIV and Sexism

In 1992 women in America still make between 59–63 cents for every dollar men make. Over four million women are battered every year in the U. S., and one out of three women will be sexually assaulted in her lifetime. The catalog of abuses and injustices goes on and on and on.

How is sexism connected to HIV? There are many ways.

> • *Much of the safe sex literature available assumes that sex is consensual, and that individuals can make free choices about sexual behavior. For many women, such is not the case.*
>
> • *Discussions about safer sex intensify a number of the contradictions that women already experience about sexuality:*
>
> —*Good girls don't.*

HIV-Related Issues—Nurturing Diversity

> *—A man's orgasm is more important than a woman's.*
>
> *—It's not respectable for a woman to assert her sexual needs.*
>
> *...and so on.*

Proclaiming the necessity of safer sex without addressing some of those underlying contradictions ignores women's realities.

- *Too much of the attention paid to women and HIV has focused on their roles as "vectors of transmission"—sex workers who could infect men, pregnant women who could infect their children—rather than the issues and needs of HIV-infected women themselves. This degrades the lives of women living with HIV.*

- *Not enough attention has been paid to the caregiver roles of women living with HIV. HIV-infected mothers, for example, may find it more difficult to access HIV services for lack of childcare resources.*

- *And even the definition of AIDS itself has worked against the needs and experiences of women with HIV. The official case definition of AIDS was built on observations of the disease's manifestations in men; little note was paid to whether the disease might manifest differently in women. It turns out that it does; for example, there are gynecological infections and complications related to HIV immunosuppression. This has led some activists to muse darkly, but not without merit, that "women don't get AIDS—they just die from it." One of the reasons this is important is that it is difficult to obtain some services or to get some disability benefits, without an official diagnosis of AIDS. Thus, women have gotten sick and died, but because their HIV-related illnesses didn't fit into "the official roster," they have been unable to get the medical attention and support they deserve.*

Background: HIV and Other Forms of Oppression

Other forms of oppression or discrimination intermingle with HIV as well.

HIV has had a disproportionate affect on the poor, both in the United States and in other parts of the world. This means that people who can least afford health resources are needing them the most. And even when HIV affects people of moderate or higher income, the experience of AIDS often drives people into poverty: the combination of mounting medical bills (and insurance premiums), lost wages, and psychosocial stress can bankrupt even financially stable families.

HIV has had a disproportionate affect on the chemically dependent, who are still seen in many sectors as morally weak, corrupt and dangerous, rather than as people struggling with another potentially life-threatening disease or condition who deserve support, assistance and above all, access to treatment resources.

The list goes on. In fact, taking all of the preceding into account, a different, non-medical picture of HIV begins to emerge: HIV has been difficult to deal with not merely because of the science involved, but because *HIV appeared, grew, and was nurtured in the cultural context of multiple oppressions, which further fed AIDSphobia, which in turn further fed other forms of oppression.* Because of this, *it is impossible to consider a rational approach to HIV without also confronting the realities of the oppression that helped make HIV so ominous, frightful, and venomous.*

HIV, Diversity, and the Workplace

What does all this mean for the workplace? A few essential points deserve to be made. First, oppression is still with us; in fact, it contaminates just about every aspect of modern life. It can rob organizations of the talents and contributions of gay men and lesbian women, people of color, heterosexual women, and others.

Second, because of the above, *homophobia, racism, sexism, and other forms of oppression are mental health issues.* It is difficult to believe that anyone is truly healthy unless they are confronting those beliefs and attitudes which limit wholeness, including homophobia, sexism, racism, and so on.

Third, the AIDS epidemic has most especially brought the issue of homophobia to the forefront, and addressing AIDS means, by implication, confronting homophobia.

Fourth, AIDS and oppression present a challenge to organizations: we can embrace the diversity that forms the essence of American life, or we can run from it. It requires some courage, for example, for businesses to condemn homophobia, and welcome gay and lesbian staff and clients, even when the surrounding community may be hostile to the idea. But the alternative is continued condemnation of people for no other reason than who they love, their identity, or the color of their skin, and losing out on the lessons that AIDS really has to teach us.

And fifth, *silence on this issue is complicity with oppression.* Human service agencies and all businesses in general need to state openly what they believe so that all staff and clients are aware of, and working toward, the realization of organizational values. The implication is clear: organizations will want to examine all areas of operations and evaluate whether they tend to promote or oppose the continuation of oppression, and thereafter put into place measures that will challenge and condemn oppression whenever and however it emerges.

Policy Recommendations

There are at least three main policy implications that derive from the previous material.

> •*First, worksites will want to examine existing organizational policies that relate to equal opportunity in employment and services. Are they sufficiently inclusive? Are sexual minorities included in the organization's equal opportunity statement? Does the policy affirm the right of clients representing diverse identities (gay men and lesbians, people of color, people with disabilities, and*

others) to equal and respectful care and service? If not, you should revise the equal opportunity statement so that it embraces such diversity.

• Second, worksites will want to review their staff and volunteer makeup and assess the degree to which it adequately corresponds to client demographics and community composition. If the organization determines that staff/volunteer make-up is too homogeneous, it should make special efforts to recruit and retain members of under-represented groups.

• And third, organizations will want to commit to the ongoing development of staff competence in relation to diversity issues. I suggest that such a commitment be integrated into policy, otherwise training and staff education is prey to the whims of whoever is "in charge" at any one moment. It should be noted that the provision of training need not involve significant expense; some organizations, for example, have enjoyed considerable success in arranging for "training trades" with other organizations—company A provides training for company B in A's area of expertise, and vice versa.

Recently, a number of Minnesota state agencies circulated the following "Personal Commitment" statement among employees, and encouraged them to sign. (The statement is from A World of Difference at 15 South 9th Street, Minneapolis, MN 55402. It has been modified slightly to include concerns about homophobia.) The names of employees who did sign were posted in a public place. The circulation of the statement and its public nature served as the basis for an organizational commitment to nurturing diversity, and thus set the groundwork for the training that followed.

I encourage organizations to use the statement in a similar way. Distribute it among staff and volunteers, and encourage individuals to sign. Make a poster-sized copy, and ask individuals to collectively affix their names to the document. Such a process helps make it clear to all that "we, as *individuals* and as an *organization*" are dedicating ourselves to equality, respect, and fair treatment of each other and all clients.

My Personal Commitment

I will support [Name of Organization] in improving race and gender relations, increasing cultural awareness, and reducing bias and prejudice by:

- *Educating myself about the rich cultural diversity in our state.*

- *Intervening to let others know that I will not tolerate ethnic jokes, racial and religious slurs, sexist and homophobic comments, or any statement or action that demeans any person or group.*

- *Being a model of language and behavior that is non-biased and inclusive of persons regardless of ethnicity, race, religion, gender, or sexual orientation.*

- *Seeking opportunities to participate with culturally diverse groups.*

- *Celebrating my own cultural and religious heritage and studying, understanding, and respecting the traditions of others.*

- *Being proactive in my home, at work, and in the community to combat racism, sexism, homophobia, and all forms of bigotry wherever they are found.*

- *Discussing controversial subjects of discrimination and prejudice, when appropriate.*

- *Joining with other organizations to support efforts to reduce discrimination.*

Signature _____

Name _____

Date _____

Chapter Nine:
SHAPING POLICY FOR BUSINESS SETTINGS

Introduction

Does the previous outline of HIV policy topics apply to for-profit, business, or corporate settings? The quick answer is yes...and no. The *essential substance* of earlier chapters will be relevant to nearly any and every kind of organization, from daycare centers to large EAPs, from the small machine shop to the Fortune 500 corporation. But for the most part, businesses will not need to concern themselves with those policy topics that seem to be related to *client service* only, unless there is an application to *employees*. In other words, corporate policy on HIV/AIDS will probably be simpler and less detailed than the HIV/AIDS policy one might find in, for example, a group home for mentally ill adults.

There are both positive and negative aspects to that fact. On the one hand, businesses will probably find that the actual development of HIV/AIDS policy will not require a great deal of effort. On the other hand (and unfortunately), too many businesses have responded to the challenge of AIDS by adopting policy that is *too limited* in scope, and therefore need to expand their thinking about the importance of truly *comprehensive* HIV policy.

The following material reexamines each of the policy topics of previous chapters from a business perspective, and spells out what businesses will need to do. It also provides case examples of successful policy development in business settings and discusses potential policy pitfalls.

Policy Topics for Businesses

Discrimination

Businesses will need to enact unambiguous policy prohibiting discrimination against any job applicant, employee, customer, or contractee simply on the basis of that person's HIV status. In addition, management will need to examine corporate health and benefits packages to make sure that they treat HIV infection and AIDS in the same manner as any other chronic or potentially life-threatening illness, such as cancer and heart disease. Employees need to know that discrimination against or mistreatment of any other employee, because of perceived or real HIV serostatus, will not be tolerated. And employees living with HIV need to know that they can freely discuss matters related to health, performance, benefits, and reasonable accommodations with appropriate personnel without fear of any form of reprisal.

HIV Antibody Testing

It is difficult to imagine any circumstances in which routine testing of employees would be warranted—and as pointed out in an earlier chapter, such an action would be highly vulnerable to legal challenge. Businesses should take a firm position against mandatory testing of job applicants or employees, while at the same time providing all employees with accurate information about community resources for HIV antibody testing.

Confidentiality

Medical information about employees, including HIV seropositivity, is legally protected, except for those rare cases allowed by statute. Businesses will need to formulate policy that safeguards the privacy of employee medical information, in addition to shielding individuals from the sometimes harmful employee-to-employee gossip and rumor that can damage the smooth functioning of workplaces. Individuals with HIV-related concerns should be encouraged to consult with their supervisor, the company's EAP program, medical staff, or benefits managers—and always with the reassurance that unnecessary disclosure to others will not occur.

Infection Control/Universal Precautions

Infection control strategies in business settings will vary widely depending on the nature of the operation. Food service enterprises, for example, will no doubt have more stringent rules than a brokerage house or travel agency. Lead federal agencies, such as the Occupational Safety and Health Administration (OSHA) and the Centers for Disease Control (CDC) should be consulted for assistance in developing operation-specific infection control policy. In most cases, specific policy has already been written, and can be adopted or adapted for your use.

Employee Education

Business management will find that it is in their best interest to provide all employees with sensitive, accurate, and effective education about HIV and AIDS. Not only can such education help prevent potential disruption in the workplace, it can help ensure that the workforce remains healthy—which, in the long run, saves money. There are many programs, curricula, and people resources available to businesses, and the cost of providing such information should be weighed against the benefits of preventing employee HIV infection and workplace crisis.

Diversity

And finally, businesses should recognize that part of the challenge of AIDS is accepting, even embracing, a diversity of individuals in the workplace. We have already seen that AIDS, at least to date, has had a disproportionate effect on homosexuals, people of color, and other societal groups that, even before AIDS, suffered discrimination in communities...and workplaces. The loss of talent and energy resulting from that discrimination has been enormous.

Businesses should view AIDS as an opportunity to review their recruitment, hiring, retention, and layoff practices to make sure that they respect and encourage the kind of diverse workforce that most experts are predicting as the reality of the future. Are gay men and lesbians protected by the corporate anti-discrimination policy? What about domestic partner benefit regulations? Does daily life and corporate culture in the workplace *honor* diversity?

Two Worksites, Two Approaches

How does reasonable advice translate into action? This is precisely the point where most managers get "stuck." Having read this far, most readers will have come to the conclusion that AIDS policy in the workplace is a desirable, even necessary, goal. Making the leap from a logical argument to an action response can feel intimidating, maybe even slightly overwhelming. Rest assured: it can be done.

It may help to review two examples of workplaces that have developed comprehensive policy and education about HIV. One is a small, family-owned business; the other, a large multinational corporation.

Acme Machine

The Acme Machine Company is a single-site, family owned and operated business employing forty people, most of whom have been with the company for a long time. Acme has a very particular and specialized market—precision tooling for large truck engines—and has therefore weathered recessionary cycles quite well.

John Allen has been an engineer with the company since the early days when the business was just a handful of people. He's a loyal employee and devoted worker; John is the kind of person who rarely takes a sick day and who always seems to inspire loyalty and innovation in others. He has a personal friendship with Trent and Luann Belli, Acme's owners. They've built the business together, and watched their children grow up together.

So Trent and Luann were understandably concerned when John began calling in sick on a fairly regular basis. They didn't say anything—they trusted John—but they talked about it with each other. Twelve sick days in a four-week period. No explanation but "the flu," "a cold," and other vague generalities.

And so on a warm day in May of 1989, Trent and Luann asked John out to lunch.

And after the usual pleasantries, Luann posed the question: "John, we're worried. You've been missing a lot of work—and that's fine, that's not an issue. But we're worried about *you*. Is something going on that you feel like talking about?"

We Are All Living With AIDS

And in spurts and rushes, John's story came tumbling out. His son, Perry, had AIDS.

Perry had called home two months earlier to tell them he had AIDS and that he was already quite sick. Despite Perry's fears of rejection, he was met only with love and concern. Based on that reaction, Perry had moved back into his parents' home so that they could provide emotional, financial, and medical assistance.

John had been staying home to care for his son, to spend time with him. He'd been terrified of telling other friends and co-workers because of his own fears of rejection. John hadn't really talked to *anybody* and was feeling sad, overwhelmed, and scared.

When John told his tale, Luann's and Trent's hearts went out to him. They'd watched Perry grow up, too, and had fond feelings for a man they considered a kind of nephew. Luann and Trent responded to John with compassion, support, and an open willingness to do whatever they could to help out.

"I'll need more time off," John replied. "I want to spend as much time as I can with Perry. He's very sick. He may not have much longer."

"Whatever you need," assured Trent. "But I don't understand why you didn't tell us before?"

"I...guess I was just...I don't know. I should have. But I was scared. You two, the rest of the folks at the plant, you all are like family and I was afraid of losing that. People do weird things with AIDS."

"Then maybe it's time for Acme to so something about it," Luann said.

John smiled. "I'm all for it. I mean, it makes me nervous—but I'm all for it."

When Trent got back to his office that afternoon, he made two phone calls. One was to the Centers for Disease Control in Atlanta. He asked them to send all the information they had on AIDS, especially AIDS in the workplace. Then he called the Education Director of the state's largest AIDS service/education organization, and asked to set up a meeting.

Three days later Trent called John into his office. "I've learned some things, John. We do need to do some things about AIDS at Acme. We need to develop policy and educate all the workers. I've contacted an AIDS organization, and they'll help. But I need your help, too. I want you to be able to share your experience with the others here. And I want you to help plan. Will you do it?"

Within ten days, Trent, Luann, and John had identified five key employees who would help plan Acme's response to AIDS. The group started out by hearing John's story—and as Luann had predicted, they responded only with encouragement and a commitment to do what they could.

Luann then outlined the next steps. First, educate the planning committee. Then, review policy and employee education needs. Then, put forward an Acme policy about AIDS, accompanied by education for all employees.

After brainstorming all the possible policy and educational considerations, the group narrowed the list down to a few key elements. Policy would have to address discrimination, confidentiality, workplace infection control, and on-going education. With help from the local AIDS project and the CDC materials, the group found it fairly easy to draft policy. Trent had Acme's lawyer review the draft statement, and got the go-ahead.

The plan was to schedule mandatory education about HIV and release the policy statement at the same time. Again working with local AIDS experts, the planning group tailored an educational agenda that would last 90 minutes.

Six weeks after issuing policy and conducting employee education, the planning group met to review their work. Policy was well-received, and employees appreciated the education, especially since it was so "personalized" with the addition of John's story. John was still taking time off to be with Perry, and his co-workers were offering to help out in a variety of different ways.

"There's just one thing," John said at the review meeting. "I think this whole AIDS thing is also about homosexuality. You all know my son is gay, and that I've learned to accept that, even embrace that. If Acme really wants to deal with AIDS, it has to deal with gayness. I know no one here would discriminate against someone who was gay or lesbian, but I think it needs to be part of our policy."

After much discussion, the committee agreed. Two weeks later, the term "sexual orientation" was added to the company's non-discrimination clause.

When Perry died three months later, Trent and Luann shut the plant down for the morning. Thirty-three of Acme's forty employees attended the memorial service.

Climates International

When Ben Shadley returned to the office that day, after attending a "Business Responds to AIDS" seminar that lasted three hours, he knew that the time had come to do something.

Ben was the Chief Benefits Manager for Climates International, a multinational home climate control company. CI had its corporate headquarters in Canada, but maintained branch offices in Hong Kong, Manila, Seoul, Sydney, and Tokyo. Over 2,000 employees made CI run, and its workforce encompassed a wide diversity of values, nationalities, languages, and occupational specialties. Ben already knew there were employees with HIV and AIDS, and he knew there was *no* plan, *no* strategy, *no* organized response to the issue.

Ben's initial concern, the reason he went to the AIDS seminar in the first place, was cost control. Proliferating cases of AIDS could demand a lot of an employee health and benefits plan, and besides, there was always the potential cost of litigation if, heaven forbid, a CI employee with AIDS were mistreated in some way. But after attending the seminar Ben realized there was a human element as well: AIDS could be a devastating disease, and people with AIDS often suffered rejection, isolation, and condemnation. CI had a moral responsibility, at the very least, not to heap additional burdens and pains on the lives of employees with AIDS.

So Ben made a decision. He knew that developing AIDS policy and education would be a lot of work, and he didn't really have anybody to spare—there was no one in his department he could tap to take on the necessary tasks without something else being neglected.

Ben decided to bring in a consultant. After calling around, Ben hired Jane Zemsky, an expert on AIDS in the workplace. He contracted with her to review the company's operations, trends and issues in AIDS, and legal concerns. He asked that she come up with a list of recommendations for how to proceed. Since he was unfamiliar with Jane's work, he didn't hire her to execute a plan—only to articulate the broad scope of one. Ben would then decide what to do next, and how.

Six weeks later Jane submitted her report. Among her major findings, Jane noted that:

* CI needed to develop AIDS policy that addressed discrimination, confidentiality, infection control, employee education, and HIV antibody testing. CI should also seriously consider adopting policy forbidding discrimination on the basis of sexual orientation.

* That policy could be formulated as a set of core principles and regulations that could then be adapted for various sites, according to local law and statute. In some cases, however, CI policy may prohibit what may be allowed by local statute; e.g., even if local laws allowed for the use of the HIV antibody test as a screening or employment tool, CI would prohibit its use for such a purpose.

* That policy should be developed with the assistance of a planning team to be composed of no more than fifteen people, representing, as much as possible, the diversity of CI's workforce. Representatives from overseas offices could participate via videoconferencing or teleconconference.

* Employee education about AIDS could be managed by designating an interested person at each location who would then work in partnership with local AIDS organizations to develop and deliver educational presentations.

* Finally, Jane noted that, in her estimation, the entire process would take about six months.

Ben was pleased with Jane's report and assembled a team at CI headquarters to begin operationalizing it. He kept Jane on for additional consulting support, though he discovered that much of the work could be done internally by sharing certain responsibilities. Six months later, Climates International issued its AIDS policy to all employees, and began conducting employee educational seminars at all sites.

Business Policy Checklist

Discrimination

_____ Does policy prohibit discrimination against job applicants, employees, customers, and contractors based on real or perceived HIV seropositivity?

_____ Does policy guarantee fair access to corporate healthcare and benefits for people with HIV disease?

HIV Antibody Testing

_____ Does policy prohibit mandatory HIV antibody testing of employees or job applicants?

_____ Does policy refer employees who wish to get tested to appropriate HIV antibody testing sites?

Confidentiality

_____ Does policy protect, according to law, the confidentiality of employee HIV status?

Infection Control/Universal Precautions

_____ Does policy spell out procedures for infection control in the workplace?

Employee Eduation

_____ Does policy provide for effective education of all employees about HIV/AIDS?

Diversity

_____ Does policy provide protections against discrimination for gays, lesbians, and other groups?

_____ Does policy articulate methods for nurturing a corporate culture that embraces workplace diversity?

Potential Traps and Pitfalls

In the process of developing and implementing comprehensive workplace HIV policy, businesses should guard against a number of common policy or strategic pitfalls. While certain obstacles to good HIV policy are also found in social service agencies, they are perhaps more likely seen in business settings. There are a number of reasons:

1. *Workplaces traditionally are not forums for discussion of certain difficult, even intimate, matters such as sex, drugs, and infectious disease.*

2. *The topic of AIDS always, at some level, forces a certain set of values to the surface—about gay and lesbian people, about sexuality and moral belief, about trust and safety.*

3. *Addressing AIDS inevitably means facing the realities of sickness and death, and such personal loss is a very uncomfortable subject to confront.*

4. *And finally (especially in this author's experience), discussions about AIDS, when conducted with people in their thirties and older, often brings up a host of fears and concerns about the safety, security—and sexuality—of our children, especially those who may be young adults and sexually active.*

Pitfall Number One: Failing to Involve Representatives from All Levels of the Organization in Policy Planning and Implementation—Line Workers and Top Management.

If HIV policy planning does not include the perspectives of both the workers affected by policy and the managers who have the power to implement policy, the process will be marked by frustration and confusion, and the result will only be partially successful. The policy planning team should reflect the diversity of the organization, while at the same time having enough vested authority to investigate problems, craft solutions, and shepherd proposals through the corporate decisionmaking process with some reasonable chance of successful action.

Pitfall Number Two: Allowing HIV Policymaking to Be Cast as a "Labor vs. Management" Debate.

An example should help illustrate. One large business that had meat-packing operations as part of its holdings developed HIV policy addressing worksite infection control. This enterprise was also characterized by lukewarm relations between labor and management, and unfortunately management did not adequately consult with union representatives in the articulation and promulgation of HIV policy. Workers reacted to the policy announcement by asserting that "management is not telling the whole truth" about AIDS in the workplace, and the policy initiative got muddled in all ensuing debates. In fact, the union ended up taking the issue to court (where their case was dismissed), and the labor/management polarization was only heightened.

Workers and unions have historically believed that business has not and does not place a high enough value on occupational safety—and the contention is not without merit. Add to that the sometimes irrational fears that people still have about casual contact and HIV transmission, and it's not surprising that labor may sometimes reply, when told by management that "there is no need to worry about HIV transmission in the workplace," with expressions of disbelief. Union representatives should always be involved in HIV policy planning.

Pitfall Number Three: Failing to Allocate the Financial and Personnel Resources Required to Develop and Implement HIV Policy.

Developing and implementing HIV policy in the workplace will require time—and ultimately, money. Freeing staff time for participation in the planning process, acquisition of materials, providing for employee education—all these carry a price tag.

It should be noted that the cost of HIV policy development and implementation is rarely excessive, that it is well within the capabilities of most any concern, and that it always has to be measured against the costs of *not* doing anything. From the outset, management should commit the financial resources necessary to carry out policy planning and action.

Pitfall Number Four: Adopting Policy Without Offering Employee Education about AIDS; Offering Employee Education Without Good Policy to Back It Up.

Some corporations have provided employees with good information about AIDS but have failed to support that education with policy. Informing workers that "there is no reason to treat people with HIV differently" in the workplace, but neglecting to undergird that information with anti-discrimination policy, won't in the long run help eliminate discrimination in business settings. And if HIV discrimination is prohibited without educating employees about the wisdom of that prohibition, anti-discrimination efforts will be undermined. HIV policy and employee education go hand-in-hand.

Pitfall Number Five: Failing to Take into Account the Needs of Certain Operations, or Regional Differences Between Operations.

Business concerns with multiple sites and operations cannot expect that a single approach—or even a single statement of policy on specific HIV topics, such as infection control—will work at every site, for each operation. There are regional variations in style that must be taken into account when doing employee education: for example, the firm's lawyer from a corporate office in New York is probably not the best person to do education on a plant floor outside Biloxi. And policymakers will find that there are state-to-state variations on some legal matters, such as confidentiality and regulations about HIV antibody testing, that will need to be incorporated into policy.

Pitfall Number Six: Approaching HIV in the Workplace as a "One-Time" Issue, Rather Than an On-Going Concern Requiring Continual Monitoring.

One CEO, when asked what the corporation had done about HIV/AIDS, confidently replied, "Oh, we've taken care of all that. We wrote the policy and had education for all employees back in '88." An examination of the business's policy on AIDS revealed some errors of fact and terminology (e.g., referring to the virus as "HTLV-III," a term that was supplanted, for good, by "HIV" some years ago), in addition to some policy positions that were no longer legally tenable. In other words, the policy, while sincerely articulated, had become worthless. And one has to ask whether employees who participated in HIV education so many years ago still remember the facts, and what new employees learn or don't learn about HIV.

In all matters related to HIV, the shifting landscape of law, healthcare management, and research needs continual monitoring. As of this writing, for example, the federal plan for healthcare restructuring has not been completely disclosed, and the details of that plan, when adopted, will almost certainly have implications for insurance, benefits, healthcare access, and many other issues. Business leaders not only need to survey current events in the world of HIV/AIDS, but translate, when necessary, those events into revised corporate policy. The task is on-going.

And if a business provides employee education about AIDS, that education should be a regular task as well. Not only are regular updates for all employees appropriate, but consideration should be given to employee turnover and ways the corporation can bring new workers up to speed on corporate policy and the essential facts about HIV/AIDS.

Pitfall Number Seven: Failing to Build Partnerships with Local AIDS Organizations and other AIDS "Stakeholders."

In most every medium and large city in the United States, Canada and Europe, one will find an HIV/AIDS education/service network. Community-based service and education organizations have been in existence for years; they have been the "front-line" in the fight against AIDS, and have accumulated enormous knowledge and expertise. Businesses that fail to tap into those networks are neglecting a truly critical resource.

AIDS service and education organizations are generally excellent resources to consult on matters such as providing comprehensive medical care and social services to people with HIV, offering support groups to employees who may be affected by HIV, and designing and delivering education programs for workers. They usually have handouts and often have video libraries. And they can assist individuals and businesses in navigating the sometimes rocky waters of insurance coverage, disability, and government programs that can assist people living with HIV disease.

What keeps businesses from forming partnerships with community-based AIDS service/education agencies? It's certainly possible that business leaders are simply unfamiliar with what's out there. More likely, it's that many businesses simply aren't accustomed to building such "private/public" partnerships, or even considering them. Then, too, a certain degree of homophobia may be involved: many AIDS service/education agencies have their roots in the gay community, and though they have become more diverse (as the epidemic began affecting many different populations), some people think of such agencies as "gay-identified" and want to keep a certain distance. None of these reasons, whether real or perceived, can justify any reservations about reaching out to groups who really *know* this epidemic, with all its intricacies.

Pitfall Number Eight: Approaching HIV Policy and Employee Education from a Purely "Scientific," Detached Position.

Some early education about HIV stuck to the "scientific angle," attempting to carefully usher audiences through complex mazes of the science of HIV disease. While understanding the facts is important, HIV educators soon learned that facts alone are not enough. Education and policy has to address the range of *emotional responses* that attend this disease, and help individuals sort through personal feelings, values, and beliefs to arrive at understanding, awareness, and compassion.

Some businesses have recruited company medical personnel to deliver "science of HIV" lectures to employees. As long as the information is comprehensible to the audience, that's fine. But it's just as important to hear from people with HIV disease—how the illness has affected their lives, what supports they need—and individuals affected by HIV: friends and family members. And it's equally important to allow dialogue, to engage people, to permit the free and open expression of feelings. Education that does not include such elements will only have limited effectiveness in the long run.

Pitfall Number Nine: "Sanitizing" Employee Education about HIV and AIDS.

One large corporation developed comprehensive HIV policy and scheduled HIV education for all its employees. As part of the education session, a videotape about AIDS was shown. The video included interviews with a number of different people with AIDS, including openly gay men and a former heroin user, and presented those interviewees in a positive, supportive light.

Some employees objected. "It's too 'gay.'" "It endorses homosexuality." "It doesn't condemn drug use strongly enough." In reality, only a few people complained, but their voices were loud enough to cause management some concern.

Unfortunately in this case, management pulled the video, and substituted one that was much more "sanitary" in the eyes of the objectors. By doing so management chose to avoid some of the more controversial aspects of AIDS—and avoiding uncomfortable topics is part of what fueled this epidemic in the first place.

AIDS is about *everybody:* gay men, white suburban married couples, drug addicts, babies, prisoners, people with hemophilia, sex workers, CEOs of corporations. Even those who feel uneasy about certain realities—homosexuality and drug use, among others—know that. Preventing HIV infection, and providing good care for people with HIV disease, demands that we squarely face *all* the issues, not just those that are comfortable and "safe."

Pitfall Number Ten: Allowing HIV Policy and Employee Education to be Framed as an "Us vs. Them" Dilemma

Some individuals and groups of people have been cast as "the bad guys" in this epidemic. One hears, for example, about bisexual men being "responsible for bringing HIV into the heterosexual bedroom," and unfortunately, some people still blame gay men (or drug users) for "starting" this epidemic.

Any education or policy that perpetuates the belief that it's all "us" (heterosexual, white, married, sober) vs. "them" (gay/bisexual, people of color, drug users) ignores the fundamental reality: in this epidemic, "Them" *is* "Us." Fostering hatred or animosity toward individuals or groups of people simply won't help in the long run—and in fact, may lead people to maintain mistaken, and potentially dangerous, attitudes (for example, "Since I'm not gay or a drug user, I'm safe.").

Ten Principles of the Workplace

In July of 1987, the Citizens Commission on AIDS for New York City and Northern New Jersey was formed. Initiated as an assembly of individuals representing business, unions, public service, and HIV/AIDS organizations, the Commission sought to stimulate informed and sensitive private sector leadership in responding to AIDS.

By February of 1988 the Commission released its first report, *Responding to AIDS: Ten Principles of the Workplace*. Thirty corporations immediately endorsed the Ten Principles—among them American Telephone and Telegraph (AT&T), Dow Jones and Company, the IBM Corporation, Johnson and Johnson, *Ms.* Magazine, and United Jersey Banks.

By January of 1991 the Ten Principles had 404 official endorsers, including corporations, health and medical groups, local governments, religious organizations, unions, foundations, and AIDS organizations. An estimated three and a half million employees are working in settings covered by the Ten Principles.

In responding to AIDS, private sector employers will want to examine, and perhaps update, their employee policies on discrimination, benefits, disability, and other matters. They should also seriously consider providing education about HIV/AIDS to employees so that workplace disruption is minimized, workers are offered valuable health information, and valued employees are retained. Other sections of this chapter address such issues.

But if you're just beginning, adoption of the Ten Principles may be a great place to start—at the highest levels of decision-making, and then, throughout the business. They can be adopted by any business or agency so wishing.

The Ten Principles are reprinted on the following page.

Ten Principles of the Workplace
The Citizens Commission on AIDS
February, 1988

1. People with AIDS or HIV (Human Immunodeficiency Virus) infection are entitled to the same rights and opportunities as people with other serious or life-threatening illnesses.

2. Employment policies must, at a minimum, comply with federal, state, and local laws and regulations.

3. Employment policies should be based on the scientific and epidemiological evidence that people with AIDS or HIV do not pose a risk of transmission of the virus to co-workers through ordinary workplace contact.

4. The highest levels of management and union leadership should unequivocally endorse nondiscriminatory employment policies and educational programs about AIDS.

5. Employers and unions should communicate their support of these policies to workers in simple, clear, and unambiguous terms.

6. Employers should provide employees with sensitive, accurate, and up-to-date education about risk reduction in their personal lives.

7. Employers have a duty to protect the confidentiality of employees' medical information.

8. To prevent work disruption and rejection by co-workers of an employee with AIDS or HIV infection, employers and unions should undertake education for all employees before such an incident occurs and as needed thereafter.

9. Employers should not require HIV screening as part of general pre-employment or workplace physical examinations.

10. In those special occupational settings where there may be a potential risk of exposure to HIV (for example, in health care, where workers may be exposed to blood or blood products), employers should provide specific, on-going education and training, as well as the necessary equipment, to reinforce appropriate infection control procedures and ensure that they are implemented.

If your business or agency decides to endorse the Ten Principles, the Citizens Commission on AIDS asks that you notify them. They can be reached at:

The Citizens Commission on AIDS
121 Sixth Avenue, 6th Floor
New York, NY 10013
(212) 925-5290.

Assessing Workplace Readiness*

Most business leaders are acutely aware that HIV illness is also a significant workplace issue. Not only are many managers concerned with the safety, health and well-being of employees, they are also aware that situations involving AIDS in the workplace, if badly handled, can prove disruptive and damage a company's ability to do business. Addressing AIDS forthrightly is not only the right thing to do in terms of human impact, it's good business.

A large number of businesses will be affected by AIDS in the coming years, and if they haven't already, they will need to develop effective policy and educational responses. But how to start?

The following checklist, developed by business, human service, and government leaders, can help. It will allow a business to gain a sense of "where we are," and, by implication, "where we need to go." It can be employed by individuals within a company who are attempting to start the process, or by AIDS Teams which may have a formal charge to "figure out what to do."

The survey should be used in the following manner:

• *Complete the survey individually. If more than one person is completing it (for example, an AIDS Policy Team), average your responses.*

• *The survey's statements revolve around four basic topics related to HIV workplace readiness: Adjusting to Chronic Illness, Discrimination, Confidentiality, and Health Maintenance.*

• *Use the five-point response scale, and circle the number corresponding to the response that best reflects your workplace's efforts to date.*

• *Respond to the statements from the perspective of your professional position.*

• *Identify what you think the "next step" should be to improve your workplace's handling of each area of concern.*

---

* Adapted from *Responding to HIV in Minnesota's Workplaces: A Guide for Chief Executives and Their Managers* (May 1992). Minnesota AIDS Funding Consortium, 1120 Norwest Center, St. Paul, MN 55101. (612) 224-5463.

Shaping Policy for Business Settings

Assessing Workplace Readiness

One: Adjusting to Chronic Illness

1   No Workplace Response   4   Good Workplace Response
2   Inadequate Workplace Response   5   Exceptional Workplace Response
3   Adequate Workplace Response

Circle One Number:

A. Workplace education about HIV describes HIV illness as a chronic condition.

           1   2   3   4   5

B. Workplace policies anticipate the potential long-term productivity of HIV-positive employees.

           1   2   3   4   5

C. The benefit plan is responsive to the chronic and cyclic nature of HIV illness.

           1   2   3   4   5

D. Managers are trained to provide reasonable accommodations for employees with HIV disease.

           1   2   3   4   5

E. Managers are trained to provide referrals to services that can help HIV-positive employees with medical case management and daily living needs.

           1   2   3   4   5

F. Employees can use bereavement leave to cope with the loss of an unrelated partner, close friend, or member of their work group.

           1   2   3   4   5

WE ARE ALL LIVING WITH AIDS

Next Steps:

Considering your responses to these statements, does your workplace need to improve its capacity to respond to HIV as a chronic illness? What one or two activities should be considered priorities for next steps?

_____
_____
_____
_____
_____
_____
_____
_____

Two: Discrimination

1	No Workplace Response	4	Good Workplace Response
2	Inadequate Workplace Response	5	Exceptional Workplace Response
3	Adequate Workplace Response		

Circle One Number:

A. Policies prohibiting discrimination due to an employee's real or perceived HIV status are clear and unambiguous.

    1   *2*   *3*   *4*   *5*

B. Education and training about discrimination are provided for all employees.

    1   *2*   *3*   *4*   *5*

C. Discrimination due to real or perceived HIV status or sexual orientation is addressed as a part of HIV education or other education and training dealing with discrimination issues.

    1   *2*   *3*   *4*   *5*

D. It has been clearly stated that employees with HIV illness will be afforded the same consideration as employees with other chronic illnesses.

    1   *2*   *3*   *4*   *5*

E. Managers have been trained to understand the workplace applications of state and federal laws protecting disabled workers.

    1   *2*   *3*   *4*   *5*

Shaping Policy for Business Settings

F. Policies prohibiting discrimination due to sexual orientation are clear and unambiguous.

1   2   3   4   5

Next Steps:

Considering your responses to these statements, does your workplace need to improve its capacity to respond to HIV discrimination? What one or two activities should be considered priorities for next steps?

_____
_____
_____
_____
_____
_____
_____
_____

Three: Confidentiality

1	No Workplace Response		4	Good Workplace Response
2	Inadequate Workplace Response		5	Exceptional Workplace Response
3	Adequate Workplace Response			

Circle One Number:

A. Procedures for handling confidential information are clearly defined.

1   2   3   4   5

B. Compliance with procedures for managing confidential medical and health information is regularly monitored.

1   2   3   4   5

C. Employees who handle confidential health and medical information have participated in HIV education and training activities.

1   2   3   4   5

D. Steps have been taken to inform and reassure all employees that medical and health information is handled confidentially.

1   2   3   4   5

E. Managers have been trained to understand and implement "need to know" standards regarding confidential medical and health information.

1   2   3   4   5

Next Steps:

Considering your responses to these statements, does your workplace need to improve its capacity to respond to HIV confidentiality? What one or two activities should be considered priorities for next steps?

_____
_____
_____
_____
_____
_____
_____
_____

Four: Health Maintenance

1	No Workplace Response	4	Good Workplace Response
2	Inadequate Workplace Response	5	Exceptional Workplace Response
3	Adequate Workplace Response		

Circle One Number:

A. Employees receive encouragement and assistance is using their benefits.

1   2   3   4   5

B. Wellness is promoted as a workplace value and employees are encouraged and assisted in using their benefits in ways that promote health maintenance.

1   2   3   4   5

C. Healthcare benefits treat all chronic illnesses equally.

1   2   3   4   5

D. Comprehensive workplace education about HIV is regularly offered to all employees.

1   2   3   4   5

Shaping Policy for Business Settings

E. The chief executive and key managers stay informed about current and proposed changes in healthcare financing.

1   2   3   4   5

Next Steps:

Considering your responses to these statements, does your workplace need to improve its capacity to respond to HIV and health maintainence? What one or two activities should be considered priorities for next steps?

_____
_____
_____
_____
_____
_____
_____

Survey Instruments

The following surveys will be useful for assessing, on a number of levels, your organization's "state of being" in relation to HIV/AIDS and its attendant issues. At the very least, you are encouraged to use the first two; you can add the additional surveys as you feel appropriate or desirable. Of course, the more information you can gather about your organization, the more effectively you can plan policy and procedures.

All the surveys should be administered anonymously, and if used, should be administered to all staff.

On subsequent pages you will find the following surveys:

1. AIDS and the Organization is designed to determine, overall, the "stage" your business or agency is at. It takes but 5–10 minutes to complete. Scoring procedures follow the survey.

2. The HIV/AIDS Questionnaire will tell you a lot about an individual's knowledge and attitudes about HIV/AIDS and HIV/AIDS-related issues. Scoring follows.

3. Beliefs and Attitudes about Bisexuality/Homosexuality will reveal aggregate attitudes about bisexual or gay men or women, and certain aspects of bisexuality and homosexuality. Research has indicated, over and over again, that there is a strong correlation between how people perceive bisexual/gay/lesbian people and how they perceive people with HIV/AIDS; if they are accepting of one group, it is very likely that they will be accepting of the other, and vice versa. At any rate, working with people with HIV/AIDS will force people, inevitably, to confront beliefs and values about bisexuality/homosexuality. Comments on interpreting the survey follow.

Much of the scoring is based on the assumption that some responses are more desirable than others, rather than absolutes of right or wrong. Desirable answers indicate, for the most part, the respondents' *degree of comfort* with a subject. The presumption is, of course, that the greater one's comfort with certain topics, the most effective she or he will be as a business or social service professional. It should be noted, however, that such is not always the case, since it is always possible that the professional is capable of stepping out of personal biases if they interfere with good job performance or client service.

Coming To Terms with AIDS: Organizational Stages

Before a business or workplace program can *change*—that is, develop appropriate rules and regulations and nurture the skills required to implement those policies—it must have a clear understanding of:

1. *Where the organization is*—an analysis *of the current situation;*
2. *Where the organization* wants to be—*a sense of* goals and vision; *and*
3. *A plan for what the organization* will do—*a strategy for getting there.*

A central part of the organization's analysis of itself, in terms of its preparedness for HIV/AIDS, will involve a determination of the business or agency's current *stage*. Most groups go through a series of clear, definable stages in their response to HIV/AIDS. An understanding of those stages can aid the professional in analyzing the organization's current condition and charting desirable futures. The work in this section is drawn from experience with hundreds of organizations—no doubt the reader will be able to recognize, somewhere in the stages, her or his organization.

There are six stages in all:

- *Consciousness*
- *Concern*
- *Crisis*
- *Containment*
- *Collaboration*
- *Commitment*

Organizations tend to move in a more or less linear fashion through the stages, starting out at the first stage and "arriving," at some point in the future, at the sixth. Each stage has distinct features, and most organizations tend to be "at" one stage at a time, but there is some fluidity between the boundaries. Each stage, in the following discussion, is outlined in turn, and described in terms of:

1. *Its* General Features;
2. *The* Feelings, Talk, and Action *that typify that stage; and*
3. *The* Precipitating Events *that often move the organization from the previous stage to the current one.*

109

Stage One: Consciousness

General Features

• Rudimentary awareness of a reality called AIDS as something "out there," in some place or setting other than the organization.
• People in the organization are also likely to believe that many of the faces of AIDS (gay men, IV drug users etc.) live elsewhere, outside of the organizational reality. This belief is rarely checked for accuracy; it is simply an unquestioned assumption, resting on the premise that "if I don't know about it, it doesn't exist."

> *"We've never had any gays working here, as far as I know. I think I'd know something like that."*
> — Supervisor in agency serving sex workers

> *"Yeah, I've heard about it, but I don't think about it very much. Until today, I wasn't even sure how it was transmitted."*
> — Counselor in agency serving adults with-developmental disabilities in a city of 60,000 people

Feelings, Talk, Action

• Very little discussion of AIDS or AIDS-related issues in the organization—no compelling reason for such discussions. When mentioned at all, it is generally in the same tones people adopt for talking about hunger in Africa: distant, regrettable, but easily ignored.
• The facts about AIDS, and the implications of those facts for organizational life, are not yet a regular part of the organization's agenda.
• It is doubtful that there is any action at all at this stage. There is nothing yet to act toward or against. AIDS is merely a part of *consciousness,* something of which people are aware, but nothing more.

Movement from Previous Stage: Precipitating Event(s)

• If there *were* a previous stage, it would have to be "never heard of AIDS at all." Now, in the 1990s, it is difficult to imagine a business or social service professional who hasn't heard at least *something*. In some ways, that is an advantage over the early 1980s: most everyone now knows that AIDS and HIV exist.

Stage Two: Concern

General Features

• A generalized awareness that "AIDS is possible here." It is no longer a mere abstraction, but a real *potential*. In this stage, it hasn't happened yet, but members of the organization are largely aware that it *could*.

Feelings, Talk, Action

• Discrete and recognizable feelings about AIDS and AIDS-related issues begin surfacing. People may become aware of their fear.

> *"Whenever I think about it I think about myself, my teenaged daughters. I don't get it."*
> —Staff person at a substance abuse treatment facility

• They may feel angry—at gay men, at the government, at society as a whole—for "making me deal with this thing; bringing it down on us."

> *"It's that whole sexual revolution thing. If it weren't for everybody jumping into bed all the time—we wouldn't have this. I've been moral, but others...."*
> —R. N. in a nursing home

• Sometimes profound and persistent feelings of guilt and shame can emerge (or reemerge), especially about past sexual or IV drug use behavior, at this stage. Those feelings may present as fears about possible acquisition of HIV, but the underlying issue is unresolved guilt.

> *"Ten years ago I had a brief affair. It was nothing, meant nothing, so I never told my husband, and he never found out about it. Now I'm sure I got AIDS from that."*
> —Night counselor in residential facility for mentally ill adults

• The range of feelings that can begin to arise will be unique to different members of the organization. Some may feel hopeless, others helpless. Some may feel sad at the toll HIV is exacting, at the "loss of collective innocence," and so on. Still others may feel relatively little or nothing.

• It is important to note that the general *concern* of this stage can have positive, as well as not-so-positive, roots: it may indicate for some, a sense of confusion and protectiveness; for others, a more compassionate *concern* that the reality of AIDS is threatening *all of us*.

• People *do* begin talking more openly about AIDS in the organization, but the dialogues are directionless, diffuse expressions of feelings for which there is little resulting action.

> *"I keep thinking we should do something to get ready, in case it*

happens, but we haven't. I don't know what we'll do."
—Nursing home administrator

• And no one is quite sure what to do, or where to start.

"I look at all this [gesturing to a stack of new rules and regulations on infection control and other matters, just received in the mail] and I can't figure it out. I don't even know where to start!"
—Administrator of a number of group homes for persons with developmental disabilities

• What little action there is in this stage is often poorly planned or carried out. Revised infection control procedures, for example, may be published, but they are unevenly implemented. Staff may be very careful with a client known to have a history of IV drug use, for example, and careless with clients with an unknown risk history. Client education is sometimes begun, but because the overall organizational focus is unclear, the education is hit-or-miss, without an underlying philosophy or goals.

Movement from Previous Stage: Precipitating Event(s)

There are a number of events that are likely to precipitate movement from *Consciousness* to *Concern*. They include, but are certainly not limited to, the following:

• The facility accepts a client who has a "high risk" history (for example, someone who has used IV drugs in the recent past), but who is nevertheless seronegative.

• The local community becomes aware of its first (known) resident with AIDS. Especially in smaller cities, this can have a dramatic effect on other residents.

• The business or facility may begin receiving a series of mandates or guidelines from local, state, provincial, or federal authorities. Even in the local absence of HIV infection, such mandates can "force the issue" of future potential.

"I didn't start thinking about it until we got infection control bulletins from the State. And I started realizing that it could happen here before long."
—Nurse in state hospital unit for profoundly disabled adults

• Staff may discover family members, even distant relatives, who have AIDS.

• Staff may begin hearing of organizations similar to theirs, with roughly the same mission and goals, that "now have people with AIDS or HIV infection" among their caseloads or on staff.

The above examples all point to a common feature: something has happened to make the *possibility* of AIDS become tangible.

Stage Three: Crisis

General Features

• Crisis is the most distinct of all the stages; it is launched by a very specific occurrence: the known presence or impending presence of HIV in the "organizational family." It matters little whether the infected person is among staff or clients, whether she or he is symptomatic. What matters is that the Human Immunodeficiency Virus is *inside the four walls of the organization.*

• Crisis does not necessarily connote visible disruption as much as a profound conflict of beliefs, norms, goals and values, all of which may play itself out on internal arenas. If everyone is acutely frightened and confused, even if they aren't talking about it, it's still a kind of crisis and demands intervention and management.

• Few organizations will be immune from some crisis in relation to HIV/AIDS. Trying to circumvent or bury AIDS-related organizational crisis will prove fruitless; in fact, if anything, such a crisis provides an extraordinary opportunity for new growth and development.

Feelings, Talk, Action

• Feelings are high in Stage Three, and often entirely unpredictable. The feelings themselves are nothing new—they will be familiar from Stage Two—but the intensity has increased. At times they threaten to, or actually do, boil over, as when staff meetings are made chaotic with sharp expressions of anger or frustration. Usually, however, they are not quite so obvious: they come out in intrastaff conversations, in supervisory meetings, in therapy settings, or indirectly through behavior or passivity.

• Some staff members may threaten to quit "if we take someone here who has AIDS."

> *"I'm going to St. James and practice nursing there, where there's no people with AIDS."*
> *"But there is. There's AIDS in St. James."*
> *"Then I'm going to Blackberry Falls. There's no AIDS there."*
> *"But there is."*
> *"[Exasperated] Then where can I go?!"*
>
> —Conversation between L.P.N. and AIDS workshop leader in a nursing home caring for the chronically mentally ill. The facility was expecting an HIV seropositive client the next day.

• Some staff members actually *do* quit, which, if they are valued employees in other ways, can be painful.

- Some staff members may threaten to refuse service to an infected client or work with an infected co-worker.

> "Sure, he can be here. But he doesn't have to be in my therapy group, does he?"
> —Clinician in a program for persons with mental illness

- Administrators may consider refusing intake for a referred client who is known seropositive. Of course, staff can always "veil" reasons for intake refusal, citing a long list of other reasons.
- Administrators or supervisors may consider refusal of employment, or restrictive employment, for staff or interviewees who are known HIV seropositive.
- Some staff members may begin covertly or overtly lobbying for their "rights," generally for "a safe working environment." Superficially this sounds reasonable, and is in fact a justified request from employees. Often though, when it comes to AIDS, this may translate into a demand for an impossible guarantee that there will never be any danger of infection for employees, any time, under any conditions.

> "I'm tired of hearing about the rights of those people. What about my rights? Can you prove there will never be a danger?"
> —Corrections officer

- Some clients, in turn, may make similar demands of staff, lobbying for their rights in relation to another infected client or staff person.
- Some staff may exhibit a tendency to overstate risk, and therefore grossly overcompensate in taking precautions.

> "They give us latex gloves and breathing tubes for CPR. I think that's not enough. We should get gowns, masks—the whole works."
> —Social worker at a juvenile correctional facility

- Some staff may demand mandatory testing of all clients and full release of test results to all staff, so that "we can protect ourselves better," or even more ambiguously, so that "we can better serve the positive client."

> "I don't get it. I work with my clients closely, over a long time. I know just about everything about them. We get close. But I'm not allowed to know the test results? That's crazy."
> —Counselor in an apartment program for developmentally disabled adults

- There may be a polarization between staff and administration, or clients and staff, because people feel "forced" into something they don't want, or that they're not being told everything they "need" to know.

> "Administration has done memos, doing workshops on all these ways you can't get AIDS. But I read the papers; I hear conflicting reports. I don't

think administration is giving us the whole story."
—Corrections officer assigned to prison drug rehab program

• There tend to be lots of hushed conversations between individuals—staff and clients—where people feed off each other's anxieties and anger.
• The business, agency, or facility may schedule "emergency" meetings or trainings with the expectation that they can "nip the problem in the bud" quickly and decisively.

"We're getting our first AIDS client tomorrow afternoon. Can you come in and do a quick one-hour training for all the staff and clients tomorrow morning?"
—Adolescent substance abuse program administrator, in a request to an AIDS service agency

• A host of AIDS-related issues may come to the fore, with a previously unknown depth and ferocity. For example, latent homophobic feelings and attitudes, or judgmental responses to sex workers, IV drug users, or other affected groups may surface.
• Or, in something of a contradiction to much of the above, the organization may experience a thorough and strained silence. It might be that no one says anything, but the tension is entirely evident.

"When Jim [a seropositive client] came, no one said anything. It was scary. You'd think people would have a lot to say, but they didn't. You could feel it, though; you could cut it with a knife."
—Night counselor at a men's substance abuse halfway house

• The list of possible organizational responses in the midst of crisis is seemingly endless. Crisis, by its very nature, generates a myriad list of options and reactions. Often AIDS-related crises elicit "negative" responses, but such is not always the case. An organization might also respond in more positive, helpful ways.
• Some staff and members of the client community, if characterized by a great deal of maturity and cohesive trust, could collectively decide to confront fears *as* fears—nothing more and nothing less—rather than as unalterable truth.
• Administrative planning may be sufficient to foresee many of the problems and dilemmas that would attend the actual presence of HIV, and already have in place contingencies that will mitigate the worst of negative responses.

Movement from Previous Stage: Precipitating Event(s)

There is, as already noted, only one event that produces Stage Three Crisis: the actual presence, or impending entry, of HIV in the organization.

Stage Four: Containment

General Features

In the face of competing demands and tangible conflict, organizations generally tend toward solutions that address the lowest common denominators. They deal with symptoms and shy away from underlying causes. In the case of AIDS, that process can be called *containment:* minimally adapting to the crisis in order to tame the worst of collective worries and fears. Because the most visible aspects of crisis have been addressed—but *not* the underlying dilemmas—the central feature of an organization in Stage Four Containment is continuing, unresolved conflict.

Feelings, Talk, Action

The feelings, talk, and action of Stage Four all tend to betray the presence of unresolved conflict of lingering dilemmas.
- Administrators may schedule on-going AIDS education for all staff and clients, but it emphasizes the epidemiological or virological aspects of HIV infection, ignoring its social, sexual, political, and ethical aspects.
- The business or agency will have in place a number of AIDS-related policies, but they are inconsistently implemented and monitored.
- Staff enacts different rules for clients who are known HIV seropositive than for those whose antibody status is not known.

> *"Well, I would expect that Dave [a seropositive client] would not be sexual with anyone any more. You can't trust him to use condoms. Of course, it's different for the other residents."*
> —Counselor in community program for mentally-ill adults

- Risk reduction education efforts may be targeted only toward clients, ignoring the sexual or drug-taking lives of staff.

> *"We have thirty clients, mentally retarded, dispersed through several group homes. We know that two of the guys are gay. We're worried that they might get infected with the AIDS virus. Can you come in and talk to the two guys about safer sex?"*
> —Program manager, in a request to an AIDS education agency

- Staff and/or clients will persist in a certain amount of "victim-blaming" about HIV infection.

> *"She knew better. Shooting up, and she knew about AIDS, but sharing her works. I mean, I feel bad that she got infected, but she can't point her*

Shaping Policy for Business Settings

finger at anyone else."
—Substance abuse counselor, referring to a client who just tested HIV+

• Attitudes about AIDS are still death-focused, rather than focused on life and healing.
• Attitudes about gay men and lesbians, or members of other HIV-affected communities, are based on uneasy tolerance.

"I know that Jack's gay, and he's an okay guy. But I have to say I feel a little funny when he brings his lover to staff parties. I just never know what to say."
—Crisis intervention counselor

• Older organizational contradictions that are somehow related to AIDS and HIV begin to reemerge. For example, too, staff working with people with mental illness or developmental disabilities are sometimes uncomfortable with the idea that their clients may be actively sexual, and may deny such activity takes place.

"Our clients don't have sex."
—Physician at a large facility for mentally-ill adults

"How can we teach our clients about safer sex when we haven't even covered basic sexuality? We've tried, but the administrator won't go for it. He's afraid of what the parents will do if they find out."
—Counselor in a group home for adults with developmental disabilities

• There are a host of old, unresolved dilemmas in the field of social services, especially about sexuality and the nature of "acceptable" sexual behavior.

Movement from Previous Stage: Precipitating Event(s)

Movement from Stage Three to Stage Four occurs not so much because of discrete events as it does by the desire to avoid some of the discomfort and anguish that Crisis can bring. There are, however, a number of factors that will predispose an organization toward a "containment" strategy in the face of AIDS-related crisis.
• The organization has little or no history of dealing with some of the thornier AIDS-related issues, i.e., sexuality and homophobia.
• The organization's administration is typified by a crisis management style that elevates narrow, short-term interests over long-term, broad considerations.
• The organization has done little or no advance training about AIDS and AIDS-related issues.
• The organization may be marked by a relative degree of mistrust among staff members; their work style might be characterized as more competitive than cooperative.
Unfortunately, many agencies reach Stage Four and stay there, without real change.

117

Since legal obligations are satisfied, and overt "crisis" has been quelled, the organization's task, on the surface, is done. Tired perhaps of dealing with crisis, afraid perhaps of doing some of the hard work that real change will require, everyone wants to get back to "business as usual." The underlying problems are still there, however—and the organization that stays in Stage Four will miss out on the deeper opportunities for growth that HIV/AIDS offers.

Stage Five: Collaboration

General Features

Collaboration is characterized by an increasing dissatisfaction with the net results of Containment, coupled with a growing ability to articulate underlying difficulties and devise the means for resolving those difficulties. In many ways, it is a transitional stage. Private disagreements and animosity are increasingly replaced with a more collaborative stance, a growing sense that everyone needs to be involved in the development of a long-term philosophy and strategy that will work. On its most basic level, people in Stage Five have begun to look beyond narrow personal fears and interests, and have begun to reexamine the organization's goals and mission in the light of a decade-long, universally-impacting disease.

Feelings, Talk, Action

As a distinctly transitional stage, Collaboration is marked by feelings, talk, and action that waver between progress and regression, between forward momentum and stagnation, between hope and resignation. What underlies the variations is a subtle change in perception.
• There is a growing awareness that homophobia, racism, sexism, and other forms of oppression underlie the AIDS/HIV issue.

> *"Every time I talk to clients about AIDS, all the 'faggot jokes' start coming out. I'm beginning to realize that we have to deal with that. It seems really difficult to talk about AIDS without talking about some of that."*
> —Counselor at a family general service agency

• Individuals come to recognize the personal issues, as such, that commonly surface when fighting AIDS: fear of mortality, filled with images of "infection" and "disease," struggles with the nature of intimacy (and so on). Such issues are increasingly identified and claimed as personal difficulties.

> *"A week after the training I'm still sorting it out. I hadn't realized*

Shaping Policy for Business Settings

how personally this all affects me, how much of my stuff it challenges."
—Assistant administrator at a vocational rehab agency,
after attending a day-long training

• Individuals come to see that with AIDS, "pulling on the threads unravels the whole fabric." That is, they will move away from specific, unrelated observations and toward more wholistic analyses.

"At first I thought it would be pretty simple, that it was all a matter of some training, maybe a policy. Now I'm beginning to realize how big and complex this all is."
—Director of a program for assault survivors

• Members of the organization catch glimpses of the *opportunity* that AIDS presents, not just the *threat*.

"The more I talk to people with AIDS the more I realize that I have a lot to learn about death, about dying—about living. This sounds weird, but I sometimes find myself grateful for that."
—School counselor

• Finally, people *begin* to imagine the unimaginable, to form organizational visions hitherto unarticulated: "an organization free of bias, nurturing everyone's individuality and uniqueness"; "an agency that serves as a model in the fight against AIDS." Members of the organization may not state the vision in precisely those terms, but the initial content will be there.

Movement from Previous Stage: Precipitating Event(s)

• The organization may experience a change in key leadership that brings on someone strong, charismatic and visionary, someone with the necessary organizational skills to realize a vision. Experience informs us that *almost every organization that moves beyond Stage Four is headed by effective, sensitive, proactive management.*

• The organization may experience the death or hear of the infection of a client or staff person who is popular, well-loved. When the client or staff person is not well-known or liked, it is easier to distance oneself from the experience; when strong attachments are present, it is much harder to "contain" the feelings. It may appear callous to diminish the sickness or death of someone—anyone—but our experience certainly bears this out: if you don't know or like someone, their sickness or death will have considerably less impact.

• In larger organizations, with a number of clients or staff who are infected or sick, their persistent lobbying and self-advocacy—stating "this is not good enough"—may force the organization out of containment.

• The organization may be forced out of complacent containment by legal action that charges discrimination or substandard treatment for those living with HIV.

Stage Six: Commitment

General Features

Stage Six is difficult to characterize, partly because there are few organizations to which one can point as models, and partly because this stage is not so neatly marked by definitive features. *Commitment* is, ultimately, a vision of the best an organization can be in the fight against HIV/AIDS.

Feelings, Talk, Action

• Rather than mere acceptance, or even resignation to fate, the organization actually *welcomes* people with HIV or AIDS—as clients and as staff. The group does so first of all because *the need exists,* and it is within the mission of every private business and social service agency to serve the well-being of its clients and staff; and secondly, the organization consciously embraces the learning and growth that can come from diversity.

• The organization is committed to developing the in-house expertise that will allow it to serve people with HIV or AIDS *well.* It will not "shunt off" the above people to AIDS-service organizations every time they experience an AIDS-related need. Thus, for example, the organization will develop and sponsor an in-house HIV-positive support group if there is a sufficient number of staff or clients.

• Necessary procedures, such as infection control, are in place, and are followed calmly, without undue fear, by all.

• The organization is committed to the on-going education of all staff and clients, aimed not at "filling your head with facts," but rather, with the goal of helping each person to develop their innate ability to separate fact from fiction, and make appropriate decisions accordingly.

• The organization recognizes and affirms that when it comes to AIDS, it's *not* a matter of "us vs. them," it's only *us*—all staff, administrators, clients. That recognition is both personal and professional.

• The organization is cognizant of the underlying realities of AIDS (homophobia, racism, sexism, fear of sexuality and intimacy, and so on) and is committed to taking progressive steps that will eventually eradicate them from organizational life.

• Staff and clients will address personal issues, like fears about mortality, *as* personal issues.

• The organization has a long-range plan addressing AIDS and AIDS-related issues that encompasses service demands, special clinical needs, resource management, education, and all other areas.

• The organization has come to recognize long-standing organizational contradictions preventing progress in the fight against HIV, and is taking active steps to resolve those contradictions.

Movement from Previous Stage: Precipitating Event(s)

No decisive event will move an agency or private sector business from Stage Five into Stage Six. It is a process. The fruits of Stage Six are likely to be achieved over time by hard work, strong leadership, and committed staff. Without those elements, Stage Six will remain elusive, unattainable.

Where would you place your business or social services group on this continuum of stages? An accurate assessment of your organization, in this regard, will be crucial to the process of policy development, and especially, implementation. An instrument designed to gauge organizational stage-status follows.

AIDS and the Organization

    Please check the description that seems to most accurately describe your organization's current approach or stance towards HIV and AIDS. *Check only one.*

    _____ We've had people (staff or clients) here with HIV or AIDS, and have done some education and policy development in response. The education isn't very interesting; it's mostly medical. Generally staff have a lot of pity for people who have AIDS because it's so sad that they're going to die. Overall, the situation seems pretty much under control.

    _____ Most people recognize that we could see AIDS in our organization, but it hasn't happened yet, as far as I know. At first, it seemed far away, but now it seems like it's getting closer and closer all the time. We probably should do more to get ready but it seems a little overwhelming. It has made me think some about whether I'm at risk, or other people I know.

    _____ There has been very little discussion about HIV/AIDS within my organization. It doesn't seem terribly likely that we would ever get anyone with AIDS here, so we've never done anything with education or policy. It's not that we don't care, it's just that it doesn't affect us.

    _____ I think working with people with AIDS has been a great learning experience for us, and in a strange way, I'm grateful. I feel like I know a lot about AIDS and am learning more all the time; it's been a personally growthful experience. I know it's made us look at some of the ways "we've always done things," and ask hard questions. More and more I value diversity: gays and straights, men and women, whites and people of color.

    _____ We've worked with people with AIDS, and have done quite a bit. More and more, however, it seems like we're missing some of the bigger issues, like how people feel about sex or gay people. A lot of beliefs and values come up when we talk about AIDS and they're not being talked about enough. I know that I've begun thinking about it differently, like maybe we can learn something from all this.

    _____ We've recently found out that someone here (staff or clients) has HIV or AIDS. It seems to have had quite an effect on people. I've noticed that some people have strong feelings about it, and there have been some problems. I don't think we really have the situation under control yet.

Shaping Policy for Business Settings

AIDS and the Organization: Scoring

Each of the statements on the survey corresponds to the perspective one would be likely to have at each of the Six Stages. Notice that the order here is different than on the survey.

____ There has been very little discussion about HIV/AIDS within my organization. It doesn't seem terribly likely that we would ever get anyone with AIDS here, so we've never done anything with education or policy. It's not that we don't care, it's just that it doesn't affect us.
This corresponds to Stage One, Consciousness. Mark here for each respondent who checked it.

____ Most people recognize that we could see AIDS in our organization, but it hasn't happened yet, as far as I know. At first, it seemed far away, but now it seems like it's getting closer and closer all the time. We probably should do more to get ready but it seems a little overwhelming. It has made me think some about whether I'm at risk, or other people I know.
This corresponds to Stage Two, Concern. Mark here for each respondent who checked it.

____ We've recently found out that someone here (staff or clients) has HIV or AIDS. It seems to have had quite an effect on people. I've noticed that some people have strong feelings about it, and there have been some problems. I don't think we really have the situation under control yet.
This corresponds to Stage Three, Crisis. Mark here for each respondent who checked it.

____ We've had people (staff or clients) here with HIV or AIDS, and have done some education and policy development in response. The education isn't very interesting; it's mostly medical. Generally staff have a lot of pity for people who have AIDS because it's so sad that they're going to die. Overall, the situation seems pretty much under control.
This corresponds to Stage Four, Containment. Mark here for each respondent who checked it.

____ We've worked with people with AIDS, and have done quite a bit. More and more, however, it seems like we're missing some of the bigger issues, like how people feel about sex or gay people. A lot of beliefs and values come up when we talk about AIDS and they're not being talked about enough. I know that I've begun thinking about it differently, like maybe we can learn something from all this.
This corresponds to Stage Five, Collaboration. Mark here for each respondent who checked it.

____ I think working with people with AIDS has been a great learning experience for us, and in a strange way, I'm grateful. I feel like I know a lot about AIDS and am learning more all the time; it's been a personally growthful experience. I know it's made us look at some of the ways "we've always done things," and ask hard questions. More and more I value diversity: gays and straights, men and women, whites and people of color.
This corresponds to Stage Six, Commitment. Mark here for each respondent who checked it.

It is quite unlikely that everyone will answer the same way. You will notice, however, a general grouping around one or two stages. That will give you a fairly accurate picture of how people in the organization see themselves, in terms of the Stages.

WE ARE ALL LIVING WITH AIDS

HIV/AIDS QUESTIONNAIRE

1. How much do you know about the Human Immunodeficiency Virus (HIV) and Acquired Immune Deficiency Syndrome (AIDS)? Circle one.

    A. *A great deal*

    B. *Some*

    C. *Very little*

    D. *Nothing*

2. Identify by a check mark the statement that best describes your feelings about HIV/AIDS.

    ____ *I don't really need to know anything about HIV/AIDS.*

    ____ *I need to learn about HIV/AIDS, but it really doesn't affect me or my family.*

    ____ *I want to learn about HIV/AIDS. It may affect me or people I love.*

    ____ *I want to learn about HIV/AIDS. It's affecting everybody.*

3. What have been your sources of information about HIV/AIDS? Circle all that apply.

    A. *Television or radio*

    B. *Newspapers or magazines*

    C. *Pamphlets or brochures*

    D. *Members of my family*

    E. *Friends or co-workers*

    F. *Teachers or professors*

    G. *Ministers or other spiritual leaders*

    H. *Doctors or other medical personnel*

    I. *Professional HIV/AIDS educators*

4. How concerned are you about acquiring HIV at work? Circle one.

    A. *I am very concerned*

    B. *I am moderately concerned*

    C. *I am a little concerned*

    D. *I'm not at all concerned*

Shaping Policy for Business Settings

5. How concerned are you about acquiring HIV because of your own sexual or drug-using behavior?
    A. Very concerned
    B. Moderately concerned
    C. A little concerned
    D. Not at all concerned

6. Have you ever known someone with HIV infection or AIDS?
    A. Yes
    B. I believe so, but I'm not sure
    C. No.

7. If "yes," that person was (circle one):
    A. A sexual or IV-drug using partner
    B. A member of my immediate family
    C. Someone in my extended family
    D. A close friend
    E. A friendly acquaintance
    F. Just someone I knew of

Circle the correct answer.

8. Currently, all blood donated for transfusions is screened for the HIV antibody.	TRUE	FALSE	UNSURE
9. You can get AIDS by drinking from the same glass as someone who has AIDS.	TRUE	FALSE	UNSURE
10. If you share IV drug injection equipment with another person you are at risk for HIV infection.	TRUE	FALSE	UNSURE
11. You can get AIDS from a mosquito bite.	TRUE	FALSE	UNSURE
12. You can get infected with HIV by donating blood.	TRUE	FALSE	UNSURE
13. A woman infected with HIV can pass the virus on to her unborn child.	TRUE	FALSE	UNSURE

14. People living with someone who is HIV-infected are at high risk for acquiring the disease. TRUE FALSE UNSURE

15. A "positive" blood test means that one is infected with HIV. TRUE FALSE UNSURE

16. Staff who are working closely with clients who are HIV-infected are at greatly elevated risk for contracting the disease. TRUE FALSE UNSURE

17. There are clinics in most states where an individual may get a confidential or anonymous HIV antibody test. TRUE FALSE UNSURE

18. You can tell just by looking at someone whether or not they are HIV-infected. TRUE FALSE UNSURE

19. Individuals can pass the AIDS virus, HIV, to others without knowing it. TRUE FALSE UNSURE

20. The AIDS virus, HIV, can be sexually transmitted from man to man, man to woman, woman to man, and woman to woman. TRUE FALSE UNSURE

21. You can get HIV-infected from French kissing. TRUE FALSE UNSURE

22. Use of condoms can significantly reduce the chance of infection, if used properly every time one has sexual intercourse. TRUE FALSE UNSURE

23. If one is not gay/bisexual or an IV drug user, one doesn't *really* need to worry about AIDS. TRUE FALSE UNSURE

24. AIDS is now curable. TRUE FALSE UNSURE

25. Tears and sweat are HIV-infectious. TRUE FALSE UNSURE

Shaping Policy for Business Settings

26. Receiving blood donations is now safe from the chance of HIV infection.   TRUE   FALSE   UNSURE

27. One should be careful about the doctor or dentist they chose, because they could have AIDS and transmit it to their patients.   TRUE   FALSE   UNSURE

	Strongly Disagree	Not Sure	Strongly Agree

Check the number that seems to correspond most accurately to your reaction to the statement.

28. Our organization should find out about the health of the people it hires.   1   2   3   4   5

29. Our organization should find out about the health of its clients.   1   2   3   4   5

30. I am entitled to know if a co-worker or client has HIV or AIDS.   1   2   3   4   5

31. I have the right to transfer if a client or co-worker has HIV or AIDS.   1   2   3   4   5

32. People with HIV/AIDS should be allowed to live in a group home.   1   2   3   4   5

33. Homosexuality should not be a cause for discrimination in any situation.   1   2   3   4   5

34. People with HIV/AIDS have the right to work in hospitals.   1   2   3   4   5

35. There are many people with HIV/AIDS who are spreading the virus on purpose.   1   2   3   4   5

36. People with HIV/AIDS should be permanently separated from the rest of society.   1   2   3   4   5

37. To some extent, people who contract HIV through sex or IV drug use deserve it.   1   2   3   4   5

	Strongly Disagree		Not Sure		Strongly Agree
38. People with HIV or AIDS should be barred from teaching.	1	2	3	4	5
39. I doubt that anyone I know will get HIV-infected.	1	2	3	4	5
40. People with HIV or AIDS have the right to anonymity.	1	2	3	4	5
41. Homosexuality is not acceptable to me.	1	2	3	4	5
42. People with HIV or AIDS should be prohibited from working with food in restaurants.	1	2	3	4	5
43. It is extremely doubtful that any of our clients will get HIV or AIDS.	1	2	3	4	5
44. IV drug users don't care about anything but their "fix."	1	2	3	4	5
45. A person with HIV who doesn't inform their sexual partner should be jailed.	1	2	3	4	5
46. I have personally changed some of my behaviors because of HIV.	1	2	3	4	5
47. Scientists who say that HIV can't be spread by casual contact don't really have all the facts they claim to have.	1	2	3	4	5
48. Doctors with HIV should always tell their patients of their infection.	1	2	3	4	5
49. There should be a law requiring testing for everyone; that way, we'll know for sure.	1	2	3	4	5
50. Homosexuality is a serious threat to our cherished values and institutions.	1	2	3	4	5

HIV/AIDS Questionnaire: Scoring

1. How much do you know about the Human Immunodeficiency Virus (HIV) and Acquired Immune Deficiency Syndrome (AIDS)? Circle one.

    A. A great deal   _____

    B. Some   _____   *Write in number of each checked.*

    C. Very little   _____

    D. Nothing   _____

2. Identify by a check mark the statement that best describes your feelings about HIV/AIDS.

    Write in number checked of each.

    ____ *I don't really need to know anything about HIV/AIDS.*

    ____ *I need to learn about HIV/AIDS, but it really doesn't affect me or my family.*

    ____ *I want to learn about HIV/AIDS. It may affect me or people I love.*

    ____ *I want to learn about HIV/AIDS. It's affecting everybody.*

3. What have been your sources of information about HIV/AIDS? Circle all that apply.

    A. Television or radio   _____

    B. Newspapers or magazines   _____

    C. Pamphlets or brochures   _____

    D. Members of my family   _____

    E. Friends or co-workers   _____

    F. Teachers or professors   _____   *Write in number of each checked.*

    G. Ministers or other spiritual leaders   _____

    H. Doctors or other medical personnel   _____

    I. Professional HIV/AIDS educators   _____

4. How concerned are you about acquiring HIV at work? Circle one.

    A. I am very concerned   _____

    B. I am moderately concerned   _____   *Write in number of each checked.*

    C. I am a little concerned   _____

    D. I'm not at all concerned   _____

5. How concerned are you about acquiring HIV because of your own sexual or drug-using behavior?
    A. Very concerned   _____
    B. Moderately concerned   _____   *Write in number of each*
    C. A little concerned   _____   *checked.*
    D. Not at all concerned   _____

6. Have you ever known someone with HIV infection or AIDS?
    A. Yes   _____
    B. I believe so, but I'm not sure   _____   *Write in number of each*
    C. No   _____   *checked.*

7. If "yes," that person was (circle one):
    A. A sexual or IV-drug using partner   _____
    B. A member of my immediate family   _____
    C. Someone in my extended family   _____   *Write in number of each*
    D. A close friend   _____   *checked.*
    E. A friendly acquaintance   _____
    F. Just someone I knew of   _____

For each, record the number of correct *responses,* incorrect *responses, and the number that checked "unsure."*

                                           Correct / Incorrect / Unsure

8. This is true in the United States.

9. False.

10. True.

11. False.

12. False. Many people get this wrong because they confuse *donating* blood with *getting* blood.

13. True.

14. False. To date, no one living with someone with AIDS has gotten infected from casual contact.

Shaping Policy for Business Settings

Correct / Incorrect / Unsure

15. True—though literally, the test only implies the presence of HIV because it detects the antibody to the virus.

16. False.

17. True.

18. False.

19. True.

20. True.

21. Though theoretically possible, it has never happened and the odds against it are astronomical.

22. True.

23. False. Identity is not the significant factor; behavior is.

24. False. Though many people with AIDS are living longer and better, there is no treatment that can *undo* the condition of AIDS.

25. False. Though they have been found to contain traces of HIV, the amount is entirely insufficient, under any conditions, to cause HIV transmission.

26. True. There's always a chance, of course, but the truth is that the U. S. blood supply is now safer than it's ever been.

27. False. As a good healthcare consumer, one should always choose a doctor or dentist with care, but as long as they are following standard infection control procedures one need not worry about HIV infection.

131

For each number, record the number of responses.
1   2   3   4   5

28. *The best answer is 1.* The organization should always find out whether the people it hires are capable of performing the job; "health status" is too vague and too easily the basis for discriminatory behavior.

29. On the face of it, this seems like a very value-free statement of concern; for example, what social service professional wouldn't care about or want to know about the health of her or his clients? But in the present context, and in the context of most discussions about HIV, it usually means "we have a right to know if our clients are HIV-infected." *Therefore, the best answer is 1.*

30. *The best answer is 1.* There is a difference between being "entitled" and curious.

31. *The best answer is 1.* Legally and ethically, there is no such right; it is based purely on prejudicial attitudes.

32. *The best answer is 5.* There is no reason they shouldn't, unless there are documented behavior problems that specifically relate to the possibility of HIV infection.

33. *The best answer is 5.* All the available research tells us, again and again, that there is no reason for excluding gay men and lesbian women from any sphere of life.

34. *The best answer is 5.* Unless one is practicing specific invasive procedures

Shaping Policy for Business Settings

| | 1 | 2 | 3 | 4 | 5 |

— and most of the time, with proper infection control, even then—healthcare professionals pose no risk of HIV infection.

35. *The best answer is 1.*

36. *The best answer is 1.*

37. *The best answer is 1.* No one, no matter who they are or what they've done, deserves HIV infection or AIDS.

38. *The best answer is 1.* There is no logical reason people with HIV or AIDS shouldn't teach or have contact with children.

39. *The best answer is 1.* The facts indicate that before long nearly everyone will know someone with HIV infection.

40. *The best answer is 5.* Everybody has the right to determine who does and does not know intimate and potentially damaging facts about their lives.

41. *The best answer is 5.* Homosexuality is a fact of life, and ought to be treated as such.

42. *The best answer is 1.* People with HIV or AIDS will not transmit the virus through food preparation.

43. *The best answer is 1.* Most everybody working in social services and the private sector will, as a matter of course, encounter a client with HIV or AIDS.

44. *The best answer is 1.* IV drug users care about many things; many, in fact, tend to be very responsible about HIV and other diseases.

1 2 3 4 5

45. This one is very complex; the best answer would probably be "it depends." If an HIV-infected person intentionally has unprotected intercourse with a lot of people and doesn't inform them so that she or he can transmit the virus— it's hard not to see such a person as malicious, dangerous, felonious. It does tend to be a "red flag" statement, however, because HIV-intolerent people want to see people with HIV "put away" and use transmission as a justification. *Therefore we will have to say there is no ideal response to this statement.*

46. *The best answer is 5.* Everyone should examine their behavior in light of HIV.

47. *The best answer is 1.* There is absolutely no reason for scientists to lie about the facts of HIV/AIDS; if anything, they tend to be conservative in their estimates and conclusions.

48. *The best answer is 3.* It really depends on the doctor, what procedures she or he is performing, and any possible risk to the patient.

49. *The best answer is 1.* Such a policy would result in millions of wasted dollars and little impact on the spread of HIV.

50. *The best answer is 1.* Though it does challenge some of the assumptions and myths we live by, it does not destroy anything we hold sacred—if anything, it broadens and deepens our values and institutions.

Beliefs and Attitudes about Bisexuality/Homosexuality

1. I believe there is homophobia in my organization:

   ____Among staff   ____Among residents/clients

   ____Among board members   ____Among volunteers

2. In your opinion, what determines a person's sexual/affectional orientation?

   ____Heredity   ____Early sexual experiences

   ____Environment (Learning)   ____Personal choice

   ____Brain chemistry or structure   ____Unknown factors

3. Does your organization currently have any lesbian, gay, or bisexual...

Staff?	____Yes	____No	____Unsure
Board members?	____Yes	____No	____Unsure
Volunteers?	____Yes	____No	____Unsure

4. In your opinion, should lesbian/gay/bisexual staff be "out of the closet?"

   ____Yes   ____No   ____Not Sure

   If "yes," to whom? (Check all that apply.)

   ____Other staff   ____Board members   ____Residents/Clients

   ____Volunteers   ____The community in general

   If "no," why not?_____

   _____

   _____

   _____

We Are All Living With AIDS

5. Do you identify yourself as bisexual, gay, or lesbian?

   ____Yes   ____No

   If "yes," are you "out" at work?

   ____Yes   ____No

   If "yes," to whom? Check all that apply.

   ____Staff   ____Board members   ____Residents/Clients

   ____Volunteers   ____The community in general

Below are a number of statements. For each, circle the letters which correspond most closely with your *honest opinion* about the statement.

Strongly Agree = SA   Agree = A   Neutral = N
Disagree = D   Strongly Disagree = SD

1. Living as a bisexual, lesbian, or   SA   A   N   D   SD
   gay man is a legitimate lifestyle.

2. In my experience, lesbians do not   SA   A   N   D   SD
   hate men, nor do gay men hate women.

3. I would not want to have a bisexual,   SA   A   N   D   SD
   lesbian, or gay friend.

4. I understand why some people   SA   A   N   D   SD
   prefer to have their emotional, sexual, and social
   needs met by someone of the same gender.

5. I am sometimes afraid that if I   SA   S   N   D   SD
   associate with a bisexual or gay man or woman,
   that he or she will "come on" to me sexually.

6. The idea of two women or two men   SA   A   N   D   SD
   involved in a sexual encounter makes me uncomfortable.

7. I think that people in social services   SA   S   N   D   SD
   and business spend too much time
   talking about homophobia and gay/lesbian/bisexual/transgender issues.

8. I am opposed to bisexuals, les-   SA   A   N   D   SD
   bians, and gay men working at jobs
   where they come into contact with children.

Shaping Policy for Business Settings

9. At times I have been worried that my feelings for someone of the same gender are stronger than they should be. SA A N D SD

10. Bisexuals, lesbians, and gay men should be protected from discrimination. SA A N D SD

11. If I associate with someone known as bisexual or gay, I worry that others will think I am also gay or bisexual. SA A N D SD

12. It makes me uncomfortable to see people of the same gender display affection in public. SA A N D SD

13. The thought of having a bisexual, lesbian, or gay son or daughter does not upset me. SA A N D SD

14. Lesbians and gay men should not have custody of their children. SA A N D SD

The following situations are based on actual incidents. In the space provided, describe in two or three sentences how you would respond:

Situation One. You are a counselor in a group home. You and Wayne, another counselor, are working together one afternoon. While you are busy with some paperwork, Wayne is talking with a new resident in the next room. Suddenly the resident, obviously upset, appears at your doorway and says, "I don't want Wayne anywhere near me—he's queer."
Your response_____

Situation Two. You are the program manager of a vocational rehabilitation program for young adults with visual impairments. For some weeks now you have been talking to the parents of a blind teenage girl; they are considering your program for their daughter. On the day they are scheduled to come in to sign the necessary paperwork for program intake, they call you, angry, and ask, "We were all ready to admit our daughter when we found out that you have homosexuals on your staff—is it true?"
Your response_____

Situation Three. You are walking past an office in which two colleagues are talking. As you pass the door, you overhear one mention the name of another co-worker, followed by the comment, "Well, what can you expect of a dyke?"
Your response_____

WE ARE ALL LIVING WITH AIDS

Beliefs and Attitudes about Bisexuality/Homosexuality: Scoring

1. I believe there is homophobia in my organization:

   Record number of responses for each.

   _____Among staff   _____Among residents/clients

   _____Among board members   _____Among volunteers

2. In your opinion, what determines a person's sexual/affectional orientation?

   Record number of responses for each.

   _____Heredity   _____Early sexual experiences

   _____Environment (Learning)   _____Personal choice

   _____Brain chemistry or structure   _____Unknown factors

3. Does your organization currently have any lesbian, gay, or bisexual...

   Record number of responses for each.

   Staff?   _____Yes   _____No   _____Unsure

   Board members?   _____Yes   _____No   _____Unsure

   Volunteers?   _____Yes   _____No   _____Unsure

4. In your opinion, should lesbian/gay/bisexual staff be "out of the closet?"

   Record number of responses for each.

   _____Yes   _____No   _____Not Sure

   If "yes," to whom? (Check all that apply.)

   _____Other staff   _____Board members   _____Residents/Clients

   _____Volunteers   _____The community in general

5. Do you identify yourself as bisexual, gay, or lesbian?

   Record number of responses for each.

   _____Yes   _____No

Shaping Policy for Business Settings

If "yes," are you "out" at work?

_____Yes   _____No

If "yes," to whom? Check all that apply.

_____Staff   _____Board members   _____Residents/Clients

_____Volunteers   _____The community in general

Below are a number of statements. For each, circle the letters which correspond most closely with your **honest opinion** about the statement.

Strongly Agree = SA   Agree = A   Neutral = N
Disagree = D   Strongly Disagree = SD

Record number of responses for each.

SA   A   N   D   SD

1. The best answer is "Strongly Agree."

2. The best answer is "Strongly Agree." The question is based on the myth that people are attracted to members of the same gender because of bad experiences with the same gender.

3. The best answer is "Strongly Disagree."

4. The best answer is "Strongly Agree."

5. The best answer is "Strongly Disagree." While it's possible, it should be of no more concern than the possibility that a friend of the opposite gender would make such a move. And if they do, the mature person could handle it with sensitivity.

6. The best answer is "Strongly Disagree," though everyone in society is taught from an early age that such acts are repulsive.

7. The best answer is "Strongly Disagree." Although it's possible that at any one facility staff may be talking about homophobia a great deal, it's not likely; most facilities see little, if any, discussion.

	SA	A	N	D	SD

8. The best answer is "Strongly Disagree." There are a number of reasons people believe this, but one of the most common is an ungrounded fear that the adult will manipulate the child sexually. The overwhelming evidence indicates that heterosexual adults are more likely to manipulate children sexually than gay or lesbian adults.

9. The best answer is "Strongly Disagree," simply because a healthy person wouldn't "worry," they would see such feelings as common, natural. It's hard to imagine, however, a teenager growing up in our society and *not* worrying about such feelings.

10. The best answer is "Strongly Agree."

11. The best answer is "Strongly Disagree," since an individual with self-confidence and high self-esteem wouldn't be concerned.

12. The best answer is "Strongly Disagree."

13. The best answer is "Strongly Disagree," though it would be natural for even a loving, accepting parent to be worried about the homophobia their child will face.

14. The best answer is "Strongly Disagree."

The following situations are based on actual incidents. In the space provided, describe in two or three sentences how you would respond. (Situations One, Two, and Three are presented, along with a personal response space.)

It would be impossible to quantify "correct" or "most desirable" responses to the three different scenarios, though the answers should be revealing. However, it should be obvious that the "best" response in each case would be one that was sensitive to the feelings of all parties involved, while at the same time taking a firm stand against homophobia.

Section Two:
POLICY FROM BEGINNING TO END

Policy Checklist

Deciding _____
Researching _____
Surveying/Assessing _____
Planning _____
Implementing _____
Evaluating _____

Chapter Ten:
TAKING ACTION

"Yeah, I've heard about it, but I don't think about it very much. Until today, I wasn't even sure how it was transmitted."

—Counselor in an agency serving developmentally-disabled adults

"I keep thinking we should do something to get ready, in case it happens here, but we haven't. I don't know what we'll do."

—Nursing home administrator

Steps in Policy Development and Implementation

The process of HIV policy development in most human service agencies and general business environments will progress along a series of discernable, tangible steps. A review of those steps, therefore, forms the logical foundation of this book.

First, the agency or business has to ***decide*** that it does indeed recognize the need for a comprehensive policy about HIV and AIDS. On the face of it such a decision seems simple; in reality, there are usually some in the organization who will advocate for HIV policy, and some who will actively or passively oppose it.

Second, the agency or business needs to ***research*** facts about HIV and AIDS, their related policy implications, and the legal and scientific premises upon which good policy rests. Part One of this book addresses most of those topics, but in some cases additional research may be required. You will need to research, for instance, those municipal, regional, and federal regulations that apply to your specific jurisdiction (if different from the material cited in Part One). Competent legal counsel should always be consulted in this process.

Third, individuals will need to ***survey and assess*** the organization as it is now. They will need to determine which policies in place already speak to aspects of HIV, and evaluate their adequacy. And they will need to find out what staff and clients know and don't know about HIV, and what beliefs and attitudes about HIV dominate the organization.

Fourth, members of the organization will need to take the research and data they have accumulated to date and begin ***planning*** for policy development. Draft policy will have to be written. A process for policy implementation will have to be articulated. And staff/client training needs should be determined, so that HIV policy, when distributed, is comprehensible to all.

Fifth, the plan will have to be ***implemented.*** Board and management approval may be required at this point, if they have not already been involved in the planning process.

And *sixth,* compliance with implemented HIV policy will have to be ***evaluated.*** If policy is not being rigorously followed, the policy itself (or aspects of its implementation) will have to be scrutinized and corrected.

1

Policy Checklist

Deciding √
Researching _____
Surveying/Assessing _____
Planning _____
Implementing _____
Evaluating _____

Step One:
DECIDING

"I didn't start thinking about it until we started getting all these bulletins about it from the state. And I started realizing that it could happen here before long."
—Nurse in a substance abuse treatment program

In the end, it always begins with one person.

A counselor attends an HIV/AIDS workshop and returns to her agency, committed to doing something about HIV. A board member finds out a family member is HIV-infected, and decides his business needs to respond. A care attendant works with a client with AIDS and is personally impacted. A manager engages in some serious reading about HIV/AIDS and realizes that it's only a matter of time before her organization comes face-to-face with AIDS. I've seen it a hundred times: in the end, it always comes down to one person who wants to do something.

I'm assuming that for your business or organization, the one-person policy catalyst will be you, the reader. And I'm assuming that you've already decided that it's important for your organization to have a comprehensive policy about HIV/AIDS. The next step is a little more difficult. How do you convince the *organization* as a whole that it's important to decide?

Decisions for change in most human service agencies and businesses originate from the top and flow down, or at the bottom (or middle) and extend upwards. The two situations are very different, and require different strategic blueprints.

> Jane was the Board Treasurer for a community mental health center in a rural county. A year earlier she found out that her brother who lived in Minneapolis had AIDS.
>
> Jane was devastated. She was frightened, confused, sad, and even angry at times. She spent a lot of time talking to her brother by phone; he was very open about what was happening with him. She read as much as she could about the disease. Every time a story came on the news about AIDS, she stopped what she was doing to listen.
>
> But for a long time, she didn't talk to anybody except her immediate family. Gradually she began talking to friends, even co-workers. Word, of course, got around, and to her surprise, she found most people supportive.
>
> Jane realized that the community health center needed to get ready for AIDS. She asked for time on the agenda at a board meeting, and shared her story. Other board members were moved and echoed her contention that the mental health center needed to act.

> Lee was a counselor in a vocational rehab program. As a gay man, Lee had seen and felt the effects of HIV/AIDS firsthand—friends had died and he knew many people who were struggling to live with HIV or AIDS. Though not infected himself, he felt passionately that society as a whole needed to address this crisis.
>
> Lee met with his boss, Marilyn, the executive director of the agency. He proposed that the agency develop HIV/AIDS policy and get training for the staff. Marilyn was swamped with work and was clearly reluctant to take on anything new. Lee left the discussion feeling discouraged.
>
> That evening, he decided to take a different approach.
>
> When he ran into Marilyn the next day he broached the subject again. At first, she seemed bothered. Then he made a proposal: "You don't have to do anything. I'll do all the work. I'll research it, check with people, and write a draft policy. All you have to do is take it to the board."
>
> Marilyn warmed to the idea, and gave Lee the go-ahead. Within a month, he had a draft policy on her desk and was helping her strategize how to carry it to the board.

If you are a board member, member of the management team, or an agency director, you are already in a position to declare the need for HIV/AIDS policy. That does not mean that everybody in your organization will *welcome* the prospect, but education and

Taking Action

training (which is within your power to schedule, and if necessary, require) can help convince others that HIV is an important topic, and that comprehensive policy is an appropriate response. But what about the reader who is *not* in such a position, and who may face opposition? Some advice from others in similar situations might be helpful:

The process may take time. The organization may need a period of education to build awareness about the need for policy.

• *One can invite speakers to conduct inservice education workshops or circulate articles about HIV/AIDS.*

• *Don't wait for someone else to take the initiative. Do the research yourself or offer to draft policy.*

• *Find out if other agencies and businesses similar to yours in mission and scope have already adopted policy about HIV. If few or none have, you can build an argument for "enhancing the leadership" of your organization by beginning to develop HIV policy. If others have implemented policy, you may be able to learn from their experience. You can also build an argument for "keeping pace" with your competitors or "being progressive" like other affiliated organizations.*

• *Raise the issue in staff and supervisory meetings. When appropriate, pose dilemmas the organization may face if it fails to prepare for HIV/AIDS.*

• *Investigate laws and rules impacting your kind of workplace, and whether any are related to HIV. The Americans with Disabilities Act (ADA), for example, will affect a vast array of programs, organizations, and service settings—and the ADA specifically prohibits discrimination against people with HIV or AIDS. A significant number of managers and board are yet still unaware of the ADA's potential impact on their organizations. Bring such laws and rules to your supervisor's attention, and suggest that "we might need to do something about this."*

• *Find out what resolutions about HIV/AIDS the professional bodies in your field have adopted. Professional bodies in developmental disabilities, mental illness, substance abuse, vocational rehabilitation, victims' rights, health care, and many other areas have all passed significant resolutions calling for action on HIV/AIDS. The National Congress of American Indians has encouraged all 140 federal tribes to adopt HIV/AIDS policy, and many leaders in the communities of color have made similar pleas. Share such statements or resolutions with others in your organization.*

•Analyze sources of support and potential opposition. Sometimes resistance to policy may have nothing to do with HIV/AIDS or its related issues. For example, an organization in the midst of financial crisis, or experiencing layoffs will be reluctant to take on new challenges that may involve an expenditure of time or money.

We Are All Living With AIDS

> Steven was the director of an outpatient substance abuse treatment program. After attending a day-long training workshop on HIV/AIDS, he was convinced that the program should develop and implement HIV/AIDS policy. He brought the issue up at the next board meeting.
>
> The board director, Gene, a recovering alcoholic who was the chief of police in town, was openly hostile to the idea and quashed the proposal. Steven was taken aback, but decided to let it drop for the moment.
>
> The next morning Steven called Gene and arranged to get together. Over lunch that day, Steven began probing gently, trying to discover why Gene (someone Steven had always known as open-minded and generous) was so adverse to the idea of HIV/AIDS policy.
>
> It turned out that a month earlier, Gene had arrested a recklessly speeding motorist. While pat-searching the motorist, Gene felt a sharp prick. It seemed that the man was an IV drug user, and Gene had poked himself with a needle the man had in his pocket.
>
> There was no way to know whether the man was HIV-infected, and Gene was terrified. The only person he had talked to was his doctor, who said that he would have to wait three months before the test would be valid. He hadn't even told his wife, but he had stopped having sex with her, coming up with weak excuses.
>
> The more Steven and Gene talked, the more relieved Gene began to feel, that he was able to share this awful secret with someone who listened and cared. Steven, for his part, pledged his support and convinced Gene that he should talk to his family, in addition to an experienced HIV/AIDS counselor.
>
> Gene did. Gradually, he began to feel less and less anxious, though he didn't feel completely relieved until his antibody test came back negative at the three-month mark. Gene and Steven decided together that they should bring in someone to talk to the board about HIV/AIDS, and the process of policy development was launched.

- Don't hesitate to assemble and activate a planning team. It may not be that everyone in the organization currently accepts the needs for an HIV/AIDS policy, but the process of initiating action, rather than passively waiting for some catalytic event, will itself be educative. It will be hard for top managers, even if they are resistant to the idea of an HIV/AIDS policy, to condemn a planning team's voluntary involvement in a project.

2

Policy Checklist

Deciding	√
Researching	√
Surveying/Assessing	____
Planning	____
Implementing	____
Evaluating	____

Step Two:

RESEARCHING

"I look at all these rules and laws and regulations about HIV, and I can't figure it out. I don't even know where to start."
—Director of a mental health facility

If the agency or business accepts the challenge of HIV/AIDS, policymakers should begin a period of self-education, followed by brainstorming and broad strategic planning. For those settings where board/management endorsement of HIV policy development is already a given, this will not require much effort.

This step is not nearly as complicated or protracted as it may appear. Board self-education, for example, might involve nothing more than making a slender packet of core reading materials available to all board members. Discussions of possible impact may take but a half hour in an all-board meeting. What is essential at this stage is that (1) everybody is brought up to the same basic level of understanding about HIV and HIV-related issues, and (2) that individuals engage in some focused dialogue about the future of HIV and the organization.

> ### *Researching: The Board and/or Management*
>
> - Board/Management Self-Education
>   - Reading materials (see Appendices and Educational Materials reading list)
>   - Board workshop conducted by local HIV/AIDS expert
>   - Videos
>   - Hearing from people living with HIV or AIDS
>   - Hearing from board representatives or managers of like organizations who have already undergone the policymaking process
>
> - Board/Management Brainstorming
>   - Impact of HIV/AIDS on our organization five, ten, twenty years from now?
>   - Staffing?
>   - Programming?
>   - Resources?
>   - Client needs?
>
> - Broad Strategic Planning
>   - What do we need to do to get ready?

Board commitment is certainly desirable, but as already suggested, it is not always the case. The reader who comes from an agency or general business where the board has not committed to a process of HIV policy development is likely to be one of two kinds of staff: first, a manager who has not yet approached a board or executives, and who may expect some resistance when doing so; or second, someone on line staff who has come to believe that policy is important, made a personal commitment to the process, but does not yet know how to proceed or what resistance to expect. Both will, of course, need to carry out some self-education about HIV, as above; a thorough reading of the materials in this book should provide the essentials.

What about strategic planning? At this point, the individuals just mentioned will be more concerned with gaining support for the process within the organization; a few ideas have already been mentioned. A good point of departure is informal conversations with one's supervisor, asserting the need for HIV policy. Informal education of other staff will also be helpful. The bottom line, however, is that creating the need for change will be up to you; one cannot expect that others will necessarily jump to the opportunity. In such a case, you may need some support and guidance yourself—don't hesitate to call local HIV/AIDS service or education organizations for help and guidance.

Whether one begins as an individual hoping for change or works with a board and executive staff already committed to change, the next step is to work toward the assembly of a formal or informal team or core group that can carry out research and, later, policy development and implementation. A team approach to HIV/AIDS policy development is highly desirable for several reasons:

- *A number of organization staff, rather than just one person, can learn about HIV and AIDS in the process, making implementation smoother.*
- *Individuals will be more committed to the success of policy if they helped create it.*
- *Soliciting diverse points of view will enable the organization to create policy that is responsive to real needs—not an abstract document.*
- *Utilizing the energy and resources of a team will help "spread the work around," so that no one individual is overwhelmed.*

In many small businesses and agencies, policy development, as well as many other program decisions, often follows an informal path. An organization with an executive director, five staff, and a small board can already function as a "team" for the purposes of HIV/AIDS policy development. And the process of policy development may indeed be assigned to a single person, providing they enjoy the support of staff and the board.

But in larger organizations the assembly of a planning team will need to be more deliberate. The following constellation can be viewed as an ideal grouping:

- Clinical Coordinator/Program Director/Top Manager
- Board representative
- Front-line, direct-service staff person
- Health education/Healthcare representative
- Client/customer representative
- For some services, a parent/guardian/significant other representative
- Support/Maintenance staff representative (e.g. cook, receptionist)

In addition, the team might want to add:
- An HIV-infected/affected person, someone from a high-impact HIV community (gay/bisexual, former IV-drug user, person with hemophilia), and an HIV/AIDS expert (your local HIV/AIDS service/education organization or your county public health office can provide recommendations for both HIV experts and people from highly-affected communities)

Once the team is assembled, it needs to do its work—develop written recommendations for policy content and its implementation, and shepherd those recommendations through the organizational process of review and adoption. First, however, it needs to carry out more research.

The First Meeting

In the first meeting of the planning team—whether that group is formally constructed or informally gathered—the facilitator or convenor (who is also perhaps the reader) will want to implement four primary objectives (as follows).

A. Make sure everyone is introduced and has an opportunity to talk about their reasons for being on the team;

B. Clearly articulate the responsibilities facing the group;

C. Help the team make some necessary decisions about research, investigation, and surveys to be carried out; and

D. Conclude the meeting with assignments for the next meeting and an outline of the agendas for coming meetings.

I suggest you make the following material from this book available to each team member before the meeting (these items are formatted in the book so as to be easily reproducible):

- "Steps to Comprehensive HIV/AIDS Policy Development" (following), and
- The "Fact Sheets" at the end of this book.

At the meeting itself, the facilitator should distribute:

- Copies of the agenda (following);
- The "HIV Policy Checklist" (following); and
- Copies of the "Research Worksheet" (following).

There are a few major decisions to be made in the meeting. First, the team should discuss, and come to some agreement about the current state of HIV policy in the organization; the "HIV Policy Checklist" can be usefully employed in that discussion. Second, team members should decide whether to survey the organization about its HIV-related knowledge and attitudes, and if so, which survey instruments to employ. Again, the "Survey Checklist" and the surveys themselves can aid in making that decision.

Finally, a member of the team should be charged with researching one or more of the HIV policy topic areas listed on the agenda (discussed in some detail earlier in this book). Perhaps the easiest way to carry out that task is to have the team member read the section of this book that corresponds to the policy area, and use the "Research Worksheet" to summarize notes and suggestions for the next meeting.

Planning Team Agenda
First Meeting

1. Select or Confirm Moderator

2. Team Member Introductions
    - Who you are
    - Perspective you bring to team
    - Feelings you have about process (e.g., enthusiasm or reservations)

3. Review of Team Tasks
    - Survey organization knowledge and attitudes about HIV/AIDS
    - Research policy needs and options (see Checklist, following)
    - Develop draft policy based on research
    - Assess sources of support/resistance within the organization or larger community
    - Articulate implementation plan, including education and training needs based on survey and assessment
    - Submit draft policy for legal review
    - Offer draft policy and implementation plan to decisionmakers for action

4. Tasks to be Carried Out
    - Research
        a. Knowledge about HIV/AIDS for team (the "Fact Sheets" packet given to each member of the team before or at the first meeting)
        b. Policy areas:
            Discrimination (Staff and Clients)
            Confidentiality
            Client Education
            Staff Education
            Infection Control
            Accidental Exposure
            HIV Antibody Testing
            Treatment/Care of HIV+ (Staff and Clients)
            Diversity

    (Members of the team should be assigned to research one or more of each of the policy areas and prepare a brief report for the next team meeting; see Research Worksheet. The materials in this book should be sufficient for most investigation needs within the United States.)

5. Open Discussion

6. Confirm Assignments and Set Next Meeting

Steps to Comprehensive HIV/AIDS Policy Development

One: Deciding

Two: Researching
- *Facts about HIV/AIDS*
- *Policy Implications of Facts*

Three: Surveying/Assessing
- *Existing Policies*
- *"Knowledge/Attitudes about HIV/AIDS"*
- *"AIDS and the Agency"*
- *"Beliefs/Attitudes about Homosexuality"*

Four: Planning
- *Drafting policy*
- *Barriers and Strategies for Overcoming Them*
- *Education/Training Plan*

Five: Implementing
- *Policy Legal Review*
- *Board/Management Approval*
- *Communication of New Policy*
- *Training/Education:*
    - *Supervisors*
    - *Direct Service Staff*
    - *Clients*
    - *Others*

Six: Evaluating

HIV Policy Checklist

Access to Services/Discrimination
___ We already have satisfactory policy in this area, and it is being implemented.
___ We already have effective policy in this area, but it is not being effectively implemented.
___ We do not have effective policy in this area.

Staff/Client Education
___ We already have satisfactory policy in this area, and it is being implemented.
___ We already have effective policy in this area, but it is not being effectively implemented.
___ We do not have effective policy in this area.

Infection Control (Including Accidental Exposure)
___ We already have satisfactory policy in this area, and it is being implemented.
___ We already have effective policy in this area, but it is not being effectively implemented.
___ We do not have effective policy in this area.

HIV Antibody Testing
___ We already have satisfactory policy in this area, and it is being implemented.
___ We already have effective policy in this area, but it is not being effectively implemented.
___ We do not have effective policy in this area

Confidentiality
___ We already have satisfactory policy in this area, and it is being implemented.
___ We already have effective policy in this area, but it is not being effectively implemented.
___ We do not have effective policy in this area.

Care and Treatment of HIV-Infected Clients/Staff
___ We already have satisfactory policy in this area, and it is being implemented.
___ We already have effective policy in this area, but it is not being effectively implemented.
___ We do not have effective policy in this area.

Diversity
___ We already have satisfactory policy in this area, and it is being implemented.
___ We already have effective policy in this area, but it is not being effectively implemented.
___ We do not have effective policy in this area.

Research Worksheet

Your task is to research one of the outlined HIV/AIDS policy areas, and prepare a report for the next planning team meeting. It is much easier than it may sound; most of what you'll need is found somewhere in *We Are All Living With AIDS*. Basically you need answer only a few questions.

What are the facts?

For example, in the area of *Discrimination,* you will want to survey appropriate local, state, federal, or other jurisdictional laws that address (directly or by implication) HIV and discrimination. For *Infection Control* you will want to review basic principles and procedures. You should be prepared to summarize your findings in an outline, either written or verbal (whichever the planning team has agreed upon).

What do the facts imply about policy?

In your research about fundamental facts you will inevitably draw some conclusions about policy in relation to those facts. For example, you may decide that your organization needs a specific way of addressing infection control, or that there need to be mechanisms for ensuring HIV confidentiality. Frame your conclusions in brief statements of recommendations.

Notes:

3

Policy Checklist

Deciding √
Researching √
Surveying/Assessing √
Planning _____
Implementing _____
Evaluating _____

Step Three:
SURVEYING/ASSESSING

"Sure, we can have people with AIDS here. But they don't have to be in my therapy group, do they?"
—Counselor in general mental health agency

"Whenever I think about it I get overwhelmed. I can't help but think about my teenaged daughters, my students, and what they're going to have to deal with."
—High school teacher

After the first meeting of the planning team, members will be gathering data in preparation for the next meeting. The primary task for all members of the planning team should be to *learn as much as they can*—and if the process takes some time, it will be time well spent.

The agenda for the second meeting of the planning team, as follows, moves the team into the third step of surveying and assessing. The main goals of the meeting are to hear reports on policy areas and to initiate surveying/assessing tasks. In addition to sharing what individuals have learned, the team will need to engage in some focused discussion about the organization as it is. (The facilitator will want to reproduce the "Survey Checklist" for team members and distribute copies at the meeting.) Several critical questions enter into that discussion.

1. *What policies do we have in place now about HIV; or what policies do we now have that might in some way be related to HIV (e.g., infection control)? Are the policies the most effective they can be?*

2. *What do staff and clients know about HIV? Where do they get their information? Is it accurate?*

3. *What beliefs and attitudes do staff and clients have about human sexuality and sexual behavior? About gay/lesbian/bisexual/transgender people? About addiction? About other issues that inevitably surface in discussion about HIV?*

4. *How do staff and clients feel generally about facing HIV/AIDS?*

The most effective way to gather such data will be to survey the organization. Several crucial survey instruments are included on page 102 and following pages: one assessing the organization's "stage" in relation to HIV/AIDS, another evaluating knowledge and attitudes about HIV, and a third canvassing beliefs and attitudes about homosexuality and bisexuality. They are highly recommended and have been refined from a variety of similar surveys in use over the past ten years. There may also be other surveys team members have seen that could be added to the list.

By the end of the second meeting the team will have decided (1) what additional information it is seeking, (2) how that information will be collected (e.g., surveys or interviews), (3) the practical mechanics of data gathering, and (4) who will be responsible for which aspects of data gathering.

Planning Team Agenda
Second Meeting

1. Reports from Research
   - Presentations
   - Feedback and Discussion

2. Decision Making: Surveying/Assessing
   - What policy is in place? Is it adequate? Is it being implemented?
   - Whether to survey staff on knowledge and attitudes, and which instrument(s) to use
       a. How will surveying be conducted?
       b. Who will photocopy, distribute?

3. Set Next Meeting Date

Taking Action

Survey Checklist

___ AIDS and the Organization

___ The HIV/AIDS Questionnaire

___ Beliefs and Attitudes about Bisexuality/Homosexuality

___ Other Surveys

4

Policy Checklist

Deciding	√
Researching	√
Surveying/Assessing	√
Planning	√
Implementing	_____
Evaluating	_____

Step Four:

PLANNING

"Every time I talk to clients about HIV and AIDS, all the 'faggot jokes' start coming out. And I'm beginning to realize that if we're going to deal with HIV, we have to address homophobia."

—Counselor in a youth crisis agency

"How can we teach our clients about safer sex when we haven't even covered basic sexuality? Whenever we do, administration and parents get uneasy."

—Counselor in a community service program

"At first I thought it was all pretty simple—that we'd just do some training for staff. But there's much more to it than that...."

—Director of a victim services program

Once the planning team has researched the facts about HIV/AIDS and gathered information about your organization's knowledge and attitudes, the team can begin developing policy and planning for its implementation. At this point the team will need to accomplish several tasks.

These tasks include:

- *Review all of the information the team has assembled*
- *Draft policy statements in each of the seven areas identified in Part One of this book*
- *Review, discuss, and reach agreement about draft policy statements*
- *Develop a plan for policy implementation that includes training of staff and clients.*

Many people find the actual process of policy writing unnecessarily intimidating. Even equipped with all the essential facts, they sit down with pen and paper and draw a blank. The truth is that there is nothing mystical about writing policy, and you should not balk at the task, even if you've never done it before. Team members can help each other in the process.

In the third meeting of the planning team, members will take on writing assignments for each of the policy areas, most probably for the area they have already researched. The two planning sheets, "Draft Policy Statement" and "Guidelines for Policy Statements," will aid individuals when they sit down to write.

In the fourth meeting, the planning team will share their draft policy statements, discuss them, and hopefully reach a broad consensus on HIV policy. Such may not be the case, and additional meetings may need to be scheduled to allow for more discussion and debate—if it takes a while, that's okay. And in the fifth meeting, or once agreement about the *content* of policy has been achieved, the group needs to discuss and plan for the implementation of policy.

The agenda, as written, is a good guide to follow in discussing implementation. First, the team should spend some time brainstorming obstacles to, and supports for, implementation. What resistance to the new policy do you anticipate? What is that resistance based on? Are there financial considerations, personnel issues, or concerns about reactions from clients or customers? All of these questions should be thoroughly reviewed and written down.

There are several different ways to approach implementation. One could, for example, simply issue new policy and expect that every member of the organization will follow it without question. Such an expectation might prove unrealistic, unless agency personnel already have advanced and uniform knowledge about HIV and sensitivity to its related issues. Another approach is to issue policy and provide training and education to staff as a follow-up to its issuance. However, this strategy will mean that training and education will be forced to respond to the immediate reactions by staff to policy, rather than follow a careful, step-by-step agenda designed to increase knowledge and sensitivity.

The best approach is to provide for an initial period of training and education so that everyone in the organization is brought "up to speed" about baseline HIV facts and issues, and then to release policy, which can be accompanied by more specialized education and training on policy implementation, staff roles and responsibilities in relation to policy, and so on.

In discussing implementation, the following questions may be helpful in generating team discussion.

1. How will policy or program guidelines in this area be disseminated to staff and/or clients?

2. Is there any education, investigation, or programming that needs to precede or accompany dissemination?

3. Who is responsible for implementation?

4. What consequences are there, if any, for "violating" policy or program guidelines in this area?

5. Will adherence to the policy or program guidelines be considered as a part of regular employee performance review?

6. How will new staff be brought into accord with policy or program guidelines in this area?

Planning Team Agenda
Third Meeting

1. Survey Results
    - Present Survey Results
    - Discussion
        a. What do survey results indicate about potential support/opposition to policy implementation?
        b. What training/education might be warranted?

2. Policy Statements
    - Assignments

3. Set Next Meeting Date

Draft Policy Statement

1. Diversity
2. Infection Control and Universal Precautions
3. Client and Staff Education
4. HIV Antibody Testing
5. Confidentiality
6. Clinical Care of HIV+ Clients and Staff
7. Discrimination & Access to Services and Benefits

Guidelines for Policy Statements

When drafting a policy statement you should attempt to respond to the following questions. If your statement answers all of them clearly and concretely, and is legally and ethically valid, the chances are that the policy will be well-written and effective.

- **Why** are we writing policy on this topic? What problem or potential problem does this policy attempt to address? What is the legal and ethical basis for policy in this area?

- **Who** does this policy pertain to? All staff, or just some of them? Clients? Is someone required to monitor policy compliance?

- **What** concretely does this policy direct individuals or the organization to do, or not do?

- **When** or under what conditions is this policy operative? If the policy statement requires an on-going activity, according to what schedule is that activity conducted?

- **Consequences** What consequences are incurred, both for individuals and the organization, if the policy is violated in some way?

Planning Team Agenda
Fourth Meeting

1. Presentation of Draft Policy Statements

2. Decisionmaking: Policy
   - Is there consensus about policy statements, or is additional discussion required?

3. Decisionmaking: Implementation
   - Group Brainstorm
       a. Obstacles to implementation
       b. Supports for implementation (see Brainstorm worksheet, following)
   - Discussion
       a. What can be done to turn obstacles into supports?
   - Decision
       a. What is our implementation plan?
       b. What training/education activities will be required to carry out that plan? (See Training/Education Plan and Staff Education Planning Sheet, following.)
       c. Who is responsible for carrying out plans?

4. Set Next Meeting Date

Brainstorming Successful Policy Implementation

Use this sheet to list the obstacles, supports, and strategies that you and your team can think of regarding policy implementation (use the following headings to arrange your ideas in columns for comparison purposes).

Obstacles to Policy	Supports for Policy	Strategies for Change

Policy Implementation Plan

Training / Education Plan

WHO is the audience? Is there more than one audience, e.g., different groupings of staff? Who is responsible for overseeing the training plan, and who will deliver the education?

WHAT is the content? Is it the same for everyone, or does it vary according to staff groupings?

WHY are we doing training? Why did we choose the content as we did—in other words, what are the goals of training?

WHEN will the training take place? Before or after new policy is released? Does timing matter?

HOW will the training/education be delivered—videos, written materials, presentations?

COST/EVALUATION What will be the cost to the organization, and how will the effectiveness of the training be evaluated? Will we conduct pre-and post-tests to measure changes in knowledge and attitudes?

WHO	WHAT	WHY	WHEN	HOW	COST / EVAL

Staff Education Planning Sheet

Staff Position:	Has Received HIV Education Covering:	Needs HIV Education Covering:

5

Policy Checklist

Deciding	√
Researching	√
Surveying/Assessing	√
Planning	√
Implementing	√
Evaluating	_____

Step Five:

IMPLEMENTING

"When Jim [an HIV-seropositive counselor] came here, he was real open about it, everybody knew, but no one said anything. You'd think people would have a lot to say, but they didn't. It was scary—the tension was so thick you could cut it with a knife."

—Director of a board and lodging facility

Having a plan for implementation of HIV policy is not the same as implementation itself. There are a few details that still need to be taken care of:

• First, the policy statements should be assembled into a coherent, overall HIV/AIDS policy package. In other words, someone needs to act as an editor. The outline sheet "Assembling the Policy Package" should help.

• Second, the proposed policy should be reviewed and approved by competent legal counsel. Don't assume that your organization's legal counsel (if you have one) is competent to review policy about HIV. Bad legal advice is perhaps worse than none. For names of lawyers knowledgeable about HIV, contact your local HIV/AIDS service organization.

171

• And third, the policy should be approved by organization management and, if your business or agency has one, the board of directors. Since the board and management have already been represented on the planning team, approval should be a formality, but it is a necessary one.

The team may want to meet again to review the final policy statement and firm up plans for implementation and staff training and education. And finally, the team should set a time to meet again, perhaps three months after the policy has been released to staff, to review and evaluate the impact and effectiveness of policy.

Planning Group Agenda

Fifth Meeting

1. Final Review of Policy Package
   - Discussion and Approval
   - Date to Submit to Decisionmakers

2. Review of Implementation Plan

3. Review of Training/Education Plan

4. Planning Group Evaluation

5. Set Date for Policy Evaluation Meeting

Taking Action

Assembling the Policy Package

The following outlines the constituent elements of a comprehensive policy package addressing all key aspects of HIV/AIDS. The order is deliberate; different topics build upon each other in a sequential fashion. The reader can use the outline as a framework for the development of organization- or agency-specific policy, and as a checklist to make sure all critical topics are addressed.

_____ **Cover letter from Board Chair or Executive Director**

The policy statement, when released to staff, should be accompanied by a cover memo as an introduction to the policy and a reinforcement of its importance. The example on the following page is particularly effective.

_____ **Preamble**

The policy should begin with a brief preamble that establishes a rationale for the policy. On the following pages are four examples.

_____ **Discrimination and Access to Services**

[Clients and Staff; Services, Employment, and Benefits]

_____ **Infection Control**

[Addressing HIV and HBV]

_____ **HIV/AIDS Education for Clients and Staff**

_____ **HIV Antibody Testing**

_____ **Accidental Exposure**

_____ **Confidentiality**

_____ **Care and Treatment of HIV-Infected Clients and Staff**

_____ **Diversity Statement**

_____ **Closing Paragraph**

173

Sample Cover Letter

To: All Shakopee Mdewankanton Sioux Community Employees
From: Leonard Prescott, Tribal Chair
Re: Attached AIDS Policy

I need to discuss with you a difficult issue all of us must come to grips with—AIDS.

You've probably heard about it on TV, read about it, talked about it with friends and co-workers. It seems like everywhere you turn, there are new reports being released, different opinions being expressed.

That makes sense, because AIDS has been designated the number one health problem of the decade. It's affecting men, women, gay people, heterosexuals, people of color, children—and those who love them. Reliable estimates indicate that over 1.5 million people in the United States are carrying the AIDS virus, and that as many as 1,000,000 people will have come down with AIDS when the 1990s are over.

You've probably also heard that AIDS is blood-borne, which means it *cannot be spread* through casual contact—touching, sneezing, coughing, sharing bathrooms or eating utensils. Because of this, there is *no danger* to an employee if he or she is working with someone who has AIDS.

Our primary concerns are ensuring that employees have access to accurate information about AIDS, and making certain that, should an employee of SMSC ever contract AIDS, that she or he is able to continue working, as long as is advisable, in an environment free of discrimination or mistreatment.

With that in mind, we have adopted the attached policy about AIDS for SMSC. I encourage all of you to read it and, should you have any questions, bring them up with your supervisor. We have scheduled employee education seminars to supplement this policy, so that there is ample time to find out about AIDS and have your concerns addressed.

It's been said before, and it's true: the only weapons we now have to fight the AIDS epidemic are education and compassion. I think we can make SMSC a place where people learn what they need to know, and treat each other with dignity and respect.

Sample Preambles

1

"It is the philosophy of _____ that all people have the right to be treated with respect and dignity. Because people with AIDS may encounter problems of discrimination and prejudice in employment and as participants in service programs, _____ has taken the responsible position of adopting the following Human Immunodeficiency Virus (HIV) Policy and Procedure Manual for its programs and businesses. The purpose of this manual is to ensure that no one will be denied employment or access to services based on her or his real or perceived HIV antibody status.

"These guidelines are intended to be an educational tool and outline the procedures that will be followed as we look at providing counseling, testing, infection control, and family support when needed. All service and employment policy pertaining to HIV and AIDS status will be consistent with current legal, epidemiological, and medical practice and thought.

"We all have a critical role to play in curbing the transmission of HIV, and assisting those in need of service and support. This is true not only for programs and businesses in large metropolitan areas, but in small communities. In the past, it may have seemed to many people that AIDS was confined to large cities or to certain segments of the population, but it is evident today that AIDS knows no boundaries or borders. Everyone will be effected in some manner by the HIV epidemic."

2

"Recognizing that HIV/AIDS may pose a significant threat to many clients seeking services from _____, and recognizing there is no basis for discrimination or separate treatment based on ungrounded fears of casual contact, we affirm the critical role of _____ in providing effective policy and education regarding HIV. The education and policy will be intended to (1) reduce the potential for discrimination against people with HIV, and (2) provide education to clients and staff that will help them reduce their risk of HIV infection.

"Since it is currently impossible to determine with perfect accuracy the HIV status of any one individual, HIV related policies operate from the assumption that all staff and residents are currently seropositive for HIV."

3

"Public and agency concerns that participants and staff in our facility be able to work and attend programming without being infected with serious communicable diseases such as AIDS and hepatitis B, require that the management adopt procedures effectively responding to these health concerns while respecting the rights of all participants and staff, including those who are infected."

4

"The _____ recognizes the employment-related rights and concerns of employees who may have HIV infection, as well as the rights of clients, to receive quality services regardless of their health condition. The _____ further recognizes its obligation as an employer to provide a safe work environment for all employees, clients, and the public at large. We therefore adopt the following policies and procedures to ensure that those rights are maintained and respected."

6

Policy Checklist

Deciding	√
Researching	√
Surveying/Assessing	√
Planning	√
Implementing	√
Evaluating	√

Step Six:

EVALUATING

"The more I talk to people living with HIV or AIDS, the more I realize that I have a lot to learn—about respecting differences, about death and dying, about living. This sounds weird, but sometimes I find myself grateful for that."
—Vocational rehabilitation counselor

Some time after the business or agency's HIV/AIDS policy has been implemented (three to six months) the planning team should evaluate the effectiveness of both the policy itself and the policy implementation process. Specifically, the team will want to determine:

- *Whether policy is clearly understood by everyone concerned,*
- *Whether organization staff comprehend and accept the philosophical basis for the policy,*
- *Whether policy, in all its aspects, is being followed strictly and consistently, and*
- *Whether any refinements or adjustments in policy need to be made.*

If policy implementation seems to be progressing smoothly, the meeting can be informal—and an opportunity to celebrate a job well done. If there are problems, a more formal approach might be required. Either way, the planning team should summarize the results of its evaluation and share them with everybody else in the organization who is affected by the HIV policy.

The agenda, following, provides a framework for the meeting. And by the way, when you've made it this far, *congratulations!*

Planning Group Agenda

Sixth Meeting

1. Evaluation Discussion
   - Is the Policy Working?
   - Are Changes in Policy or Implementation Warranted?

2. Summarize Evaluation
   - Who Will Write a Summary and Distribute?

3. Celebrate!

Chapter Eleven:
SAMPLE POLICIES

On the following pages you will find a series of policy statements currently in use by a variety of organizations. In presenting them I have resisted the temptation to provide many more. Since the goal of this book is to give the reader everything she or he needs to create comprehensive policy about HIV, I believed I should include a wide range of policy statements that would be appropriate for every setting, under any condition. But when I began to put them all together, I realized it would add, quite easily, 200 pages to the current volume, and would make the work something I very much wanted to avoid—intimidating.

You will, therefore, have to do some adapting. But don't be too concerned: as I have said already, the core of policy will remain the same, across organizational environments. Use the following as a template from which to start, not as an end-product.

A few additional points should be made about the following:

• *There are a handful of complete policy statements, employed in different settings. But none of them, in my opinion, is really complete by itself. The addition of a policy statement on diversity would serve them all. You may decide to "mix-and-match" according to your needs and goals.*

• *The one exception I have made to the inclusion of a number of policy statements about a specific topic within HIV is in the area of infection control. While I believe infection control policy is a relatively straightforward matter, it can seem complex. I am hoping that the addition of a number of policies, each appropriate for a certain kind of setting, will simplify the policymaker's task.*

• *Finally, I want to underline the caution against merely borrowing someone else's policy without undergoing the organizational steps previously outlined. Policy without an organization-wide commitment to compliance is hollow, and will doubtless be undermined in many subtle and overt ways.*

179

ABC Agency
HIV/AIDS Policy Statement

Recognizing that HIV/AIDS may pose a significant threat to many clients seeking services from ABC Agency, and recognizing that there is no basis for discrimination or separate treatment based on ungrounded fears of casual contact, we affirm the critical role of ABC Agency in providing effective policy and education regarding HIV. This education and policy will be intended to (1) reduce the potential for discrimination against people affected by HIV, and (2) provide education to clients and staff that will help them to reduce their risk for HIV infection.

Since it is currently impossible to determine with perfect accuracy the HIV status of any one individual, HIV-related policies operate from the assumption that all staff and residents are currently seropositive for HIV.

Access To Services

ABC Agency will not discriminate against or offer substandard services or treatment to staff or clients based on their HIV antibody status, diagnosis of AIDS, or perception of risk for HIV infection. No prospective client or staff member shall be required to disclose their HIV antibody status or be required to submit to an HIV antibody test as a prerequisite to receiving services or employment.

Education

Client Education: All clients receiving services from ABC Agency will receive HIV education appropriate to their level of contact with the agency. (See attached sheet for guidelines specific to each program.)

Staff Education: Quarterly inservices will be offered by the HIV Educator. Inservices will cover information regarding HIV transmission and risk reduction, HIV antibody testing issues, orientation to existing HIV policy, and issues specific to HIV-affected women.

HIV Antibody Testing

In relation to HIV antibody testing issues, the primary role of ABC Agency is to provide information or referrals that will assist each client in deciding what is desirable and appropriate in her or his unique case. Clients who wish to discuss the option of HIV antibody testing will be encouraged to discuss concerns with appropriate staff, and may be referred to either the ABC Agency HIV Educator or the Minnesota AIDSLine for further assistance.

Confidentiality

With regard to clients on whom records may be kept (i.e., clients seeking services from the Mental Health Clinic or the Chemical Dependency program), a one page statement regarding client HIV antibody status (see attached) will be provided to clients upon orientation to the program. After the client reviews the statement, it will be included in her or his file. There will be no further charting of the client's HIV antibody status.

With regard to all clients seeking services from ABC Agency, staff will only disclose a client's HIV antibody status on a "need to know" basis. Staff will not disclose a client's HIV antibody status to other clients or outside the agency, except as provided for by law.

Infection Control

Since it is currently impossible to determine with complete accuracy an individual's HIV antibody status, universal precautions shall be consistently observed by all staff and clients, as recommended by the Centers for Disease Control. Universal precautions apply to the following bodily fluids: blood, semen, vaginal secretions, and bodily fluids containing visible blood. Latex gloves shall be worn when cleaning up any of the bodily fluids listed above, as in the event of an accident.

Oak Manors, Inc.
AIDS Policy/Procedures

Policy

Precautions shall be consistent for all clients as recommended by the Centers for Disease Control because medical history and examination cannot reliably identify all persons infected with Human Immunodeficiency Virus (HIV-l), hepatitis B Virus (HBV), or other blood-borne pathogens.

Purpose

To prevent the spread of HIV-l, HBV, and other blood-borne pathogens through contact with blood and certain bodily fluids (infected blood, semen, vaginal secretions and other bodily fluids containing visible blood). Also to protect HIV-infected persons from the acquisition of other infections.

Infection Control

Assume seropositivity for all clients. No isolation of known HBV or HIV-infected clients except protective isolation to prevent exposure to potentially infectious agents.

Protective garments such as vinyl or latex gloves are to be used by personnel in direct contact with blood, semen, and vaginal secretions; general purpose utility gloves shall be used for housekeeping chores involving potential contact.

Gowns, eye protection, and masks must be worn by personnel in direct contact with bodily fluids containing visible blood. Hands must be thoroughly washed immediately after contact with bodily fluids to which universal precautions apply.

Access to Services

No person shall be denied treatment services based solely on having tested positive for HIV-l or receiving a diagnosis of AIDS, or be discriminated against in any way inside or outside the treatment program.

Confidentiality

Staff trained for "Confidentiality Crisis" resulting from client self-disclosure.

Confidentiality assured all HIV-l clients and staff. Internal disclosure on a "need to know" basis only.

Inservice training on law and case studies regarding confidentiality.

Chart information about client HIV-l status will be written in the most general, euphemistic terms, e.g. "client talked about sexuality concerns," "we discussed client health issues," etc. HIV-l seropositivity data recorded in a medical file is accessed only by program nurses and physicians, and not typically requested or released in a standard Request for Release form.

Procedures

Testing for seropositivity will be at the client's request and can be performed by any physician in any clinic or hospital or at any of the eight state-sponsored counseling and testing sites.

A comprehensive AIDS education plan will be integrated into all new employee orientation.

Inservice workshops (at least twice a year) will include: precautions for healthcare workers and residential facilities; basic facts about HIV and AIDS; and how to utilize local health agencies in our AIDS education process.

AIDS education, with emphasis on behavioral changes, will be given all clients.

Medical Aspects classes, AIDS videos, and Risk-Reduction counseling—classroom setting and individually—will be given all clients.

An AIDS Risk Assessment will be included in the client's Vulnerability Assessment.

A Caring Agency, Inc.
HIV/AIDS Policy

Subject: HIV Prevention

Purpose

Prevention of HIV transmission in the client population of A Caring Agency, Inc. via dissemination of information.

Policy

A Caring Agency, Inc. Medical Staff will routinely inform clients of the transmission and prevention of the HIV virus.

Responsibility

It is the responsibility of the Nursing Supervisor to coordinate the presentation of educational materials/lectures regarding HIV.

Procedure

During admission the Nurse on duty will issue handouts on the nature of AIDS, transmission of HIV, and prevention of HIV infection or reinfection. For clients with poor reading levels, the Nurse on duty should read the information aloud to the client. Clients who can read will be asked to read the handouts during the admission process. After the client has read the handouts, the Nurse on duty will administer the HIV/AIDS questionnaire.

Additionally, at least once every four weeks the Nursing Supervisor will present an educational lecture to clients regarding HIV. A videotaped recording will also be kept on file for clients to view if necessary.

What is AIDS?

AIDS stands for Acquired Immune Deficiency Syndrome.

AIDS is a serious disease believed to be caused by a virus. The virus is called HIV.

Sample Policies

The virus weakens the body's immune system. The immune system normally works to protect us from diseases. Without protection, we are open to serious illnesses that are normally not a problem. The virus can also affect brain cells.

AIDS has a very high death rate—over one-half of the people with AIDS have died.

How Do You Get HIV?

HIV is spread by infected bodily fluids (blood, semen, or vaginal secretions) getting directly into the body of someone else (sexual intercourse, blood transfusions before 1985, sharing needles and syringes for shooting drugs, an infected mother to her unborn baby). HIV is not spread by everyday, casual contact. You can't get HIV from: • toilets • food/water • sneezes/coughs • shaking hands • hugging • donating blood • doorknobs • telephones • chairs • mosquitoes • silverware • pens • swimming pools • combs • pets, etc., etc., etc.

Who Is At Risk?

HIV affects men, women, and children of all races. Anyone who engages in high-risk behavior (defined above) with an HIV-infected person is at risk for HIV infection.

Safer Sex

Safer sex is:

- *Showing concern and love for yourself and your partner.*
- *Completely enjoying sex while reducing your risk of giving or getting sexually-transmitted diseases like HIV, syphilis, gonorrhea, and others.*
- *Sexual activity where no semen, vaginal secretions, or blood goes from one partner to the other.*

Safer Sex Guidelines

Safe or Very Low Risk:

- *Sexual fantasies of any kind*
- *Sex talk*
- *Flirting*
- *Hugging*
- *Social (dry) kissing*
- *Body massage*
- *Body licking (on healthy, unbroken skin)*

- *Consensual showing off/watching*
- *Masturbation (together or alone)*
- *Use of personal sex toys*
- *Bathing together*

Probably Safe/Possibly Risky:
- *French kissing*
- *Vaginal intercourse with condom (safer with spermicide, even safer if combined with a cervical barrier—e.g., diaphragm, cap, or sponge)*
- *Anal intercourse with a condom (safer to withdraw before ejaculation)*
- *Oral-vaginal sex (cunnilingus—safer with latex barrier, riskier during menstruation)*
- *Oral-anal sex with a latex barrier*
- *Oral-penile sex (fellatio) without ejaculation*
- *Oral-penile sex with ejaculation wearing a condom*
- *Contact with urine on unbroken skin*
- *Manual vaginal intercourse with a latex glove*
- *Drinking or getting high (both alter judgment)*

Unsafe:
- *Vaginal intercourse without a condom*
- *Anal intercourse without a condom*
- *Swallowing semen*
- *Unprotected oral-anal intercourse (fisting)*
- *Unprotected manual vaginal intercourse*
- *Sharing menstrual blood*
- *Sharing needles or blood while piercing or shooting drugs*

If you have questions about Safer Sex or AIDS call the AIDS Hotline, [give local, regional, and/or national hotline numbers].

SUBJECT: Administration of AIDS Questionnaire

Purpose:

To check the spread of HIV virus at A Caring Agency, Inc. facilities.

Policy:

It is the policy of A Caring Agency, Inc. to assist all clients entering A Caring Agency, Inc. in determining the advisability of HIV antibody testing.

Responsibility:

It is the responsibility of the admitting Nurse to administer an HIV/AIDS questionnaire.

Procedure:

After the admitting Nurse has issued AIDS educational handouts to the client and the client has either read them or the Nurse has read them to her/him, the admitting Nurse will administer the AIDS questionnaire. As part of this questionnaire, the question "Do you have reason to believe that you have been exposed to HIV?" will be asked. If the client answers affirmatively the client will be asked about the presence of clinical symptoms as well as the circumstances under which the exposure might have occurred (i.e., sexual contact, needles, etc.). This information, recorded on the AIDS questionnaire, will be maintained in a separate file and given to the Nursing Supervisor to review. If the client decides that an HIV antibody test is advisable given the circumstances of possible exposure and clinical symptoms, the Nursing Supervisor will consult with the Medical Director or her/his designate. After a consultation with the Medical Director, a referral for testing may be made if deemed appropriate by the Medical Director.

SUBJECT: Confidentiality of A Caring Agency, Inc. Clients and HIV

Purpose:

To protect the confidentiality of A Caring Agency, Inc. clients regarding HIV.

Policy:

It is the policy of A Caring Agency, Inc. to keep confidential all information regarding suspected presence or absence of HIV in any given client.

Responsibility:

It is the responsibility of A Caring Agency, Inc. Nursing Supervisor to maintain all AIDS questionnaires administered to A Caring Agency, Inc. clients in a separate, locked file in her office.

Procedure:

After administering the AIDS questionnaire the Nurse on duty will place the questionnaire in a sealed envelope and address it to the Nursing Supervisor. The Nurse on duty will record in the client record only that the AIDS questionnaire was administered. Under no circumstances should the Nurse on duty record any AIDS clinical symptoms or other responses in the client's medical file. The Nursing Supervisor will maintain the questionnaire in a locked file in her office. Only authorized persons, such as the Medical Director or the Administrator of A Caring Agency, Inc. will have access to these files. Access to the file by other staff must be approved by the A Caring Agency, Inc. Administrator.

Sample Policies

SUBJECT: Education for Clients With HIV

Purpose:

To prevent the spread of HIV by A Caring Agency, Inc. clients.

Policy:

It is the policy of A Caring Agency, Inc. to provide education concerning transmission of HIV to all clients testing positive on an HIV antibody test.

Responsibility:

It is the responsibility of the Nursing Supervisor to instruct any client testing positive of the U. S. Public Health Services recommendations regarding the prevention of the spread of HIV.

Procedure:

Upon receiving knowledge of positive HIV antibody test results in an A Caring Agency, Inc. client, the Nursing Supervisor will schedule an interview with that client. She will go over the following recommendations from the Public Health Service of the U. S. Department of Health and Human Services:

- *If you do have sexual intercourse, use a condom.*
- *Do not share needles for the injection of intravenous drugs.*
- *People at increased risk for AIDS should not donate blood, organs, semen, or breast milk.*
- *Women who have a positive HIV antibody test, or who may be at higher risk of HIV infection, should consider the risk to their babies before planning a pregnancy. A woman can transmit HIV to her unborn child.*

People with positive HIV antibody tests should observe the following additional recommendations:

- *A regular medical evaluation, follow-up, and counseling should be sought.*
- *Do not share toothbrushes, razors, or other implements that could become contaminated with blood.*

Anytown Municipal Hospital
Anytown, U. S. A.
Approved Policy on HIV/AIDS

Confidentiality Policy

Anytown Municipal Hospital employees have access to a variety of confidential information including patient/client records, sensitive hospital operating data, and employee information. This information is available on a "need-to-know" basis to authorized personnel through patient charts and other records. All hospital employees who are authorized access to this confidential information are expected to maintain confidentiality. Failure to do so will result in disciplinary action. The extent of disciplinary action, up to and including involuntary termination, will be determined on a case-by-case basis.

Procedure

Disciplinary action will be taken if unauthorized personnel access confidential records; if employees who observed unauthorized personnel accessing confidential records fail to notify their supervisor; or if any employee gives out any confidential information to others who do not have a "need to know."

A department head or supervisor considering disciplinary action for breach of confidentiality or accessing any confidential information should contact the Administrator to discuss disciplinary action. Necessary documentation and the appropriate type of disciplinary action will be determined by the Department Head/Supervisor and the Administrator.

Body Substance Isolation Policy

Body Substance Isolation shall be used in the care of all patients.

Purpose

To prevent disease transmission. To protect healthcare workers and patients from disease transmission.

Procedure

1. All healthcare workers shall routinely use appropriate barrier precautions to prevent skin and mucous membrane exposure when contact with blood or other bodily fluids of any patient is anticipated. Bodily fluids include blood, urine, feces, saliva, semen, mucous, vomitus, wound drainage, nonintact skin, amniotic fluid, and breast milk.

2. Gloves should be worn for touching blood and bodily fluids, mucous membranes, or non-intact skin of all patients, for handling items or surfaces soiled with blood or bodily fluids, and for performing venipuncture. Gloves should be changed after contact with each patient and during the care of one patient when various procedures are carried out.

3. Masks and protective eyewear shall be worn during procedures that are likely to generate droplets of blood or other bodily fluids to prevent exposure of mucous membranes of the mouth, nose, and eyes.

4. Gowns should be worn during procedures that are likely to generate splashes of blood or bodily fluids.

5. Hands and other skin surfaces should be washed immediately and thoroughly if contaminated with blood or other bodily fluids. Hands should be washed immediately after gloves are removed.

6. All healthcare workers should take precautions to prevent injuries caused by needles, scalpels, and other sharp instruments or devices. To prevent needlestick injuries, needles should not be recapped, bent, or broken by hand. After use, disposable needles and syringes should be placed in a puncture-resistant container. If recapping of needles must be done, a one-handed capping procedure should be used.

7. For emergency resuscitation, ambubags or face masks should be used.

8. Precautions for Invasive Procedure (surgical entry into tissues, cavities or organs, or repair of major traumatic injuries—in O. R., E. R., delivery, outpatient, and inpatient settings)—the precautions listed above combined with the precautions listed below should be the minimum precautions for all such invasive procedures:

- *Routine use of barrier precautions to prevent skin and mucous membrane contact with blood and bodily fluids of all patients.*
- *Gloves and surgical masks must be worn.*
- *Protective eyewear for procedures that commonly result in generation of droplets or splashing of blood/bodily fluids.*
- *Gowns should be worn to prevent splashing of blood/bodily fluids on clothes.*

- *Gown and gloves should be worn during and after vaginal and C-section deliveries, gloves when doing post-delivery care of the umbilical cord, and when doing any type of post-delivery care until baby is clean and dry.*

- *If a glove is torn or a needlestick or other injury occurs, the glove should be removed promptly and the needle or instrument involved should also be removed from the sterile field.*

Disposal of Used Needles, Syringes, and Glassware

Purpose

To provide for safe disposal of needles, syringes, and glassware.

Policy

To protect personnel, patients, and visitors from accidental skin punctures.

Procedure

1. All healthcare workers should take precautions to prevent injuries caused by needles, scalpels, and other sharp instruments or devices.

2. To prevent needlestick injuries, needles should not be recapped, bent, or broken by hand. After use, disposable needles and syringes should be placed in a puncture-resistant container. If recapping of needles must be done, a one-handed capping procedure should be used.

3. When filled, the plastic container should be closed, taped, and labeled "contaminated needles" and disposed of by housekeeping personnel.

Accidental Needlestick/ Other Accidental Exposure to Bodily Fluids Policy

The follow-up procedures will be carried out whenever a healthcare worker is involved in a parenteral or mucous membrane exposure or to blood or other bodily fluids.

Purpose

To provide follow-up and appropriate treatment following accidental needlestick or accidental exposure to bodily fluids.

Sample Policies

Procedure

1. Cleanse exposed area with soap and water, and rinse thoroughly.

2. Report incident to supervisor and complete an employee incident form.

3. If it is determined that the needle or instrument was contaminated and the skin was punctured or mucous membrane exposure occurred, the following steps will be taken:

Table 1. Recommendations for Hepatitis B Prophylaxis After Percutaneous Exposure

Source	Exposed Person — Unvaccinated	Exposed Person — Vaccinated
HBsAg positive	1. One dose of HBIG immediately. 2. Initiate hepatitis B vaccine series.	1. Test exposed person for anti-HBs. 2. If inadequate antibody (<10 sample ratio units by RIA or negative by EIA) give one dose of HBIG immediately plus hepatitis B vaccine booster dose.
Known source High risk of being HBsAg positive	1. Test source for HBsAg; if positive, give one dose of HBIG immediately. 2. Initiate hepatitis B vaccine series.	1. Test source for HBsAg only if exposed person is vaccine nonresponder; if source is HBsAg positive, give one dose of HBIG immediately plus hepatitis vaccine booster dose.
Low risk of being HBsAg positive	1. Test source for HBsAg; if positive, give one dose of HBIG immediately. 2. Initiate hepatitis B vaccine series.	Nothing required.
Unknown source	1. One dose of HBIG immediately. 2. Initiate hepatitis vaccine series.	Nothing required.

*Table 2. Recommendations for HIV Follow-up
After Parenteral or Mucous Membrane Exposure to Bodily Fluids*

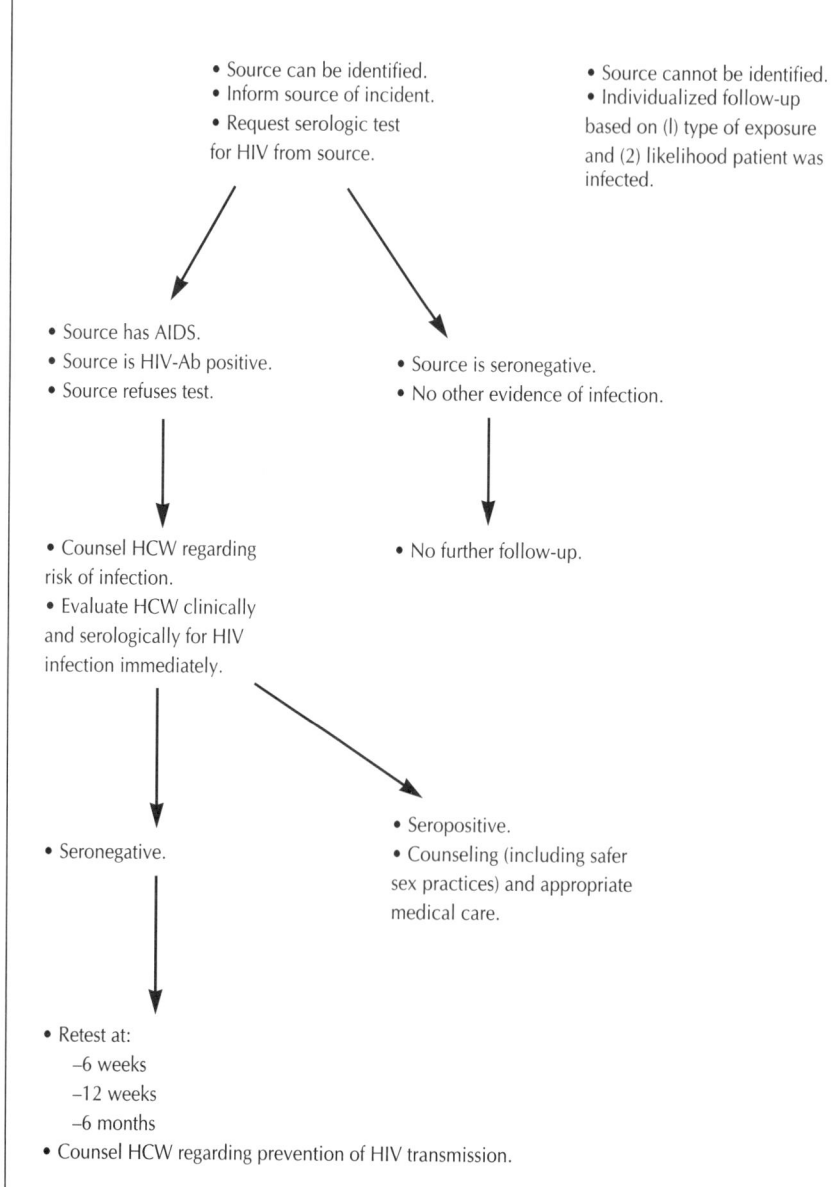

- Source can be identified.
- Inform source of incident.
- Request serologic test for HIV from source.

- Source cannot be identified.
- Individualized follow-up based on (l) type of exposure and (2) likelihood patient was infected.

- Source has AIDS.
- Source is HIV-Ab positive.
- Source refuses test.

- Source is seronegative.
- No other evidence of infection.

- Counsel HCW regarding risk of infection.
- Evaluate HCW clinically and serologically for HIV infection immediately.

- No further follow-up.

- Seronegative.

- Seropositive.
- Counseling (including safer sex practices) and appropriate medical care.

- Retest at:
  – 6 weeks
  – 12 weeks
  – 6 months
- Counsel HCW regarding prevention of HIV transmission.

Sample Policies

Table 3. Examples of Recommended Personal Protective Equipment for Worker Protection Against HIV/HBV Transmission[1] in Prehospital[2] Settings

Task/Activity	Gloves	Gown	Mask[3]	Protective Eyewear
Bleeding control with with spurting blood	Yes	Yes	Yes	Yes
Bleeding control with minimal bleeding	Yes	No	No	No
Emergency childbirth	Yes	Yes	Yes, if splashing is likely	Yes, if splashing is likely
Blood drawing	At certain times	No	No	No
Starting an Intravenous (IV) line	Yes	No	No	No
Endotrachceal Intubation, esophageal obturator use	Yes	No	No, unless splashing is likely	No, unless splashing is likely
Oral/nasal suctioning, manually cleaning airway	Yes[4]	No	No, unless splashing is likely	No, unless splashing is likely
Handling and cleaning instruments with microbial contamination-	Yes	No, unless soiling is likely	No	No
Measuring blood pressure	No	No	No	No
Measuring temperature	No	No	No	No
Giving an injection	No	No	No	No

1 The examples provided in this table are based on application of universal precautions. Universal precautions are intended to supplement rather than replace recommendations for routine infection control, such as handwashing and using gloves to prevent gross microbial contamination of hands (e.g., contact with urine or feces).

2 Defined as setting where delivery of emergency health care takes place away from a hospital or other healthcare facility.

3. Refers to protective masks to prevent exposure of mucous membranes to blood or other potentially contaminated bodily fluids.

4 While not clearly necessary to prevent HIV or HBV transmission unless blood is present, gloves are recommended to prevent transmission of other agents (e.g., Herpes simplex).

Care of the Patient with Human Immunodeficiency Virus (HIV)

DEFINITION

HIV-infected individuals include:

- *Those with Acquired Immune Deficiency Syndrome (AIDS).*
- *Those diagnosed by their physicians as having other illnesses due to infection with HIV.*
- *Those who have virologic or serologic evidence of infection with HIV but who are not ill.*

The HIV virus can cause the disease AIDS. In individuals with AIDS, the body's immune system is not functioning normally. Because the immune system is impaired, individuals with AIDS are subject to unusual infections and malignancies not usually seen in a healthy person.

The HIV virus is transmitted through sexual contact, parenteral exposure to infected blood and blood products, and perinatal transmission from mother to neonate. HIV has been isolated from blood, semen, vaginal secretions, saliva, tears, breast milk, urine, brain tissue, marrow and colorectal cells and is likely to be isolated from other bodily fluids and excretions, but epidemiologic evidence has implicated only blood, semen, and vaginal secretions in transmission.

PATIENT CARE PRECAUTIONS

(1) Blood and Bodily Fluid Precautions (same as for hepatitis B). If a patient has another infection or condition requiring additional precautions, then these should be added according to the Disease Specific Isolation Precautions.

(2) A private room is not necessary unless the patient's hygiene is poor, or as may be mandated by the presence of other infections requiring a private room.

(3) In the event of respiratory arrest, artificial ventilation should be performed with pocket masks until other means of ventilation, such as EOA or intubation, are available. These masks have been strategically located throughout the hospital for immediate availability.

(4) The use of gowns is recommended only if soiling of clothing with blood or bodily fluids is anticipated.

(5) Masks are not routinely necessary for the care of infected patients. However, the use of masks is recommended for healthcare personnel who have direct, sustained contact with a person who is coughing extensively or a patient who is intubated and being suctioned.

(6) The use of nonsterile gloves is recommended if contact with blood or bodily

Sample Policies

fluids containing visible blood or any bodily fluid to which universal precautions apply (i.e. semen, vaginal secretions, tissues, cerebrospinal fluid, synovial fluid, pleural fluid, peritoneal fluid, pericardial fluid, and amniotic fluid). This recommendation is particularly important for personnel who have cuts or abrasions on their hands.

(7) Hands must be washed routinely when caring for infected patients, especially if they are contaminated with blood, bodily fluids, secretions, or excretions. This precaution should be observed regardless of the use of gloves.

(8) The use of protective eyewear, such as goggles, is recommended in situations where the splatter of blood, bloody secretions, or bodily fluids is possible. This is particularly recommended in the performance of procedures such as endotracheal intubation, bronchoscopy, or GI endoscopy. Precautions during other surgical procedures will be judged on an individual basis.

(9) Needles and syringes should be disposable and disposed of in the rigid puncture-resistant containers provided in each room. Needles should not be recapped and should not be purposely bent or broken by hand or any other means.

(10) Extraordinary care should be taken to avoid accidental wounds from needles or other sharp instruments. Should a needle stick or exchange of bodily fluids occur, follow needle stick protocol.

(11) Blood and other specimens should be labeled prominently with a warning such as "Blood/Bodily Fluid Precautions." All blood specimens should be placed in a second container, such as an impervious bag, for transport. The container or bag should be examined carefully for leaks or cracks and labeled as previously stated.

(12) Special precautions for linen and other laundry are not necessary unless soiling has occurred or as mandated by the presence of other infections. When soiled with blood, bodily fluids, secretions or excretions, it should be bagged, labeled, and processed according to existing policy regarding linens from patients on isolation precautions.

(13) Nondisposable articles contaminated with blood or bodily fluids should be bagged and labeled and sent for reprocessing according to existing policy regarding nondisposable articles from patients on isolation precautions. Disposable items contaminated with blood or bodily fluids should be bagged and labeled and disposed of in accordance with the policy for disposal of infectious waste.

(14) No special precautions for dishes are necessary.

(15) Patients with HIV infection who are being transported require no special precautions other than blood/bodily fluid precautions, unless mandated by the presence of other infections. Personnel in the area to which the patient is to be taken should be notified of precautions to be used.

(16) Decontamination of surgical equipment (endoscopes, etc.) should be accomplished by the same sterilization as those currently used for equipment used for patients with hepatitis B. Invasive patient care equipment should be disposable or should be sterilized. Lensed instruments should be sterilized with ethylene oxide. Ventilator tubing should be either disposable or sterilized before reuse. Instruments that come in contact with blood, secretions, excretions, or tissues (including laryngoscope and endotracheal tubes) should be sterilized before reuse.

(17) Blood spills should be cleaned up promptly with a solution of 5:25 percent

sodium hypochlorite (household bleach) diluted 1:10 water (prepared daily). Gloves should be worn and good handwashing protocol followed as stated previously.

(18) Patients with HIV infection who must undergo dental procedures should be managed just as patients known to be carriers of HBsAg (hepatitis). The use of protective eyewear, masks, and nonsterile gloves is recommended. Dental instruments must, of course, be sterilized after such procedures.

(19) As part of immediate post-mortem care, patients with HIV infection should be identified "Blood/Bodily Fluid Precautions," and that identification should remain with the body when delivered to morticians.

(20) These precautions also apply to the management of HIV-infected patients in ambulatory care settings, including outpatient clinics and emergency departments. Segregated examining rooms are not recommended. These patients will use the same waiting areas and bathroom facilities as other patients unless the presence of other infections may require special precautions.

PRECAUTIONS IN CLINICAL LABORATORIES

(1) Universal precautions will be taken.

(2) Mechanical pipetting devices must be used for the manipulation of all liquids in the laboratory. Mouth pipetting must not be allowed.

(3) Needles and syringes should be handled as described previously.

(4) Laboratory coats, protective attire should be worn while working with potentially infectious materials and should be removed before leaving the laboratory.

(5) Gloves should be worn when handling blood, tissue specimens, blood-soiled items, bodily fluids, excretions and secretions, as well as surfaces, materials, and objects contaminated by them.

(6) All procedures and manipulations of potentially infectious material should be performed in order to minimize the creation of droplets and aerosols. Procedures that have a high potential for creating aerosols or infectious droplets include centrifuging, blending, sonicating, vigorous mixing, and harvesting infected tissues from animals or embryonated eggs. Such procedures should be carried out in biological safety cabinets (Class II). Whenever centrifugation of blood or bodily fluids from patients is necessary, the use of centrifuge safety cups is recommended.

(7) Eating, drinking, and smoking should be prohibited in the immediate laboratory work area.

(8) Laboratory work surfaces should be decontaminated with appropriate cleaners. Infectious waste from the laboratory should be processed according to established hospital policy for disposal of infectious waste.

(10) Tissue or serum specimens to be stored should be clearly and permanently labeled as biohazardous.

(11) All personnel should wash their hands following completion of laboratory activities, after removal of protective clothing, and before leaving the laboratory.

Sample Policies

PERSONNEL MANAGEMENT

At this time there is no evidence that the risks in caring for an HIV-infected patient are any greater than the risks associated with caring for any other sick person, therefore, no employee is excused on their own request from providing care to these patients as assigned. Employees who believe they may be at increased risk because they are immunosuppressed or have other clinical conditions that may confer an increased risk of acquiring an infection should discuss their work with the infection control nurse and their personal physician. If the physician determines that the employee is indeed at an increased risk, or that there are certain work assignments that the employee should not accept in relation to the care of an HIV-infected patient, a written recommendation should be provided to the hospital for appropriate action in accordance with personnel policies.

CONFIDENTIALITY

Patient confidentiality must be observed. Communication must specifically identify the precautions, not the diagnosis, necessary to provide patient care safely. The designation "Blood/Bodily Fluid Precautions" is imperative in alerting all involved in the patient's care as to the precautions necessary. Do not identify the diagnosis of AIDS, but do identify specifically the precautions needed. Any break in this patient confidentiality is grounds for dismissal as outlined in personnel policies.

CONSENT FOR TESTING BLOOD

The HIV antibody test should only be performed after the patient or person designated to be responsible for the patient's medical decisions is consulted and permission obtained to have HIV antibody testing done. A consent form follows.

WE ARE ALL LIVING WITH AIDS

Patient Authorization
Human Immunodeficiency Virus (HIV) Testing

I, _____, a patient of Dr. _____, at the Anytown Municipal Hospital, hereby authorize the Anytown Municipal Hospital to test my blood for the presence of the Human Immunodeficiency Virus (HIV), which is the probable causative agent of AIDS (Acquired Immune Deficiency Syndrome). I have read the information given to me and have been informed of the nature of these blood tests, their benefits and risks, and have been given the opportunity to ask questions about the blood tests. I understand that my physician will notify me of the results of the blood tests and the results will be explained to me.

Subject to the foregoing, the hospital, to the best of its ability, will not disclose the results of these tests to others, except to the extent required by law or except to the extent such a disclosure is required to safeguard the well-being of patients and employees at the Anytown Municipal Hospital.

On this basis, I authorize the Anytown Municipal Hospital to perform the blood tests for the Human Immunodeficiency Virus (HIV).

Patient Signature   Date

Witness   Date

Guidelines for Obtaining Consent for HIV Testing (Non-Healthcare Worker Exposure)

I. Consent

a. Patient is to be informed, knowingly and voluntarily, to consent prior to testing procedure. The general consent signed on admission to hospital gives permission for routine diagnostic tests and procedures. The HIV antibody test cannot be considered routine due to the implications and consequences if test results are positive.

b. Consent is to be obtained by the patient's physician or other qualified Healthcare Worker and noted in the chart (i.e. someone who is able to counsel the patient with regard to positive or negative test results).

c. Consent is to be obtained from a competent patient or representative who is best able to convey the patient's wishes (i.e., in no particular order, a companion or close friend, spouse, parents, adult child, sibling, other relative, guardian, attorney, or power of attorney; a court-appointed guardian would take precedence over all others, including relatives).

d. Minor patient consent is to be obtained from patient, legal guardian, other legally-appointed representative, or in accordance with Minnesota law.

e. Testing with no informed consent (in case of incompetent or minor patient) may take place providing the patient's physician has a timely and clinical basis for ordering the testing, a second physician is consulted and concurs, and data is documented in the patient's chart.

II. Information to be given to the patient prior to informed consent and test procedure:

a. Blood will be tested to detect antibodies to the Human Immunodeficiency Virus, which is the probable causative agent of AIDS.

b. The test will not give a diagnosis of AIDS, but an exposure to the virus.

c. The test is performed by withdrawing blood and using a substance to test the blood.

d. The test can possibly result in false positives or false negatives if exposure has been so recent that the body has not had time to develop measurable antibodies.

e. If initial test results are positive, further evaluations will be used before a positive diagnosis is made.

f. Confidential testing is available at various sites in Minnesota, including St. Paul, Minneapolis, St. Cloud, Rochester, Duluth, and Mankato. The patient may opt for confidential testing or refuse testing.

g. Modes of transmission of HIV include:

1. Sexual contact with an HIV-infected person,

2. Sharing IV drug equipment with an HIV-infected person,

3. Receiving blood or blood products contaminated with HIV, and

4. HIV-infected mother to child during pregnancy/childbirth.

h. If test results are negative and the person fits into category 1 or 2 above, counseling may be given or arranged for, such counseling to include a discussion on behavior practices for preventing infection.

> *1. Counseling should be done by properly trained healthcare workers because of the implications and consequences of test results.*

    i. If test results are positive and it is confirmed there has been exposure to HIV, it is recommended by the AHA and the U. S. Public Health Service that HIV seropositive people alert their past (5–10 years) and present sexual contacts about their possible infection with HIV.

> *1. In order to prevent further transmission of HIV it is recommended to refrain from donating blood, plasma, body tissue or sperm, to protect sexual partners from contact with bodily fluids by using condoms during sexual intercourse, and to avoid pregnancy.*

> *2. It is recommended there be a psychosocial and medical follow-up to include health protection and living with a compromised immune system.*

    j. Inform each person why the test is being recommended for them and the significance of positive or negative test results.

    k. Test results will be released to those healthcare workers directly responsible for care and treatment and to the Minnesota Department of Health as described by law.

> *1. Unauthorized release of HIV status can lead to institutional or individual liability.*

> *2. The CDC recommends that the physician or health department should use confidential measures to notify partners if HIV positive people are unwilling to do so. (Physicians could possibly be held liable by the third party for allowing them to be endangered.)*

    l. Any questions regarding the blood test, its benefits, or risks may be asked and answered before consent is given.

    m. Consent is not to be a substitute for discussion with the patient, as she or he may not understand terms and may want more information than is included on the consent form. A patient who does not understand the consent form is an uninformed patient.

    n. Oral consents with documentation in the patient's chart by the physician may be legally sufficient, but it is advisable to have a written consent.

    o. Patient notification of test results is appropriately done by the physician. There should be discussion of the test results, regardless of results, to provide opportunity for patient education.

References: *AHA Report,* November 1987
Health One AIDS Task Force Recommendations, October 1988
AIDS Issues and Updates, July 1988
AIDS Memorandum #4, November 1988

Consent for Communicable Disease Blood Testing

I, _____, a patient of Dr. _____, at the Anytown Municipal Hospital, understand that a hospital employee has been exposed to my blood or bodily fluids. Because of this exposure there is a chance that a communicable disease may have been transmitted. I hereby authorize the Anytown Municipal Hospital to test my blood for the presence of these communicable conditions: Human Immunodeficiency Virus (HIV) antibody and Hepatitis. I have been informed about the nature of these blood tests, their benefits and risks, and have been given the opportunity to ask questions about the blood tests. I understand that my physician will notify me of the results of the blood tests and that the results will be explained to me.

Subject to the foregoing, the hospital, to the best of its ability, will not disclose the results of these tests to others except to the extent required by law or except to the extent such a disclosure is required in order to safeguard the well-being of patients and employees at the Anytown Municipal Hospital.

On this basis, I authorize the Anytown Municipal Hospital to perform the blood tests for the communicable diseases described above. I also understand that these tests will be performed at no charge to me or to my insurance company.

_____

Patient signature   Date

_____

Witness   Date

CAREPLACE
HIV/AIDS Policy Statement

Recognizing that HIV/AIDS may pose a significant risk to chemically-dependent residents, and recognizing that there is no basis for discrimination or separate treatment based on ungrounded fears of casual contact, we affirm the critical role of CAREPLACE in providing effective policy and education regarding HIV and related issues such as homophobia that will (l) reduce the potential for discrimination against people affected by HIV and, (2) help residents and staff obtain and maintain good health status and remain free of HIV infection.

Since it is currently impossible to determine with perfect accuracy the HIV status of any one individual, HIV-related policies operate from the assumption that all staff and residents are currently seropositive for HIV and HBV. The following policy statements serve to support the above positions:

Access to Services

CAREPLACE will not discriminate against or offer substandard services or treatment to staff or residents based on HIV infection, diagnosis of AIDS, or perception of risk of HIV transmission.

Education

CAREPLACE will provide HIV-related education, with an emphasis on behavior change for risk reduction, in a formal manner to clients every three months. As a part of orientation new employees of CAREPLACE will read *HIV-l Guidelines for Chemical Dependency Treatment and Care Programs in Minnesota*.

Every effort will be made to provide employees with the opportunity to attend an HIV-related training within the first six months of their employment.

HIV Antibody Testing

In relation to HIV antibody testing issues, the primary role of CAREPLACE is to provide information or referrals that aid each resident in deciding what is desirable and appropriate in his or her unique case. Therefore,

l. At each intake interview new residents will be provided with a one-page fact sheet outlining testing facts and options (see attached About the HIV Antibody Test*). In addition, the fact sheet will be explained verbally to assure resident understanding.*

2. Residents at any point who wish to discuss individual matters of whether or not they want to be tested for HIV antibody will be encouraged to discuss concerns with program staff and will be referred to the Minnesota AIDSLine for counseling assistance.

Sample Policies

Confidentiality

A one-page statement regarding client HIV status (see attached *Program Statement About HIV/AIDS*) will be provided to and reviewed with residents upon admission. After review, a summary statement will be inserted in the resident file (see attached *Client HIV Status*). Staff disclosure of a resident's HIV status to other clients or outside the agency, except as provided for by law, shall be grounds for disciplinary action.

Infection Control

1. Policy

Universal precautions shall be consistently used for all clients as recommended by the Centers for Disease Control because medical history and examination cannot reliably identify all persons infected with HIV-l, HBV, or other blood-borne pathogens. Specific matters of infection control not addressed in the remainder of this policy shall be handled according to the attached *Infection Control Policy for Residents*, Residential Facilities Manual, Policy Number 6701.

2. Definitions

A. Universal Precautions: Procedures intended to prevent parenteral, mucous membrane, and non-intact skin exposure of healthcare workers to blood-borne pathogens.

1. Bodily Fluids to Which Universal Precautions Do Apply:

    a. Blood is the single most important source of HIV-l, HBV, and other blood-borne pathogens in the occupational setting.

    b. Semen and vaginal secretions.

    c. Other bodily fluids containing visible blood.

2. Bodily fluids to Which Universal Precautions Do Not Apply:

    a. Saliva: General infection control practices already in existence, including using gloves for digital examination of mucous membranes, suctioning, oral hygiene, and handwashing after exposure to saliva should further minimize the minute risk, if any, for salivary transmission. Gloves need not be worn when feeding clients or when wiping saliva from skin.

    b. Feces.

    c. Nasal secretions.

    d. Sweat.

    e. Tears.

    f. Urine.

g. *Vomitus, unless it contains visible blood.*

The risk of transmission of HIV-l and HBV from these fluids and materials is extremely low or non-existent.

3. Procedures

A. Room Assignments: Isolation is not necessary for known HIV- and HBV-infected residents. They may use common house areas and bathroom facilities, unless the presence of other communicable infections requires special precautions. Clients with known HIV-l infection shall receive protective isolation only to prevent their exposure to potentially infectious agents. However, it may be prudent to provide HIV-infected residents with private rooms if they are coughing, non-compliant with hygiene and treatment instructions, or cannot be adequately instructed in blood, secretion, and enteric precautions. When a double or larger room is used, the additional client(s) will not be an impaired host(s) (e.g., another client with a known HIV-l infection who might be susceptible to potential infections).

B. Protective Garments: The following protective garments are to be used as specified:

1. Gloves: Personnel in direct contact with blood, semen and vaginal secretions, and other bodily fluids containing visible blood shall wear vinyl or latex gloves. Gloves must be changed between client contacts. Hands will be washed after removing gloves. General purpose utility gloves (e.g., rubber gloves) shall be used for housekeeping chores involving potential blood contact or for decontamination procedures. Utility gloves may be decontaminated and reused, but must be discarded if they are peeling, cracked, discolored or have punctures, tears, or other evidence of deterioration.

2. Handwashing: Hands and other skin surfaces contaminated with blood, bodily fluids containing visible blood, or other bodily fluids to which universal precautions apply must be thoroughly washed immediately after contact.

C. Equipment:

1. Precautions must be taken by all personnel to prevent injuries caused by needles, scalpels, and other sharp objects or devices. All needles and syringes are to be disposed of in rigid wall puncture-resistant containers. Needles are not to be resheathed or clipped after use before being discarded in the container. The container must be handled carefully to prevent accidental injury to either staff or residents.

D. Dishes: Standard dishwashing procedures shall be maintained for all residents.

E. Housekeeping: Environmental surfaces contaminated with blood or other bodily fluids shall be immediately cleaned with bleach and water.

F. Urine Specimen Collection: All employees handling urine samples shall wear gloves.

G. Personal items: Residents will be instructed upon admission not to share personal items such as razors, toothbrushes, etc.

About The HIV Antibody Test ("the AIDS Test")

There are some important things you should know about the HIV Antibody Test (what a lot of people incorrectly call "the AIDS Test") as a client here at Careplace.

First of all, you deserve to know where we stand. Careplace believes that:

1. It's up to the individual to decide whether they want to get tested. It's not our place to tell you what you should do, because there are many things to think about, and so many things about your life or situation that make it unique. Careplace staff can help by giving facts and counseling, but we won't tell you what to do.

2. If you have been tested, you don't have to tell us the results. If you choose to get tested during treatment, you still don't have to tell us. That's private information, and you decide what you want to do with it.

3. If you have questions or concerns about testing, ask your counselor; she or he will be glad to help, and will keep it confidential. And you can always call the Minnesota AIDSline at 870-0700. You don't have to give your name when you call and trained volunteers will answer your questions or talk to you about your concerns.

Secondly, there are a few things about the test itself, and the testing process, that you should know about:

1. The test itself is a blood test. That is, a nurse or a doctor will draw a blood sample for lab work. It takes a while (7–10 days) before the results come back.

2. The test doesn't tell you if you have AIDS. If the test comes back "positive," that means you are probably carrying the virus, or germ, that can lead to AIDS. You can carry the virus (called HIV) without being or feeling at all sick, just like you can be carrying cold germs without actually having a cold.

3. If the test comes back positive, it won't tell you when the HIV—the virus—got inside your body. It could have been six months ago or six years ago.

4. Having a positive test result doesn't mean you're going to die of AIDS. It means there are some medical matters that you will need to pay attention to.

5. And having a "negative" test result doesn't necessarily mean that you don't have the virus inside your body. There are some problems connected with the test that don't always make negative results 100% correct.

6. There are a number of different places to get tested, each of which has advantages and disadvantages. Depending on where you go, there are differences in how much you will have to pay, whether you will get counseling, and what happens to the results of your test. Because of that, if you do decide to get tested, it's really important to talk over the options beforehand with someone who knows.

7. Whether or not you get tested, you should know that the most important thing any of us can do is to avoid getting the virus inside our bodies in the first place. That means never sharing needles and practicing safer sex. Getting tested, without changing some of the things that might put us at risk, is the wrong way to go about it. That's why Careplace offers education programs on AIDS for all clients while they are in treatment.

Program Statement About HIV/AIDS

AIDS, and the virus that can cause AIDS (HIV), are in some ways very hard to detect. Someone can look fine—perfectly healthy—and be carrying the HIV virus. In fact, most people carrying the virus don't even know they have it. Even the so-called "AIDS test" can't tell you for sure whether someone is carrying the virus. If someone tells you that they "had the AIDS test and came up clean," the test might not be right. It is even possible that they might be lying. There's no way to know for sure who's carrying the HIV virus and who's not. That's an important point, since you don't have to actually have AIDS to pass it on to other people. You only have to be carrying the virus.

Because it's hard to tell, doctors recommend that we assume that everyone we come in contact with is carrying the virus. That means friends, people you know, and other residents here at CAREPLACE. And it certainly means everyone you have sex with or share needles with.

And it means you. We are not saying this to make you scared; you are probably not carrying the virus. But it makes sense to assume that you are. That's why this program assumes that everybody—all the staff, all the residents—is carrying the HIV virus. We make that assumption in the education about AIDS that we do, in how we talk about AIDS. We make that assumption in infection control (stopping the spread of diseases and germs). So if you were to accidentally cut yourself and bleed on a surface, we would assume that your blood has HIV in it, and we would put on rubber gloves before mopping it up (as we would for any resident or staff person). And we caution you not to share razors, toothbrushes, or anything else that might have blood, semen, or vaginal fluids (the liquids that can pass on HIV) in it.

Again, we don't want to scare you. It's just that this is the only way to really be safe.

We should also say that we believe that people with AIDS, or who are carrying the HIV virus, should be treated in a loving and caring way. If someone tells you they have AIDS or are carrying the AIDS virus, remember that what they told you is confidential; if you start telling other people without that person's permission, some really hurtful things could happen to that person. So keep it to yourself, unless you have permission. And if you have AIDS or are carrying the HIV virus, feel free to talk to your counselor about your concerns and feelings. We will help you however we can and will not tell other people without your permission.

And if you have any questions about AIDS, ask your counselor; she or he would be glad to help. Or you can call the Minnesota AIDSline, without having to tell them who you are, at (612) 870-0700.

Client HIV Status

❝ *The best epidemiological and medical evidence about HIV-l infection and AIDS suggests that since it is extremely difficult to know with certainty who is HIV-l-infected and who is not, individuals and medical/social service providers ought to assume that everyone with whom they come in contact with is HIV-l seropositive (carrying the Human Immunodeficiency Virus).*

❝ *Therefore, CAREPLACE acts as if every client, including the person identified in this case file, is HIV-l seropositive. This assumption is made for the purposes of infection control, risk reduction education, maintenance of confidentiality, prevention of discrimination, and all other areas of programming. This does not suggest that CAREPLACE has definite knowledge of the HIV-l seropositivity or seronegativity of the client identified herein, or any other client. It only indicates the wisdom of assuming seropositivity.*

❝ *This statement will be found in the file of every resident at CAREPLACE, and all new residents are instructed in its content.* ❞

Turnaround House, Inc.
HIV Virus Guideline

Reference: *Human Immunodeficiency Virus (HIV-1) Guidelines for Chemical Dependency Treatment and Care Programs in Minnesota* (Sept. 1989).

1. Purpose:

To establish policy on access to services and general information relative to HIV-1 positive residents.

2. Access Policy:

No resident should be denied services, or offered substandard services, because of real or perceived HIV-1 antibody status. There is no valid ethical, clinical, epidemiological, or legal reason to refuse admission for a person with the HIV-1 antibody who is otherwise qualified for services.

3. Education:

Education that emphasizes behavioral change is one of the only tools presently available in the fight against transmission of HIV-1. Education can be effective in changing knowledge, attitudes, and behaviors. Staff will be afforded this education through workshops and inservice settings.

4. Infection Control/Universal Precautions:

There is a minute risk of HIV-1 exposure through occupational exposure to blood, semen, and vaginal secretions. High-risk behavior within the program is not condoned by staff or residents and is reason for termination of employment and residency.

5. Risk Reduction:

The basic premise of risk reduction is that the blood, semen, and/or vaginal secretions of one person must not get inside the body of another person. Transfer of blood, semen, or vaginal secretions can be reduced or eliminated by adopting a number of strategies, i.e., reduce or eliminate the risk of sexual transmission and sharing of injection equipment.

6. Confidentiality:

HIV-1 Information Management. A "need to know" will be the criterion for disclosure between residents and specific staff through verbal communications. There will be no charting of HIV-1 status until unanswered questions about what is appropriate, legally and clinically, have been resolved at other levels of authority. Any further questions about confidentiality that may arise should be directed to the Executive Director.

Sample Policies

Human Immunodeficiency Virus (HIV-l) Policy and Procedure Manual

May 1990

It is the philosophy of the Shakopee Mdewakanton Sioux Community that all people have the right to be treated with respect and dignity. Because people with AIDS may encounter problems of discrimination and prejudice in employment and as participants in service programs, the Shakopee Mdewakanton Sioux Community (SMSC) has taken the responsible action of adopting the following Human Immunodeficiency Virus (HIV-l) Policy and Procedure Manual for its tribal programs and businesses. The purpose of this manual is to ensure that no one will be denied employment or access to services, based on real or perceived HIV-l antibody status.

These guidelines are intended to be an educational tool and to outline the procedures that will be followed as we look at providing counseling, testing, infection control, and family support when needed. All service and employment policy pertaining to HIV-l and AIDS status will be consistent with current legal, epidemiological, clinical, and medical practice and thought.

Review of these guidelines, along with inservice training, will be mandatory for all program administrators, business managers, and direct service providers. Personnel in these areas will be available to all employees and Community members to supply information, when requested, and to provide support, as needed. We all have a critical role to play in curbing the transmission of HIV-l, and assisting those in need of service and support. This is true not only for programs and businesses in large metropolitan areas, but also in small communities. In the past, it may have seemed to many people that AIDS was confined to large cities, or to certain segments of the population, but it is evident today that AIDS knows no boundaries or borders. Everyone will be effected in some manner by the HIV-l epidemic. The Shakopee Mdewakanton Sioux Community is one of the first reservations in the nation to confront this crisis, using the only method of prevention currently available—education.

SHAKOPEE MDEWAKANTON SIOUX COMMUNITY— RESOLUTION 1-04-90-008

WHEREAS,   The General Council is the governing body of the Shakopee Mdewakanton Sioux Community and has the authority under the Constitution for the Community to promulgate resolutions governing the conduct of business in the Community; and

WHEREAS,   Believing that every member and tribal employee of the Shakopee Mdewakanton Sioux Community is valued—that every one of us is important; and

We Are All Living With AIDS

WHEREAS, Believing that we all have certain rights, including the right to health and freedom from preventable disease, the right to respect for our uniqueness, and the rights to be free of discrimination, unfair treatment, or harassment; and

WHEREAS, Knowing that AIDS is a potentially devastating disease, both because of the illnesses it can involve and because people with AIDS suffer rejection, persecution, and mistreatment; and

WHEREAS, Knowing that there is no risk to others in our Community if someone happens to have AIDS or is infected with the so-called AIDS virus (HIV), unless individuals share needles or have unsafe sex with that person; and

WHEREAS, Believing that it is important that all members of the Community and all tribal employees get accurate information about how they can reduce their chance of getting infected with the HIV virus;

THERE BE IT RESOLVED, The Shakopee Mdewakanton Sioux Community adopts the attached *Human Immunodeficiency Virus (HIV-1) Guidelines for Chemical Dependency Treatment and Care Programs in Minnesota* as the basis for its policies and procedures related to all aspects of AIDS.

The *Guidelines* address five different areas of AIDS, which can be summarized as follows:

1. **Discrimination.** *We will not discriminate against anybody with AIDS or HIV in services or employment. Not only is such discrimination morally wrong, it is also against state and federal law.*

2. **Education.** *We will make available educational programs and resources to all Community members and tribal employees that inform people how they can reduce their chances of getting HIV and address fears and concerns related to HIV.*

3. **Infection Control.** *"Infection control" means controlling the spread of disease in the workplace. In the case of AIDS, it means looking at those settings where people may come into contact with HIV infectious bodily fluids. The Community, therefore, will follow standard infection control procedures in dental, medical, and daycare settings to reduce the extremely remote possibility of HIV infection in those settings.*

4. **Antibody Testing ("the AIDS Test").** *The Community does not support mandatory testing, believing that no one should be forced to take the test. Because there are complicated issues related to the decision to get tested, indi-*

viduals should decide for themselves whether they want to get tested. Staff will provide solid information about the advantages and disadvantages to testing, as well as resources, for those people who have questions. We believe, for a number of reasons, that people who do decide to get tested should go to one of the confidential Counseling and Testing Sites operated by the Minnesota Department of Health.

    5.   **Confidentiality.** We should all work to protect the privacy of people. Rumors about AIDS can have a terrible effect on individuals, and may not even be true. In addition, professionals are responsible for meeting all the requirements of state and federal laws related to confidentiality.

In light of this resolution, appropriate and specific policy will be implemented in all areas of the Community, including Community Center programs and all business operations.

This resolution is one we make with each other, as a community, and extends beyond the term of any particular tribal government; it is binding on us, our children, and our children's children so that we might live in health and mutual respect and dignity.

SMSC AIDS Policy:
Guidelines for Supervisors

1. Remember that an employee's health condition is personal and confidential, and precautions should always be taken to protect information regarding an employee's health condition.

2. Contact _____ if you believe that you or other employees need information about AIDS or other life-threatening illnesses, or if you need further guidance managing a situation that involves an employee with such an illness.

3. If a supervisor has a reasonable basis to believe that an employee with a life-threatening illness is unable to perform the duties of his or her position, the supervisor may request the employee undergo a medical clarification examination. The results of the examination will guide future personnel decisions affecting that employee.

4. If warranted, make reasonable accommodation for employees with life-threatening illnesses, consistent with the needs of the work unit.

5. Make a reasonable attempt to transfer employees with life-threatening illnesses who request a transfer and are experiencing undue emotional stress.

6. Be sensitive and responsive to co-workers' concerns, and emphasize the need for education. At the same time, no special consideration beyond normal transfer requests should be given to employees who feel threatened by a co-worker's life-threatening illness.

It should be made clear that mistreatment, harassment, malicious gossip, or hurtful actions in the workplace will not be tolerated.

7. Employees with AIDS or other life-threatening illnesses are entitled to full coverage under SMSC's policies on sick leave, medical leave of absence, disability benefits, and equal employment opportunity. Should questions arise on such matters, contact the Personnel Administrator.

8. Be sensitive to the fact that continued employment for an employee with a life-threatening illness may sometimes be therapeutically important in the remission or recovery process, or may help prolong the employee's life.

Summary

Equal Access to Services/Employment/Benefits

No one will be denied services, or offered substandard services, because of real or perceived HIV+ antibody status. There is no valid ethical, epidemiological, or legal reason for any Community program or business to refuse admission for a person who is antibody HIV-1+ who is otherwise qualified for service or employment.

The Shakopee Mdewakanton Sioux Community (SMSC) adopts a policy statement that explicitly acknowledges full access to services and employment for persons who are HIV-1+ who are otherwise qualified. In addition, programs will endeavor to educate all Community members and program staff, with the cooperation of Personnel, about nondiscrimination law as it relates to HIV-1 and AIDS.

HIV-1 Education

Education that emphasizes behavioral change is one of the only tools presently available in the fight against the transmission of HIV-1. Though difficult, education can be effective in changing knowledge, attitudes, and behaviors.

SMSC programs will provide education on HIV-1 for all staff, all clients, and all Community members. Education will be integrated smoothly into the existing program format and philosophy and will include, at the very least, an explanation of the nature and action of HIV-1, the facts about transmission, and personal and occupational risk-reduction strategies.

Infection Control/Universal Precautions

There is a minute risk of HIV-1 exposure through occupational exposure to blood, semen, and vaginal secretions. Despite the fact that it is extremely unlikely that such exposure would take place in SMSC programs and businesses, it is sensible for general hygienic reasons and to control infection of other blood-borne pathogens such as the hepatitis B Virus, to adopt simple, accessible infection control procedures and protocols in treatment programs and in all client service settings and business places.

SMSC programs and businesses adopt, as a matter of policy, an infection control plan appropriate to the programs and businesses. The policies reproduced in this volume will be made available to all Community members and employees and they will be the source of SMSC education, employment standards, and Community service related to HIV-l.

HIV-l Antibody Testing

The current HIV-l antibody test has both potential advantages and limitations. The HIV-l antibody test will not be required as a precondition for employment or services. Persons thinking of getting the test should carefully weigh a number of critical factors before getting the test. SMSC health and social service staff working with clients have a role to play in helping the client (1) to decide whether or not to be tested, (2) to learn about resources for testing and their respective advantages and disadvantages, and (3) to provide adequate and appropriate follow-up counseling, or referral for counseling, before and after testing.

SMSC programs and businesses will make clear to all staff and clients their stance on HIV-l antibody testing. SMSC health and social service staff will help clients reach uniquely appropriate decisions on the question of being tested, rather than forcing one recommendation over another. Programs and businesses will endeavor to protect client confidentiality in the entire process of test decisionmaking and actual testing, and will endeavor to make sure that no client comes to harm because of a positive test result.

Confidentiality and HIV-l Information Management

Since a great deal of potential harm can come to clients whose HIV-l positive antibody status is inappropriately or illegally disclosed to third parties, SMSC programs and businesses will scrupulously guard the confidentiality of client and staff HIV-l status.

SMSC programs have developed and adopted policies that address specific questions about HIV-l antibody status and confidentiality. The policies address issues such as who needs to know when a client self-reports HIV-l seropositivity, program and business responsibilities and liabilities in relation to HIV-1 status information, third party disclosure, charting protocol of HIV-1 status, and other matters. Specific recommendations on confidentiality questions are contained in these Guidelines.

COUNTY POLICY STATEMENT
Policy Statement Regarding AIDS in the Workplace

TO: Department and Agency Heads

FROM: County Commissioner

Introduction

The topic of AIDS (Acquired Immunodeficiency Syndrome) has been receiving a great deal of public attention and discussion. According to the latest information available from the United States Public Health Service, Centers for Disease Control and the State Department of Health, AIDS is not a disease that can be spread by casual contact. The kind of non-sexual person-to-person contact that normally occurs among employees, clients, students, inmates and the general public in the course of providing public service does not pose a risk for transmission of HIV (Human Immunodeficiency Virus), the virus associated with AIDS.

In light of the many concerns, questions, and apprehensions of employees and the public at large regarding AIDS, it is appropriate to communicate to you the policy of the County as an employer regarding the presence of AIDS in the workplace.

General Statement

The County recognizes the employment-related rights and concerns of employees who may have HIV or AIDS, as well as the rights of inmates, residents of county facilities, students, and the public at large to continue to receive quality services regardless of their health condition. The County further acknowledges its obligation as an employer to provide a safe work environment for all employees, clients, and the public at large. Therefore, it is the policy of the County that it will not discriminate against any individual applicant, employee, or client because she or he may be HIV-infected. HIV/AIDS will be treated the same as any illness in the workplace.

In order to address concerns regarding the transmission of this virus, the County hereby adopts the Centers for Disease Control Guidelines for AIDS in the Workplace.

Employees

No employee shall be required to submit to any test to determine HIV infection as a requirement to begin or maintain employment with the County. The County recognizes that employees with HIV or AIDS may wish to continue working. As long as employees are able to meet acceptable performance and attendance standards and medical evidence indicates that their employment is not a threat to themselves or others, employees shall not be denied continued employment solely because of their medical condition. If determined necessary, an effort will be made to modify an employee's duties based on medical recommendations of the employee's and/or the county's physician. Such determinations shall be made on a case-by-case basis.

The County further recognizes that an employee's health condition is personal and confidential. In the event an employee is absent from work because of an AIDS-related illness, the same confidentiality requirements that apply to any medical condition apply. Therefore, reasonable steps will be taken to protect such information from being disclosed inappropriately.

Co-workers

The County acknowledges that co-workers of employees with HIV infection or AIDS may have concerns for their own health and safety. For that reason, managers and supervisors are to pursue all reasonable and appropriate actions which would ensure that an employee's health condition does not present a health or safety threat to co-workers or the public. Further, while managers and supervisors should be sensitive to co-workers' concerns, where it has been determined that there is no health or safety risk, those employees who feel threatened will not be allowed to refuse to work. To alleviate fears or concerns, County agencies shall provide their employees with informational materials which would address those fears or concerns.

Employees Providing Services to Individuals who may be HIV-Infected

The County acknowledges that there are certain employees who may be required to provide services to individuals with HIV or AIDS. In order to ensure that such employees are able to provide those services in a safe and healthful manner, the affected agencies shall develop policies which address this issue and provide appropriate educational materials/programs to these employees. In doing so, agencies are advised to incorporate the Centers for Disease Control Guidelines on AIDS in the Workplace as they have been adopted by the County. Appropriate and adequate information and training will provide safeguards to both the employee and the agency as employer should any disputes about work requirements arise.

Implementation of this Policy

Implementation of this policy is intended to be consistent with County personnel rules and administrative procedures, County plans, and labor agreements. Managers, supervisors, and employees are encouraged to avail themselves of related educational opportunities. Additionally, agencies should use the resources of the Employee Assistance Program, the Department of Health, and community support services as appropriate.

Implementation Plan

I. Objectives:

A. The Department of Employee Relations will provide training and other resources to all County managers and supervisors.

B. A Personnel Response Team within Employee Relations will be available to assist all agency staff with HIV-related employment issues in County government.

C. Employee Relations will provide agency personnel staff with information and training models which will be used for the general education of employees. Several County agencies have developed internal AIDS policies and materials such as videotapes which can be used in educational programs, and a list of such materials will be made available to personnel staff. The Department will also provide materials such as a workplace poster with a list of AIDS information resources, suggested newsletter articles, and assistance in developing agency-specific training.

2. Timetable:

A. By August 15, Employee Relations will conduct a pilot training for managers and supervisors, to include:

- *Essential facts about HIV and AIDS;*
- *Review of legal and administrative issues;*
- *County policy and implementation; and*
- *Outline of training for employees.*

B. By September 1, Employee Relations will begin conducting training for all managers and supervisors.

C. By January 1, Employee Relations will begin conducting training for all County employees.

D. By June 1, all County agencies will have in place appropriate policy on HIV and HIV-related issues.

Sample Policies

HIV Antibody Testing Policy
Yellowstone Treatment Center, Yellowstone Regional Medical Center

Yellowstone Treatment Center is governed by Federal (42 Code) and state guidelines regarding the release of confidential information.

Clients entering the treatment program are immediately directed to focus on their substance abuse issues. We adhere to the principle that substance abuse is the focal point of treatment.

There is no documented evidence that HIV antibody testing enhances or inhibits client recovery in substance abuse treatment. Clients will be referred for HIV antibody testing only after complete pre-test counseling has taken place.

Pre-test counseling will include:

- *A description of the HIV antibody test;*
- *An explanation of disclosure laws applicable to alcohol and drug programs;*
- *An outline of the potential benefits and drawbacks of HIV antibody testing;*
- *A description of how documentation in the medical record will occur;*
- *A discussion of the client's motives for testing; and*
- *A summary of available counseling and testing sites.*

Pre-Test Counseling

1. What is the HIV antibody test?
   A. The initial blood test is an enzyme linked immunosorbent assay (ELISA or EIA) which determines the presence of HIV antibodies in the blood.
   If HIV antibodies are detected, then the next step is to have the blood tested through another procedure called the Western Blot. The Western Blot will determine the accuracy of the ELISA. One can be only either HIV positive or HIV negative. It can take up to six months after exposure to HIV to accurately confirm HIV seropositivity. The ELISA and Western Blot procedures do not indicate that one has AIDS, they only indicate the presence of antibodies to HIV. Testing can not be considered reliable unless the individual has waited for six months after high-risk behavior which could have resulted in acquisition of HIV.

2. Disclosure Laws
   Even under federal guidelines regarding confidentiality, there are two ways in which disclosure of your antibody test results can be made:
   A. Upon receiving the client's written consent; or
   B. Upon receiving a court order commanding the program to release the information.

3. Potential Benefits and Drawbacks of HIV Antibody Testing
   A. Early detection of HIV can allow for better medical intervention.
   B. Early detection of HIV can lead to lifestyle and behavior changes which will support the maintenance of long-term health and well-being.
   C. Experiencing the testing process may help raise awareness about the importance of behavior change.
   D. Testing may relieve anxiety.
   E. Clients may have mistaken ideas about what the test is and what it does.
   F. Clients may not be emotionally prepared to learn of potential HIV seropositivity.
   G. Testing may minimize the importance of on-going behavior change.
   H. Clients in substance abuse treatment may find testing diversionary from immediate recovery tasks.

4. Documentation in the Medical Record
   At present any authorization (order) to test for the HIV antibody, and the results of that test, are entered in the client's medical record. The medical record is a permanent, legal document, and may be requested by insurance carriers for the purpose of establishing the presence of a preexisting condition.

5. The following questions will be posed and discussed with the client who requests HIV antibody testing.
   A. What do you know about the test, how it works, what it does and does not do?
   B. What are your motives for getting tested?
   C. How will you respond if your results come back HIV seropositive?
   D. Do you feel emotionally prepared to hear the test results?
   E. Is this your choice or someone else's recommendation?

6. Counseling and Testing Sites (CTS)
   All clients who wish to defer testing until after they are discharged will be referred to the appropriate CTS in Minnesota.

Sample Policies

Crisis Concern Services
HIV/AIDS Policy

PROGRAM: The program is located in the Tri-County metro area serving African-American men and women in the Tri-County area. This is an information and referral program also providing counseling, aftercare, follow-up, and court diversion.

POLICY: The program will provide services to all clients having problems related to alcohol use regardless of disability, including HIV infection.

PURPOSE: To provide information and referral services for individuals infected with HIV and to protect other staff and clients. To prevent the spread of HIV/HBV and other blood-borne pathogens through contact with blood and certain bodily fluids.

EDUCATION: The program will provide education to all clients and staff about issues and policies relating to confidentiality so that inadvertent violation is prevented.

CARE: The HIV-infected client shall receive the same level of effective care as those clients who are not HIV-infected.

PRIVACY: Upon client disclosure, HIV status will be charted in only the most general euphemistic terms.

TESTING: The client shall not be required to take an HIV-antibody test. Counselors will provide appropriate referrals for testing. Staff will assist clients in individual decision-making regarding HIV-antibody testing.

REPORTING: The program will follow State Statute, section 144.4175, subdivision 1. This subdivision states that knowledge or reasonable cause to believe that a client is a health threat to others is cause to report that information to the Commissioner of Health.

RESOURCES: All staff will make full use of existing HIV-related community services in providing comprehensive education and service to clients.

Brown Printing Company
Corporate Policy

Subject:	HIV/AIDS in the Workplace
Issued By:	Jim Rifenbergh
Authority:	President
Depts. Affected:	All
Effective:	Immediately

Purpose

The topic of AIDS (Acquired Immunodeficiency Syndrome) has received increasing public attention and discussion. According to current information available from the U. S. Public Health Service, Centers for Disease Control (CDC) and the Minnesota Department of Health, AIDS is not a disease that can be transmitted through casual contact. The kind of personal conduct in the course of our business does not pose a risk for the transmission of the Human Immunodeficiency Virus (HIV), the virus which can cause AIDS.

In light of many concerns, questions, and anxieties of employees and the public at large regarding AIDS, it is appropriate to define a policy regarding AIDS in the workplace.

Policy

The Company recognizes the employment-related concerns of employees who may be HIV-infected as well as the rights of other individuals as related to our obligations as an employer to provide a safe working environment for all employees, customers, and individuals who visit our facilities for business reasons.

It is the policy of Brown Printing Company that we will not discriminate against any individual, applicant, employee, or customer because she/he may be HIV infected or have AIDS. HIV disease will be treated the same as any illness in the workplace pursuant to the CDC Guidelines.

Specifics

1. No employee shall be required to submit to any test to determine the presence of HIV as a requirement to begin or maintain employment with the Company.

2. The Company recognizes that employees with HIV disease may wish to continue working. Therefore, as long as those individuals are able to meet established performance and attendance standards *and* as long as medical evidence indicates that their condition is not a threat to others, employees shall not be denied continued employment solely because of their medical condition.

3. If determined to be necessary, efforts will be made to modify an employee's duties based on the recommendations of the Company's medical director or the director's designated representative. Such determinations shall be made on a case-by-case basis.

4. The Company recognizes that an employee's health condition is personal and confidential. Therefore, all reasonable steps shall be taken to protect such information from being disclosed inappropriately.

5. We acknowledge the fact that employees may have concerns for their own health and safety if a co-worker has HIV/AIDS. As is the case with other health and safety issues, supervisors and managers are to rely on guidance from the Personnel Department to pursue reasonable and appropriate actions to ensure that an employee's health condition does not present a health or safety threat to co-workers or to authorized visitors to our facilities.

6. While managers and supervisors should be sensitive to the concerns of fellow employees, where it has been determined that there is no health or safety risk, an individual who feels threatened by a fellow employee's health condition will *not* be allowed to refuse work assignments. To alleviate concerns or fears, we will attempt to provide employees with published information which would address those fears or concerns.

7. According to the CDC Guidelines on AIDS in the Workplace, people who administer first aid or medical assistance should assume automatically that *every* person is HIV-infected when rendering assistance. Appropriate information and training will be provided to members of the Employee Health Center (EHC) Team.

8. Equipment contaminated with blood or other bodily fluids of any worker, regardless of HIV-infection status, should be cleaned with soap and water or a detergent. A disinfectant solution or a fresh solution of household bleach should be used to wipe the area after cleaning.

9. Employees with specific questions should address them to the Personnel Manager at each facility.

10. Questions may be referred on to the Director of Industrial Relations for further resolution when required.

Cedarwood Community College

Policy on Acquired Immunodeficiency Syndrome (AIDS) and Human Immunodeficiency Virus (HIV)

Definitions

- Acquired Immunodeficiency Syndrome (AIDS): A potentially life-threatening and incurable (though sometimes treatable) disease.
- Human Immunodeficiency Virus (HIV): The infectious virus widely held to be the causative agent of AIDS (previously termed Human T-Lymphotropic Virus, Type III—HTLV-III).

Basic Facts

- HIV is an infectious virus, and AIDS is a disease. They are not moral conditions.
- AIDS can develop as a result of HIV infection.
- Information concerning the transmission of the virus HIV has not changed since 1982.
- The consensus of authoritative medical opinion is that HIV is spread through (1) the direct exchange of infective bodily fluids (blood, semen, and vaginal fluids) during insertive sexual contact, (2) the sharing of infective drug injection equipment by intravenous drug users, (3) the receipt of infective blood or blood component products, and (4) transmission from an infected mother to an infant during pregnancy or childbirth.
- The time between infection with HIV and the onset of symptoms varies from person to person. Symptoms will appear, at the earliest, six months after infection; on the other hand, some people have been living with HIV since the early eighties and have yet to show symptoms of disease.
- There is an HIV antibody test available which can infer the presence of the virus. It cannot be said to be accurate, however, unless individuals wait for six months after their last possible exposure to HIV.
- For each person diagnosed with AIDS, there are anywhere from 50–100 people who are HIV-infected.
- Diagnostic AIDS is still uncommon among high school students and persons in their early twenties. That is because most people who become HIV-infected as adolescents will not get sick until they are in their late twenties or thirties (or perhaps longer). The rate of HIV infection among adolescents is significant, and growing rapidly.
- There is presently no medical justification for restricting the enrollment of students or the employment of staff who have HIV or AIDS.
- The consensus of medical opinion is that the HIV is not a readily communicable disease. The virus is not spread by casual contact.
- Current medical knowledge concludes that students or employees with HIV or AIDS do not pose a health risk to others in academic settings.

• In Minnesota, discrimination against people with HIV or AIDS is prohibited under the state Human Rights Act, Chapter 363. It is also prohibited by the federal Americans with Disabilities Act and Section 504 of the federal Rehabilitation Act of 1973 (amended).

• Persons wishing to avoid HIV infection or reinfection are advised to avoid sharing drug injection equipment and to either abstain from insertive sex or use latex condoms consistently whenever engaging in anal, vaginal, or oral intercourse.

Legal Issues

The following statements are from a document prepared by the American Council on Education (ACE). The author is Sheldon Elliot Steinbach, General Council of the ACE, who worked extensively with legal experts in the development of the document.

• It is highly unlikely that a school, acting conscientiously on the basis of the best currently-available medical information, would be held liable simply because one student or employee transmitted the virus to another.

• A school could suspend a person with HIV who engages in conduct known to infect others.

• On the basis of medical information, the routine segregation or exclusion of persons with HIV or general disclosure of their identity to faculty and students is unwarranted, in addition to being in conflict with state and federal laws regarding discrimination and data privacy.

• In every individual case, verifiable risks and benefits to both (1) the person with HIV and (2) other students and employees are to be weighed.

• Mandatory HIV antibody testing of students or employees, or dismissal of persons with HIV or AIDS even in occupations involving close contact with others, is not justified.

• When transmission does occur among students or staff, it is most probably the result of private behaviors for which the college should not be held responsible.

Procedures

College Attendance

• Unless medical evidence clearly indicates that any situation would produce an unreasonable risk for the person diagnosed with HIV or AIDS or for others coming into contact with the person, (1) a student should be allowed to attend college and participate in college activities in an unrestricted manner and (2) an employee should be permitted to remain engaged in normal work activity.

• The college should respond individually to situations involving special concerns or questions.

• Any decisions involving the restriction of a student's attendance or participation in activities, or an employee's involvement in work, will be made only by the College President, following a recommendation by the First Response Team (see below).

- Neither the admissions process nor the hiring process should involve questions concerning a person's sexual orientation.
- Neither the admissions process nor the hiring process should involve any required or requested HIV testing or screening.
- The college may not ask whether a prospective or current employee or student has HIV or AIDS. However, if an employee has a pattern of excessive sick leave use, the employer may request a doctor's statement about the nature of the illness and its severity.
- The college must provide "reasonable accommodation" for students and employees living with disabilities, including those caused by HIV disease. Decisions regarding "reasonable accommodation" should be made on a case-by-case basis.

First Response Team

- A First Response Team has been established, comprised of State Department of Health officials and the State Attorney General's office.
- The First Response Team should be contacted in situations involving special concerns or questions.
- The recommended procedure for utilizing the First Response Team is as follows:

   (1) Contact the State Community College System office

   (2) Contact the State Department of Health

   (3) Contact the State Attorney General's Office

- The First Response Team should make recommendations directly to the college president.

Privacy

Regarding data privacy as it pertains to persons having AIDS or HIV:
- Any information shared with college officials by students, staff, parents, and medical personnel regarding an individual's HIV status should be absolutely private.
- No information about a person's HIV status should be entered on (1) the student's educational records, or (2) the employee's employment records.
- The number of individuals aware of an individual's medical condition should be kept to a minimum.
- Notification of a person's medical condition should be made to no one except those involved in making the recommendation or decision in a given situation.

Educating the Cedarwood College Community on HIV/AIDS

- Materials and resources (medical, health promotion, and counseling support) on HIV and AIDS are available in the College Health Service Office for all students and employees.

- Presentors on the subject of AIDS will be included in the health/wellness programs sponsored by the College Health Service during the school year.
- Courses at Cedarwood that include AIDS information as part of their course content are currently offered in the following areas: Public Health, Nursing, Human Services, Law Enforcement, and Science. Contact the College Health Service for a complete listing of these courses.
- Audiotapes and videotapes on AIDS have been purchased and are available in the library for employees and students.
- Articles on AIDS will be published in the student newspaper and weekly student newsletter.
- The College Health Service Nurse has been designated the campus resource person who can provide overall information on policies and procedures related to AIDS.
- State Counseling and Testing Sites provide counseling and a blood test which detects the presence of antibody to HIV. Contact the College Health Service Office, the State Department of Health, or the statewide AIDS hotline for further information.

State College Coordinating Board Policies and Regulations:

Requirements for All Colleges Regarding Acquired Immunodeficiency Syndrome (AIDS)

Board Policy

The following requirements are in effect regarding (1) the establishment of an AIDS education program, and (2) the procedures to be followed when a person is diagnosed as having AIDS or being infected with HIV.

Educational Program

1. Every college shall have an educational program concerning HIV and AIDS.
2. Educational programs shall be operational no later than winter quarter 1988.

Procedure for Responding To Any Situation Where A Person Is Diagnosed As Having AIDS Or As Being Infected With HIV

The following guidelines will be followed when dealing with persons who have been diagnosed as having AIDS or being infected with HIV:

1. Unless medical evidence indicates that any situation would produce an unreasonable risk for the person diagnosed as having AIDS or being infected with HIV or for others coming into contact with the person, (a) a student will be allowed to attend college and participate in college activities in an unrestricted manner, and (b) an employee will be permitted to remain engaged in normal work activity.

2. The college will respond individually to situations involving special concerns or questions.

3. Any decisions regarding the restriction of a student's attendance or participation in activities, or an employee's involvement in work will be made by the college president. The president shall make such a decision only after receiving medical advice from the State Department of Health and legal advice from the State Attorney General's Office.

4. Any decisions negatively affecting a student's college status shall be open to appeal to the chancellor or her or his designee. The decision of the chancellor or her or his designee shall be final, and will be made only after receiving medical advice from the State Department of Health and legal advice from the State Attorney General's Office.

5. Neither the admissions process nor the hiring process shall involve any required or requested testing or screening.

6. Any information shared with college officials by students, employees, parents, and medical personnel regarding an individual's HIV serostatus shall be absolutely private.

7. Notification of a person's medical condition shall be made to no one except those persons officially involved in making recommendations or decisions involving the particular case.

8. No information regarding a person's condition shall be entered on (a) the student's educational records or (b) the employee's employment records.

9. Colleges shall provide "reasonable accommodation" for students and employees who are disabled. Decisions regarding "reasonable accommodation" should be made on an individual case basis.

Affiliated Arts Alliance
HIV/AIDS Policy

3.0 POLICY ON AIDS AND OTHER LIFE-THREATENING, CHRONIC, OR POTENTIALLY DISABLING ILLNESS

The Affiliated Arts Alliance (AAA) is dedicated to maintaining a safe and healthy work environment for all its employees. Affiliated Arts Alliance employees with HIV disease or other life-threatening, chronic, or potentially disabling illness will be managed with sensitivity and in a non-discriminatory manner consistent with AAA's Affirmative Action Policy and all federal, state, and local laws.

Life-threatening, chronic, or potentially disabling illnesses include, among others, arthritis, cancer, heart disease, hepatitis, diabetes, respiratory disease, asthma, kidney or lung disease, HIV disease, and stroke.

Chronic illnesses are characterized by their long duration, and/or by frequent recurrence that are constantly weakening, handicapping, and/or psychologically troubling. Life-threatening illnesses are considered catastrophic or terminal in nature.

As their health permits, AAA employees with life-threatening, chronic, or potentially disabling illnesses may wish to continue working. In such instances an employee's ability to work must be evaluated by the employee's physician, who will be asked to fill out an Ability to Work Statement supplied by the Affiliated Arts Alliance. As long as an employee's medical condition permits the employee to perform her or his job without endangering the employee's or others' health, the AAA will provide reasonable work accommodations to assist the employee in continuing work.

Ill or disabled employees will be entitled to remain in the same job classification and work location unless:

* Remaining in that job classification or work location would seriously endanger the health of the employee or co-workers;

* The ill or disabled employee is unable to adhere to acceptable performance standards for his or her position as defined by position description; or

* Accommodating the employee imposes undue financial or administrative burdens on the AAA or has serious adverse effect on the AAA's programs or operations.

The Personnel Manager is responsible for evaluating and adjudicating any change in work status or reasonable accommodation for an Affiliated Arts Alliance employee.

3.1 AIDS AND HIV EXPLAINED

In light of employee and general public concerns, it is appropriate to the AAA to relay specific information regarding HIV illness and its impact on the workplace.

AIDS, or Acquired Immune Deficiency Syndrome, is a disease that may result from infection with the Human Immunodeficiency Virus (HIV). HIV weakens the human immune system so that it cannot fend off unusual infections or cancers.

The Centers for Disease Control (CDC) of the United States Public Health Service defines AIDS as a disease that corresponds to a list of specific infections, cancers, and other maladies that may result from HIV immunosuppression.

There have been a large number of people with AIDS. There is an even larger number of people who are HIV-infected, but who do not manifest the symptoms of AIDS as specified by the CDC. They may show no signs of illness, and may be unaware of HIV infection, but they can pass the virus on to others. They may or may not get sick in coming years.

Current scientific research concludes that HIV is transmitted only through certain, specific ways:

- *Through sexual contact involving exchange of blood, semen, or vaginal fluids with an HIV-infected person;*
- *Through direct blood-to-blood contact with an infected person; e.g., by sharing drug injection equipment; or*
- *Through pregnancy, childbirth, or breastfeeding from an HIV-infected mother to her child.*

Non-sexual person-to-person contact that normally occurs among employees or the general public does not transmit HIV.

The AAA is not an authority on HIV and is not responsible for an employee's interpretation or actions taken as a result of the information in this policy or in any education program provided by the AAA about this illness.

The Affiliated Arts Alliance will not require job applicants or employees to undergo HIV antibody testing as a condition of job consideration or employment.

3.2 CONFIDENTIALITY

Health data on AAA employees, in verbal and written form, is private. Such data is not to be disclosed to the general public or other employees unless specific legal obligations pertain. Employees who have such information about other employees will be held accountable for maintaining the confidentiality of such information.

3.3 EMPLOYEE BENEFITS DURING LIFE-THREATENING, CHRONIC, OR POTENTIALLY DISABLING ILLNESS

The Affiliated Arts Alliance renegotiates health, dental, life, and accidental-death-or-dismemberment insurance coverage for its employees on an annual basis. The benefits available to an employee during a life-threatening, chronic, or potentially disabling illness will depend on the terms of the insurance contract for all employees at the time of the employee's illness.

As outlined earlier, the AAA will pay a full-time employee for ten consecutive work days missed due to a prolonged illness or disability. Part-time employees do not receive paid sick days.

After an absence of ten consecutive work days in any calendar year as a result of sickness or disability, all part- or full-time employees must submit an Absence Report Form to the Personnel Manager, and thereafter apply for an unpaid Medical Leave of Absence, accompanied by an Ability to Work Form completed by the employee's physician.

Infection Control/Universal Precautions Sample Policies

[This policy statement, from the Minnesota Department of Human Services, and reviewed by the Minnesota Department of Health, is appropriate for residential programs. Non-residential programs that provide a heightened level of care, such as daycare programs, can use it as well, but should, before adopting it, eliminate those sections or paragraphs that have nothing to do with program practice. Daycare centers should also attach to their policy statement the procedural paper, *Daily Care of the Child with Acquired Immunodeficiency Virus (AIDS) Human Immunodeficiency Virus (HIV) Infection, and Related Conditions;* it is found on page 383 of this book.]

RESIDENTIAL FACILITIES MANUAL
Policy Number: 6701
21 October 1988

PATIENT/RESIDENT CARE
General Infection Control Policies for Residents

1. POLICY

Universal precautions shall be consistently used for all clients as recommended by the Centers for Disease Control because medical history and examination cannot reliably identify all persons infected with Human Immunodeficiency Virus (HIV), hepatitis B Virus (HBV), or other blood-borne pathogens.

2. AUTHORITY:

A. Minnesota Statutes Sections 144.12 (1986) (Department of Health Authority to Control Infectious Diseases); 144.651 (1986) (Patients and Residents Bill of Rights); 144.68 and 144.69 (Suppl. 1987) (Records, Reports and Privacy Rights); 145.36 (1986) (Willful Exposure to Disease); Chapter 182 (1986 and Suppl. 1987) (Occupational Safety and Health Act); 246.01 (1986) (Powers of the Department of Human Services' Commissioners); Chapter 253B (1986 and Suppl. 1987) (Civil Commitment Act); 626.557 (1986 and Suppl. 1987) (Vulnerable Adult Abuse Reporting Act); 246.017 (1986) (Duties of Department of Human Services' Medical Director).

B. Minnesota Department of Human Services Rules 9515.1000 to 9515.2600 (Cost of Care for Residents in a State Hospital); 9525.0210 to 9525.0430 (Residential Facilities for Persons with Mental Retardation); 9530.2500 to 9530.4000 (Residential Facilities for Inebriate and Drug Dependent Persons); 9520.0500 to 9520.0690 (Residential Facilities for Adult Mentally Ill Persons); 9545.0900 to 9545.1090 (Child Care Institutions); 9555.8000 to 9555.8500 (Vulnerable Adult Abuse Reporting).

C. Minnesota Department of Health Rules for Health Care and Residential Facilities 4655.0090 to 4655.9900 (nursing and boarding care homes); 4640.0100 to 4640.6400 (hospitals); 4665.0100 to 4655.9900 (supervised living facilities).

D. Centers for Disease Control, Recommendations for Prevention of HIV Transmission in Health Care Settings, MMWR 1987, 36 (Supplement No. 2S); Centers for Disease Control, Update: Universal Precautions for Prevention of Transmission of Human Immunodeficiency Virus, Hepatitis B Virus, and other Bloodborne Pathogens in Health Care Settings, MMWR 1988, 37 (Supplement No. 24).

3. PURPOSE

A. To prevent the spread of HIV, HBV, and other blood-borne pathogens through contact with blood and certain bodily fluids at the Department's residential facilities.

B. To protect HIV-infected persons from the acquisition of other infections.

4. DEFINITIONS

A. Universal Precautions: Procedures intended to prevent parenteral, mucous membrane, and non-intact skin exposure of healthcare workers to blood-borne pathogens.

1. Bodily Fluids to Which Universal Precautions Do Apply:

a. Blood is the single most important source of HIV, HBV, and other blood-borne pathogens in the occupational setting.

b. Semen and vaginal secretions.

c. Other bodily fluids containing visible blood.

d. Tissues and the following bodily fluids: cerebrospinal fluid, synovial fluid, pleural fluid, peritoneal fluid, pericardial fluid, amniotic fluid.

2. Bodily Fluids to Which Universal Precautions Do Not Apply:

a. Saliva: General infection control practices already in existence, including using gloves for digital examination of mucous membranes, suctioning, oral hygiene, and handwashing after exposure to saliva should further minimize the minute risk, if any, for salivary transmission. Gloves need not be worn when feeding clients or when wiping saliva from skin.

b. Feces.

c. Nasal secretions.

d. Sweat.

e. Tears.

f. Urine.

g. Vomitus, unless it contains visible blood.

The risk of transmission of HIV and HBV from these fluids and materials is extremely low or non-existent.

3. Universal precautions are intended to supplement rather than replace recommendations for routine infection control, such as handwashing and using gloves to prevent gross microbial contamination of hands. Because specifying the types of barriers needed for every possible clinical situation is impractical, sound judgment must be exercised. Implementation does not eliminate the need for other category or disease-specific isolation precautions, such as enteric precautions for infectious diarrhea or isolation for pulmonary tuberculosis.

5. RESPONSIBILITIES:

A. Chief Executive Officers:
Develop and implement facility policies and procedures in consultation with the Medical Director and Infection Control Nurse.

6. PROCEDURES:

A. Room Assignments: Isolation is not necessary for known HBV and HIV-infected clients. They may use common waiting areas and bathroom facilities, unless the presence of other communicable infections requires special precautions. Clients with known HIV infection shall receive protective isolation only to prevent their exposure to potentially infectious agents. However, it may be prudent to provide HIV-infected clients with private rooms if they are coughing, non-compliant with hygiene and treatment instructions, or cannot be adequately instructed in blood, secretion, and enteric precautions. When a double or larger room is used, the additional client(s) will not be an impaired host(s) (e.g., another client with a known HIV infection who might be susceptible to potential infections).

B. Protective Garments: The following protective garments are to be used as specified:

1. *Gloves:* Personnel in direct contact with blood, semen and vaginal secretions, and other bodily fluids containing visible blood, shall wear vinyl or latex gloves. Gloves must be changed between client contacts. Hands shall be washed after removing gloves. General purpose utility gloves (e.g., rubber household gloves) shall be used for housekeeping chores involving potential blood contact, for instrument cleaning, and for decontamination procedures. Utility gloves may be decontaminated and reused, but must be discarded if they are peeling, cracked, discolored, or have punctures, tears, or other evidence of deterioration.

2. *Gowns:* Personnel in direct contact with blood, semen and vaginal secretions, and other bodily fluids containing visible blood, must wear gowns. Water-protective barrier gowns or plastic aprons are recommended when exposure to large volumes of bodily fluid is expected.

3. *Handwashing:* Hands and other skin surfaces contaminated with blood, bodily fluids containing visible blood, or other bodily fluids to which universal precautions apply must be thoroughly washed immediately after contact.

4. *Eye Protection and Masks:* In certain rare instances, such as when a splash of bodily fluids is likely, eye protection and masks should be used.

C. Specimens: Blood and bodily fluids to which universal precautions apply shall be placed in an impervious bag or container for transport. A 1:10 dilution of bleach or hospital-approved disinfectant shall be used to clean the outside of visibly soiled containers.

D. Equipment:

    1. Precautions must be taken by all personnel to prevent injuries caused by needles, scalpels, and other sharp instruments or devices. All needles and syringes are to be disposed of in rigid wall puncture-resistant containers. Needles are not to be resheathed or clipped after use before being discarded in the container. The container must be handled carefully to prevent accidental injury to either staff or clients.

    2. The following procedures must be implemented for equipment used commonly by all clients: (a) lensed instruments should be sterilized with ethylene oxide; (b) respiratory therapy tubing should be disposable or sterilized before reuse; (c) instruments which come in contact with blood or secretions must be sterilized before reuse, including anesthesia instruments, i.e., laryngoscopes and tracheal tubes. All reusable items should be transported in impervious bags or containers. Scheduling procedures, as appropriate, for the end of the day to allow for overnight sterilization (e.g., endoscope) should be considered.

    3. All disposable contaminated items (visibly soiled with blood or bodily fluids) are considered infectious wastes and must be bagged before disposal, in accordance with facility procedures for infectious waste. Non-disposable contaminated items are to be bagged and labeled prior to decontamination.

E. Linen: Soiled linen shall be handled as little as possible, and with minimum agitation to prevent contamination to persons bagging it. All soiled linen should be bagged at the location where it is used; it should not be sorted or rinsed in client areas. Linen soiled with blood or bodily fluids must be transported in bags that prevent leakage. If hot water is used, linen should be washed with detergent in water at least 160 degrees F for 25 minutes. If low-temperature water laundry cycles (less than 158 degrees F) are used, chemicals suitable for low-temperature washing at proper-use concentrations must be used.

F. Dishes: Standard dishwashing procedures shall be maintained for all residents.

G. Cardiopulmonary Resuscitation: An AMBU-BAG and oral airway shall be available for CPR even though current knowledge suggests the passage of HBV or HIV by this means has not occurred.

H. Housekeeping: Environmental surfaces contaminated with blood or other bodily fluids shall be immediately cleaned with chemical germicides approved for use as "hospital disinfectants."

I. Dental Care:

    1. Personnel shall wear latex gloves, masks, and protective eyewear (i.e., glasses, goggles, face shields) when performing dental procedures on all clients because contamination of saliva with blood is predictable; trauma to healthcare workers' hands is common; and blood spattering may occur.

    2. Instruments used in the mouths of all residents (e.g., mirrors, drills, etc.) shall be disinfected after use according to the manufacturer's instructions.

J. Laboratories:

    1. Use of gloves is recommended for performing phlebotomy and is mandatory

when healthcare workers have cuts, scratches, or other breaks in their skin.

2. Gloves shall be used in situations in which the healthcare worker judges that hand contamination with blood may occur; for example, when performing phlebotomy on an uncooperative client.

3. Gloves shall be used when performing finger-sticks.

4. Gloves shall be used when persons are receiving training in phlebotomy.

5. Mechanical pipetting devices are to be used for the manipulation of all liquids in the laboratory. Mouth pipetting is not permitted.

6. Needles and syringes are to be handled as required in 6-D-(1), above.

7. Laboratory coats, gowns, or uniforms shall be worn while working with potentially infectious materials and appropriately discarded before leaving the laboratory.

8. All employees processing blood and bodily fluids shall wear gloves and aprons. Gloves and aprons shall be changed and hands washed after completing specimen processing.

Reviewers: Residential Program Management Division Director, Medical Director, Department of Human Services; and the State Epidemiologist, AIDS Epidemiology Unit Supervisor, Acute Disease Epidemiology Section, Minnesota Department of Health.

Recommendations for Prevention of HIV Transmission in Healthcare Settings

Reprinted from *Morbidity and Mortality Weekly Report* 1987; 36 (no. 2S)

Introduction

Human Immunodeficiency Virus (HIV), the virus that is believed to cause Acquired Immunodeficiency Syndrome (AIDS), is transmitted through sexual contact and exposure to infected blood or blood components and perinatally from mother to neonate.

HIV has been isolated from blood, semen, vaginal secretions, saliva, tears, breast milk, cerebrospinal fluid, amniotic fluid, and urine and is likely to be isolated from other bodily fluids, secretions, and excretions. However, epidemiologic evidence has implicated only blood, semen, vaginal secretions, and possibly breast milk in transmission.

The increasing prevalence of HIV increases the risk that healthcare workers will be exposed to blood from patients infected with HIV, especially when blood and bodily-fluid precautions are not followed for all patients. Thus, this document emphasizes the need for healthcare workers to consider *all* patients as potentially infected with HIV and/or other blood-borne pathogens and to adhere rigorously to infection-control precautions for minimizing the risk of exposure to blood and bodily fluids of all patients.

The recommendations contained in this document consolidate and update CDC recommendations published earlier for preventing HIV transmission in healthcare settings: precautions for clinical and laboratory staffs (1) and precautions for healthcare workers and allied professionals (2); recommendations for preventing HIV transmission in the workplace (3) and during invasive procedures (4); recommendations for preventing possible transmission of HIV from tears (5); and recommendations for providing dialysis treatment for HIV-infected patients (6). These recommendations also update portions of the *Guidelines for Isolation Precautions in Hospitals* (7) and reemphasize some of the recommendations contained in *Infection Control Practices for Dentistry* (8). The recommendations contained in this document have been developed for use in healthcare settings and emphasize the need to treat blood and other bodily fluids from all patients as potentially infective. These same prudent precautions also should be taken in other settings in which persons may be exposed to blood or other bodily fluids.

Sample Policies

Definition of Healthcare Workers

Healthcare workers are defined as persons, including students and trainees, whose activities involve contact with patients or with blood or other bodily fluids from patients in a healthcare setting.

Healthcare Workers with AIDS

As of July 10, 1987, a total of 1,875 (5.8%) of 32,395 adults with AIDS, who had been reported to the CDC national surveillance system and for whom occupational information was available, reported being employed in a healthcare or clinical laboratory setting. In comparison, 6.8 million persons—representing 5.6% of the U.S. Labor force—were employed in health services. Of the healthcare workers with AIDS, 95% have been reported to exhibit high-risk behavior; for the remaining 5%, the means of HIV acquisition was undetermined. Healthcare workers with AIDS were significantly more likely than other workers to have an undetermined risk (5% versus 3%, respectively). For both healthcare and non-healthcare workers with AIDS, the proportion with an undetermined risk has not increased since 1982.

AIDS patients initially reported as not belonging to recognized risk groups are investigated by state and local health departments to determine whether possible risk factors exist. Of all healthcare workers with AIDS reported to CDC who were initially characterized as not having an identified risk and for whom follow-up information was available, 66% have been reclassified because risk factors were identified or because the patient was found not to meet the surveillance case definition for AIDS. Of the 87 healthcare workers currently categorized as having no identifiable risk, information is incomplete on 16 (18%) because of death or refusal to be interviewed; 38 (44%) are still being investigated. The remaining 33 (38%) healthcare workers were interviewed or had other follow-up information available. The occupations of these 33 were as follows: five physicians (15%), three of whom were surgeons; one dentist (3%); three nurses (9%); nine nursing assistants (27%); seven housekeeping or maintenance workers (21%); three clinical laboratory technicians (9%); one therapist (3%); and four others who did not have contact with patients (12%). Although 15 of these 33 healthcare workers reported parenteral and/or other non-needlestick exposure to blood or bodily fluids from patients in the 10 years preceding their diagnosis of AIDS, none of these exposures involved a patient with AIDS or known HIV infection.

Risk to Healthcare Workers of Acquiring HIV In Healthcare Settings

Healthcare workers with documented percutaneous or mucous-membrane exposures to blood or bodily fluids of HIV-infected patients have been prospectively evaluated to determine the risk of infection after such exposures. As of June 30, 1987, 883 healthcare workers have been tested for antibody to HIV in an ongoing surveillance project conducted by the CDC (9). Of these, 708 (80%) had percutaneous exposures to blood, and 175 (20%) had a mucous membrane or an open wound contaminated by blood or bodily fluids. Of 396 healthcare workers, each of whom had only a convalescent-phase serum sample obtained and tested 90 days post-exposure, one (for whom heterosexual transmission could not be ruled out) was seropositive for HIV antibody. For 425 additional healthcare workers, both acute and convalescent-phase serum samples were obtained and tested; none of 74 healthcare workers with nonpercutaneous exposure seroconverted, and three (0.9%) of 351 with percutaneous exposures seroconverted. None of these three healthcare workers had other documented risk factors for infection.

Two other prospective studies to assess the risk of nosocomial acquisition of HIV infection for healthcare workers are ongoing in the United States. As of April 30, 1987, 332 healthcare workers with a total of 453 needlestick or mucous-membrane exposures to the blood or other bodily fluids of HIV-infected patients were tested for HIV antibody at the National Institutes of Health (10). These exposed workers included 103 with needlestick injuries and 229 with mucous-membrane exposures; none had seroconverted. A similar study at the University of California of 129 healthcare workers with documented needlestick injuries or mucous-membrane exposures to blood or other body fluids from patients with HIV infection has not identified any seroconversions (11). Results of a prospective study in the United Kingdom identified no evidence of transmission among 150 healthcare workers with parenteral or mucous-membrane exposure to blood or other bodily fluids, secretions, or excretions from patients with HIV infection (12).

In addition to healthcare workers enrolled in prospective studies, eight persons who provided care to infected patients and denied other risk factors have been reported to have acquired HIV infection. Three of these healthcare workers had needlestick exposures to blood from infected patients (13–15). Two were persons who provided nursing care to infected persons; although neither sustained a needlestick, both had extensive contact with blood or other bodily fluids, and neither observed recommended barrier precautions (16, 17). The other three were healthcare workers with non-needlestick exposures to blood from infected patients (18). Although the exact route of transmission for these last three infections is not known, all three persons had direct contact of their skin with blood from infected patients, all had skin lesions that may have been contaminated by blood, and one also had a mucous-membrane exposure.

A total of 1,231 dentists and hygienists, many of whom practiced in areas with many AIDS cases, participated in a study to determine the prevalence of antibody to HIV; one dentist (0.1%) had HIV antibody. Although no exposure to a known HIV-infected person could be documented, epidemiologic investigation did not identify any other risk factor for infection. The infected dentist, who also had a history of sustaining needlestick injuries and trauma to his hands, did not routinely wear gloves when providing dental care (19).

Sample Policies

Precautions to Prevent Transmission of HIV

Universal Precautions

Since medical history and examination cannot reliably identify all patients infected with HIV or other blood-borne pathogens, blood and bodily-fluid precautions should be consistently used for all patients. This approach, previously recommended by CDC (3,4), and referred to as "universal blood and bodily-fluid precautions" or "universal precautions," should be used in the care of all patients, especially including those in emergency-care settings in which the risk of blood exposure is increased and the infection status of the patient is usually unknown (20).

1. All healthcare workers should routinely use appropriate barrier precautions to prevent skin and mucous-membrane exposure when contact with blood or other bodily fluids of any patient is anticipated. Gloves should be worn for touching blood and bodily fluids, mucous membranes, or non-intact skin of all patients, for handling items or surfaces soiled with blood or bodily fluids, and for performing venipuncture and other vascular access procedures. Gloves should be changed after contact with each patient. Masks and protective eyewear or face shields should be worn during procedures that are likely to generate droplets of blood or other bodily fluids to prevent exposure of mucous membranes of the mouth, nose, and eyes. Gowns or aprons should be worn during procedures that are likely to generate splashes of blood or other bodily fluids.

2. Hands and other skin surfaces should be washed immediately and thoroughly if contaminated with blood or other bodily fluids. Hands should be washed immediately after gloves are removed.

3. All healthcare workers should take precautions to prevent injuries caused by needles, scalpels, and other sharp instruments or devices during procedures; when cleaning used instruments; during disposal of used needles; and when handling sharp instruments after procedures. To prevent needlestick injuries, needles should not be recapped, purposely bent or broken by hand, removed from disposable syringes, or otherwise manipulated by hand. After they are used, disposable syringes and needles, scalpel blades, and other sharp items should be placed in puncture-resistant containers for disposal; the puncture-resistant containers should be located as close as practical to the use area. Large-bore reusable needles should be placed in a puncture-resistant container for transport to the reprocessing area.

4. Although saliva has not been implicated in HIV transmission, to minimize the need for emergency mouth-to-mouth resuscitation, mouthpieces, resuscitation bags, or other ventilation devices should be available for use in areas in which the need for resuscitation is predictable.

5. Healthcare workers who have exudative lesions or weeping dermatitis should refrain from all direct patient care and from handling patient-care equipment until the condition resolves.

6. Pregnant healthcare workers are not known to be at greater risk of contracting HIV infection than healthcare workers who are not pregnant; however, if a healthcare worker develops HIV infection during pregnancy, the infant is at risk of infection resulting from perinatal transmission. Because of this risk, pregnant healthcare workers should be especially familiar with and strictly adhere to precautions to minimize the risk of HIV transmission.

Implementation of universal blood and bodily-fluid precautions for all patients eliminates the need for use of the isolation category of "Blood and Bodily Fluid Precautions" previously recommended by CDC (7) for patients known or suspected to be infected with bloodborne pathogens. Isolation precautions (e.g., enteric, "AFB" [7]) should be used as necessary if associated conditions, such as infectious diarrhea or tuberculosis, are diagnosed or suspected.

Precautions for Invasive Procedures

In this document, an invasive procedure is defined as surgical entry into tissues, cavities, or organs or repair of major traumatic injuries (1) in an operating or delivery room, emergency department or outpatient setting, including both physicians' and dentists' offices; (2) cardiac catheterization and angiographic procedures; (3) a vaginal or cesarean delivery or other invasive obstetric procedure during which bleeding may occur; or (4) the manipulation, cutting, or removal of any oral or perioral tissues, including tooth structure, during which bleeding occurs or the potential for bleeding exists. The universal blood and bodily-fluid precautions listed above, combined with the precautions listed below should be the minimum precautions for all such invasive procedures.

1. All healthcare workers who participate in invasive procedures must routinely use appropriate barrier precautions to prevent skin and mucous-membrane contact with blood and other bodily fluids of all patients. Gloves and surgical masks must be worn for all invasive procedures. Protective eyewear or face shields should be worn for procedures that commonly result in the generation of droplets, splashing of blood or other bodily fluids, or the generation of bone chips. Gowns or aprons made of materials that provide an effective barrier should be worn during invasive procedures that are likely to result in the splashing of blood or other bodily fluids. All healthcare workers who perform or assist in vaginal or cesarean deliveries should wear gloves and gowns when handling the placenta or the infant until blood and amniotic fluid have been removed from the infant's skin and should wear gloves during postdelivery care of the umbilical cord.

2. If a glove is torn or a needlestick or other injury occurs, the glove should be removed and a new glove used as promptly as patient safety permits; the needle or instrument involved in the incident should also be removed from the sterile field.

Sample Policies

Precautions for Dentistry

Blood, saliva, and gingival fluid from all dental patients should be considered infective. Special emphasis should be placed on the following precautions for preventing transmission of blood-borne pathogens in dental practice in both institutional and non-institutional settings.

1. In addition to wearing gloves for contact with oral mucous membranes of all patients, all dental workers should wear surgical masks and protective eyewear or chin-length plastic face shields during dental procedures in which splashing or spattering of blood, saliva, or gingival fluids is likely. Rubber dams, high-speed evacuation, and proper patient positioning, when appropriate, should be utilized to minimize generation of droplets and spatter.

2. Handpieces should be sterilized after use with each patient, since blood, saliva, or gingival fluid of patients may be aspirated into the handpiece or waterline. Handpieces that cannot be sterilized should at least be flushed, the outside surface cleaned and wiped with a suitable chemical germicide, and then rinsed. Handpieces should be flushed at the beginning of the day and after use with each patient. Manufacturers' recommendations should be followed for use and maintenance of waterlines and check valve and for flushing of handpieces. The same precautions should be used for ultrasonic scalers and air/water syringes.

3. Blood and saliva should be thoroughly and carefully cleaned from material that has been used in the mouth (e.g., impaction materials, bite registration), especially before polishing and grinding intra-oral devices. Contaminated materials, impressions, and intra-oral devices should also be cleaned and disinfected before being handled in the dental laboratory and before they are placed in the patient's mouth. Because of the increasing variety of dental materials used intra-orally, dental workers should consult with manufacturers as to the stability of specific materials when using disinfection procedures.

4. Dental equipment and surfaces that are difficult to disinfect (e.g., light handles or X-ray unit heads) and that may become contaminated should be wrapped with impervious-backed paper, aluminum foil, or clear plastic wrap. The covering should be removed and discarded, and clean coverings should be put in place after use with each patient.

General infection-control precautions are more specifically addressed in previous recommendations for infection-control practices for dentistry (8).

Precautions for Autopsies or Mortician Services

In addition to the universal blood and bodily-fluid precautions listed above, the following precautions should be used by persons performing postmortem procedures:

1. All persons performing or assisting in postmortem procedures should wear gloves, masks, protective eyewear, gowns, and waterproof aprons.

2. Instruments and surfaces contaminated during postmortem procedures should be decontaminated with an appropriate chemical germicide.

Precautions for Dialysis

Patients with end-stage renal disease who are undergoing maintenance dialysis and who have HIV infection can be dialyzed in hospital-based or free-standing dialysis units using conventional infection-control precautions (21). Universal blood and bodily-fluid precautions should be used when dialyzing all patients.

Strategies for disinfecting the dialysis fluid pathways of the hemodialysis machine are targeted to control bacterial contamination and generally consist of using 500–750 parts per million (ppm) of sodium hypochlorite (household bleach) for 30–40 minutes or 1.5%–2.0% formaldehyde overnight. In addition, several chemical germicides formulated to disinfect dialysis machines are commercially available. None of these protocols or procedures need to be changed for dialyzing patients infected with HIV.

Patients infected with HIV can be dialyzed by either hemodialysis or peritoneal dialysis and do not need to be isolated from other patients. The type of dialysis treatment (i.e., hemodialysis or peritoneal dialysis) should be based on the needs of the patient. The dialyzer may be discarded after each use. Alternatively, centers that use dialyzers (i.e., a specific single-use dialyzer is issued to a specific patient, removed, cleaned, disinfected, and reused several times on the same patient only) may include HIV-infected patients in the dialysis program. An individual dialyzer must never be used on more than one patient.

Precautions for Laboratories

Blood and other bodily fluids from all patients should be considered infective. To supplement the universal blood and bodily-fluid precautions listed above, the following precautions are recommended for healthcare workers in clinical laboratories.

1. All specimens of blood and bodily fluids should be put in a well-constructed container with a secure lid to prevent leaking during transport. Care should be taken when collecting each specimen to avoid contaminating the outside of the container and of the lab-

oratory form accompanying the specimen.

2. All persons processing blood and bodily-fluid specimens (e.g., removing tops from vacuum tubes) should wear gloves. Masks and protective eyewear should be worn if mucous-membrane contact with blood or bodily fluids is anticipated. Gloves should be changed and hands washed after completion of specimen processing.

3. For routine procedures, such as histologic and pathologic studies or microbiologic culturing, a biological safety cabinet is not necessary. However, biological safety cabinets (Class I or II) should be used whenever procedures are conducted that have a high potential for generating droplets. These include activities such as blending, sonicating, and vigorous mixing.

4. Mechanical pipetting devices should be used for manipulating all liquids in the laboratory. Mouth pipetting must not be done.

5. Use of needles and syringes should be limited to situations in which there is no alternative, and the recommendations for preventing injuries with needles outlined under universal precautions should be followed.

6. Laboratory work surfaces should be decontaminated with an appropriate chemical germicide after a spill of blood or other bodily fluids and when work activities are completed.

7. Contaminated materials used in laboratory tests should be decontaminated before reprocessing or be placed in bags and disposed of in accordance with institutional policies for disposal of infective waste (2e8). Scientific equipment that has been contaminated with blood or other bodily fluids should be decontaminated and cleaned before being repaired in the laboratory or transported to the manufacturer.

8. All persons should wash their hands after completing laboratory activities and should remove protective clothing before leaving the laboratory.

Implementation of universal blood and bodily-fluid precautions for all patients eliminates the need for warning labels on specimens since blood and other bodily fluids from all patients should be considered infective.

Environmental Considerations for HIV Transmission

No environmentally mediated mode of HIV transmission has been documented. Nevertheless, the precautions described below should be taken routinely in the care of all patients.

Sterilization and Disinfection

Standard sterilization and disinfection procedures for patient care equipment currently recommended for use (2S, 26) in a variety of healthcare settings including hospitals, medical and dental clinics and offices, hemodialysis centers, emergency care facilities, and long-term nursing care facilities are adequate to sterilize or disinfect instruments, devices, or other items contaminated with blood or other bodily fluids, from persons infected with blood-borne pathogens including HIV (21,23).

Instruments or devices that enter sterile tissue or the vascular system of any patient or through which blood flows should be sterilized before reuse. Devices or items that contact intact mucous membranes should be sterilized or receive high-level disinfection, a procedure that kills vegetative organisms and viruses but not necessarily large numbers of bacterial spores. Chemical germicides that are registered with the U.S. Environmental Protection Agency (EPA) as "sterilants" may be used either for sterilization or for high-level disinfection depending on contact time.

Contact lenses used in trial fittings should be disinfected after each fitting by using a hydrogen peroxide contact lens disinfecting system or, if compatible, with heat (78° C or 172.4–176.0° F) for 10 minutes.

Medical devices, or instruments that require sterilization or disinfection should be thoroughly cleaned before being exposed to the germicide, and the manufacturer's instructions for the use of the germicide should be followed. Further, it is important that the manufacturer's specifications for compatibility of the medical device with chemical germicides be closely followed. Information on specific label claims of commercial germicides can be obtained by writing to the Disinfectants Branch, Office of Pesticides, Environmental Protection Agency, 401 M Street SW, Washington, D.C. 20460.

Studies have shown that HIV is inactivated rapidly after being exposed to commonly-used chemical germicides at concentrations that are much lower than used in practice (27–30). Embalming fluids are similar to the types of chemical germicides that have been tested and found to completely inactivate HIV. In addition to commercially-available chemical germicides, a solution of sodium hypochlorite (household bleach) prepared daily is an inexpensive and effective germicide. Concentrations ranging from approximately 500 ppm (1:100 dilution of household bleach) sodium hypochlorite to 5,000 ppm (1:10 dilution of household bleach) are effective depending on the amount of organic material (e.g., blood, mucus) present on the surface to be cleaned and disinfected. Commercially available chemical germicides may be more compatible with certain medical devices that might be corroded by repeated exposure to sodium hypochlorite, especially to the 1:10 dilution.

Survival of HIV in the Environment

The most extensive study on the survival of HIV after drying involved greatly concentrated HIV samples, i.e., 10 million tissue-culture infectious doses per milliliter (31). This concentration is at least 100,000 times greater than that typically found in the blood or serum of patients with HIV infection. HIV was detectable by tissue culture techniques 1–3 days after drying, but the rate of inactivation was rapid. Studies performed at CDC have also shown that drying HIV causes a rapid (within several hours) 1–2 log (90–99%) reduction in HIV concentration. In tissue culture fluid, cell-free HIV could be detected up to 15 days at room temperature, up to 11 days at 37° C (98.6° F) and up to 1 day if the HIV was cell-associated.

When considered in the context of environmental conditions in healthcare facilities, these results do not require any changes in currently recommended sterilization, disinfection, or housekeeping strategies. When medical devices are contaminated with blood or other bodily fluids, existing recommendations include the cleaning of these instruments, followed by disinfection or sterilization, depending on the type of medical device. These protocols assume "worst-case" conditions of extreme virologic and microbiological contamination, and whether viruses have been inactivated after drying plays no role in formulating these strategies. Consequently, no changes in published procedures for cleaning, disinfecting, or sterilizing need to be made.

Housekeeping

Environmental surfaces such as walls, floors, and other surfaces are not associated with transmission of infections to patients or healthcare workers. Therefore, extraordinary attempts to disinfect or sterilize these environmental surfaces are not necessary. However, cleaning and removal of soil should be done routinely.

Cleaning schedules and methods vary according to the area of the hospital or institution, type of surface to be cleaned, and the amount and type of soil present. Horizontal surfaces (e.g., bedside tables and hard-surfaced flooring) in patient care areas are usually cleaned on a regular basis, when soiling or spills occur, and when a patient is discharged. Cleaning of walls, blinds, and curtains is recommended only if they are visibly soiled. Disinfectant fogging is an unsatisfactory method of decontaminating air and surfaces and is not recommended.

Disinfectant-detergent formulations registered by EPA can be used for cleaning environmental surfaces, but the actual physical removal of microorganisms by scrubbing is probably at least as important as any antimicrobial effect of the cleaning agent used. Therefore, cost, safety, and acceptability by housekeepers can be the main criteria for selecting any such registered agent. The manufacturers' instructions for appropriate use should be followed.

Cleaning and Decontaminating Spills of Blood or Other Bodily Fluids

Chemical germicides that are approved for use as "hospital disinfectants" can be used to decontaminate spills of blood and other bodily fluids. Strategies for decontaminating spills of blood and other bodily fluids in a patient-care setting are different than for spills of cultures or other materials in clinical, public health, or research laboratories. In patient care areas, visible material should first be removed and then the area should be decontaminated. With large spills of cultures or concentrated infectious agents in the laboratory, the contaminated area should be flooded with a liquid germicide before cleaning, then decontaminated with fresh germicidal chemical. In both settings, gloves should be worn during the cleaning and decontaminating procedures.

Laundry

Although soiled linen has been identified as a source of large numbers of certain pathogenic microorganisms, the risk of actual disease transmission is negligible. Rather than rigid procedures and specifications, hygienic and commonsense storage and processing of clean and soiled linen are recommended (26). Soiled linen should be handled as little as possible and with minimum agitation to prevent gross microbial contamination of the air and of persons handling the linen. All soiled linen should be bagged at the location where it was used; it should not be sorted or rinsed in patient care areas. Linen soiled with blood or bodily fluids should be placed and transported in bags that prevent leakage. If hot water is used, linen should be washed with detergent in water at least 71° C (160° F) for 25 minutes. If low-temperature (<70° C) laundry cycles are used, chemicals suitable for low-temperature washing at proper-use concentration should be used.

Infective Waste

There is no epidemiologic evidence to suggest that most hospital waste is any more infective than residential waste. Moreover, there is no epidemiologic evidence that hospital waste has caused disease in the community as a result of improper disposal. Therefore, identifying wastes for which special precautions are indicated is largely a matter of judgment about the relative risk of disease transmission. The most practical approach to the management of infective waste is to identify those wastes with the potential for causing infection during handling and disposal and for which some special precautions appear prudent. Hospital wastes for which special precautions appear prudent include microbiology laboratory waste, pathology waste, and blood specimens or blood products. While any item that has had contact with blood, exudates, or secretions may be potentially infective, it is not usually considered practical or necessary to treat all such waste as infective (23,26). Infective waste, in general, should either be incinerated or should be autoclaved before disposal in a sanitary landfill. Bulk blood, suctioned fluids, excretions, and secretions may be carefully poured down a drain connected to a sanitary sewer. Sanitary sewers may also be used to dispose of other infectious wastes capable of being ground and flushed into the sewer.

Implementation of Recommended Precautions

Employers of healthcare workers should ensure that policies exist for:

1. Initial orientation and continuing education and training of all healthcare workers—including students and trainees—on the epidemiology, mode of transmission, and prevention of HIV and other blood-borne infections and the need for routine use of universal blood and bodily-fluid precautions for all patients.

2. Provision of equipment and supplies necessary to minimize the risk of infection with HIV and other blood-borne pathogens.

3. Monitoring adherence to recommended protective measures. When monitoring reveals a failure to follow recommended precautions, then counseling, education, and/or retraining should be provided and, if necessary, appropriate disciplinary action should be considered.

Professional associations and labor organizations, through continuing education efforts, should emphasize the need for healthcare workers to follow recommended precautions.

Serologic Testing for HIV Infection

Background

A person is identified as infected with HIV when a sequence of tests, starting with repeated enzyme immunoassays (EIA) and including a Western blot or similar, more specific assay, are repeatedly active. Persons infected with HIV usually develop antibody against the virus within 12 weeks after infection.

The sensitivity of the currently licensed EIA tests is at least 99% when they are performed under optimal laboratory conditions on serum specimens from persons infected for > 12 weeks. Optimal laboratory conditions include the use of reliable reagents, provision of continuing education of personnel, quality control of procedures, and participation in performance evaluation programs. Given this performance, the probability of a false-negative test is remote except during the first several weeks after infection, before detectable antibody is present. The proportion of infected persons with a false-negative test attributed to absence of antibody in the early stages of infection is dependent on both the incidence and prevalence of HIV infection in a population (Table 1).

Table 1. Estimated number of patients infected with HIV not detected by HIV-antibody testing in a hypothetical hospital with 10,000/year*

Beginning prevalence of HIV infection	Annual incidence of HIV infection	Approximate number of HIV-infected patients	Approximate number of HIV-infected patients not detected
5.0%	1.0%	550	17–18
5.0%	0.5%	525	11–12
1.0%	0.2%	110	3–4
1.0%	0.1%	105	2–3
0.1%	0.02%	11	0–1
0.1%	0.01%	11	0–1

* The estimates are based on the following assumptions: (1) the sensitivity of the screening test is 99% (i.e., 99% of HIV-infected persons with antibody will be detected); (2) persons infected with HIV will not develop detectable antibody (seroconvert) until 6 weeks (1.5 months) after infection; (3) new infections occur at an equal rate throughout the year; and (4) calculations of the number of HIV-infected persons in the patient population are based on the mid-year prevalence, which is the beginning prevalence plus half the annual incidence of infection.

The efficacy of the currently licensed EIA tests is approximately 99% when repeatedly reactive tests are considered. Repeat testing of initially reactive specimens by EIA is required to reduce the likelihood of laboratory error. To increase further the specificity of serologic testing, laboratories must use a supplemental test, most often the Western blot, to validate repeatedly reactive EIA results. Under optimal laboratory conditions, the sensitivity of the Western blot test is comparable to or greater than that of a repeatedly reactive EIA, and the Western blot is highly specific when strict criteria are used to interpret the test results. The testing sequence of a repeatedly reactive EIA and a positive Western blot test is highly predictive of HIV infection, even in a population with a low prevalence of infection (Table 2). If the Western blot test result is indeterminate, the testing is considered equivocal for HIV infection. When this occurs, the Western blot test should be repeated on the same serum sample and, if still indeterminate, the testing sequence should be repeated on a sample collected 3–6 months later. Use of other supplemental tests may aid in the interpreting of results on samples that are frequently indeterminate by Western blot.

Table 2. Predictive value of positive HIV-antibody tests in hypothetical populations with different prevalences of infection

	Prevalence of infection	Predictive value of positive test*
Repeatedly reactive enzyme immunoassay (EIA)**	0.2%	28.41%
	2.0%	80.16%
	20.0%	98.02%
Repeatedly reactive EIA followed by positive Western Blot (WB)***	0.2%	99.75%
	2.0%	99.97%
	20.0%	99.99%

* Proportion of persons with positive test results who are actually infected with HIV.
** Assumes EIA sensitivity of 99.0% and specificity of 99.5%.
*** Assumes WB sensitivity of 99.0% and specificity of 99.9%.

Testing of Patients

Previous CDC recommendations have emphasized the value of HIV serologic testing of patients for: (1) management of parenteral or mucous-membrane exposure of healthcare workers, (2) patient diagnosis and management, and (3) counseling and serologic testing to prevent and control HIV transmission in the community. In addition, more recent recommendations have stated that hospitals, in conjunction with state and local health departments, should periodically determine the prevalence of HIV infection among patients from age groups at highest risk of infection (32).

Adherence to universal blood and bodily-fluid precautions recommended for the care of all patients will minimize the risk of transmission of HIV and other blood-borne pathogens from patients to healthcare workers. The utility of routine HIV serologic testing of patients as an adjunct to universal precautions is unknown. Results of such testing may not be available in emergency or outpatient settings. In addition, some recently-infected patients will not have detectable antibody to HIV (Table 1).

Personnel in some hospitals have advocated serologic testing of patients in settings in which exposure of healthcare workers to large amounts of patients' blood may be anticipated. Specific patients for whom serologic testing has ben advocated include those undergoing major operative procedures and those undergoing treatment in critical care units, especially if they have conditions involving uncontrolled bleeding. Decisions regarding the need to establish testing programs for patients should be made by physicians or individual institutions. In addition, when deemed appropriate, testing of individual patients may be performed on agreement between the patient and the physician providing care.

In addition to the universal precautions recommended for all patients, certain additional precautions for the care of HIV-infected patients undergoing major surgical operations have been proposed by personnel in some hospitals. For example, surgical procedures on an HIV-infected patient might be altered so that hand-to-hand passing of sharp instruments would be eliminated; stapling instruments rather than hand-suturing equipment might be used to perform tissue approximation; electrocautery devices rather than scalpels might be used as cutting instruments; and, even though uncomfortable, gowns that totally prevent seepage of blood onto the skin of members of the operative team might be worn. While such modifications might further minimize the risk of HIV infection for members of the operative team, some of these techniques could result in prolongation of operative time and could potentially have an adverse effect on the patient.

Testing programs, if developed, should include the following principles:
- *Obtaining consent for testing.*

- *Informing patients of test results, and providing counseling for seropositive patients by properly trained persons.*

- *Assuring that confidentiality safeguards are in place to limit knowledge of test results to those directly involved in the care of infected patients or as required by law.*

- *Assuring that identification of infected patients will not result in denial of needed care or provision of suboptimal care.*

- *Evaluating prospectively (l) the efficacy of the program in reducing the incidence of parenteral, mucous-membrane, or significant cutaneous exposures of healthcare workers to the blood or other bodily fluids of HIV-infected patients and (2) the effect of modified procedures on patients.*

Testing of Healthcare Workers

Although transmission of HIV from infected healthcare workers to patients has not been reported, transmission during invasive procedures remains a possibility. Transmission of hepatitis B (HBV), a blood-borne agent with a considerably greater potential for nosocomial transmission from healthcare workers to patients, has been documented. Such transmission has occurred in situations (e.g., oral and gynecologic surgery) in which healthcare workers, when tested, had very high concentrations of HBV in their blood (at least 100 million infectious virus particles per milliliter, a concentration much higher than occurs with HIV infection), and the healthcare workers sustained a puncture wound while performing invasive procedures or had exudative or weeping lesions or microlacerations that allowed virus to contaminate instruments or open wounds of patients (33, 34).

The hepatitis B experience indicates that only those healthcare workers who perform certain types of invasive procedures have transmitted HBV to patients. Adherence to recommendations in this document will minimize the risk of transmission of HIV and other blood-borne pathogens from healthcare workers to patients during invasive procedures. Since transmission of HIV from infected healthcare workers performing invasive procedures to their patients has not been reported and would be expected to occur only very rarely, if at all, the utility of routine testing of such healthcare workers to prevent transmission of HIV cannot be assessed. If consideration is given to developing a serologic testing program for healthcare workers who perform invasive procedures, the frequency of testing, as well as the issues of consent, confidentiality, and consequences of test results—as previously outlined for testing programs for patients—must be addressed.

Management of Infected Healthcare Workers

Healthcare workers with impaired immune systems resulting from HIV infection or other causes are at increased risk of acquiring or experiencing serious complications of infectious disease. Of particular concern is the risk of severe infection following exposure to patients with infectious diseases that are easily transmitted if appropriate precautions are not taken (e.g., measles, varicella). Any healthcare worker with an impaired immune system should be counseled about the potential risk associated with taking care of patients with any transmissible infection and should continue to follow existing recommendations for infection control to minimize risk of exposure to other infectious agents (7, 35). Recommendations of the Immunization Practices Advisory Committee (ACIP) and institutional policies concerning requirements for vaccinating healthcare workers with live-virus vaccines (e.g., measles, rubella) should also be considered.

The question of whether workers infected with HIV, especially those who perform invasive procedures, can adequately and safely be allowed to perform patient care duties or whether their work assignments should be changed must be determined on an individual basis. These decisions should be made by the healthcare worker's personal physician(s) in conjunction with the medical directors and personnel health service staff of the employing institution or hospital.

Management of Exposures

If a healthcare worker has a parenteral (e.g., needlestick or cut) or a mucous membrane (e.g., splash to the eye or mouth) exposure to blood or other bodily fluids or has a cutaneous exposure involving large amounts of blood or prolonged contact with blood—especially when the exposed skin is chapped, abraded, or afflicted with dermatitis—the source patient should be informed of the incident and tested for serologic evidence of HIV infection after consent is obtained. Policies should be developed for testing source patients in situations in which consent cannot be obtained (e.g., an unconscious patient).

If the source patient has AIDS, is positive for HIV antibody, or refuses the test, the healthcare worker should be counseled regarding the risk of infection and evaluated clinically and serologically for evidence of HIV infection as soon as possible after the exposure. The healthcare worker should be advised to report and seek medical evaluation for any acute febrile illness that occurs within 12 weeks after the exposure. Such an illness, particularly one characterized by fever, rash or lymphadenopathy, may be indicative of recent HIV infection. Seronegative healthcare workers should be retested 6 weeks post-exposure and on a periodic basis thereafter (e.g., 12 weeks and 6 months after exposure) to determine whether transmission has occurred. During this follow-up period, especially the first 6–12 weeks after exposure when most infected persons are expected to seroconvert, exposed healthcare workers should follow U.S. Public Health Service (PHS) recommendations for preventing transmission of HIV (36, 37).

No further follow-up of a healthcare worker exposed to infection as described above is necessary if the source patient is seronegative unless the source patient is at high risk of HIV infection. In the latter case, a subsequent specimen (e.g., 12 weeks following exposure) may be obtained from the healthcare worker for antibody testing. If the source patient cannot be identified, decisions regarding appropriate follow-up should be individualized. Serologic testing should be available to all healthcare workers who are concerned that they may have been infected with HIV.

If a patient has a parenteral or mucous membrane exposure to blood or other bodily fluid of a healthcare worker, the patient should be informed of the incident and the same procedure outlined above for management of exposures should be followed for both the source healthcare worker and the exposed patient.

References

1. Centers for Disease Control. Acquired immunodeficiency syndrome (AIDS): Precautions for clinical and laboratory staffs. *MMWR* 1982; 31:577-80.

2. Centers for Disease Control. Acquired immunodeficiency syndrome (AIDS): Precautions for health-care workers and allied professionals. *MMWR* 1983; 32:450-1.

Sample Policies

3. Centers for Disease Control. Recommendations for preventing transmission of infection with human T-lymphotropic virus type III/lymphadenopathy-associated virus in the workplace. *MMWR* 1985; 34:681-6, 691-5.

4. Centers for Disease Control. Recommendations for preventing transmission of infection with human T-lymphotropic virus type III/lymphadenopathy-associated virus during invasive procedures. *MMWR* 1986; 35:221-3.

5. Centers for Disease Control. Recommendations for preventing possible transmission of human T-lymphotropic virus type III/lymphadenopathy-associated virus from tears. *MMWR* 1985; 34:533-4.

6. Centers for Disease Control. Recommendations for providing dialysis treatment to patients infected with human T-lymphotropic virus type III/lymphadenopathy-associated virus infection. *MMWR* 1986; 35:376-8, 383.

7. Garner JS, Simmons BP. Guideline for isolation precautions in hospitals. *Infect Control* 1983; 4 (suppl):245-325.

8. Centers for Disease Control. Recommended infection control practices for dentistry. *MMWR* 1986; 35:237-42.

9. McCray E, The Cooperative Needlestick Surveillance Group. Occupational risk of the acquired immunodeficiency syndrome among health care workers. *N. Engl. J. Med.* 1986; 314:1127-32.

10. Henderson DK, Saah AJ, Zak BJ, et al. Risk of nosocomial infection with human T-cell lymphotropic virus type III/lymphadenopathy-associated virus in a large cohort of intensively exposed health care workers. *Ann Intern Med* 1986;104:6447.

11. Gerberding JL, Bryant-LeBlanc CE, Nelson K, et al. Risk of transmitting the human immunodeficiency virus, cytomegalovirus, and hepatitis B virus to health care workers exposed to patients with AIDS and AIDS-related conditions. *J Infect Dis* 1987; 156:1-8.

12. McEvoy M, Porter K, Mortimer P, Simmons N, Shanson D. Prospective study of clinical, laboratory, and ancillary staff with accidental exposures to blood or body fluids from patients infected with HIV. *Br Med J* 1987; 294:1595-7.

13. Anonymous. Needlestick transmission of HTLV-III from a patient infected in Africa. *Lancet* 1984; 2:1376-7.

14. Oskenhendler E, Harzic M, Le Roux JM, Rabian C, Clauvel JP. HIV infection with seroconversion after a superficial needlestick injury to the finger [Letter]. *N Engl J Med* 1986; 315:582.

15. Neisson-Vernant C, Arfi S, Mathez D, Leibowitch J, Monplaisir N. Needlestick HIV seroconversion in a nurse [Letter]. *Lancet* 1986; 2:814.

16. Grint P, McEvoy M. Two associated cases of the acquired immune deficiency syndrome (AIDS). *PHLS Commun Dis Rep* 1985; 42:4.

17. Centers for Disease Control. Apparent transmission of human T-lymphotropic virus type III/lymphadenopathy-associated virus from a child to a mother providing health care. *MMWR* 1986; 35:76-9.

18. Centers for Disease Control. Update: Human immunodeficiency virus infections in health-care workers exposed to blood of infected patients. *MMWR* 1987; 36:285-9.

19. Kline RS, Phelan J, Friedland GH, et al. Low occupational risk for HIV infection for dental professionals [Abstract. In: Abstracts from the III International Conference on AIDS, 1-5 June 1985. Washington, DC: 155].

20. Baker JL, Kelen GD, Sivertson KT, Quinn TC. Unsuspected human immunodeficiency virus in critically ill emergency patients. *JAMA* 1987; 257:2609-11.

21. Favero MS. Dialysis-associated diseases and their control. In: Bennett JV, Brachman PS, eds. *Hospital infections.* Boston: Little, Brown and Company, 1985:267-84.

22. Richardson JH, Barkley WE, eds. Biosafety in microbiological and biomedical laboratories, 1984. Washington, DC: US Department of Health and Human Services, Public Health Service, HHS publication no. (CDC) 84-8395.

23. Centers for Disease Control. Human T-lymphotropic virus type III/lymphadenopathy-associated virus: Agent summary statement. *MMWR* 1986; 35:540-2, 547-9.

24. Environmental Protection Agency. EPA guide for infectious waste management. Washington, DC: U.S. Environmental Protection Agency, May 1986 (publication no. EPA/530-SW-86-014).

25. Favero MS. Sterilization, disinfection, and antisepsis in the hospital. In: Manual of clinical microbiology. 4th ed. Washington, DC: American Society for Microbiology, 1985; 129-37.

26. Garner JS, Favero MS. Guideline for handwashing and hospital environmental control, 1985. Atlanta: Public Health Service, Centers for Disease Control, 1985. HHS publication no. 99-1117.

27. Spire B, Montagnier L, Barre-Sinoussi F, Chermann JC. Inactivation of Lymphadenopathy associated virus

by chemical disinfectants. *Lancet* 1984; 2:899-901.

28. Martin LS, McDougal JS, Loskoski SL. Disinfection and inactivation of the human T Lymphotropic virus type III/lymphadenopathy-associated virus. *J Infect Dis* 1985; 152:400-3.

29. McDougal JS, Martin LS, Cort SP, et al. Thermal inactivation of the acquired immunodeficiency syndrome virus III/lymphadenopathy-associated virus, with special reference to antihemophilic factor. *J Clin Invest* 1985; 76:875-7.

30. Spire B, Barre-Sinoussi F, Dormont D, Montagnier L, Chermann JC. Inactivation of lymphadenopathy-associated virus by heat, gamma rays, and ultraviolet light. *Lancet* 1985; 1:188-9.

31. Resnik L, Veren K, Salahuddin SZ, Tondreau S, Markham PD. Stability and inactivation of HTLV-III/LAV under clinical and laboratory environments. *JAMA* 1986; 255:1887-91.

32. Centers for Disease Control. Public Health Service (PHS) guidelines for counseling and antibody testing to prevent HIV infection and AIDS. *MMWR* 1987; 36:509-515.

33. Kane MA, Lettau LA. Transmission of HBV from dental personnel to patients. *J Am Dent Assoc* 1985;110:634-6.

34. Lettau LA, Smith JD, Williams D, et al. Transmission of hepatitis B virus with resultant restriction of surgical practice. *JAMA* 1986; 255:934-7.

35. Williams WW. Guideline for infection control in hospital personnel. *Infect Control* 1983; 4(suppl):326-49.

36. Centers for Disease Control. Prevention of acquired immune deficiency syndrome (AIDS): Report of inter-agency recommendations. *MMWR* 1983; 32:101-3.

37. Centers for Disease Control. Provisional Public Health Service inter-agency recommendations for screening donated blood and plasma for antibody to the virus causing acquired immunodeficiency syndrome. *MMWR* 1985; 34:1-5.

Sample Policies

Compliance Assistance Guideline for the February 27, 1990 OSHA Instruction CPL 2-2.44B

Enforcement Procedures for Occupational Exposure to Hepatitis B Virus and Human Immunodeficiency Virus

U. S. Department of Labor, Occupational Safety and Health Administration.

Compliance Assistance Guidelines, for the February 27, 1990 OSHA Instruction CPL 2-2.44B Enforcement Procedures for Occupational Exposure to Hepatitis B Virus and Human Immunodeficiency Virus. U.S. Department of Labor Occupational Safety and Health Administration, Gerard F. Scannell, Assistant Secretary.

Introduction

The intent of this guideline is to offer employers assistance in understanding the Occupational Safety and Health Administration's (OSHA) requirements for preventing occupational exposure to hepatitis B virus (HBV) and human immunodeficiency virus (HIV). SEE: OSHA Instruction CPL 2-2.44B, February 27, 1990, Enforcement Procedures for Occupational Exposure to Hepatitis B Virus (HBV) and Human Immunodeficiency Virus (HIV) for the complete text.

OSHA Instruction CPL 2-2.44B sets forth the enforcement procedures and interpretations of OSHA requirements with respect to the protection of workers who are exposed to blood or other potentially infectious materials. The OSHA requirements currently being enforced include section 5(a)(1) of the Occupational Safety and Health Act of 1970, the general duty clause, and certain general OSHA standards. The Instruction will be superseded after OSHA promulgates a standard on occupational exposure to blood-borne pathogens.

Appropriate measures have been taken to ensure that the information contained in this pamphlet is current, reliable, and accurate. This document is published as a guide to assist in compliance with the Occupational Safety and Health Act of 1970 (OSHA Act). It is not intended, however, to be a substitute for the OSHA Act and OSHA standards. In the event of a conflict, the OSHA Act and OSHA standards apply.

Workers at risk are those whose work may involve exposure to blood or other potentially infectious materials. They include but are not limited to:

    Physicians   Dentists and other dental workers
    Nurses   Laboratory and blood bank technologists

257

Pathologists
Research laboratory scientists
Dialysis personnel
Funeral service personnel
Medical examiners
Some laundry workers

Phlebotomists
Medical technologists
Paramedics
Emergency medical technicians
Some maintenance personnel
Some housekeepers

Infection Control Program

Employees incur risk of infection and subsequent illness each time they are exposed to blood or other potentially infectious materials. Therefore, the infection control program (ICP) is the core element used to reduce worker risk by minimizing or eliminating employee exposure incidents to blood-borne pathogens, such as HBV and HIV. An ICP is the establishment's oral or written policy for implementation of procedures relating to the control of infectious disease hazards.

ICP Components

Exposure Determination
Control Methods
   (A) Universal Precautions
   (B) Engineering Controls
   (C) Work Practice Controls
   (D) Personal Protective Equipment
HBV Vaccination
Post-Exposure Evaluation and Follow-up
Infectious Waste Disposal
Tags, Labels, and Bags
Housekeeping Practices
Laundry Practices
Training and Education of Employees
Recordkeeping

Exposure Determination

CONSIDERATIONS:

• *The employer shall identify all employees who are directly exposed or whose jobs have the likelihood of exposure to blood or other potentially infectious materials.*

• *Fluids that have been recognized by the Centers for Disease Control (CDC) as directly linked to the transmission of HBV and/or HIV are: blood, blood products, semen, vaginal secretions, cerebrospinal fluid, synovial fluid, pleural fluid, peritoneal fluid, pericardial fluid, amniotic fluid, concentrated HIV and HBV viruses, and saliva in dental settings.*

* *The employer shall make an exposure determination without regard to the use of personal protective equipment.*

Control Methods

A. Universal Precautions

The term "universal precautions" refers to a method of infection control in which all human blood and other potentially infectious materials are treated as if known to be infectious for HIV and HBV.
CONSIDERATIONS:

* *Universal precautions do not apply to feces, nasal secretions, sputum, sweat, tears, urine, or vomitus unless they contain visible blood.*

B. Engineering Controls

An engineering control is the use of available technology and devices to isolate or remove hazards from the worker.
CONSIDERATIONS:

* *Engineering controls should be used in preference to other control methods to eliminate or minimize worker exposure to blood or other potentially infectious materials.*

* *Engineering controls must be examined and maintained or replaced on a regular scheduled basis to ensure their effectiveness.*

* *Examples of engineering controls include but are not limited to: puncture-resistant sharps containers, splash guards, mechanical pipetting, and self-sheathing needles.*

C. Work Practice Controls

Work practice controls are alterations in the manner in which a task is performed in an effort to reduce the likelihood of a worker's exposure to blood or other potentially infectious materials.
CONSIDERATIONS:

* *Hands shall be washed after removing gloves or as soon as possible after contact with bodily fluids.*

* *All personal protective equipment (PPE) should be removed immediately, or as soon as possible upon leaving the work area, and placed in an appropriately*

designated area or container for storage, washing, decontamination, or disposal.

• Used needles and other sharps shall not be sheared, bent, broken, recapped, or resheathed by hand.

• All procedures involving blood or other potentially infectious materials shall be performed in such a manner as to minimize splashing and spraying.

D. Personal Protective Equipment

Personal protective equipment is specialized clothing or equipment used by workers to protect themselves from direct exposure to blood or other potentially infectious materials.
CONSIDERATIONS:

• The employer shall provide and assure employee use of appropriate personal protective equipment such as, but not limited to, gloves; gowns, laboratory coats, fluid-resistant aprons, head and foot coverings; face shields or masks and eye protection; and mouthpieces, resuscitation bags, pocket masks, or other ventilation devices when there is a potential for exposure to blood or other potentially infectious materials.

• The employer shall assure that appropriate personal protective equipment is available in a variety of sizes and readily accessible.

• The employer shall provide for the cleaning, laundering, or disposal of personal protective equipment.

• The employer shall repair or replace required personal protective equipment as needed to maintain its effectiveness.

• Surgical or examination gloves shall be replaced when visibly soiled, torn, or punctured, or when their integrity is compromised. They shall not be washed or disinfected for re-use.

• Utility gloves may be cleaned and disinfected for re-use if they show no signs of deterioration.

HBV Vaccination

CONSIDERATIONS:

• The HBV vaccination shall be offered, at no cost, to all employees whose jobs involve the risk of directly contacting blood or other potentially infectious materials.

• Vaccinations shall be given according to recommendations for standard medical practice.

Post-Exposure Evaluation and Follow-up

CONSIDERATIONS:

• Following a report of an exposure incident, the employer shall make available to the employee a confidential medical evaluation and follow-up of the incident.

• The employer shall document the route of exposure, HBV and HIV status of the source patient(s), if known, and the circumstances under which the exposure occurred.

• The employer shall notify the source patient(s) of the incident and attempt to obtain consent to collect and test the source's blood to determine the presence of HIV and/or HBV infection.

• The employer shall offer to collect a blood sample from the exposed worker as soon as possible after the exposure incident for determination of HIV and/or HBV status.

• The employer shall offer repeat HIV testing to exposed employees six weeks post-exposure and on a periodic basis thereafter (12 weeks and 6 months after exposure).

• Follow-up of the exposed worker shall include counseling, medical evaluation of any acute febrile illness that occurs within twelve weeks post-exposure, and use of safe and effective post-exposure measures according to recommendations for standard medical practice.

Infectious Waste Disposal

CONSIDERATIONS:

• Disposal of all infectious waste shall be in accordance with applicable Federal, State, and local regulations.

• All infectious waste shall be placed in closable, leakproof containers or bags that are color-coded, labeled, or tagged.

• Disposable syringes, needles, scalpel blades, and other sharp items shall be placed in puncture-resistant containers for disposal.

• Puncture-resistant sharps containers shall be easily accessible to workers and located in areas where they are commonly used.

• Double-bagging prior to handling, storing, and/or transporting infectious waste is necessary if the outside of a bag is contaminated with blood or other potentially infectious materials.

• Lab specimens of bodily fluids shall be transported in a container that will prevent leaking and disposed of in accordance with institutional policies and regulatory requirements.

Tags, Labels, and Bags

CONSIDERATIONS:

- *Tags that comply with 29 CFR 1910.145 (f) shall be used to identify the presence of an actual or potential biological hazard.*

- *Tags shall contain the word "BIOHAZARD" or the biological hazard symbol and state the specific hazardous condition or the instructions to be communicated to employees.*

- *The word and message must be understandable to all employees who may be exposed to the identified hazard.*

- *Labels/tags may be an integral part of the container or affixed as close as safely possible to their respective hazards by string, wire, or adhesive to prevent their loss or unintentional removal.*

- *Red bags or red containers may be substituted for labels on containers of infectious waste.*

- *All employees shall be informed of the meaning of various labels, tags, and color-coding systems.*

Housekeeping Practices

CONSIDERATIONS:

- *The employer shall assure that the worksite is maintained in a clean and sanitary condition.*

- *The employer shall determine and implement an appropriate cleaning schedule for rooms where bodily fluids are present. Schedules shall be as frequent as necessary depending on the area of the institution, the type of surface to be cleaned, and the amount and type of soil present.*

- *The employer shall ensure that housekeeping workers wear appropriate PPE including general-purpose utility gloves during all cleaning of blood or other potentially infectious materials and during decontaminating procedures.*

- *Initial clean-up of blood or other potentially infectious materials shall be followed with the use of an approved hospital disinfectant chemical germicide that is tuberculocidal or a solution of 5.25 percent sodium hypochlorite (household bleach) diluted between 1:10 and 1:100 with water.*

- *Equipment contaminated with blood or other potentially infectious materials shall be checked routinely and decontaminated if possible prior to servicing or shipping.*

Laundry Practices

CONSIDERATIONS:

* *The employer shall ensure that laundry workers wear protective gloves and other appropriate personal protective equipment to prevent exposure to blood or other potentially infectious materials during handling and sorting of linen. Laundry that is contaminated with blood or other potentially infectious materials or that may contain contaminated needles or sharps shall be treated as if it were HBV/HIV infectious and handled as little as possible with a minimum of agitation.*

* *Contaminated laundry shall be bagged at the location where it was used and shall not be sorted or rinsed in patient areas.*

* *Contaminated laundry shall be placed and transported in bags that are labeled or color coded and that prevent liquid seepage if such a potential exists.*

Training and Education of Employees

CONSIDERATIONS:

* *The employer shall ensure that all employees with exposure to blood or other potentially infectious materials participate in a training and education program.*

* *Material appropriate in content and vocabulary to educational level, literacy, and language background of employees shall be used.*

* *The training program shall contain the following elements:*

—*A general explanation of the epidemiology and symptoms of HBV and HIV.*

—*An explanation of the modes of transmission of HBV and HIV.*

—*An explanation of the employer's infection control program.*

—*An explanation of the use and limitations of methods of control that may prevent or reduce exposure, including universal precautions, engineering controls, work practices, and personal protective equipment.*

—*An explanation of the basis for selection of personal protective equipment.*

—*Information on the HBV vaccine, including its efficacy, safety, and the benefits of being vaccinated.*

—*An explanation of the procedure to follow if an exposure incident occurs, method of reporting the incident, and the medical follow-up.*

Recordkeeping

* The employer shall track each worker's reported exposure incident to blood or other potentially infectious materials.

• Needlestick injuries shall be included on the OSHA 200 occupational injury and illness log if medical treatment such as gamma globulin, hepatitis B immune globulin, or hepatitis B vaccine is prescribed and administered by licensed medical personnel.

• HBV and HIV shall be recorded on the OSHA 200 log if the illnesses can be traced back to an injury or other exposure incident.

Sources

1. Centers for Disease Control: "Protection Against Viral Hepatitis; Recommendations of the Immunization Practices Advisory Committee." *MMWR* 39:1-26, February 9,1990.

2. Centers for Disease Control: "Recommendations and Reports Guidelines for Prevention of Transmission of Human Immunodeficiency Virus and Hepatitis B Virus to Health Care Workers and Public Safety Workers." *MMWR* 37 (24): 376-387, June 24,1988.

3. Centers for Disease Control: "Perspectives in Disease Prevention and Health Promotion." *MMWR* 37 (24): 376-387, June 24,1988.

4. Centers for Disease Control: "Recommendations for Prevention of HIV Transmission in Health Care Settings." *MMWR* 36: 3s- 1 8s, August 21, 1987.

5. Department of Labor-Occupational Safety and Health Administration: "Occupational Exposure to Bloodborne Pathogens; Proposed Rule and Notice of Hearing." *Fed Regis:* 54, May 30, 1989.

6. U.S. Department of Labor, OSHA Instruction CPL 2-2.44B, "Enforcement Procedures for Occupational Exposure to Hepatitis B Virus (HBV) and Human Immunodeficiency Virus (HIV)," February 27, 1990.

Related OSHA Publications

Single free copies of the following publications can be obtained from the OSHA Publications Office, U.S. Department of Labor, 200 Constitution Avenue, N.W., Room N-3101, Washington, D.C. 20210. Send a self-addressed mailing label with your request.

1. OSHA-2056 *All About OSHA.*
2. OSHA-2098 *OSHA Inspection.*
3. OSHA-3021 *OSHA: Employee Workplace Rights.*
4. OSHA-3000 *Employer Rights & Responsibilities Following An OSHA Inspection.*

Section Three:
SPECIAL POLICY CONSIDERATIONS FOR PARTICULAR POPULATIONS

SPECIAL POLICY CONSIDERATIONS FOR PARTICULAR POPULATIONS

Because the issue of HIV/AIDS policymaking is so important for businesses and human service organizations to address, I have asked a variety of contributors, all experts in their workplace specialties, to address HIV/AIDS policy as it pertains to their particular working environment and to special populations. Not all of this material will be of use to you or to your particular workplace, but one or more of the "articles" within this Section will be helpful to you:

HIV, Children, and Family Law—Legal and Policy Issues for Care Providers

Agencies Serving the Severely and Persistently Mentally Ill

Employee Assistance Programs

Arts Organizations: Arts Over AIDS—Education and Policy Initiatives

Substance Abuse Treatment and Care Programs

Primary Healthcare Settings

Special Note for Healthcare Workers

Community Mental Health Centers

Homeless Populations: Homelessness and HIV—Problems and Recommendations

Cultural Communities

Native American Communities

HIV/AIDS and Correctional Facilities

Agencies Serving People with Developmental Disabilities

Agencies Serving Adolescents

Disability in the Workplace

Religious Institutions

School/Educational Settings

Women's Programs

HIV, Children, and Family Law
Legal and Policy Issues for Care Providers

Earl C. Pike

The reality of children living with HIV infection and AIDS requires a revisitation of family law and a discussion of its application to HIV. Providers of services to children will need to be cognizant of such issues; they will invariably arise in the process of delivering services and may grow in importance in the coming years as more and more children live with HIV infection and AIDS.

It should be noted at the outset that family law varies, sometimes greatly, from state to state or territory to territory. For example, lesbians and gay men are unable to legally adopt children in many states, and a woman's unrestricted access to abortion services has been, in the past decade, curtailed in a number of locales. The following cannot even attempt to outline the state-by-state differences in family law and its application to HIV; it can, however, summarize central themes in family law and its potential impact on children and families living with HIV disease.

Marriage

Several states in the U. S. have passed laws requiring premarital HIV antibody testing. Numerous questions about such obligations surface immediately, not the least of which is the accuracy of testing as a screening procedure when the window period for HIV seroconversion is so long. The overriding constitutionality of such requirements has not yet been established, and as a practical matter, many couples simply cross a state border to avoid the requirement. To date, no statute exists prohibiting marriage if one partner is known to be HIV seropositive, though the possibility of such legislation cannot be ruled out.

The marriage relationship carries both legal privileges and legal obligations, among them, the duty of partners to support each other. In the past ten years there has been considerable disparity of opinions among state courts as to whether the legal obligation to provide mutual support maintains in the presence of a so-called "terminal" illness. Since in many cases the medical costs associated with HIV disease are astronomical, questions have been raised about the legal obligation of a healthy partner to share the financial burdens of an ill partner, and about such situations as a basis for divorce. Again, as a practical matter, there is no universal legal standard on such matters, and we can expect that some couples may be forced to divorce if only to survive the financial burdens of chronic disease.

And although one of the privileges of marriage is the opportunity to engage in sexual activity with one's spouse, it should be noted that there is at least one case where the state has intervened to cancel that right: the case of inmates. While the U. S. Supreme Court has upheld the freedom of inmates to marry. the New York Court of Appeals has ruled that a state department of corrections department may deny conjugal rights to prisoners with AIDS, even though such visits are permitted to all other married partners.

Finally, we should acknowledge the obvious: in 49 states, same-gender marriages are prohibited. (The Hawaiian court ruled in 1993 that such a prohibition is unconstitutional, leaving the door open in that state for same-gender marriage.) Questions of the life-partner obligations and rights of same-gender couples are hopelessly muddled from state to state; such couples should *always* consult with gay-sensitive legal counsel about their concerns.

Divorce and Annulment

HIV and AIDS may affect matters of marital dissolution in three ways: as grounds for divorce, as a consideration in property distribution, and as a factor in maintenance awards.

If an HIV-positive spouse engages in sexual intercourse without notifying his or her partner of the infection, grounds for divorce may be established. Such judgements have already been rendered, based on cruelty, when one spouse has proven that the other spouse infected them with a sexually-transmitted disease. From a legal point of view, HIV exposure could satisfy the same criteria. In a similar vein, annulment actions may raise questions as to whether deliberate concealment of HIV seropositivity is demonstration of misrepresentation or fraud, thereby invalidating the marriage contract.

In the distribution of property, many states allow a court to evaluate the "fault" of either party in granting its award. Conceivably, infecting a spouse with HIV (when one's HIV status is known and withheld) could be considered such "fault," and may therefore enter into decisions about property distribution at divorce.

And since maintenance awards are modifiable in most states, AIDS may be relevant in applications for reduced financial support from a spouse who has AIDS, or in requests for increased financial support to a divorced spouse whose capacity for self-support is diminished due to HIV infection or AIDS.

Child Custody and Visitation

HIV and AIDS have already impacted a significant number of cases involving child custody and visitation. Courts have been far from consistent in their decisions on such matters; some have displayed a tendency to react from hysteria and a lack of sound judicial reasoning, rather than medical fact. When children are involved, couples should always endeavor to come to reasonable agreements about custody and visitation before courtroom battles ensue; if they cannot, competent legal assistance is mandatory.

HIV may enter into child custody and visitation cases in several contexts, including the initial custody determination at the time of divorce, moves for modification of custody after it has already been established, and efforts to limit or prohibit visitation. Hovering around these questions is another: whether HIV antibody testing can be ordered by the court, and if so, under what circumstances—and here a distinction must be made between cases where a parent is alleged to be HIV-infected and those cases where HIV infection has been medically established.

Courts are supposed to make decisions about custody based on "the best interests of the child," which is, unfortunately, a vague standard in practice. That test should be applied no less in cases involving HIV or AIDS. And cases involving parents with HIV or AIDS should be treated no differently than other cases where a parent has a disability. The great body of law in such situations contends that disability, by itself, is not grounds for denying or modifying custody, but rather must be evaluated in terms of how it affects the child or children in question. This body of law asserts that the relevant question is not disability per se, but the parent's ability to care for the child and the child's ability to adapt to the parent's disability.

Some cases have forwarded the medically unwarranted claim that a child is in "danger" because of casual contact, such as would occur in a shared residence, because a parent is HIV-infected. Again, a few courts have responded hysterically by requiring supervised visitation, the prohibition of a kiss or hug, or by barring visitation altogether.

Such examples point to the potential volatility of family law as it relates to HIV and custody or visitation decisions. Again, parents in such circumstances should seek and secure the best legal counsel they can find.

Child Abuse and Neglect

In situations involving potential abuse and neglect, HIV and AIDS may be relevant factors. A parent with an AIDS-related disability may be perceived as unable to care for a child, thus prompting state intervention in the form of a neglect proceeding. (This may be particularly likely given the concentration of HIV in communities of color, which are the primary targets of state intervention in child-rearing matters.) In all such cases AIDS should be evaluated like any other disability; by itself, HIV infection and AIDS should not be grounds for a neglect determination.

And while a parent with HIV or AIDS may experience heightened stress, which can increase the potential for abuse, court decisions about child abuse should be based on the behavioral patterns of abuse rather than any underlying emotional condition which may contribute to them.

Adoption

HIV and AIDS can create a number of dilemmas in the process of adoption, including the right and ability of people with HIV to adopt children, disclosure of the HIV status of a child placed for adoption, and efforts to terminate an adoption if the child or parent is later found to be HIV-positive. As with many other areas of family law and HIV, these dilemmas are compounded by questions of mandatory HIV antibody testing and the authority under which such testing is ordered.

Some factors have been deemed relevant in determining whether a potential adoptive parent is qualified. In other non-HIV related cases these have included disability (child or adult) and age (to the degree that age is seen as an indicator of life expectancy). Progressive cases have ruled that age or disability only become important insofar as they affect the child, but it's hard to imagine that a court supervising an adoption by an HIV-positive adult would not take that condition into account.

It is the question of HIV antibody testing of children that is most problematic. In theory, an adoption agency, as the legal custodian of the child, could order HIV antibody testing, but many have been reluctant to do so, fearing that it will only further damage their ability to place hard-to-place children. At issue is not only the possibility that prospective parents may have little knowledge about AIDS and may therefore refuse a placement based on hysteria rather than fact, but also considerations of an adult's ability to care for a child with chronic disease. This is a problem intensified by the fact that larger cities may well experience future crises, if they haven't already, because of the difficulties in finding placements for HIV-positive children. The problem is given an absurd twist when gay or lesbian adults (many having already experienced the tragedy of AIDS in their communities) have been more than willing to adopt HIV-positive children, but are legally barred from adopting children in many states.

HIV may also emerge as a critical issue in questions of adoption subsidies, since all states now have adoption subsidy laws. Again, preplacement HIV antibody testing becomes an issue: subsidies, which may seem reasonable when a child appears healthy, can prove inadequate if the child has a chronic disease.

Foster Care and HIV

The same questions about HIV antibody testing surface in foster care placement. Since children in child welfare services are entitled to a variety of services, including medical care, testing may be helpful in planning for the "best interests of the child." Some authorities, including the Centers for Disease Control and Prevention and the Child Welfare League of America, have asserted that foster parents have the right to know the HIV status of the child because of its impact on the daily care of the child. Again, possible ill-informed reactions on the part of foster parents must be factored into the equation.

Abortion and Sterilization

Unfortunately, some judges may assert that a pregnant HIV-positive woman should abort rather than risk giving birth to an HIV-infected infant. One overriding principle should govern such cases: the constitutionally-protected right of a woman to choose whether to bear a child. The right to privacy, derived from the Fourteenth Amendment to the U. S. Constitution, cannot permit coerced or forced termination of pregnancy for any reason.

The same standard applies to involuntary sterilization of HIV-positive women. Sterilization should not, and constitutionally cannot, be imposed to prevent the birth of a possibly HIV-infected baby any more than it could if hemophilia or sickle-cell anemia were involved.

Conclusion

One major current runs through the preceding discussion: in family law cases such as adoption and child custody, HIV or AIDS must be considered in the same manner as any other disability. That is, the operative question is not the mere presence or absence of disability, but rather the actual effects the disability will have, as established by medical fact rather than ignorance.

Issues related to testing are a little more complex, but in most of the preceding illustrations, the same universal standard has to be applied: what is in the best, long-term interests of the child? If it cannot be demonstrated that testing in an individual case is beneficial (rather than a matter of simple curiosity), then testing has questionable value.

Once again, and in all matters related to family law, all parties are advised to secure competent legal counsel from someone who is well-versed in HIV and its related legal implications.

Agencies Serving the Severely and Persistently Mentally Ill

Karen Helfand, M.A.

Karen Helfand has worked for over six years in the fields of mental health and HIV/AIDS. She is the former program director for a Rule 36 facility (a residential facility for persons with chronic mental illness) in Minneapolis. In 1991 she received a grant from the Minnesota AIDS Funding Consortium to create a task force addressing homelessness and HIV/AIDS.

General Concerns

- Severely and persistently mentally ill clients may have problems with concentration, short attention span, hypersexual episodes, short-term memory loss, comprehension of complex material, and low impulse control.
- Some clients may also be highly vulnerable to sexual exploitation.
- There may be a tendency to view some clients as asexual because of behavior or affect. Some clients may present a strong and compelling set of religious delusions that suggest asexuality; the professional should remember that belief and behavior do not always coincide.
- Clients who self-injure may, depending on the nature of the self-injurious behavior, be at elevated risk of HIV or HBV infection because of bleeding or open wounds.
- Some pharmaceuticals prescribed for mental illness may effect sexual desire and/or performance, therefore leading to changed patterns of sexual expression.

Special Concerns When Presenting Material to Clients

- Clients may generalize information when discussing needle use. Be specific: it is *street* drugs, not the medications they may receive through injection, that is of concern. If clients are worried or delusional that they will acquire HIV through prescription injections, review or show them how needles are disposed of in the facility.
- Clients may also present unusual delusions about ways they may acquire HIV infection, e.g., "because of the armadillos." Those beliefs need to be addressed respectfully.
- Educational material must be concrete. An explanation of a point should consist of four or five words, with a complementary drawing.
- Effective HIV education for clients includes the components that follow.
    1. Individual intervention at intake
        A. Short sexual history

B. Explanation of agency HIV policy

C. How to access condoms and who on staff can answer questions about HIV/AIDS

D. A short, easy-to-read pamphlet on HIV transmission

2. Group sessions once a month

A. Focus on relationships, boundaries, and appropriate drug use

B. Use role playing and visual aids

C. Provide behavioral incentives for group attendance

3. Follow-up counseling for clients

A. During crisis or after HIV antibody test

Policy Considerations

Confidentiality

- The facility will need to have policy around note-taking on the client's HIV status and medical records for testing.
- A client's sexual history should be kept confidential. Gay or lesbian clients can be ostracized from the main group of residents because of the belief that "all gays have AIDS."
- Records sent to hospitals and other residences should not include HIV testing information.

Infection Control

- Clients should know where condoms can be accessed.
- Disposable gloves and bleach should be readily available for emergencies (e.g., if a client engages in self-cutting).
- Needles should be disposed of in a locked area.

HIV Antibody Testing

- The facility will need to account for client competence to give free and informed consent.
- A client may have a court-appointed guardian who may need to be consulted—and perhaps educated—about the HIV antibody test.

Special Policy Considerations for Particular Populations

• The facility will need to ensure confidential testing, and adequate pre-/post-test counseling.

Duty to Warn

• Policy needs to be developed for clients with HIV or other STDs who are sexually active within the facility.

• Questions to be raised include (1) has the client informed her or his partner of their HIV infection or STD, and (2) is the client competent to inform his or her partner?

• Policy needs to address whether the facility has a duty to warn the client without HIV [see chapter on *Confidentiality* in the *Policy Areas* section].

Client Rights and Responsibilities

• Clients should receive a written copy of the facility's policy on HIV antibody testing, drug use, and sexual behavior in the facility.

State Department of Human Services Licensing

• Facilities should check with State Licensing authorities to ensure that HIV policies are consistent with their requirements.

Employee Assistance Programs

Pat Lamb, M. S.
Cargill Corporation

Pat Lamb is an Employee Assistance counselor with the Cargill Corporation where she helped develop AIDS policy and education. She has also worked at St. Cloud Hospital and Journey Home, a substance abuse treatment program for women.

Typically, on a policy level, business has responded to HIV in the workplace as they would any other serious or life-threatening illness. However, this stance may not address all the many facets of the issue or allow for factual information to aid business in dealing with HIV in a responsible and humane manner. Employee Assistance Program (EAP) counseling can serve as a valuable referral source for the employee. Other concerns related to EAPs and appropriate management of HIV in the workplace include the following.

1. Confidentiality

Employee Assistance Programs are confidential services provided to employees and their family members. Information regarding the use of an EAP is *not* part of personnel records, nor is information discussed or released without the written consent of the service user.

2. Education

EAP services can assist in HIV training and education for managers and supervisors, addressing both general HIV considerations and site-specific concerns. Educational efforts can tap into international, national, and local HIV resources (such as the Centers for Disease Control program on AIDS in the workplace), and can be offered to employees on both an individual and work group basis.

3. Crisis Intervention

Even though there is no risk of HIV transmission to co-workers through ordinary workplace contact, there is still a great deal of misinformation and fear regarding casual contact. When such fears threaten to disrupt workplace activities, EAP counselors can be called upon to offer timely, sensitive, and accurate information to employees so that work disturbance and rejection/harassment by co-workers is minimized.

Special Policy Considerations for Particular Populations

4. Case Management

All too often HIV seropositive employees go "out of plan" and deplete their own financial resources before they will draw upon the health insurance plan—often because of fears of discrimination if the employer "finds out." Therefore, the employee may not receive timely case management and is not apprised of various treatment options, such as nutrition strategies, experimental medication regimes, and HIV-specific resources. EAPs can both encourage appropriate use of health insurance benefits and provide reassurance about confidentiality and discrimination fears.

5. Partnerships

The EAP can serve as an intermediary to ensure that employees receive supportive services on whatever level they require—not only for the HIV-infected employee, but for her or his co-workers, family, and significant others as well. EAPs are often a safe haven for employees to obtain advocacy services that will result in effective, appropriate care. Company policies and attitudes about HIV/AIDS can create an atmosphere that allows the HIV-positive employee to self-disclose HIV status, but until that sense of safety permeates the business, EAPs and social service agencies can form alliances to assure support for the HIV-positive employee.

Arts Organizations
Arts Over AIDS: Education and Policy Initiatives

Mariann Johnson

Mariann Johnson has worked in arts administration for over ten years. From 1989 to 1992 she worked as a consultant and trainer with M. T. Johnson and Associates, engaged in strategic planning, program design and development, marketing, and management services for nonprofit organizations. She has served as a staff person to Arts Over AIDS, and as a consultant to the Minnesota AIDS Funding Consortium.

In the Spring of 1988, a concerned group of Twin Cities artists, funders, and arts administrators founded Arts Over AIDS (AOA). As an ad hoc working group, AOA committed itself to engaging the arts community in proactive HIV programming and educational initiatives.

Later that same year, AOA developed the *Minnesota Arts Community AIDS Resolution*. The resolution was designed as a tool to focus attention on the need for life-affirming HIV education and policies in the workplace.

In signing the resolution, boards and staffs of area arts organizations dedicated themselves to creating educational programming, personnel policies, and organizational guidelines that would demonstrate a compassionate response to people living with HIV. In light of their historic community role, organizations also pledged themselves to promote and support HIV/AIDS education for the public.

The Arts Community AIDS Resolution was circulated at the first AOA meeting attended by over 150 members of the arts community. By the Spring of 1992, thirty-seven arts organizations had signed the document, and the majority had, at least to some degree, implemented its provisions for education, policy, and organizational guidelines.

In evaluating the effectiveness of the resolution, Arts Over AIDS found that it had served as a powerful organizational catalyst to address HIV workplace issues. Almost two-thirds of the organizations that signed the resolution indicated they would not have introduced HIV workplace initiatives without the resolution.

However, most of the organizations also reported some problems in establishing HIV-specific policy and educational programming. AOA reviewed those reports, and has offered key recommendations for organizations interested in developed HIV policy and educational programming in the workplace. Those recommendations follow:

✓ Be Willing to Confront Organizational Apathy and Inertia

In working with arts (and other nonprofit) organizations, it is important to understand that inertia may exist not because organizations are indifferent to HIV, but because they may not consider HIV an urgent organizational priority.

The majority of people living with HIV are between 20–45 years of age and currently employed. Additionally, as many as one million Americans may be HIV infected, with 50,000 new infections occurring each year. If your organization has not yet been affected by HIV, chances are that it will. It is crucial to develop workplace HIV policy *before* you need it—the emotional, financial, and legal toll of dealing with the issue could put overwhelming stress on organizations of static or limited resources.

✓ When Creating HIV/AIDS Policy, Include Other Disabilities or Catastrophic Illnesses

When beginning to create policy or expand upon existing policies, think of wider employee concerns and needs. Singling out HIV, and ignoring other health concerns, may be considered discriminatory. Many of the signers of the AOA resolution reported that it pushed their boards and directors to reexamine personnel policies to ensure protection of staff rights and well-being in *all* situations.

✓ Given Your Organization's Resources and Capacity, Do What You Can NOW to Address HIV in Your Workplace

In evaluating the effectiveness of the *Arts Community AIDS Resolution,* AOA discovered that organizational capacities to implement HIV policy and education varied greatly. For instance, some of the smaller organizations had no written policy or health insurance, and became discouraged by the perceived enormity of writing their first personnel policies. A few of the larger organizations failed to implement educational programs because they assumed it would be too costly.

In some cases, addressing workplace HIV issues provided the impetus for a few AOA organizations to begin taking steps toward creating personnel policies and examining health insurance options. Many organizations were able to locate community volunteers who provided free or low-cost policy consultation or HIV education, while others collaborated with other organizations to save money and time in formulating HIV policy and educational programming.

Do what you can now given your organization's resources, and if necessary, plan to address the issue more completely in future policy, benefit analysis, or long-range planning efforts.

✓ The Highest Levels of Board and Management Must Endorse and Actively Support Your HIV Workplace Efforts

That level is critical; it underlines the seriousness with which the organization is addressing the issue. It also makes it more likely that programs and policies will be implemented consistently. Those AOA organizations that enjoyed the most success in implementing workplace HIV policy and education were those that had at least one staff person assigned to the project, and who had the full support of the executive director and/or the board of directors.

Substance Abuse Treatment and Care Programs

Earl C. Pike

Substance abuse (or chemical dependency) treatment and care programs in Minnesota have already received considerable direction and guidance from the Department of Human Services (DHS) about HIV policy development. *The Human Immunodeficiency Virus (HIV-1) Guidelines for Chemical Dependency Treatment and Care Programs in Minnesota,* published by DHS in 1989 and updated in 1992, provide critical facts and recommendations about all key areas of HIV policy and programming. Substance abuse treatment providers in other locales will also find it useful; it serves as the basis for policy on substance abuse and HIV for six other states.

Substance abuse treatment providers in Minnesota should also be aware that new state legislation requires provider compliance with certain requirements related to HIV. Now, as a condition for license application or re-licensure, substance abuse treatment providers must:

- *"...orient all chemical dependency [substance abuse] treatment staff and clients to the HIV minimum standards." "HIV minimum standards means...HIV education to clients, completion of HIV training by all new and existing staff, provision for referral to individual HIV counseling and services for all clients, and the implementation of written policies and procedures for working with HIV-infected clients."*
- *provide for "in-service training... to all staff on at least an annual basis...."*
- *"...maintain a list of referral sources for the purpose of making necessary referrals of clients to HIV-related services...," to be "... updated at least annually."*
- *"...develop and follow written policies and procedures, consistent with HIV minimum standards...."*

Substance abuse providers wishing copies of *HIV Minimum Standards for Chemical Dependency Treatment Programs in Minnesota: Compliance Guidelines* can contact the Chemical Dependency Program Division (CDPD) of DHS at (612) 296-3991. The CDPD can also assist with policy development and training needs.

Primary Healthcare Settings

Earl C. Pike

It is difficult to imagine primary healthcare institutions in the 1990s that haven't completed significant policy and educational tasks related to HIV. But there are. While most hospitals in high-incidence regions have prepared for the reality of HIV and AIDS, some smaller institutions (and especially community clinics) in less populated areas have yet to encounter (as far as they know) patients with HIV or AIDS, and therefore have not considered the full range of policy issues such institutions must face. We know, however, that no institution will remain untouched by this epidemic, and practical experience tells us that the more an institution anticipates and plans for AIDS, the more effectively it will manage HIV and HIV-related dilemmas.

Primary healthcare settings need policy and procedures about a number of topics related to HIV and AIDS. They include, at the very least, the following.

• **Charting**

How is HIV-related data, such as lab tests, recorded on a patient's chart? Is the charting method consistent with regulations by certification bodies?

• **Clinical Protocols**

Are there standard clinical protocols to be followed in cases of known or suspected HIV infection? Are they in line with good medical practice?

• **Confidentiality and Data Privacy**

How is data about patient serostatus managed internally, and in relation to external bodies? Does data privacy practice fully comply with all relevant confidentiality laws and protect, to the fullest, patient privacy?

• **Consent for Testing**

Is true consent for HIV antibody or antigen testing fully established, clear to all patients, and documented?

Special Policy Considerations for Particular Populations

• Death Management

When a patient dies of AIDS, are there any special considerations for family/significant other support, removal of the body, or other matters?

• Discharge of HIV-Infected Patients

When HIV-infected patients are discharged, are there any follow-up procedures for on-going medical monitoring, provision of case management, or establishment of links with community-based AIDS service organizations?

• Employee Benefits

Does policy guarantee full access to employee healthcare services and benefits for healthcare workers with HIV or AIDS?

• Employee Education

How will employees be educated about AIDS? How will their knowledge of HIV and AIDS be kept current and timely?

• Experimental Drugs and Treatments

What is the institution's policy on use of experimental drugs and treatments for management of HIV disease? How will the institution interact with current AIDS clinical trials? How will the institution interact with non-traditional healthcare practitioners, such as acupuncturists and massage therapists?

• HIV Antibody and Antigen Testing Protocol

How will HIV antibody and antigen testing be managed? Will comprehensive pre- and post-test counseling be provided? Is the testing protocol in line with that recommended by the Centers for Disease Control?

• HIV Data Disclosure and Partner Notification

Under what conditions will patient serostatus information be released to third parties? How will that information be conveyed? Are there situations in which it is necessary to notify a patient's partner(s) of the patient's HIV seropositivity?

• HIV Infection and Drug Dependency

Are there special considerations to be addressed when caring for an HIV-infected patient who is also drug dependent or recovering from drug dependency?

• **HIV Infection and Pre-/Post-Natal Care**

Are there special considerations to be addressed in the provision of pre- and post-natal care to women with HIV disease?

• **HIV- and HBV-Infected Healthcare Workers**

How will the institution handle, with intelligence and sensitivity, cases of HIV- and HBV-infected healthcare workers within the institution? Is the institution bound by any laws or statutes governing management of such cases?

• **HIV/AIDS Patient Care**

How will patients with HIV be cared for in the primary healthcare setting? Under what conditions, if any, will isolation be recommended?

• **Hospice Care**

If the institution provides hospice services, how is AIDS integrated into those services?

• **Infection Control and Universal Precautions**

Are there infection control policies addressing every possible institutional procedure? Are those policies being followed rigorously?

• **Invasive Procedures**

Are there special protocols regarding infection control during invasive procedures?

• **Management of Occupational Exposure**

If a healthcare worker is occupationally exposed to HIV or HBV, how does the institution respond? Is that response consistent with recommendations from the Centers for Disease Control?

• **Patient/Employee Discrimination and Access to Services/Employment**

Are there clear policies prohibiting HIV-based discrimination in the provision of or access to services, in applications for employment, and in hiring?

• Reporting Requirements

Is the healthcare setting bound by laws or statutes mandating reporting of cases of HIV infection? Do physicians follow requirements for reporting cases of AIDS to federal authorities?

• Tuberculosis

Any finally, does the institution have an effective tuberculosis control plan in place?

Primary healthcare institutions will find a wealth of resources available to them to assist in developing comprehensive HIV policy and procedures. Some applicable policy statements are included in *We Are All Living With AIDS*; examples of others are available from local and national health bodies and medical societies. Of these, the Centers for Disease Control in Atlanta, Georgia will probably prove most valuable.

A good (though brief) general volume for hospitals is Lawrence Corey's *AIDS: Problems and Prospects: A Hospital Practice Book* (New York, Norton Medical Books, 1993.). It is composed of a series of overview articles that appeared in the pages of *Hospital Practice* magazine.

An excellent manual for addressing pediatric HIV and AIDS in healthcare institutions was prepared in 1990 by Dorothy Allbritten (Director of Child Health Analysis, National Association of Children's Hospitals and Related Institutions). The manual, *Children with HIV/AIDS: A Sourcebook for Caring,* includes an outline of strategic steps for the establishment of pediatric AIDS services in hospitals, and highlights several model healthcare institutions that have responded effectively to pediatric AIDS. *Children with HIV/AIDS* is available from the National Pediatric HIV Resource Center; write to them at 15 Ninth Street, Newark, NJ 07107 or call (201) 268-8251.

Special Note for Healthcare Workers

Earl C. Pike

Healthcare workers of various specialties may have special obligations—beyond the universal responsibilities of infection control and good, sensitive patient care—in relation to HIV. Diagnostic AIDS, for example, is a reportable condition, and physicians must report cases to appropriate health authorities. Generally, healthcare workers are cognizant of their responsibilities and have received information and/or training about those obligations.

A number of jurisdictions have now adopted legislation addressing concerns about HIV- and/or HBV-infected healthcare workers. You should check with your own jurisdictional authority to find out what laws or statutes may pertain. Minnesota, again, can serve as an example of one state's approach.

The 1992 Minnesota Legislature amended Minnesota Statutes, 1990, Chapter 214 to "promote the health and safety of patients and regulated persons by reducing the risk of infection in the provision of health care." The major provisions of the law include the following:

• Continuing education in infection control is required for certain healthcare workers, as specified by licensing board rules;

• Healthcare workers must report serious breaches of infection control which they observe to the appropriate licensing board or a designated official of the entity where the breach occurred;

• Licensing boards may inspect private practice settings (clinics, etc.) in order to determine compliance with infection control procedures;

• Healthcare workers diagnosed with HIV or hepatitis B virus (HBV; with a positive test for hepatitis B antigen) must file a confidential report with the Commissioner of Health, and a person or institution required to report HIV or HBV status to the Minnesota Department of Health (MDH) must also alert the Commissioner if the person or institution knows that the reported person is also a healthcare worker covered by this law; and

• MDH must review and evaluate the practice of reported healthcare workers, determine whether practice restrictions are necessary, and develop an appropriate monitoring plan. Healthcare workers may choose to work with their licensing board rather than MDH.

Special Policy Considerations for Particular Populations

The various provisions of the bill would apply only to licensed dental hygienists, dentists, physicians, nurses, podiatrists, registered dental assistants, physician's assistants, and for the infection control provisions, chiropractors. The bill does not call for mandatory testing of healthcare workers. Rather, it attempts to establish voluntary procedures by which the medical practices of HIV- and HBV-infected healthcare workers can be managed and monitored to meet the best interests of healthcare workers and their patients.

What does this mean specifically?

First, healthcare *workers who fall into one of the occupational categories listed above,* and who are or who find out they are HIV- or HBV-seropositive, must self-report to the Minnesota Department of Health. Therefore, if a nurse receives a positive HIV antibody test, she or he must notify MDH. Staff who do *not* fall into one of the occupational categories listed above are not required to make such a report. Some staff may also have an obligation to self-report HIV- or HBV-seropositivity to an appropriate authority at their employing institution, but that will depend on the policies in place at that institution.

Second, employers of HIV- or HBV-infected healthcare workers regulated by the law will want to contact MDH for advice and direction when they learn of their employees' HIV- or HBV-seropositivity. It should be noted, however, that there is no reason to do so *unless* the employee is a licensed healthcare worker who falls into one of the categories listed above.

For further information about the law, contact the Acute Disease Epidemiology Section of MDH at (612) 623-5414.

Community Mental Health Centers

Terry Backhaus, R. N., and Ann Graupman

Terry Backhaus is a psychiatric nurse and serves as the AIDS Resource Person for West Central Community Services Center in Willmar, Minnesota. She has been working with people with HIV or AIDS since 1984, and has been leading a rural AIDS Support Group since 1989. She also serves on her county's AIDS Task Force. Ann Graupman is supervisor of Outreach Services at West Central Community Services Center, serving primarily people of color through the provision of victim services.

As we began developing an HIV/AIDS policy for a large multifaceted community mental health center, we had two goals in mind:

1. To ensure that all HIV-infected/affected clients and/or staff would be met with a comfortable and competent agency, regardless of individual needs or circumstances. It was our contention that individuals have the right to control whether, when, and to whom their HIV status was divulged.

2. To create an HIV policy that would apply to all units and programs within our mental health center, as opposed to the creation of separate policies for each unit.

Our agency is in rural Minnesota and serves a six-county area, a consideration that played a key role in the development of our HIV policy. Issues such as confidentiality take on additional values and parameters in areas where inadvertent disclosure of HIV status may literally mean that "the whole town knows."

The following points should be kept in mind when writing HIV/AIDS policy for community mental health centers.

Confidentiality

• A community mental health center is *not* a medical facility. It would be a mistake to fashion policy on confidentiality using the needs and rules of medical facilities as an absolute model (though many requirements would remain the same for both kinds of agency.)

• A client's HIV status is generally self-reported. We do not have actual lab test results in our charts.

• All staff from all programs will generally have access to a client's chart.

• An obvious question follows: how can a comprehensive mental health agency maintain confidentiality within the facility? That is, how can we make sure that *only* staff who have a compelling need to know a client's HIV status will have access to that information?

• There is an overriding need to prevent third-party redisclosure of a client's self-reported HIV status.

• If a client's HIV seropositivity is documented in her or his chart, a specific release of information should be created, to be signed on each occasion of outgoing correspondence, giving the client knowledge and control over whether or not they want this part of their record shared with other professionals.

• Should incoming correspondence from outside agencies be reviewed for the presence of documented HIV status? If HIV status is mentioned, will this become a permanent part of the client's chart? Who within the agency will be responsible for reviewing incoming correspondence?

Duty to Warn

• Because we are not a medical facility and our psychiatrists generally do not order an HIV antibody test, a duty to warn would be invoked only rarely, if at all.

• If a specific threat to an individual is noted, and therefore a possible invocation of duty to warn, legal counsel will be sought on procedural matters.

HIV Antibody Testing

• The agency should identify a specific counseling and testing site to which it will refer clients and staff. Ideally it should be one that is confidential or anonymous.

• The agency should communicate with that site so accurate information can be given to individuals about hours, schedules, fees, and procedures.

Education

• The agency should identify an individual or team to serve as the agency HIV resource person. The individual or team needs to:

1. Be competent and comfortable with the subject matter;

2. Stay educated and well-informed about HIV and HIV-related issues;

3. Have a variety of accurate resource materials available, such as books, brochures, videos, key journals, and referral/resource manuals;

4. Organize a system to assure that all programs within the community mental health agency are providing HIV education to clients by fitting it into their current format and treatment philosophy;

5. Be available to provide HIV education to any or all program staff and clients;

6. Maintain AIDS education materials in public areas, such as lobbies and client lounges;

7. Be available to respond to client and staff questions and concerns; and

8. Ensure that HIV-competent therapists are available to meet the numerous HIV and HIV-related needs of clients.

• For clients and staff seeking further information or counseling support about risk reduction strategies, additional referral sites should be identified, such as:

1. A counseling and testing site,

2. State and national AIDS hotline numbers,

3. State and local AIDS service organizations, and

4. Local offices of Planned Parenthood, or similar community resources.

Our goal was to make our agency a safe place to discuss, and get supportive help about, HIV and all its related issues. We do not force or pressure individuals to talk or self-disclose; we create the safety, and the discussion comes naturally afterwards. Such an atmosphere can only be established through comprehensive HIV policy and education for all programs, staff, and clients.

Special Policy Considerations for Particular Populations

Homeless Populations

Homelessness and HIV: Problems and Recommendations

The Report of the Task Force on Homelessness and HIV/AIDS
Earl Pike
Karen Helfand, Project Coordinator

The following report on problems associated with HIV and homelessness in Minnesota, and recommendations for addressing those problems, comes out of a deliberate process of research, discussion, and integration of ideas. That process began with the formation of a Task Force representing a range of agencies working with the homeless. That Task Force met a number of times under a structured concrete agenda designed to clearly delineate problems and solutions and come to consensus on those items. The report is also informed by comments made by homeless people with HIV who were contacted and interviewed about their experiences, as people with HIV, in shelters. The report does not claim to be final or conclusive; some data, such as the number of people with HIV who are accessing shelters, is simply not available. But it is a comprehensive start, and does provide concrete and realizable recommendations that will aid homeless-serving agencies in any locale to deal with HIV comprehensively, sensitively, and proactively.

Introduction: HIV/AIDS

As of this writing (1992), over 200,000 people have been diagnosed with Acquired Immunodeficiency Syndrome (AIDS) and some 1.5 million people are living with the Human Immunodeficiency Virus (HIV) in the United States. Even those numbers fail to truly reflect the seriousness of the crisis. For example:

• *AIDS is now the* third leading *cause of death for men between the ages of 25 and 44.*

• *In New York City, AIDS is the* leading *cause of death among women of the same age group.*

• *Because of poverty, reduced access to appropriate education and health care, and other factors, African Americans and Hispanics are getting diagnosed at a rate 2 to 3 times higher than European Americans.*

• *HIV continues to devastate gay/lesbian/bisexual/transgender communities throughout the United States.*

• *In Minnesota, over 1,097 people have been diagnosed with AIDS as of April 1, 1992. It is estimated that between 4,000 and 17,000 people in Minnesota are HIV-infected.*

• *In 1990, the cost of treating people with AIDS in the United States was 5.8 billion dollars. In 1993, it will be nearly twice that.*

* *As many as a million people will have been diagnosed with AIDS in the United States by the year 2000; around the world, it will be 10 million.*

* *Some important advances in the medical treatment of HIV, such as the development of partially effective anti-virals, have led to dramatic improvements in the length and quality of life for many people with HIV. But there is as yet no cure or vaccine, and neither are likely in the near future.*

Clearly, HIV is going to be around for some time to come, and in many ways, society hasn't yet even begun to feel its collective or cumulative impact. For care providers of every kind, this means that the role of education—to prevent new cases of infection, reduce unnecessary hysteria, and ensure that people with HIV are treated with dignity—is still paramount. It is nearly a cliche to say that education is the most potent weapon available, but it is true. The crisis also calls upon human service professionals across the board to work with each other and Community Based Organizations (CBOs) working in HIV/AIDS to maximize limited resources and provide coordinated, sensitive care for clients living with HIV.

Homelessness and HIV

Many people are at risk of becoming homeless due to the adverse effects of HIV disease on physical, economic, and social well-being. For example, a 1986 study conducted by the AIDS Shelter Project of New York found that one year after receiving a diagnosis of AIDS, more than 30% of gay men and 50% of IV drug users were homeless (Steven R. Lane, MD, MPH and Richard Levine, MD. "Caring for Homeless People with HIV Disease," *Focus: A Guide to AIDS Research and Counseling.* Vol. 5, No. 5, April 1990).

At the same time, people who are homeless may engage in behaviors that are known to increase the chances of HIV infection:

* *An estimated 30–60% of homeless people use and/or abuse alcohol or drugs. Any drug use impairs judgement about safer sex, and sharing of drug injection equipment remains common.*

* *The rate of sexually-transmitted diseases, a partial indicator of sexual activity, continues to increase. In poverty, people may exchange sex for money, a place to sleep, food, or drugs.*

* *And about 25–30% of homeless people have some form of mental illness, which may make it more difficult to avoid or change behaviors that put them at risk.*

Homelessness itself may also compound the virulence of HIV disease since it is associated with exposure to the elements and violence, poor hygiene and nutrition, increased exposure to infectious disease, and inadequate environments for rest and self-care. In San Francisco's Health Care for the Homeless AIDS Outreach Program it is common for patients to have well-advanced HIV disease and be suffering from catastrophic psychosocial problems by the time they seek care (as cited in "Caring for Homeless People with HIV Disease").

Special Policy Considerations for Particular Populations

In all, there may be as many as 20,000 homeless people living with AIDS or *symptomatic* HIV disease in the United States; that number is only going to increase in the coming years (cited in "Caring for Homeless People with HIV Disease"). And there are likely many more people with *asymptomatic* HIV infection who are homeless.

Homelessness and HIV: Problems

The Task Force divided the problems associated with HIV and homelessness into three sections. They address those problems only in the context of the broad shelter system; the needs and problems of homeless people who do not access that system are not discussed.

Among staff, several important points were noted:

• There is insufficient education of shelter staff on all aspects of HIV, including the nature of HIV illness, transmission concerns, risk reduction strategies (personal and occupational), client education strategies, and current treatment/care options and resources for people with HIV illness. Some staff remain unconvinced of the need for such education in the first place.

• There is little continuity of educational content when and where it is provided. Staff are gathering their information from a variety of sources that may be contradictory or provide a fragmented picture of HIV.

• Because of educational deficiencies, staff may be overly concerned about the possibility of occupational HIV infection. While all staff have the right to work in environments that are free of unnecessary hazards, shelter workers are not at high risk of contracting HIV infection on the job.

• Staff may be unaware of the roles they can or should be playing, both in terms of educating clients to reduce risk of infection (or reinfection), and in terms of their responsibilities when working with clients living with HIV. Beyond general roles and responsibilities, they are usually unaware of their specific obligations in regards to confidentiality, discrimination, infection control, referral, and information dissemination.

Among clients,

• As with staff, knowledge about HIV is probably, at best, patchy, and at times, incorrect.

• Clients may find it difficult to adhere to risk-reduction strategies, even when they know what they are, because of the effects of substance abuse, mental illness, or relationship violence.

• People with HIV, as well as non-infected individuals, may be reluctant to raise questions, concerns, or needs around HIV based on fears of discrimination or rejection.

• With little income, clients will find it difficult to purchase supplies, such as condoms or clean needles, that are required to practice HIV risk reduction.

- With little income, clients may find it problematic to access existing supportive services when they are living with HIV. On top of that, they may be unaware of the range of resources that are available and how they can be accessed.

- Limited transportation services make it difficult for clients with HIV to access services that are geographically spread out.

- Clients living with HIV and struggling with immediate survival issues such as the need for food, clothing and shelter, report finding it difficult to address and respond to their HIV status as a larger, longer-term issue.

- Clients living with HIV may feel isolated and alone. Dependent on the system, as well as the assistance provided by friends and family, they may be extremely reluctant to disclose their HIV status to anyone.

- Available literature may not respond to the language, culture, or gender realities of clients' lives.

On the institutional/funding level,

- There is no widespread awareness of a priority need for, and content of, comprehensive HIV/AIDS policy in shelters and other homeless-serving agencies. Where there is the awareness, there is insufficient assistance that will help administrators translate an intangible sense of need into a concrete plan of action.

- There is little sense of coordinated policy, educational strategy, or planning between sites in the larger system. One of the practical problems this raises is that service users who access multiple shelter/homeless-serving sites may come away with conflicting perceptions of HIV and AIDS because different programs present information in different ways, or emphasize varying parts of the mass of data available about HIV.

- Shelters may view persons with HIV as the domain of existing HIV/AIDS Service Organizations, where HIV-infected clients can be "dumped."

- Some practices, such as free distribution of latex condoms or bleach kits for cleaning syringes, are in direct contrast with organizational values in some sites, even though there may be a staff awareness that availability of condoms and bleach is important.

- Shelters have traditionally struggled with environmental issues related to cleanliness, health, and safety. Tuberculosis and Hepatitis A and B are already concerns; HIV may seem like just another problem to add to an already overflowing agenda of health-related challenges. Or institutions may believe, inaccurately, that they have to provide absolutely sterile environments in order to ensure HIV safety.

- Shelters have also struggled with high turnover because of low pay and high job stress. Developing the HIV sophistication of staff is difficult under such circumstances.

Special Policy Considerations for Particular Populations

• *Issues such as sexuality, homosexuality, and chemical use still make many institutions, including social service agencies, uneasy. The general strategy has been to avoid direct confrontation of such issues for fear that controversy might result.*

Homelessness and HIV: Recommendations

Several points about the following Task Force recommendations need to be made before they are outlined.

First, as the previous discussion of problems indicates, strategies for change ought to be as systemically-based as possible. That is, they should adapt the shelter system as a whole to HIV, focusing on consistency of approaches and standards and taking a long-term perspective.

Second, we have endeavored to make recommendations as concrete as possible. Proposals that suggest, for example, "education for all staff," may hint at important goals, but they are generally too vague to propel action.

Third, we have attempted to limit recommendations (except in the funding section) to those ideas that are realizable within the present system, and without assuming an infusion of new financial resources. If a shelter first has to raise money to do something, it is less likely to be done.

In relation to *funding*, we make the following recommendations:

• *Fund-granting or contract-making bodies, such as foundations and governmental agencies, can play a critical role by requiring certain minimal standards in relation to HIV as a condition of funding. Those standards should include (at a minimum) that the organization, perhaps in conjunction with satellite services such as the Homeless Health Team:*

1. Have an HIV non-discrimination policy;

2. Make information about HIV available to all clients;

3. Have in policy a referral-for-care strategy for clients with HIV; and

4. Provide annual inservice updates on HIV and AIDS for all staff.

In order to facilitate this process, the fund- or contract-making body that makes such requirements of grantees or contractees should make available to them, in written form, sample policies, especially in relation to numbers 1 and 3 above.

• *The Task Force is well aware that increased funding for a number of programs in education and health care would be desirable, but it is also aware that the funding environment is, at the moment, conservative. We therefore recommend that local counties, the United Way, area foundations, AIDS funding consortiums, and other grant-making bodies make available funds for the development of pilot projects to develop effective educational outreach strategies for homeless people accessing shelter systems. We would also encourage funding for a pilot project, perhaps as a joint project of the Homeless Health Team and existing HIV Case Management Programs, to develop effective case management and care coordination methods for people with HIV who are transient or homeless. The Task Force intends to meet again to begin designing such a program for possible funding. In the meantime, it is essential that current HIV case management programs work closely with the Homeless Health Team and other such groups, to make sure that the needs of homeless people with HIV are being addressed and met.*

• *The Shelter Plus Program, since it contains provisions related to homelessness and HIV, should be tracked over the next year in order to gather additional data that will be helpful in program design and funding needs and allocations.*

In the institutional (shelter system) arena, we make the following recommendations:

• *Every shelter or facility serving the homeless can and should have comprehensive HIV policy that addresses the following topics:*

1. *Discrimination;*

2. *Infection Control;*

3. *Client and Staff Education;*

4. *HIV Antibody Counseling and Testing;*

5. *Confidentiality and HIV Data Management; and*

6. *Homophobia and Other Diversity Issues.*

A model for such comprehensive policy development already exists in substance abuse treatment programs through DHS's HIV Guidelines for Chemical Dependency Treatment and Care Programs in Minnesota *(1989, 1990); shelters should borrow freely from the policy recommendations of that document.*

• *Every shelter should have in place a plan for working with clients who are HIV-infected or who have AIDS. That plan should address:*

1. *Shelter staff responsibilities;*

2. *How the shelter will work with or refer to healthcare providers and CBOs working with AIDS to meet the client's medical and psychosocial needs; and*

3. *How the shelter will manage client confidentiality, especially in terms of the "street grapevine."*

• *Shelters have a responsibility to ensure that homeless clients can access risk reduction equipment such as condoms and bleach kits. Distribution should be done in a manner that will not embarrass clients, and at no cost to them. Direct distribution of such equipment by the shelter is best, but if such distribution conflicts with a shelter's deeply-held organizational values, shelter staff should be able to inform clients where condoms and bleach kits can be acquired.*

Special Policy Considerations for Particular Populations

Some shelters have taken the approach of bringing in an outside HIV educator who distributes condoms, thus allowing the shelter to avoid direct distribution. We think this is a good resolution of the dilemma.

- *Shelters should work together to develop a common HIV educational curriculum for their clients in order to reduce message confusion. One way to accomplish this task is to hold a day-long retreat/workshop, with representatives from each shelter, whose sole purpose is to develop such a curriculum by day's end. One scheduling possibility is to add a day at the beginning or conclusion of the Minnesota Coalition for the Homeless Conference in May.*

- *Shelters can demonstrate their openness to HIV issues by publicly displaying brochures, pamphlets and posters, including material on HIV discrimination. The Task Force also encourages HIV education agencies to develop and disseminate materials that specifically target homeless people.*

- *All staff in shelters should become HIV competent through shelter-hosted training and instruction. Shelters can make use of community resources in providing that instruction or training. Such training should be conducted:*

   1. As part of the orientation of new employees;

   2. On a sustained basis as part of inservice education; and

   3. With the expectation that demonstration of HIV competence becomes a part of an employee's performance requirements, to be considered when conducting performance evaluations.

   Such training should also address critical HIV-related issues such as homophobia, chemical abuse, and the effects of race, gender, and class.

On the individual *staff* level, the Task Force recommends the following:

- *All staff should recognize their position as role models for clients and other staff. That means that staff should demonstrate openness and sensitivity to HIV issues, people with HIV, and groups of people commonly associated with HIV, such as gay men and lesbian women, people of color, sex workers, and others. That also means that staff will openly challenge attitudes or behaviors, on the part of other staff or clients, that are insensitive or injurious to people with HIV.*

- *Staff should address HIV in intake interviews in a manner that:*

   1. Makes it safe for clients to ask questions or voice concerns, should they have them; and

   2. Makes it safe for clients living with HIV or AIDS to disclose that fact, should they choose to do so, and ask for assistance.

- *All staff should rigorously guard the confidentiality of clients with HIV. If staff have concerns about someone with HIV, they should discuss those con-*

cerns with their supervisor rather than peer staff or clients.

• *And finally, staff should reexamine any personal attitudes they may hold that equate HIV infection or AIDS with death. The role of staff is to assist people with HIV in* living, *not dying.*

Task Force Members

Karen Helfand, Chair
    Homeless AIDS Task Force
Theresa Cain
    Minnesota AIDS Project
Bob Eidser
    Union Gospel Mission
Fraser Nelson
    AIDS/STD Prevention Services Section
Mary Hall
Wendy Pederson
    Access
Earl Pike
    Chemical Dependency Program Division
    Minnesota Department of Human Services
Julie Sailor
    Homeless Health Team
Kathy Wederspahn
    Midwest Farmworker Employment and Training
Lisa Brannan
    Homeless Health Team
Karen Clark
    MN State Representative
Peter Hiniker
    Hennepin County Human Services
Gino Nelson
    Minnesota Department of Health
Linda Peters
    Catholic Charities
Sandra Richardson
    Family Shelter
Dave Schultz
    Mental Health Division
    MN Department of Human Services

Cultural Communities

Earl C. Pike

Cultural communities, such as African Americans, Asians, Chicanos/Latinos, Native Americans, and others, each have unique needs and cultural realities when it comes to HIV policy and education. From a global perspective, the diversity of culturally-competent approaches required to fight the epidemic is astounding. But the cost of failure to take those cultural differences into account is equally astounding, measured in the loss of lives and futures that have already occured because policies and educational messages did not respect an individual's cultural reality, and were therefore ignored.

It is beyond the boundaries of this book (indeed, it is another couple of books altogether) to outline with any reasonable specificity the "dos and don'ts" of HIV policy and programming for the entire rainbow of cultural communities. One example, surveying some considerations for HIV work in Native American communities, follows. There are, in addition, two essential resources for those planning to develop HIV policy and education in other cultural communities. The first is the **National Minority AIDS Council** (NMAC) in Washington, DC (see page 393 for their address and phone number). The NMAC has functioned as a coalition of many cultural communities, and has amassed a wealth of resources and practical experience.

And the second is the **WHO Global Program on AIDS** (see page 394 for their address), which specializes in transnational, transcultural programming. Most states and provinces also have community-based organizations engaged in targeted work in cultural communities, and they should be contacted for local advice and assistance.

Native American Communities

Yako Myers

Yako Meyers is a Minneapolis woman who provides consultation on sexuality, HIV, and traditional teachings. She relates her roots and influences as follows: "I'm Mohawk [Indian]. My father is Mayan and Paino. I was adopted about twelve years ago by an Anishainabe spiritual leader. So for the past twelve years I've been immersed in the Ojibwe way of life, the bimadiswin, or living life to the fullest, and for the last five years I've been immersed in my Mohawk ancestry. I'm turtle clan on the Mohawk side. Through my adoption, through my grandmother, and through my vision quest I'm gaiaska—the gull, which is one of spiritual leadership. My clan is also the moral code keeper. The two go hand in hand."

HIV/AIDS policy development for Native Americans or Native American organizations must address several important issues.

Traditional/Cultural Aspects

- No one should ever make assumptions about clients' beliefs or value systems. Those that hold for many of dominant culture origins may not hold true for Native Americans.
- Some clients may possess a great deal of tribal consciousness, and be active in tribal affairs. Others may be totally unaware of their ethnicity. Still others have learned to "live in both worlds," and will behave differently in varying settings. The mere fact that someone is "Indian" will not tell you which is true.
- One should always inquire about the client's cultural background. For instance, is she or he Ojibwe? Lakota? Dakota? Oneida? These distinctions may be lost to most white Americans, but to Native Americans, they are significant, and speak of rich and complex histories.
- Tribal identity (or the lack of it) greatly influences how your client thinks, feels, behaves, responds, and how she or he perceives her or his environment.

Family Aspects

- The concept of family, in Native American culture, includes blood family, extended family, and intentional family. One's "family" is often a wide circle of associations.
- These various family associations will have a significant impact on your client's sense of self, identity, and belonging.
- Often, intentional and/or extended family will have as much, if not more, influence on your client.
- While these realities may prevail for many families, they are particularly evident in Native American communities.

Spiritual Aspects

- Respect for your clients' spiritual needs is essential to their wellness and sense of well-being.
- Among Native people there are many spiritual paths. Some are traditional, some are Judeo-Christian, some fall somewhere in between.
- Traditional paths include spiritual elders and healers, sweat lodges, pipe ceremonies, and the use of sage, cedar, and sweet grass—among many others.
- The need for personal spiritual objects is vital to some Native Americans and clients should not be discouraged or forbidden from having these objects.

Other Aspects (Things to Remember)

- Not all Native Americans will emote or respond on the cues familiar to white Americans.
- Not all Native Americans will look you directly in the eye. Often, eye contact is seen as a signal of disrespect; avoiding one's eyes is seen as respectful.
- Body language is critical to most Native Americans. The professional who says one thing, but whose body communicates in a different way, will quickly lose the trust of the client.
- In one-to-one sessions with Native American clients, professionals need to understand that simply *being* with the client, in silence, can be as effective as urging the client to speak or engage in dialogue.

HIV/AIDS and Correctional Facilities

Norma Denbrook

Norma Denbrook is Coordinator of the Corrections AIDS Prevention Program (CAPP) of the Hennepin County [Minnesota] Community Health Department. CAPP recently received a national award from the U. S. Department of Health and Human Services for outstanding and innovative programming in HIV/AIDS.

Introduction

The corrections system in the United States encompasses a wide array of programs, populations, personnel, and politics. It would be impossible to lay out, in the space of a few pages, HIV policy and education recommendations for every kind of institution and every governmental jurisdiction. But it is entirely feasible to sketch out broad and overriding guidelines that can help focus the policy and educational efforts of individual institutions, and additional specific advice (on matters such as infection control, management of HIV antibody testing, and others) is readily available from a handful of centralized sources.

Policy and Education Planning

Correctional institutions just starting the process of HIV policy and education planning should begin by going outside the institution and building collaborative partnerships with other key agencies and governmental bodies. At the very least, planning should include representation and input from:

- *the state or county department of corrections;*
- *the state or county department of health;*
- *the state or county attorney general's office;*
- *the state or county substance abuse authority;*
- *correctional personnel unions;*
- *correctional personnel professional organizations;*
- *affected inmates; and*
- *local or state community-based AIDS service/education organizations (ASOs).*

Some facilities may hesitate to involve input from inmates or community-based

ASOs. That hesitation is understandable, but exclusion of those perspectives is at the least unwise, and at worst will only tend to sabotage the success of educational and policy efforts. HIV-infected/affected inmates can share invaluable insights about the practical problems of living with HIV disease while incarcerated, and community-based ASOs have accumulated a wealth of knowledge about AIDS as a result of a decade of front-line, hands-on work. Those points of view are simply too useful to ignore.

HIV Education

HIV education in correctional facilities has been underway for a number of years now, and the combined experience of a number of educational programs points to certain, inviolable conclusions.

First, facility administration needs to actively support the nature and scope of educational endeavors. Without that support, the goals of HIV education will be undermined at lower operational levels.

Second, the authority for, as well as the content and process of HIV education, needs to be written into policy. HIV education is far too critical to be left to purely individual efforts within the institution; policy encodes that education as an organizational, rather than purely personal, responsibility. Besides, HIV educators in correctional settings deserve the support of policy backing and guiding their work.

Third, all staff within the facility should be trained about AIDS, and about the specific content and methodologies to be employed in inmate education. All prison staff, including guards, medical personnel, operations staff, and social service professionals should deliver unified, consistent messages about HIV to inmates. The goal of an informed, responsible inmate population will be seriously impaired if the HIV educator tells an inmate one thing, and a guard, five minutes later, contradicts that message.

Fourth, education about HIV and AIDS should address affective as well as cognitive levels of learning, and presented in the context of broader, affirming education about sexual health, other sexually-transmitted diseases (STDs), and chemical use. Merely focusing on pathology tends to have a minimal effect on changing behavior.

Fifth, education will need to be modified to meet the needs, codes, cultures, and styles of inmate subpopulations. Female inmates will require (and deserve) education that speaks to women's realities, and will therefore be different than education offered to men. Education for openly gay inmates will differ in overt and covert ways from that provided to heterosexuals. While it usually is impossible to separate inmates into neat and entirely separate categories, HIV education demands a special sensitivity to personal diversity.

And *sixth,* the hiring or assignment of staff who will conduct HIV education should be approached as a critical task, with every effort made to secure highly qualified people who can relate to both inmates and staff, who are comfortable with all aspects of AIDS (including sexuality and drug use), and who "know their stuff." Perhaps the most important thing a correctional facility can do to guarantee effective HIV education is to assign only the most competent person(s) to the job.

In March of 1991 the National Committee on AIDS, after extensive hearings and site visits, released its report on *HIV Disease in Correctional Facilities.* In that document the Commission made twelve recommendations for AIDS programs in correctional facilities. They are worthy of serious study and application to all correctional settings. (The recommendations were developed for the Commission in August of 1990 by Nicholas Freudenberg, Professor of Community Health Education and Executive Director, Center for Community Action to Prevent AIDS, Hunter College School of Health Sciences, CUNY; and AIDS Education Consultant, Montefiore Rikers Island Prison Health Services.)

1. All inmates should participate in a mandatory AIDS information and education session upon entry into the system.

2. All correctional and prison health staff should be required to participate in AIDS education programs.

3. All inmates should have the opportunity to request confidential HIV antibody testing and counseling.

4. Inmates should have the opportunity to participate in ongoing groups that provide information and support about risk reduction.

5. Peer educators can play an important role in prison AIDS prevention programs.

6. Prison officials need to create a social environment that supports risk reduction and humane treatment towards those living with HIV or AIDS.

7. Inmates need to learn skills that will protect them against HIV infection both inside and outside the correctional system. [All inmates, and especially those living with HIV, also need to learn skills in health maintenance.]

8. Prevention programs also need to be closely linked to health and social services for inmates with HIV/AIDS.

9. Prevention programs need to address the specific needs of female inmates.

10. Prisoners should be included in planning and implementing AIDS prevention programs.

11. AIDS education programs should be developed for all institutions in the correctional system.

12. Correctional systems, prison health services, AIDS organizations, prisoners' rights groups, and public health professionals need to work together to create effective AIDS prevention programs in correctional settings.

HIV Policy

A host of procedural and policy questions come immediately to the surface when considering the management of HIV disease in corrections populations. They include, but are certainly not limited to, concerns about the following.

- *Medical management of HIV disease and financing of care;*
- *The impact of TB and certain other opportunistic infections associated with HIV disease;*
- *Inmate access to clinical trials for new AIDS treatments;*
- *Substance use and HIV disease;*
- *Sexual behavior, sodomy, and HIV;*
- *Screening and testing for the HIV antibody;*
- *Housing and segregation;*
- *Potential violence against and harassment of inmates with HIV;*
- *Transmission and facility liability; and*
- *Transfer, discharge, and early release of inmates with HIV.*

Once again, the National Commission of AIDS/HIV Disease in Correctional Facilities makes a series of excellent recommendations on HIV policy and procedures which can be utilized as a yardstick to measure the adequacy of facility policy. Those guidelines include the following.

I. Medical Care

- *Asymptomatic HIV infection is a serious medical condition requiring regular medical attention and in many cases aggressive prophylactic treatment.*
- *Medical, nursing, inpatient and outpatient services for inmates with HIV disease should, at a minimum, be equal to prevailing standards of care for people living with HIV disease in the community at large.*
- *Correctional facilities should immediately address the controllable subsidiary epidemics of sexually-transmitted diseases and tuberculosis. Infection control protocols established by the U. S. Public Health Service, Centers for Disease Control, should be strictly followed. Universal precautions should be integrated into institutional procedures.*
- *Because of the complex and rapidly changing nature of HIV treatment protocols, quality assurance mechanisms should be implemented to review periodically the adequacy and efficacy of prison medical care. "Adequate care*

includes, but is not limited to meaningful access to HIV testing; regular examinations by physicians with sufficient training to diagnose and treat HIV infection and HIV-related illnesses; a full examination at the time infection is diagnosed, and subsequently as medically indicated; access to necessary specialist care where appropriate; T-cell monitoring at the intervals prescribed by the U. S. Public Health Service; timely, consistent and appropriate access to necessary medications, including prophylactic drug therapies approved by the Food and Drug Administration or recommended by federal health authorities; access to dental care; access to mental health care; access to meaningful drug treatment on demand; clean, hygienic housing facilities; and appropriate diets." *(from* HIV Disease in Correctional Facilities*)*

• *Medical information revealed in the course of treatment should be rigorously protected from disclosure to non-treating personnel.*

II. Identification

• *Voluntary HIV antibody testing and counseling, in a confidential/anonymous basis, should be available to all prisoners who request it. HIV antibody testing and counseling should be conducted according to protocols established by the Centers for Disease Control (CDC).*

• *Mandatory HIV antibody testing or screening should not be employed.*

III. Information and Education

In addition to the preceding,

• *HIV education should be a high priority, and include components targeting behaviors that put people at risk, alleviating unfounded fears of HIV infection, and informing everyone in the facility of available medical care.*

• *Inmates and staff need live, interactive HIV education from credible, competent educators at regular intervals. Reliance solely on written materials and videotapes is not sufficient. All education should be culturally and linguistically appropriate.*

• *HIV education to reduce HIV infection from injection equipment sharing and sexual intercourse should be explicit, and include clear advice about resources available in the prison setting that can be employed to reduce risk, even where those behaviors occur in violation of prison regulations or applicable law.*

• *Condom distribution should be a part of an overall health promotion and HIV prevention effort in all correctional systems.*

• *Because inmates may distrust information offered by prison authorities, outside organizations, including health departments and ASOs, should be involved in the development and presentation of HIV education.*

* *Continuing education programs on HIV should be mandatory for all medical and social service personnel in institutions.*

* *Support groups for prisoners living with HIV disease should be offered, promoted, and encouraged. Correctional systems should work cooperatively with community-based ASOs in providing support services and counseling to bridge the gap between institutions and the community, and to provide follow-up services as inmates return to the community.*

IV. Management

* *Discrimination and punitive treatment of people with HIV disease discourages them from seeking education, testing and treatment, thus compromising efforts to prevent new HIV infections and to treat persons living with HIV disease.*

* *Prisoners should not be isolated or housed in special units solely because of their HIV status.*

* *Prisoners with HIV disease should be permitted to participate in all prison programs and jobs for which they are otherwise qualified, including positions in food or health services, in keeping with CDC guidelines.*

* *HIV-related information in the possession of medical providers should be released to prison authorities only under extraordinary circumstances, and for the benefit of the patient. Staff should be trained to protect the privacy of inmate medical data. Work rules prohibiting release of HIV-related information should be strictly enforced.*

* *Jails and prisons should have written HIV management policies and treatment protocols that reflect the most current medical and scientific information. These policies should be reviewed regularly.*

V. Release

* *HIV disease should not be a reason to further punish any prisoner. Release should not be capriciously denied merely because of HIV serostatus.*

* *To maintain continuity of care during the transition from prison to the community, every inmate with HIV disease should be assisted in finding medical care and support services in the community. This should include assisting prisoners in enrolling in hospital- or community-based case management services prior to release.*

* *Prisons and jails should have workable early-discharge and medical furlough programs providing for the timely release of inmates whose incarceration is no longer medically appropriate.*

Resources

In the area of HIV and correctional facilities, one resource stands amidst a number of others: the AIDS Clearinghouse of the National Institute of Justice (U. S. Department of Justice) and its comprehensive publication, *AIDS in Correctional Facilities: Issues and Options*. The NIJ AIDS Clearinghouse can provide information and guidance on all aspects of HIV in jails and prisons. Other resources from local, state, provincial, and federal corrections offices can be contacted for further information.

These sources largely reflect "official," governmental perspectives on the problem of HIV in prisons. Other organizations, such as the ACLU, have published material highlighting sanctioned abuse of, and discrimination against, inmates with HIV, as well as mismanagement and inadequate care in the provision of medical services to inmates with HIV or AIDS. This work deserves serious review and consideration.

Special Policy Considerations for Particular Populations

Agencies Serving People with Developmental Disabilities

The Division for Persons with Developmental Disabilities (DPDD) of the Minnesota Department of Human Services (DHS) has issued policy guidelines for service providers, titled *Human Immunodeficiency Virus (HIV) Guidelines for Minnesota Programs Serving Persons with Developmental Disabilities*. The Guidelines were developed with the key input of service providers, provider organizations, HIV/AIDS organizations, and state and federal offices. The following, excerpted directly from the Guidelines, summarizes the policy recommendations.

A. Access to Services

Basic Principle

No one should be denied services, or offered sub-standard services, because of real or perceived HIV antibody status. There is no valid ethical, clinical, epidemiological, or legal reason for service programs to refuse admission for a person who is HIV antibody positive who is otherwise qualified for that service.

Recommendation(s)

That providers of services to people with developmental disabilities adopt a policy statement that explicitly acknowledges full access to services and employment for people who are HIV antibody positive who are otherwise qualified. Such a statement can be added to a program's existing non-discrimination clause, or addressed separately in a statement about AIDS and other chronic diseases. In addition, programs should educate all staff about non-discrimination law as it relates to HIV and AIDS, making it clear that discriminatory behavior is illegal and will not be tolerated.

B. HIV Education

Basic Principle

Education that emphasizes behavioral change is one of the only tools presently available in the fight against transmission of HIV. Though difficult, education can be effective in changing knowledge, attitudes, and behaviors. All program participants in developmental disability service programs, and the staff who work in them, deserve the best education that can be provided.

Recommendation(s)

That service programs provide education on HIV for all staff and all program participants, including board and family members. Education should be integrated smoothly into existing program format and philosophy, and include at the very least, an explanation of the nature and action of HIV, the facts about transmission, and personal and occupational risk reduction strategies. The provision of HIV education should be a matter of policy that dictates the frequency of that education, and which designates personnel responsible for its planning and delivery.

C. Sexuality Education

Basic Principle

The fundamental goal of sexuality education is the promotion of sexual health—and that goal has become even more compelling in the face of the HIV/AIDS epidemic. All people—staff, program participants, and their families—need and deserve accurate information and sensitive guidance about sexuality and sexual expression, in a manner that affirms our innate nature as sexual beings and our right to make healthy decisions about sexual self-expression. These *Guidelines* also validate the individual's right to sexual self-pleasuring and to engage in consensual and healthy sexual behavior with others of either gender.

Recommendations(s)

Programs should follow the "Sexuality Policy Checklist" at the end of Chapter VI to develop and implement program policy about sexuality and sexuality education. Programs should also consider the designation of a staff member as the program's Sexuality Resource Person to research and coordinate education efforts.

D. Infection Control

Basic Principle

There is a minute risk of HIV exposure through occupational exposure to blood, semen, and vaginal secretions. Despite the fact that it is extremely unlikely that such exposure would take place in most programs serving people with developmental disabilities, it is sensible for general hygienic reasons and to control infection of other blood-borne pathogens such as hepatitis B virus, to adopt simple, accessible infection control procedures and protocols.

Recommendation(s)

That service programs ought to adopt, as a matter of policy, an infection control plan appropriate to the program. Nonresidential programs will have different infection control guidelines than residential programs; the policies reproduced in this volume should be consulted. In addition, some programs will need to adopt policies and procedures that comply with OSHA requirements about blood-borne pathogens.

Special Policy Considerations for Particular Populations

E. HIV Antibody Testing

Basic Principle

The current HIV antibody test has both potential advantages and limitations. The HIV antibody test should *not* be required as a precondition for employment or services. Persons thinking of getting the test should carefully weigh a number of critical factors before getting the test. Service providers have a role to play in helping the program participant: (1) to decide whether or not to be tested, (2) to learn about resources for testing and their respective advantages and disadvantages, and (3) to provide adequate and appropriate follow-up counseling, or referral for counseling, after testing. Third-party decisionmakers should not make capricious decisions about HIV antibody testing; they should carefully weigh all facts and options.

Recommendation(s)

That providers of services to people with developmental disabilities should adopt policy that clarifies for all staff and program participants the program stance on HIV antibody testing. Staff should help service users reach uniquely appropriate decisions on the question of being tested, rather than forcing one recommendation over another. Third-party decisionmakers should base their deliberations on a thorough acquaintance with the facts and options. Service programs should endeavor to protect individual confidentiality in the entire process of test decisionmaking and actual testing, and should endeavor to make sure that no person comes to harm because of a positive test result. On-site testing is generally not advisable for service programs.

F. Confidentiality and HIV Information Management

Basic Principle

Since a great deal of potential harm can come to people whose HIV positive antibody status is inappropriately or illegally disclosed to third parties, service programs should scrupulously guard the confidentiality of service user and staff HIV status.

Recommendation(s)

That service programs develop and adopt policy that addresses specific questions about HIV antibody status and confidentiality. Policy should address issues such as who needs to know when a program participant self-reports HIV seropositivity, program responsibilities and liabilities in relation to HIV status information, third party disclosure, charting protocols of HIV status, and other matters. Specific recommendations on confidentiality questions are contained in the body of these *Guidelines*.

Agencies Serving Adolescents

Kevin Cwayna, M.D.

Kevin Cwayna has worked at the Youth and AIDS Project of the University of Minnesota and the Comprehensive Hemophilia Treatment Center. He is the author of *Knowing Where the Fountains Are: Stories and Stark Realities of Homeless Youth* (Minneapolis, Deaconess Press, 1993) on HIV and homeless youth.

General Policy

• The most effective way to encourage youth to act responsibly and respectfully around HIV is to *present* information and policy in a manner that is open, responsible, and respectful.

• Adolescents with HIV can stay healthy for many years. All policies should assume that HIV-infected youth, unless displaying active clinical deterioration, will live full lives for a significant period of time.

• Youth-serving agencies are already familiar with multi-tiered accountability—to youth, parents/guardians, and governmental licensing boards. Our policies on HIV must be clear and acceptable to all three factions.

• There is rarely a justifiable basis to disclose the HIV seropositivity of a youth to parents, other youth, the State, or peripheral employees.

• There is rarely any justifiable basis to make significant programmatic or service adjustments for HIV-infected asymptomatic youth.

• There are occasional reasons to adjust services or programs to meet the needs of HIV-infected youth who are displaying clinical symptoms of illness. Such adjustments must be based on the symptoms, ability limitations, or medical compliance of HIV-infected youth.

Baseline Assumptions

• Youth are sexual and their sexualities encompass the same range of sexual identities present in the adult population. Whether or not she or he is sexually active, every youth is dealing with their identity as a gay, lesbian, bisexual, transgender, or heterosexual person. Professionals should address such issues proactively by providing information, emotional support, and safety for individual exploration.

• Many youth do or will use illicit drugs and alcohol. They may also experiment with injectable drugs.

• Youth will search out and find answers to pressing personal questions—including questions about HIV and other STDs, sexuality, and drugs. If no reliable information is forthcoming they will believe what they hear on the streets or from peers, what makes sense to them, or what they want to believe. Withholding accurate information only encourages youth to answer their questions through other, less accurate and potentially dangerous, means.

• Youth who grow up in cultures characterized by open, life-long discussion about sexuality experience fewer STDs and unwanted pregnancies. Unrestricted discussions of sexuality will promote responsible sexual behavior.

Legal Considerations

• Always consult with qualified legal counsel for specific advice on policy questions.

• In the State of Minnesota, the provision of STD (including HIV) health services does not generally require parental permission. Youth, however, may be responsible for financial costs incurred. This is also true in many other states and other areas of jurisdiction.

• Agencies are not required to inform parents of HIV infection or transmission risks.

• Reporting requirements in Minnesota (and many other jurisdictional areas) are strict but narrow. Unless your agency has *direct* medical evidence of HIV infection (such as HIV antibody test results), you are not required to "report" a case to the Minnesota Department of Health or other public health authorities.

Disability in the Workplace

Carlton Hogan

Carlton Hogan is the Training Coordinator for the Community Programs for Clinical Research on AIDS (Statistical Center), and is the Editor of *PWAlive, A Journal By, For, and About People with AIDS* published out of the Twin Cities. He has been living with AIDS for a number of years, and is a leading activist and pioneer in the AIDS community in Minnesota.

The nature of the role of people with disabilities in the work force is hardly a new question: it is only in the last few centuries or so, with the advent of an industrialized society, that many of those who are currently labeled "disabled" have been diverted from the work force in great numbers. Previously, even those who were completely unable to participate in manual labor needed to make some kind of contribution to the society that sustained them. Many primitive and aboriginal cultures had special roles for people with disabilities; often they were wise men and women, shamans, oracles, curators of sacred knowledge, or otherwise dedicated to religious communities, remembering and passing down sacred lore that others in a sustenance-based culture did not have the time to learn.

More recently, there has been a tendency to "warehouse" people with disabilities. Ironically, in a wealthy culture that can afford to feed even those who are not productive, we have retrogressed rather than advanced in the judicious utility of all of society's members.

The passage of the Americans with Disabilities Act (ADA) has triggered a wave of speculation, anxiety, and concern. Such broad sweeping legislation offers fertile ground for hypothesis—many people with disabilities, and activists for disability rights, hope that the ADA will make substantial process toward a truly equitable workplace where all Americans are given an opportunity to make their best possible contribution.

On the other side of the coin, many business owners, human resource officers, and workplace supervisors regard the ADA with a great deal less enthusiasm. They fear undue burdens as a result of physical plant conversion, "quotas" (real or implicit) for workers with disabilities, and abuse of legal protections by the disabled. An example of the latter might be a substandard worker who is nonetheless unfirable, or a marginally less attractive job applicant who is able to secure the position by virtue of disability.

Addressing these concerns and beliefs is far beyond the scope of this article. I personally would probably fall in the first camp, which advocates for people with disabilities: all of the possible amendments to "business as usual" would probably be quite minor and have numerous subsidiary benefits. Far more importantly, I think that both sides of this debate are making a fundamental error in the basic assumptions that drive their rhetoric.

Both camps, to one degree or another, frame their discourse mainly in the context that a job or career is something that the employee either does or does not have a right or privilege to. The implicit assumption is that an opportunity for employment, first and foremost, is of benefit to the person who is being employed, who has been "given" this chance through the largesse of the organization. The organization in question may indisputably need "someone" to fill the job, but the selection of one particular individual over another is a process which will ultimately confer a greater improvement in fortune to the individual than to the organization.

Positing this analysis as representing the true state of affairs, the ADA doesn't make sense as anything more than a profoundly humanitarian gesture, where national productivity and quality would suffer significantly as a result of what really would not be much different from vocational rehabilitation. The employee with disabilities would reap the advantages of employment and salary, and the company would thereby suffer.

Such an analysis is a lopsided and myopic one. In truth, employment is an exchange, a contract where both sides hopefully benefit—each has a specific role, with attendant constraints and responsibilities. Ideally, there should be a symmetry between the needs and contributions of the parties involved. An essential component of this is the individuality of the workers, who bring with them certain specific and necessary skills, knowledge, and attitudes. A diversity in the members of the work force complements a diversity in need.

Often, particularly as the United States moves more in the direction of a service-oriented, non-manual labor economy, a specific disability may have little or no impact on those certain attributes that are needed in a particular position. The route that a "disabled" individual will take to get to the solution of a situation may deviate from what a person of "normal" ability might take. But as the job market becomes more and more specialized, gross and inexact definitions of "disability" and "ability" may no longer serve.

Undergirding this entire argument is the assumption that a person with disabilities is a unique, functional (within certain parameters) human being, who is undoubtedly good at *something*. Tragically, many people may never find that "something" they are good at. Many people with disabilities either have found, or are in the process of finding, what it is they are good at. People with disabilities, as all people, come to the work force with a wide range of experience and specialization. Some had thriving careers before becoming disabled; others have learned their craft post-disability. And yet a third group exists: newcomers to the work force, eagerly seeking an opportunity to participate in society and become more self-reliant.

In a professional position that requires years of dedication to master the requisite skills and vocabulary, unless the disability directly affects an essential skill with no available work around, a suitably-qualified person with disabilities may possess unique proficiency and accumulated wisdom, even in the cases where the normal "tools of the trade" may need to be modified or substituted for. The degree to which the expected and normative apparatus of the work environment can be successfully modified to aid productivity is limitless. In some of the most trivial cases, such as a person of limited mobility in a desk job, the problem may be only one of access, quickly remedied with a judiciously placed ramp or hand-hold.

It is equally true of the person who is a novice to the work force or to a new career as it is of the highly skilled professional that a dedication and willingness to learn are critical assets, sometimes counting for more than previous experience or knowledge. The commitment and aspiration of a person with disabilities in taking on a position which may be a little more taxing or inconvenient is clear testament to a willingness and desire to work, as well as to a strength of character that may bode well for all future endeavors.

Especially in a social climate that devalues persons who are impaired in any sense, tacitly encourages persons with disabilities to "take it easy," and offers at least some minimal assurance of sustenance if unable to work, those who actively pursue employment (and possible great challenges) are displaying not only bravery, but great creativity in seeking to find a definition of themselves far different from the cultural norm. In offering any person a unique opportunity to expand their horizons, those who rise to meet the challenge in the face of considerable adversity have already distinguished themselves from the pack, affirming the value in taking such a risk. Regardless of eventual outcome, they have already clearly defined themselves as courageous, committed, and creative.

People with disabilities may also bring a unique sensitivity and sensibility to the workplace. A specific understanding of disability issues may make them invaluable in organizations that make the disabled their clients or customers. More generally, the more creative among persons with disabilities may be able to translate their experience to a greater understanding of all adversity. A keen understanding of barriers to traditional social goals and behaviors can be extrapolated to any number of situations in which an individual's horizons are adversely delimited. Their transcendence of conventional limits may make them more prone to seeking unorthodox or innovative solutions, or may simply give them the ability to believe that such solutions might exist when others doubt.

This is not to say that hiring people with disabilities is any more "foolproof" than the hiring of any other applicant. Aptitude in any particular job reflects a mix of practical skills and knowledge, interpersonal attributes and talents, and dedication to the particular mission or goal at hand. Obviously, having a disability guarantees none of those things. However, if a person is willing to strive mightily to transcend what might appear to be their "lot in life," the least that any rational or practical culture can do is assist in such a valuable undertaking, especially when the vast majority of effort will be made by the individual.

And again, I feel obligated to reiterate that a physical status that may be defined in the grossest, least specific terms as a "disability" may have no impact whatsoever on the requirements of a particular position. I have already cited the case of the mobility-impaired worker in a desk job. There is also the blind worker who uses the phone in their avocation, the deaf worker at the computer terminal, and others whose primary activity is entirely unaffected by a "disability." In truth, in the context of the workplace, this term may have limited relevance or applicability. This is not a new concept—venerable traditions like the blind piano tuner are reminders that "disability" is at best a relative term.

The above examples of the blind person on the phone and the deaf person at a computer terminal are merely the most obvious, least ingenious scenarios. Technological solutions broaden the horizons even further. With the assistance of almost trivial adaptations, we now have the deaf worker conversing on the phone via TDD or relay service, the blind worker with a braille-equipped computer, and the telecommuter. I call these solutions "trivial" in that they truly are insignificant in comparison to the human factor—the adjustments to normal routine and the willingness to overcome organizational inertia that are required to pursue previously-untried strategies.

One of the biggest barriers may have nothing to do with the innate skills or capabilities of the "disabled" worker. The attitudes and beliefs of co-workers and management may be far more crippling than any physical deficit. This is especially true in the case of a chronic disease, such as HIV disease. There certainly may be intervals where the concerned individual is functionally uncompromised, yet there also may be stretches where the worker may have some varying degree of impairment. An ideal solution has the flexibility to accommodate a varying degree of stamina and ability, allowing the concerned employee the ability to always participate to the limit of their capability. Such a scheme would offer opportunities to defer, delay, or transfer assignments at times of infirmity.

Such situations can be difficult to arrange, in that limits and responsibilities are variable, based on a very subjective assessment coming from the worker herself or himself. Trust is an essential component in such a situation. There must be a willingness to believe that the worker has full intentions of giving their best shot, even though they sometimes may not be able to do so. Obviously, if the employee is perceived as "shirking" key duties, the situation will rapidly deteriorate.

Part of the administrative overhead in such a situation is creating viable mechanisms for transferring or otherwise dealing with essential components of the workload. If there are deadlines to be missed, there needs to be some form of infrastructure to ensure that other employees are made aware of the necessary duties, and given the background and pre-existing components of the work so as to be able to smoothly pick up the ball. These need to be proactively designed at a time when the person with disabilities is well, so as to avoid having the onus of responsibility remain on the afflicted worker. Allowing someone who is feeling poorly to go home is no great favor if they are left scurrying to find a replacement and worrying about the completion of the task at hand. It is not only the specific task itself that must be transferred; the timeline, monitoring and precursor components, whether they be physical materials or information, also need to be transferred as part of a cohesive unit. For example, a completed report is of little use if it is not delivered to the proper person, at the proper time, with the proper supporting documents. A completed frame is useless if you do not know the proper picture to mount in it.

There needs to be a certain brutal honesty in developing strategies to deal with such situations. There must be no denial, no evading the unpleasant reality that such methods may not be needed at crucial times. It is difficult for all parties to admit that the worst may happen, but effective planning mandates the consideration of exactly such scenarios. The employee who is worth keeping in the workplace is exactly the employee who will be responsible in seeing a project completed properly. Not creating such structures penalizes such an individual, who can not take advantage of any flexibilities in a system if to do so is to compromise the mission or quality of their workplace. When they go home for a day, they must be able to leave work completely behind, and not take stress or worry about the completion of their endeavors with them. If such safety mechanisms are not built in, a common scenario will be that the worker will not leave when they have to, or will push themselves to collapse, obviating the entire benefit of flexible scheduling.

Often problems of stamina or strength can be accommodated by the use of split shifts, telecommuting (where applicable), and other forms of working from home. An important principle in all of these strategies is that although guidance must come from the worker with disabilities herself or himself, *it is not their responsibility to initiate the process of making adaptations.* In many cases workers have simply been unaware of the options available to them. This has been more than the natural reticence to appear demanding or selfish. Sometimes it simply never occurs to the worker that things do not always need be done in the traditional manner. Simple, minor alterations of the workplace may have a huge benefit, but never cross the mind of the employee. In one case, the computer of an employee with progressive eye disease was fitted with a non-glare filter. They had not previously heard of such a thing, and it ended up improving their workday substantially.

Sometimes overburden can be less of a problem than the converse. A person with an intermittent chronic disability may end up suffering for lack of work or challenge. Particularly in the period when coming back from a period of infirmity, the employee may find too little available to challenge and stimulate them. Work will be steered in other directions, invitations to meetings will not be extended, assignments may be thinned down or trivialized, all out of the most benevolent concern. Persons will intercept assignments and messages and alter schedules in a nonproductive manner because they fear that the individual with disabilities is not capable of participating, or that it may be too hard on them. Again, this is an area where trust is paramount. The employee's assessment of their own capabilities and strengths must be elicited in order to be able to best take advantage of what they currently have to offer. And again, this should not be done in crisis mode, but should be planned for in advance. The possibilities of a varying degree of ability must be discussed forthrightly, so that the individual does not feel bored or patronized when they are underestimated.

The hardest thing about any of this planning is dealing with multiple events of convalescence and recovery. People have a very hard time adjusting to the varying ability and energy of the worker with disabilities, and find adapting to the changes in their condition disconcerting. It is sometimes hard to believe in the recovery of a person who is seriously or mortally ill. Often a degree of grieving will begin to occur far in advance of mortality. If and when the concerned person recovers, no one quite knows how to interact with a person that they believed "lost." Once better, other workers wish to believe that the problem is over, and things will eternally remain as they once were. A more typical situation, of course, is much more cyclic in nature, with the worker experiencing a wide range of degrees of functionality. If not adequately discussed and understood by all concerned, the cumulative emotional toll of all of these adjustments can be devastating.

Some of these adaptations may sound overwhelming. But I believe that all of these strategies are already common, to one degree or another. Workers have always covered for each other in times of crisis and have often self-negotiated reciprocal arrangements to facilitate vagaries of scheduling and external conflicts. I have heard of situations where workers have sought to "pool" sick days on behalf of a convalescent peer. What may need to happen in many sites is merely for management to begin to condone and support behaviors that are already present, or to provide enough education and support to defuse the fear and anxiety that may be preventing such camaraderie.

Many times the presence of an employee with HIV or other chronic disease can be an invaluable opportunity to do extremely effective education in the workplace. The reality of the situation lends a certain clarity and importance to subject matter that might seem superfluous under other circumstances. The fear of infection via an HIV positive co-worker can be turned into an advantage and an opportunity to do HIV risk-reduction education. Working with a fellow employee suffering from cardiac disease can open a discussion on nutritional and other strategies for preserving cardiovascular health. An employee with breast cancer might inspire the offer of mammograms to interested employees. These subjects may have once been seen as outside the domain of the workplace environment. Now, with more workplaces self-insuring and offering a gamut of facilitory services such as mini-clinics and day care, there seems to be an expanded perception of the role of the employer in the general welfare of employees.

Such educational efforts tend to have multiple payoffs. Other employees may adopt health behaviors that will substantially improve their health and well-being. Equally important, submerged anxiety that is almost always present in the company of someone with chronic illness will be brought to the surface and defused. With the clear understanding of the rest of the work force, the adaptation to facilitate the participation of the disabled employee can be made more specific and appropriate. A clear understanding of the limits and abilities of their co-worker will help employees be appropriately helpful and specific to the need at hand. A lack of assistance in a difficult activity may be daunting, but too much doting and inappropriate assistance may become patronizing, offensive, and destructive to morale.

In all of these scenarios, there is an essential component of self-determination that must be mentioned. That critical factor is confidentiality. Any worker with a physical disability is entitled to keep that knowledge to themselves, or restricted to a small group of preselected individuals, as permitted or curtailed by law. Many strategies for accommodating a disability may become more difficult if other employees are not apprised of the reason. Resentment or confusion may arise. Nonetheless, the mandate to the employer to follow the wishes of the concerned employee is paramount, and data privacy laws are clear on the prohibitions against sharing medical information about an employee with her or his co-workers.

This problem is not insurmountable. In some cases the disability may be clearly visible, obviating the need to explicitly verbalize what all can plainly see. In other cases, it may be less prominent and could totally escape a casual inspection. In many cases, an employee may be willing to disclose their true situation to some limited group if it can be plainly demonstrated that to do so will facilitate a more comfortable and accommodating workplace. Other times, they may elect to keep the information more private, as is their right. Whichever the case may be, management is obligated to work with that individual to facilitate their participation, regardless of the decision that is made about disclosure. More often than not, the concerned employee may see the benefits in notifying at least a carefully-chosen group.

Those sites that elect strict compliance with the ADA should have few problems. At least in companies employing fifty or more, the workplace should already have been made "disability-friendly," irrespective of the current presence or absence of employees with disabilities. Of course not all workplaces will elect to comply fully, at least at first, with the entire ADA bill, untested practically or legislatively. Other, smaller establishments may find it financially imprudent to make adaptations until a clear necessity manifests. One thing is clear: over the next decade, all workplaces in the United States will have made significant progress toward being acceptable environments for people with disabilities. This is likely to have numerous subsidiary benefits—not only will the participation of unique and gifted individuals be assured, but community relations will also profit. Clients or customers with disabilities, some of them completely hidden, will feel more welcome. The loved ones, colleagues, and friends of persons with disabilities will understand the nature of the modifications, and likely approve. A positive role model will be held up for the community and may serve to catalyze similar efforts by others.

Apprehension in the face of such possible change is to be expected. What is clear is that the minor alterations necessary to facilitate the participation of persons with disabilities will be trivial in comparison to other relatively recent innovations, like the 40-hour workweek, minimum wage, and OSHA standards for worker safety. It is essential that any such innovation is implemented by the majority of employers relatively simultaneously. Although the net benefits to society of a humane workplace are considerable, shortsighted organizations may see a financial benefit in not complying, especially when their competitors are engaged in making the necessary changes.

I do want to keep the focus clearly on the bigger picture because the alternative to making these reasonable accommodations is far more expensive. The cost of barring from the work force persons who are willing and able to work will be passed on in innumerable ways. Not only will these costs manifest in taxes, but in multitudinous other ways, as other workers who are the family or loved ones of persons with disabilities divert substantial portions of their income to their upkeep, rather than spending on consumer goods and other household needs. The cost of maintaining persons in an institution, even of the crudest and most inhumane "warehouse" type, will never be as inexpensive as independent or semi-independent living. That factor alone, leaving aside the loss of productivity implicit in such an approach, clearly indicates that creating job opportunities for people with disabilities is not only humane, but financially prudent. A key word in all of this is "reasonable" accommodation. No one is expecting employers to become philanthropists or welfare bureaus. The ADA's intention is to encourage a new way to think of the "disabled"—as potential assets, rather than as de facto liabilities.

In the short space of this article I have been able to only crudely sketch out the most surface and basic aspects of adapting the workplace to facilitate participation by people with HIV disease and other disabilities. This piece is not intended to have the answers, or even to pose all the questions. In any area, there are many community-based organizations as well as entities like the Department of Vocational Rehabilitation with substantial experience in these questions. Corporations with success in hiring and retaining employees with disabilities should operate in a mentor capacity to those just beginning. Useful practical knowledge might be as likely to come from those working in ergonomics or human potential as it is from persons working in fields more traditionally associated with disabilities, such as Vocational Rehab. The transition to a more efficient, humane workplace will not come easily. There will undoubtedly be great challenges and setbacks. What is clear is that the ADA heralds a quiet revolution in the workplace. With commitment and vision, workplaces in the United States, Canada, and other jurisdictions will reap the benefits of progress toward a more advanced, humane, and productive society.

Special Policy Considerations for Particular Populations

Religious Institutions

In addition to adoption of relevant policy as outlined earlier in this book, religious institutions should seriously consider adopting a policy statement that spells out their formal response, as a faith community, to HIV and AIDS.

One such statement is the Atlanta Declaration. The Atlanta Declaration was adopted on December 4, 1989 at the Carter Center of Emory University in Atlanta, Georgia. Its signers were participants in a national religious leader's consultation, and represented congregations from the African Methodist Episcopal Church, the American Baptist Churches in the U. S. A., the Church of the Brethren, the Episcopal Church, the Evangelical Lutheran Church in America, the Presbyterian Church USA, the Reformed Church in America, the Reorganized Church of the Latter Day Saints, the Roman Catholic Church, the Southern Baptist Convention, the Unitarian Universalist Association, the United Church of Christ, the United Methodist Church, the Fellowship of Metropolitan Community Churches, numerous Jewish congregations and bodies, and a number of community religious organizations.

The Atlanta Declaration

"We Are Living with AIDS: An Interfaith Call to Hope and Action"

We come together as members of different faiths. Our traditions teach us different ways to embrace God. We represent humanity's wide range of ways to be human. Across our diversity, however, AIDS magnifies the fact that we are also one. AIDS is not only an affliction of individuals or particular groups. AIDS is an affliction of the whole human family.

Our religious vision proclaims that living with AIDS/HIV is a condition in which we must all participate actively. It is a scandal that many people living with AIDS/HIV suffer and grieve in secret. We seek hope amidst the moral and biological tragedies of this epidemic in order to pass on hope for generations to come.

The tragedy of the Human Immunodeficiency Virus epidemic has confronted each of us personally, each of our religious institutions, as well as the whole society with the need for a new understanding of the interconnectedness between physical disease and social responsibility. It calls for creative action among all our institutions—medical, social, economic, political and religious—for the purpose of providing systemic compassionate attention to the epidemic. The religious community in particular is faced with these extended responsibilities:

1. To embody and proclaim hope, life, and healing in the midst of suffering;

2. To assure that all those who are affected by the epidemic will have access to compassion, non-judgmental care, respect, support, and assistance;

3. To generate a prophetic vision of society in which the "general welfare" becomes the abiding obligation of public, private, and voluntary sectors of society;

4. To provide accurate and comprehensive information for the public regarding HIV transmission, related behavior patterns, and means of prevention; and

5. To transform public attitudes and policies so that adequate care and appropriate preventative measures will be available for all people in need.

Fulfilling these responsibilities will require of us new commitments as individuals, as religious bodies, and as a nation.

As Individuals:

Because we are relatives, friends, and neighbors of persons with AIDS/HIV, and are ourselves persons living with AIDS/HIV, we commit ourselves to personal ministries of care for those infected with and those affected by HIV;
Because we are members and leaders of religious institutions, we commit ourselves to the work of insuring that our institutions renew their calling to ministries of health and healing;
Because we are citizens of this nation, we commit ourselves to establishing public policies through which all citizens contribute to the care of persons with AIDS and to the health and well-being of the nation as a whole.

As Religious Bodies:

Because the presence of HIV calls us to mutual cooperation, we commit ourselves to work within interfaith coalitions whenever and wherever feasible;
Because the needs in local communities are so great, we commit ourselves to promote and support local interfaith coalitions for education, provision of care, community service, public policy, and specialized training for religious professionals and laity in care and counseling;
Because religious professionals, faith communities, and the public need accurate and comprehensive education, we commit ourselves to provide accurate and complete infor-

mation about the transmission and prevention of AIDS/HIV disease; and we commit ourselves to produce and promote culturally and linguistically appropriate HIV-related educational materials—audio, video, and printed—in a context that promotes individual self-esteem, teaches the fundamental goodness of human sexuality, and supports the integrity of responsible, caring intimate relationships.

As Citizens:

Because the President's Commission on the HIV Epidemic has issued a comprehensive, balanced and informed report based upon the expertise of hundreds of America's best scientists, as well as the testimony of many other professionals and persons living with AIDS/HIV, we call for immediate implementation of its recommendations;

Because HIV is a threat to the life and health of all people in the nation, we call upon the President to demonstrate moral and political leadership in assuring adequate care for all who are afflicted and responsible federal action including the ends of:

- *protection against HIV-related discrimination in all forms,*
- *expanding of drug treatment programs to include all who choose them,*
- *for all HIV infected persons:*

    a. elimination of mandatory segregation and isolation in prisons as well as provision of humane and professional medical care,

    b. assuring decent, appropriate, and affordable housing for the homeless,

    c. establishing comprehensive, affordable, and accessible medical care,

- *insuring expeditious approval by the Food and Drug Administration of AIDS/HIV treatments, expeditious experimental drug trials, easier access to promising AIDS/HIV treatments, and wider availability of new drugs to persons with AIDS/HIV,*
- *expanding the availability of residential healthcare facilities, hospices, and affordable home care for persons with AIDS/HIV,*
- *encouraging the prudent use of voluntary HIV antibody testing with the strictest of safeguards whether anonymous or confidential as used for medical evaluation, epidemiological, or prevention modalities,*
- *advocating for the continuation of comprehensive prevention and risk-reduction programs for drug users including the distribution of AIDS prevention information and materials, including bleach for the sterilization of hypodermic needles,*
- *allowing otherwise eligible foreign nationals, without regard to their HIV status, access to visitation and/or citizenship in the United States.*

As A People Dedicated to a Future of Hope:

Because the barriers among us based on religion, race, class, gender, and sexual orientation which continue to generate fear, persecution, and violence are intensified by the HIV pandemic, we call upon all sectors of our society, particularly our faith communities, to adopt as the highest priority the elimination of racism, classism, sexism, and homophobia;

Because America's businesses and industries must address the presence of AIDS, we call upon its leaders to endorse and implement the "Ten Principles for the Workplace" and we commit our institutions to adopting these principles;

Because the presence of AIDS/HIV creates special needs among different groups of people, we call for all sectors of society to contribute to support for infected infants and children in need of foster care or adoption services, to support HIV-infected women who suffer discrimination from many sources, for families who need community care;

Because economic disparity and the poverty it engenders is a major contributing factor in the AIDS epidemic, and a barrier to prevention and treatment, we call upon all sectors of society to seek ways of eliminating poverty in a commitment to a future of hope and security.

Finally, **we commit** ourselves to calling for accountability on the part of this nation's public officials and corporate leaders. It is a time for envisioning a new society, one committed to the health and welfare of all its people, and united in anticipation for that time when we will know that to respond to today's crisis is our only hope for tomorrow.

Special Policy Considerations for Particular Populations

School/Educational Settings

National Recommendations

The Sex Information and Education Council of the U. S. (SIECUS) recently concluded an extensive survey of all state education agencies about HIV programming, and a content analysis for thirty-four state curricula/guidelines. In the process, *Future Directions: HIV/AIDS Education in the Schools* (1992) provides some important guidance for schools wishing to develop comprehensive educational and policy responses for HIV/AIDS. For a complete copy of *Future Directions: HIV/AIDS Education in the Nation's Schools,* write to: SIECUS, 130 West 42nd Street, Suite 2500, New York, NY 10036. Their phone number is (212) 819-9770.

A state-by-state review of school-based HIV efforts is impossible in the present context, but *Future Directions* offers a series of concrete recommendations for schools and school-based programs, in addition to highlighting several model efforts.

In its recommendations, *Future Directions* proposes that:

• *All states support HIV/AIDS education by enacting legislation that requires a developmentally-appropriate, scoped, and sequenced HIV/AIDS education for all grades K–12.*

• *All states adopt policies that require HIV/AIDS education as part of comprehensive health education and provide direction on program implementation and evaluation, including curriculum selection and recommendations, program monitoring, and teacher preparation.*

• *State HIV/AIDS education advisory committees be formed by state education agencies to assist in the design and implementation of programs.*

• *State advisory committees include representatives from both the state education agency and state health department, medical personnel, parents, teachers, students, a school curriculum specialist, and affected communities.*

• *Efforts be made to maintain consistent composition and membership of state HIV/AIDS advisory committees.*

• *Local advisory committees be formed at the local school district level to assist in program evaluation and technical assistance.*

• *All states implement HIV/AIDS education programs at the local level. All states establish local advisory committees within school districts.*

• *The primary function of the state HIV/AIDS education advisory committee* would be to develop or review and select the K–12 HIV/AIDS education curriculum and guidelines for statewide distribution.

- HIV/AIDS education be integrated within comprehensive health education programs as well as implemented as an important interdisciplinary subject of instruction in other domains.

- The state education agency or state board of education assist all teachers responsible for HIV/AIDS education by providing on-going technical assistance; annual inservice training should be required of all teachers.

- All teachers responsible for HIV/AIDS education instruction be certified in health education and certified, by special training, in HIV/AIDS education.

- All state HIV/AIDS education programs include provisions for state monitoring to ensure and mandate enforcement at the local level and provisions for the development and implementation of evaluation criteria to determine program effectiveness.

- Parents be encouraged to actively participate in all stages of program development and implementation and retain the option of excusing their children from all or part of the HIV/AIDS education program.

- The HIV/AIDS education curriculum be comprehensive and thorough and be adequately integrated within the general health education curriculum.

- The HIV/AIDS education curriculum provides a good developmental framework, adequately sequenced with a sufficient primary grade foundation.

- All state HIV/AIDS education programs cover the three learning domains: cognitive and informational, affective and values clarification, and skills-building.

- The HIV/AIDS education curriculum provides an accurate information base about HIV/AIDS epidemiology, transmission and prevention, on the relative risks of various sexual behaviors, and on safer sex behaviors; the HIV/AIDS education curriculum should provide learning opportunities to clarify values and beliefs about HIV/AIDS and sexuality.

- HIV/AIDS education curriculum provides a thorough skills-based approach to HIV/AIDS education and includes developmentally-appropriate learning opportunities to provide practice and simulation of HIV-prevention behaviors, including risk evaluation, assertiveness, decision making, problem solving, communication, condom use, negotiation, and refusal skills.

- The HIV/AIDS education program encourages sexual abstinence, drug abstinence, and consistent condom use, and provides "balanced messages" about sexual abstinence and safer sex practices.

- The HIV/AIDS education curriculum provides practical information on condom use: how to properly use condoms, dispose of them, and where to buy them.

Special Policy Considerations for Particular Populations

- *The HIV/AIDS curriculum provides information on low-risk, noncoital sexual behaviors, with an emphasis on sexual risk assessment and reduction.*

- *The HIV/AIDS education curriculum accurately defines sexual orientation, and provides learning opportunities to address issues of sexual orientation.*

- *The HIV/AIDS education curriculum emphasizes that persons with HIV and/or AIDS need the support of family and friends and acknowledge that they can lead satisfying and productive lives as active participants in society.*

Using these recommendations as a guide, the SIECUS report graded only three states as "exemplary" on a scorecard of state HIV curricula/guidelines.

The **Massachusetts** Department of Education has adopted a state policy recommending HIV/AIDS education at every grade level, and encouraging that it be integrated into a comprehensive health education program with a special interdisciplinary emphasis. This policy stresses a skills-building approach with condom availability at the secondary level.

The state guideline is a thorough and useful framework for integration within health education. It is developmentally appropriate with an adequate placement of topics sequenced K–12.

This guideline represents an adequate skills-building approach designed to help young people to exercise responsibility and incorporate preventive behaviors regarding sexual relationships. It sufficiently covers the cognitive, affective, and skills-building learning domains, providing information and learning opportunities for each, and emphasizing the ability to discriminate between healthy and harmful sexual behaviors. Topic areas include the history, nature, and incidence of HIV infection, transmission, and prevention; compassion for persons with HIV and/or AIDS; and self-esteem.

Highlights of the **Massachusetts** program include an excellent and balanced approach to sexual/drug abstinence and condom use information; sexual risk assessment with an emphasis on low-risk, noncoital behaviors; respect for persons of different cultures; affirmation of one's sexual orientation with respect for the sexual orientation of others; and compassion for persons with HIV and/or AIDS. It provides an accurate and positive approach to sexuality as a natural and healthy part of human life, presenting information and skills-building opportunities within the context of affirmative messages about dating and sexual relationships.

The inadequacies of the **Massachusetts** program include the absence of practical information about condom use, some gaps in learning opportunities for skills-building (such as problem solving and sexual negotiation), and its failure to mention that HIV was transmitted via blood transfusions prior to 1985.

New Jersey, which has a state policy requiring HIV/AIDS education, utilizes a "stand alone" comprehensive HIV/AIDS curriculum, developmentally appropriate with an appropriate placement of topics sequenced K–12. This curriculum represents a thorough skills-building approach designed to help young people exercise responsibility and incorporate prevention behaviors regarding sexual relationships. It sufficiently covers the three learning domains, providing thorough information and learning opportunities for each.

Curriculum topic areas include the history, nature, and incidence of HIV infection, transmission, and prevention; safer sex; HIV antibody testing; individual risk-taking behaviors; the range of sexual risk behaviors; compassion for persons with HIV and/or AIDS; and self-esteem.

Highlights of the **New Jersey** program include a balanced approach to abstinence and condom use information; abstinence from sexual behaviors and drugs, long-term sexual fidelity within or prior to marriage, and condom use are approached with equal importance and thoroughness; extensive safer sex information with emphasis on condom use, including the practical issues of using, disposing, and purchasing condoms; sexual risk assessment with emphasis on low-risk, noncoital behaviors and on the ability to discriminate between healthy and harmful sexual behaviors; and a thorough skills-building approach that includes learning opportunities for evaluating risky behaviors, assertiveness, decision making, communicating, negotiating about sexual decisions, sexual limit-setting, and resisting negative peer pressure.

The curriculum represents an excellent integration of HIV/AIDS education within the sexually-transmitted diseases component of health education, including information on medical treatment for persons with HIV and/or AIDS. It provides an accurate and positive approach to sexuality issues and to sexual orientation, and focuses on respect for people of different sexual values and orientation.

The only inadequacy of the **New Jersey** curriculum was the inclusion of an ARC vs. AIDS diagnosis, which is not in keeping with current diagnostic classifications of HIV disease.

South Carolina state law requires HIV/AIDS education. Material reviewed included extensive curriculum guidelines with additional resource material.

The state's curriculum guidelines are developmentally-appropriate, with an appropriate placement of topics sequenced K–12, representing a thorough skills-building approach that will help young people to exercise responsibility and incorporate prevention behaviors regarding sexual relationships. Guidelines sufficiently cover the three learning domains, providing thorough information and learning opportunities for each.

Areas thoroughly covered include the history, incidence, and nature of HIV/AIDS infection, transmission (including acupuncture needle use), and prevention; safer sex; HIV testing; individual risk-taking behaviors; the range of sexually risky behaviors; compassion for persons with HIV and/or AIDS; and self-esteem.

Highlights of the **South Carolina** curriculum include a balanced approach to condom use and abstinence (abstinence from sexual behaviors and drugs, long-term monogamous relationships, and condom use are approached with equal importance and thoroughness); extensive safer sex information with emphasis on condom use, including the practical issues of using, disposing, and purchasing condoms; sexual risk assessment with emphasis on low-risk, noncoital behaviors and on the ability to discriminate between healthy and harmful sexual behaviors; and thorough skills-building approach that includes learning opportunities for evaluating risky behaviors, assertiveness, decision making, communicating, negotiating about sexual decisions, sexual limit-setting, resisting negative peer pressure, and consistently practicing preventive behaviors.

The **South Carolina** guidelines represent an excellent integration of HIV/AIDS education within the sexually-transmitted diseases component of health education, including information on medical treatment for persons with HIV and/or AIDS. It provides an

Special Policy Considerations for Particular Populations

accurate and positive approach to sexuality issues and to sexual orientation, and focuses on respect for people of different sexual values and orientation. The guidelines include an excellent series of learning opportunities, with the objective of increasing cultural sensitivity in teaching HIV/AIDS prevention.

The only inadequacy of the curriculum guidelines is the discussion of high-risk persons (homosexuals and IV drug users), encouraging the idea that only certain groups of people can become infected.

Minnesota

Minnesota State Statute 121.203 (1988) directs the Commissioner of Education, in consultation with the Commissioner of Health, to "assist districts in developing and implementing a program to prevent and reduce the risk of acquired immune deficiency syndrome."

As the statewide system for professional and technical assistance to Minnesota schools, the Minnesota Department of Education (MDE) is assisting in preventing the spread of HIV through the implementation of comprehensive HIV prevention programs in all school districts. The department is working to support an infrastructure that:

1. Promotes strategies for positive behavior formation and behavior change which will reduce risk of HIV transmission among learners; and

2. Contributes to a community climate which facilitates positive and diversified responses to the reality of HIV infection.

To that end, MDE has developed a number of resources which will prove useful to school districts as they approach the task of comprehensive HIV/AIDS policy development. Foremost among these are:

• School District AIDS Policy Development: Part I: Federal and State Guidelines, *and*

• School District AIDS Policy Development: Part II: Resources.

These resources can be obtained by contacting the address or phone number below.

Staff at the AIDS Prevention and Risk Reduction Unit can also aid school districts in developing plans and policies related to HIV. Feel free to contact them for consultation.

> AIDS Prevention and Risk Reduction Unit
> Learner Support Systems
> Division of Development and Partnership
> Minnesota Department of Education
> 550 Cedar Street
> St. Paul, MN 55101
> (612) 296-5825

Women's Programs

Cindy Zegers, M.A.

Cindy Zegers has worked in a variety of roles in AIDS for over six years. She is a founder of the WOMAN Network and producer of the nationally-distributed *AIDS and Addiction,* a videotape about chemical dependency, recovery, and HIV.

As a member of the Women and Children of Minnesota AIDS/HIV Network, a chemical dependency practitioner, a caregiver of people living with HIV/AIDS, and a health educator, my work for the past six years has focused primarily on women. Of those women, 80% have children and/or partners and other family members who are significantly impacted by their illness. The demands on women—as workers, as mothers and partners, as people who care for others and who are struggling to stay strong for others as well as themselves—are intense.

The historic sexism in our culture has served to disempower women, regardless of their class, race, or professional status. This point cannot be overstressed. In the case of HIV, collective response to the epidemic has focused largely on men—women with HIV have yet to receive their due in terms of care and services. Twelve years into the epidemic, women constitute the fastest growing subgroup of people newly diagnosed with HIV. Yet care, treatment, social services, housing, and childcare for women (and their children) are sorely lacking.

The problems facing women and children with HIV are complex. Today, 80% of HIV-infected women are women of color, who are often economically disadvantaged. Basic needs such as food, clothing, shelter, and the well-being of children may be more pressing than the necessity to address the possibility of chronic disease.

As a result, those developing HIV policy and education in agencies serving women should keep the following considerations in mind:

* *Women do not often perceive themselves to be at risk for HIV infection.*
* *Pervasive sexism and specific cultural norms may sabotage women's efforts to implement safer sex behaviors that will reduce the risk of HIV infection.*
* *Many women, especially single mothers, live with the reality of insufficient access to comprehensive medical insurance and good medical care.*
* *Especially in recent years, women who are drug users may avoid seeking*

Special Policy Considerations for Particular Populations

care for fear that children will be removed from the household.

- *Drug treatment services that will accommodate childcare needs for women with children are scarce.*
- *Women with HIV who become pregnant sometimes fear involuntary abortion and/or sterilization. Counseling about pregnancy and abortion needs to be value-neutral, covering thoroughly the available information, risks, resources, and options.*
- *Care providers may not be sensitive to the diversity of cultural norms regarding sexuality and pregnancy, especially for women with HIV.*
- *Since the beginning of the epidemic, women have had a great deal of difficulty accessing clinical trials of new, experimental, and possibly health-enhancing drugs to treat HIV disease.*
- *Women with HIV often report being unable to find child care so that they can attend to HIV-related needs, such as clinic visits or support group participation.*
- *Families may face the very real possibility that older children will be orphaned if one or both parents dies of AIDS.*
- *Women with HIV, especially if they have children, often have a hard time locating reasonable housing that is responsive to HIV-related needs.*
- *Children in families where HIV is present may encounter prejudicial stigma in schools and among peers.*
- *Children of HIV-infected parents often have few resources for emotional support outside the family.*
- *And of course, all women daily survive the realities of rape and violence. Living with HIV on top of those dangers can be overwhelming.*

Counseling should be supportive, compassionate, and empowering if individuals are to make wise decisions about what is best for them and their families. Providers of services need to be especially aware of services that can meet the particular, gender-specific needs of women with HIV and women who want to reduce their risk of HIV infection.

Section Four:
SUPPORT MATERIALS

Resource Sheet: About HIV and AIDS

Most Americans are acquainted with the general facts about the Human Immunodeficiency Virus (HIV) and Acquired Immune Deficiency Syndrome (AIDS). But a number of common perceptions, arising in great part from unreliable reporting, give rise to confusion and doubt. Those beliefs certainly include the following ideas—the kinds of assertions one hears in the barber shop, at the grocery store, in everyday talk.

They can't say anything for sure because the facts keep changing. It is certainly true that some of what is known about HIV/AIDS is changing, but it is equally untrue that nothing can be asserted with absolute confidence. The fact of changing information is only logical: massive research about HIV and AIDS is now underway, and it will continually augment our collective understanding. But what is being learned only augments our basic knowledge. There is a body of facts about HIV/AIDS that is as true now as it was ten years ago, and will be true in the future. We can count on it.

They're not telling us the whole truth about this disease. No other disease in recent memory has come under such massive public scrutiny. In fact, researchers in the area sometimes complain of having to do their work under such intense review. It is extremely doubtful that anyone—scientists, public officials, activists—is withholding critical data about HIV/AIDS. If anything, sometimes *too* much is reported: a scientific study that has not been properly validated, a purported breakthrough that is wildly overstated.

This disease is being ruled by special interest groups. There are, to be sure, groups with a "special interest" in this epidemic. Gay men, for example, have felt the devastation of its impact that few heterosexuals can even imagine. The medical community is profoundly impacted. Some communities are reeling under the damage caused by HIV and AIDS. But those groups or communities do not *control* the HIV/AIDS agenda. It's too widespread, with too many implications, to fall under anybody's exclusive domain. Everyone has a stake in the epidemic, and *everyone* has a position to forward. In reasoned political and social debate, all those voices can be heard.

It's too complicated—only the scientists understand this thing. HIV/AIDS is doubtless one of the most complex illnesses we've faced. And in the very beginning most people were entirely baffled. But it is not too complicated for nearly everyone, even small children, to understand. It's complexity has to do with its detailed effects on the human organism, not its basics. And it should be noted that thousands of people living with HIV and AIDS have been educating themselves about the disease for years; their understanding rivals that of many medical personnel. The basics are within nearly everyone's grasp, and might be most easily understood if placed in historical context.

In 1981 doctors on the two coasts of the United States began reporting cases of highly unusual infection and disease among otherwise healthy young men. Two particular features of those reported cases gave a small group of doctors cause for concern. First, they were seeing kinds of infections or diseases rarely seen among that age group or population

335

before. Second, the *severity* of those diseases or infections was sometimes astonishing. In fact, in the beginning, patients were sometimes dying before the physician even had a chance to engage in comprehensive study or diagnosis.

Compounding the confusion was the fact that those early cases were nearly all among gay men or intravenous drug users. Researchers struggled to determine the cause of this new cluster of diseases and understand more fully its effects.

When reported cases began to include hemophiliacs (who must use blood products to stay healthy) and transfusion recipients, the connection became increasingly obvious. It seemed that blood and other bodily fluids with a high white blood cell count were responsible for transmission of this new disease. It also became clear that somehow the immune systems of patients had been dangerously compromised; that people were getting sick and dying of *secondary diseases and infections* that resulted from a *primary collapse* of the body's natural defenses.

It appeared that all of the people who were getting sick with this disease were infected with a virus that acted directly on the body's immune system, rendering it sometimes helpless against common and uncommon diseases and infections. That virus was isolated, and named. It was HIV. At the same time a name for the disease itself came into consistent usage. It was AIDS.

The name itself reveals a lot about the disease. It is "Acquired" because people "get it" by engaging in specific behaviors with HIV-infected persons; it doesn't "just happen," and it is not spread through casual contact. It is "Immunodeficiency" because it depletes the strength of the body's immunity. And it is "Syndrome" because it is not just one sign or symptom; instead, it manifests itself as a number of secondary symptoms, diseases, and infections that result from immunosuppression.

Finally, researchers began to note that some people with AIDS had probably been carrying HIV for a long time (sometimes years) before they got sick, while others got sick comparatively soon (six months or less) after infection with HIV had presumably occurred. During the time that patients had been *infected* but free of overt symptoms, they had also been *infectious,* capable of passing HIV to others through specific behaviors. This realization was disturbing and frightening, since it meant that people could otherwise look and feel healthy and still transmit the virus. It also raised the question, which has not yet been fully answered, of how many of those who were infected, but asymptomatic, would go on to develop AIDS or AIDS-related illnesses over the course of time.

The general public is accustomed to thinking strictly in terms of AIDS itself as the sole cause for concern, but this last fact casts a broader perspective. What actually happens is something like this: People acquire the virus, HIV, through very specific sexual and blood-sharing behaviors. (At that point the person is termed "HIV+," "HIV seropositive," or "HIV-infected." The terms all mean the same thing.) But the body does not display external signs of that infection right away. Instead, HIV "hides out," waiting sometimes for many years to take direct action against the immune system. At some point, probably because of the presence of one or more co-factors, the virus begins attacking key elements of the immune system. The fact that the body has been generating an antibody that attempts to ward off HIV is insufficient by itself because that antibody is ultimately ineffective against HIV. The term "co-factors" indicates something else that has to take place before the virus is effectively "activated." Co-factors are not the same as behaviors that led to infection in the first place. For example, poor nutrition or high levels of chemical use may be common co-factors that explain why one person harboring a cold virus gets sick, while another doesn't. HIV may act in the same way. Typical advice to people newly-tested HIV+ is to reduce stress, decrease or eliminate chemical or alcohol use, get plenty of rest, and improve diet and exercise regimens. All of those things may be significant co-factors explaining why some HIV seropositive persons get sick, and others seem to remain healthy for a very long time. The research, however, is not yet all in; scientists continue to learn more about what may "trigger" viral activity in the case of HIV.

Because immunity is depleted, people may begin getting sick with a number of "opportunistic" infections ("opportunistic" indicates that they are infections that "seize the opportunity" of weakened immunity in order to take hold). Common opportunistic infections associated with HIV-related illness include Pneumocystis Carinii pneumonia (or PCP, not to be confused with the drug phencyclidine), a rare form of parasitic pneumonia that leaves the patient with a persistent fever, dry cough, and shortness of breath; and Kaposi's Sarcoma (or KS), a rare form of cancer that is usually signaled by a purplish skin rash with lesions. Other infections include:

- *Candidiasis (commonly known as thrush), a fungal infection in the mouth or esophagus;*
- *Cryptosporidiosis, an infection caused by a parasite that lodges in the intestines, causing severe diarrhea;*
- *Cytomegalovirus (CMV), a virus that causes mild to severe flu-like symptoms;*
- *herpes zoster (commonly known as shingles), which are small and painful blisters on the skin that follow nerve pathways;*
- *lymphadenopathy, an enlargement of the lymph nodes in the neck or groin; and*
- *Toxoplasmosis, a parasitic infection that generates fevers and other symptoms.*

When people get one or more of the preceding symptoms, or other symptoms related to HIV, does that mean they have moved from being HIV+ to having AIDS? Not necessarily. In order to have an *epidemiological* diagnosis of AIDS itself, the individual must evidence a number of *particular infections or cancers,* according to guidelines established by the Centers for Disease Control. And the diagnostic guidelines for AIDS have, in fact, changed several times since the beginning of the epidemic, and are likely to change again in the near future. Women with AIDS, for example, have experienced a number of gynecological complications related to HIV immunosuppression that are not yet included in the official diagnostic criteria for AIDS. The guidelines, therefore, are imperfect.

Between the point when people are first infected with HIV and the point when they meet the case definition required for a diagnosis of AIDS, there is a wide range of clinical possibilities. Since there are myriad opportunistic infections—some relatively "mild" and others comparatively severe—and since individuals with HIV infection could be experiencing any possible combination of those infections, it would be most accurate to refer to a "spectrum of infection" when talking about how people with HIV do and do not get sick. In other words, if asymptomatic HIV seropositivity were placed at one end of a continuum and "has AIDS and is currently extremely ill" were placed at the other end, people with HIV infection could fall anywhere along the continuum. The "spectrum of infection" reveals that AIDS is not an "either/or" disease, but rather a range of conditions related to HIV infection. It is impossible in any individual case to predict to what degree, if at all, people with asymptomatic HIV infection will "progress" along the spectrum of infection, or what specific opportunistic infections, if any, they will experience.

One more point about HIV/AIDS and how it works needs to be made to conclude this section. A medical diagnosis of AIDS does not necessarily tell us about the patient's present condition or physical well-being. People have been diagnosed with cancer, for example, and then experienced long periods of remission during which they felt and functioned normally.

HIV/AIDS can work in the same way. A person may be diagnosed with AIDS because of a bout with Pneumocystis Carinii pneumonia, for example, and upon recovery feel otherwise fine and healthy for months or even years afterwards, but the diagnosis of AIDS still remains. When people meet people with AIDS for the first time, they may expect to see someone who appears obviously sickly. The point is, that may be the case, and it may *not*. The same holds true for persons who have developed symptoms related to HIV infection, but who do not have a clinical diagnosis of AIDS—we may expect that because "they don't really have AIDS," they would not be terribly sick. In fact they may be quite ill, but simply haven't developed the particular symptoms or infections required for a clinical diagnosis of AIDS. Again, there is a range of conditions associated with HIV infection.

Resource Sheet: Evaluating AIDS Data and Media Reporting

How does one know when reading texts about HIV and AIDS whether the information is reliable and accurate? That is a difficult question to answer, because even leading researchers—whose names alone *should* give a document credibility—have made spurious claims, and much information is couched in complex scientific (e.g., inaccessible) or unnecessarily vague language.

There are, however, a few questions that can be asked about any piece of data, reporting, or text that might help evaluate its credibility.

1. What is the source? Where is it printed, and by whom is it written? Is the source generally reliable on such matters?

2. What implications have been drawn from the data, and are those implications valid? For example, some writers may contend that we have something to fear from casual contact, since HIV has been isolated in saliva. But the amount contained in saliva is simply insufficient for transmission. Merely reporting that saliva contains HIV, therefore, is generally irresponsible.

3. When research or speculation is presented, has it been replicated elsewhere? Keep in mind that there are currently thousands of experiments now underway on HIV and that, given the sheer numbers, it is always possible for any one experiment to yield bizarre results. But the scientific method generally says that an experiment is not valid unless it is replicated exactly—preferably many times—by others.

4. What political viewpoint, if any, underlies the presentation? How does that viewpoint shape the selection of information to be presented, to be highlighted, to be glossed over, or to be ignored?

5. Are statistics employed in a manner that conforms to accepted techniques? Keep in mind that there are many ways to "lie" with statistics.

6. What date of publication appears on the material? The facts in some early reports about AIDS, for example, have been superseded by more accurate reporting; older data cannot be said to remain valid (on the other hand, it still may be).

7. How is the data placed in an overall presentation of information? For example, epidemiological reporting on HIV infection among gay men, when placed in the context of a more subjective account of "common homosexual behavior, such as fisting or licking feces," will give the data an entirely different spin.

8. How does the text characterize human sexuality and the varieties of human sexual behavior and experience? What values are attached to those characterizations? Do they condemn sexuality or celebrate it?

9. To what ideology of addiction does the material subscribe? What picture does it paint of drug-taking, addicts, and the process of recovery from addiction?

10. What images of various identities are projected by the text? How does it portray gay and bisexual men and women, people of color, and other HIV high-impact communities? Does the material make the reader afraid of communities of people, or the HIV pathogen?

11. How does the reporting represent the experience of people living with HIV or AIDS? Does it support the common, but incorrect assumption that HIV = AIDS = Death, or does it underscore the fullness and diversity of individual experience?

12. One way to evaluate material is to examine the impressions it leaves in the reader's mind. If you were to read something, put it aside, and write down the first five words that sprang to mind from your reading, what would those words be? Are they the words—the images—you want conveyed?

13. Finally, if you are still unsure, to whom will you turn—your local AIDSline, the Centers for Disease Control, etc.—for "the real scoop?" Why?

Resource Sheet: How HIV Is Transmitted

Despite public confusion, there is solid, reliable information about how HIV is transmitted and how it's not. But mass media reporting on transmission hasn't always put the facts of transmission into proper perspective. In some instances it has detailed extremely rare cases as if they were commonplace. Understanding a few basic principles of transmission will help balance the picture.

1. HIV is a very fragile virus. Once outside of the human body, it does not live long at all, generally no more than several minutes. While inside the body the virus can be very powerful; once it's exposed to the environment it is essentially deactivated in a very short period of time. This is not to indicate that if one should encounter spilled blood, one should estimate the amount of time it has been there before touching it. Universal precautions should always be observed (see the Resource Sheet on "Infection Control"). It is to say, however, that the fragility of the virus makes it hard to acquire.

2. HIV has to effectively "get out of" one body and "get into" another body before the necessary preconditions for transmission are met. Fortunately, that is somewhat difficult to accomplish for two reasons. First, one's intact skin is a perfect barrier, and even if HIV-infected blood were to come into direct contact with unbroken skin, it could not pass through into the body and infect the individual. Secondly, HIV is not an airborne virus. It is not passed by coughing, sneezing, or breathing the same air as an HIV-infected person.

3. Despite the fact that common advice has warned people against sharing "bodily fluids," the reality is that there are only a few specific bodily fluids that have been implicated in HIV transmission. They are blood, semen, vaginal secretions (meaning the lubrication inside a woman's vagina, and not menstrual blood, which would be included under "blood"), and to a much lesser degree, breast milk. The virus has been detected in body fluids such as saliva, but the amount of HIV therein is simply not sufficient for transmission.

HIV is not easy to acquire. Transmission requires certain specific behaviors or actions. While rare, almost "freakish" incidents of transmission could certainly occur, one need not worry about such cases. This is not to diminish, by any means, the tragic experience of those few people who were infected by such "freakish" means. Their ordeal is indeed heartbreaking, as it often is for every person struggling with AIDS. It is only to suggest that there is a reasonable hierarchy of risk.

So when some less accurate reporting implies that one could get infected by, for example, shaking hands with an infected person or even kissing, it fails to make clear how extraordinary such events would be. Such reports are grossly misleading. Unfortunately, some people have taken this information and become worried about casual contact when they really need to pay attention to other behaviors known to account for HIV transmission.

In short, HIV is not spread by casual contact of any kind: touching, shaking hands, kissing (since kissing by itself is extremely unlikely to involve an exchange of blood, semen, or vaginal secretions), and other contact. Nor is it spread by coughing or sneezing, or sharing combs, eating utensils, towels, or soap. Uninfected people can safely use the same showers, bathtubs, and toilets as infected persons. And there never has been any danger from mosquitoes or other insects or animals. Even transfusions, which were responsible for a number of early cases of infection, are now safe because blood available for donation in the United States has been screened for the presence of HIV since April, 1985.

What is *not* safe, and what has been implicated in nearly every single reported case of AIDS, is a small set of specific sexual and blood-sharing behaviors. They include:

1. Anal intercourse,

2. Vaginal intercourse,

3. Oral sex (The act of swallowing infected semen, blood, or vaginal secretions is not what transmits HIV; enzymes in the stomach kill the virus. One would have to have an opening of some kind in the mouth in order for HIV to "get inside" and potentially infect.),

4. Pregnancy, from HIV+ mother to baby (There have been several documented cases of HIV transmission linked to breast milk, but there have been a number of cases of HIV-infected mothers breastfeeding their babies without infection taking place. This is an area that requires more study. In the meantime, HIV+ mothers are advised not to breastfeed.), and

5. Needle-sharing and the sharing of other drug injection equipment. (It is certainly possible, of course, that sharing needles for other purposes could transmit HIV. Blood-sharing rituals, such as blood brother/sister pacts, or the amateur use of unsterilized needles for tattooing or ear piercing, could result in infection. No such cases have been documented to date, however.)

The degree to which the preceding behaviors have been implicated in HIV transmission allows us to assert that if we could alter the sexual and injection equipment sharing behavior of everyone in the United States so that behaviors were within known risk reduction guidelines, transmission of HIV in the United States would virtually stop. There would continue to be, of course, rare and exceptional cases, but they would not negate this central thesis.

Resource Sheet: Safer Sex and Risk Reduction

To prevent HIV infection, individuals must choose among a range of specific strategies, each of which presents some difficulty. Since there is no danger of HIV infection from casual contact, we will address those behaviors—sex and drug use—that are known to be risk factors for HIV acquisition.

First, individuals can choose not to have oral, vaginal, or anal sex. As a strategy this is often recommended, but it has its shortcomings. If one has already had unprotected intercourse, for example, she or he may already be HIV infected. And many tend to hear the recommendation of abstinence as a short-term commitment; in the context of HIV prevention, abstinence as a strategy means that one will not have oral, vaginal, or anal sex with anyone *until a successful vaccine is made available,* which may be many years away. For many people such a commitment is understandably impossible to make. It is critical, especially when talking to adolescents, who tend to view time in spans of weeks and months rather than years and decades, to be clear about the meaning of abstinence as a risk reduction strategy for HIV infection.

Second, individuals can enter into a monogamous relationship and avoid sex with anyone other than their primary partner. For many people, this strategy will work quite well. But again, it needs to be clarified. Monogamy as a risk-reduction strategy for the prevention of HIV infection implies two things:

A. Neither partner has had unprotected sex or shared drug injection equipment with anyone before. The oft-heard statement contending that "every time you have sex with someone you're also having sex with everyone they've had sex with, and so on" is absolutely true.

B. The relationship will last, and remain monogamous until a successful vaccine is developed. As an ideal, this is certainly sincere; no one enters into a committed relationship thinking it will only last a short duration. Despite best intentions, however, relationships do end, and marriages end up in divorce. Many people in our society tend to practice what is termed "serial monogamy," that is, they are faithful to their current partners even though they may have a number of partners over their lifetime. Serial monogamy is not the same as strict monogamy when it comes to HIV prevention.

Third, if individuals choose to be sexually active they can reduce their risk of HIV infection by practicing safer sex. Safer sex indicates two things:

1. Sexual activity, such as fondling or mutual masturbation, that does not involve the exchange of blood, semen, or vaginal secretions; or

2. The correct use of a latex condom or other effective barrier every time one has intercourse.

343

Condoms are not foolproof. They do not eliminate risk, but they can help reduce it significantly. The key to effectiveness is proper use, and use every time one has intercourse. For some people, such consistency is difficult. For many, condoms seem awkward, embarrassing, or uncomfortable. Even the thought of having to buy them in a small town pharmacy, where one knows the druggist, can be enough to deter their use. But for those people, and there are many, unable or unwilling to adhere to abstinence or strict monogamy, safer sex is the most effective tool available against HIV infection.

Fourth, individuals can avoid injectable drugs, or, at the very least, avoid sharing drug injection equipment. It may appear on the surface hypocritical to even mention a strategy that sounds like "safe injectable drug use," and can put the drug/alcohol abuse educator in an uncomfortable position. Nevertheless, there are people injecting heroin, cocaine, methedrine, and other drugs who cannot or will not, for the moment, discontinue use. For them our best hope is to keep them free of life-threatening diseases such as AIDS so that they might live to someday seek help or treatment.

Fifth, and finally, individuals can avoid mixing any drug or alcohol use with sexual activity. Even armed with a good "plan" for HIV risk reduction, it has been noted that chemical use impairs judgment and diminishes one's capacity to adhere to prearranged commitments.

There are a few strategies, some commonly presented, that simply don't work to prevent HIV infection:

A. Having sex only with "people I know" or "people from good backgrounds." The truth is that anyone who has engaged in certain behaviors with an HIV-infected person can, themselves, become HIV-infected. Behaviorally, the HIV is a democratic virus.

B. Asking people to disclose their sexual or drug-taking history. As a strategy this only encourages people to withhold the truth and is, at the least, extremely uncomfortable or embarrassing for most. In addition, it leads to the presumption that someone who has had multiple sexual partners is infected, and someone who hasn't is not. Only the HIV antibody test can determine with any accuracy an individual's HIV status.

C. Getting the HIV antibody test. There are many reasons one might rationally consider getting tested, but it's important to note that getting the test, by itself, does nothing to prevent HIV infection. The test is a diagnostic instrument, not a risk-prevention strategy.

Making choices among the available options is a very personal responsibility. For some, abstinence will prove to be the only viable alternative. Others may choose to have intercourse, but use condoms. The only way individuals can make a reasonable decision is by weighing *all the available facts* and measuring them against their own values, beliefs, and traditions.

Resource Sheet: HIV Antibody Testing

The HIV Antibody Test

When health officials speak of the HIV antibody test, they are generally referring to two specific test procedures which determine the presence or absence of the HIV antibody. The first is the EIA, or the Enzyme-linked Immunosorbent Assay (also referred to as "ELISA"). The second is the Western Blot, which is more exacting and expensive than the EIA. The Western Blot is generally used to confirm a positive EIA test result. The tests require only that a healthcare professional draw a small sample of blood from the patient.

The HIV antibody test is often referred to as "the AIDS test," especially among the general public. Providers are strongly encouraged to refer to the test as "the HIV antibody test" with clients. Too many people have formed dangerously inaccurate impressions of what the test is and does; correct terminology is critical to good education. It is *not* a test that tells the patient whether she or he has AIDS. Nor can it indicate at what point in the past the person may have become infected. Nor can it predict when, or to what degree, the individual may experience symptoms related to AIDS. *All the test does is indicate, with considerable reliability, whether or not the person is currently producing the HIV antibody.* It should be noted that testing technology is constantly evolving and improving. For example, a new antigen test—which detects the presence of the virus directly, rather than just the HIV antibody—is now available, and in limited use. New technologies may change test protocols and testing considerations in the future. It is not advisable, however, to wait for such changes before drafting appropriate policy.

When an individual has unprotected sex, or shares drug injection equipment with someone who is infected, the HIV virus may pass into his or her bloodstream. At that point the body begins manufacturing an antibody in an attempt to counteract the infection. In the case of HIV, the antibody the body generates is ineffective; it is incapable of destroying the virus. That is one of the main practical ways that HIV is different from other viral infections. It is also why, to a certain degree, AIDS is a life-threatening illness.

The infected person's body doesn't manufacture the HIV antibody immediately after infection. The antibody is produced over time. Some individuals produce detectable levels of the antibody as soon as two weeks after infection; others may take up to six months (and in rare cases, even longer) to produce a detectable amount. Even those parameters cannot be said to be absolutely reliable. It is commonly assumed that people are either HIV seropositive or HIV seronegative, and that there is no middle ground between the two poles. In fact, there is. At any one time the individual may be in the process of what is termed "seroconversion." When an individual is seroconverting, he or she has been infected with HIV, and the body is responding. Unless seroconversion is complete—that is, unless the individual's body has developed enough detectable HIV antibody—the HIV antibody test is invalid. It is because of the preceding that some difficulties arise in relation to the HIV antibody test.

First, as mentioned, the EIA and Western Blot both detect the antibody to HIV, not the actual presence of the virus itself. They assume that the virus is present because a specific antibody that is trying to counteract HIV is present at sufficient levels to be noted by the test.

Second, since infected individuals manufacture the HIV antibody at a variable rate, the test results cannot be said to be reliable unless the individual has waited six months after engaging in any high-risk behavior that may have resulted in exposure to HIV. A client coming into a substance abuse program who was sharing needles a month before and who is immediately tested may receive a negative test result and still be infected simply because the body hasn't had sufficient time to manufacture a detectable level of the antibody. In other words, she or he could be currently seroconverting. This is one of the primary *technical* reasons why mandatory testing is ineffective as a means of determining universally who currently carries HIV. The "window period" of six months, during which time the body develops an antibody in sufficient quantity to be discovered by the EIA or Western Blot, would mean that at least some of the results of that mandatory testing would be erroneous.

Testing Options

As one jurisdictional example, in Minnesota there are two main avenues available for the individual who wants the HIV antibody test.

Testing can be conducted by virtually any physician, in any clinic or hospital, at the individual's request, or testing can be conducted confidentially at any one of eight Counseling and Testing Sites (CTSs) maintained by the Minnesota Department of Health.

In both cases, a healthcare professional will draw blood from the patient. That sample is sent to an off-site laboratory where the EIA and/or Western Blot protocols are performed. The results are then relayed back to the site where the blood was drawn for reporting to the individual. Turnaround time is approximately ten days to two weeks.

Minnesota law requires that the identity of all HIV seropositive people be reported to the Minnesota Department of Health by the testing agent (whether a private physician or a CTS), or by physicians providing medical treatment for HIV-infected individuals. This reporting is done for the purposes of epidemiological surveillance and partner notification, and is similar to the reporting of other conditions, such as Sexually Transmitted Diseases and tuberculosis. "Partner notification" refers to the process by which sexual or IV drug partners of HIV-infected persons are informed of their possible exposure to HIV. When an individual tests HIV+, his or her name is forwarded to the AIDS/STD Prevention Services Section of the Minnesota Department of Health. Names so forwarded are kept confidential by the Department; in fact, they are even exempt from a court order demanding release. At that point a staff person in the AIDS Prevention Services Section (APPS) will contact the HIV+ individual and request his or her assistance in developing a plan to notify the individual's sexual or IV drug partners that they may have been exposed to HIV. Compliance with that request is completely voluntary, and the contact is always made in a manner that will not disclose the HIV-infected individual's identity to third parties. And if the person who is HIV+ is uncomfortable, for whatever reason, informing past sexual or IV partners of their possible exposure, APPS staff can inform those partners in a manner that will not disclose the identity of the person who is HIV+. In addition, cases of AIDS, as defined by specific criteria set out by the U. S. Public Health Service, must be reported to the Minnesota Department of Health.

Resource Sheet: Discrimination

People with HIV and AIDS face discrimination in all aspects of their lives, sometimes on a daily basis. They have been driven out of their homes, jobs, and communities. They have been harassed and attacked. They have been kicked out of schools and restaurants, even social service agencies, for no other reason than their diagnosis. And they have often suffered that discrimination while simultaneously trying to fight against a disease that can rob them of energy and the will to fight back, in the first place.

It's not fair.

Not only that, it's almost always against the law. Several major federal and state laws clearly condemn and outlaw discrimination against people with disabilities or perceived disabilities, including HIV infection and AIDS. For example:

The Federal Rehabilitation Act of 1973, which applies to any program receiving federal money directly or indirectly (therefore covering almost every social service program in the country) prohibits discrimination against people with disabilities, people with a history of disability, or people perceived to have disabilities. The law covers access to services and employment, and was specifically amended in 1988 to include AIDS.

The Americans with Disabilities Act, passed in 1990, applies to programs that do not receive federal money and essentially makes the same point as the Federal Rehabilitation Act. Though its schedule of implementation is somewhat complicated, it is probably the most sweeping piece of legislation in U.S. history to protect the rights of the disabled.

AIDS is included in the Act. Many states, provinces, and territories also have laws forbidding discrimination against people with disabilities, including HIV infection and AIDS.

For the private sector business and social service professional, all this legislation indicates that one cannot treat people with HIV infection or AIDS in a manner that is discriminatory. It would be wrong—and illegal—to refuse services to a person with HIV if they met all the other qualifications of a program. It would be wrong—and illegal—to deny employment to a person with AIDS if that person were the best candidate for the position. It would be wrong—and illegal—to separate clients with HIV from other clients, unless there was a compelling medical or behavioral reason to do so. And it would be wrong—and illegal—to treat people with HIV infection or AIDS with anything less than the full legal and ethical rights they, and all people, deserve.

Resource Sheet: Confidentiality

Living with HIV is a very personal thing. Some people with HIV are reluctant to tell others because of their own shame or embarrassment—feelings no doubt learned from society at large. Others are hesitant to speak openly of their HIV because they fear losing jobs, security, friends and family, neighborhood security, or parenting rights. They have noted that many people with HIV have been subject to harassment, rejection, discrimination and violence, and they don't want the same things to happen to them. And some don't discuss it with many people simply because it is personal, and there are always issues of trust and safety in the disclosure.

People living with HIV have a right to tell who they want, and to withhold that information from others. With only a few, certain exceptions codified in law, no one else has the right to do that for them. From a legal point of view, providers of human services and employers should note that an employee's or client's HIV status is private medical information, and is accorded no less (and no more) privacy than any other medical information.

If a client or employee does want to disclose her or his HIV seropositivity to others, you can be helpful to that person by helping them carry out that disclosure in a conscious, planful manner—so that the individual is left feeling in charge of his or her own destiny. But we should never pressure someone to self-disclose HIV because we believe that "talking it through is good," or any similar reason. Everybody's different, and each individual has to figure it out in her or his own way.

And if you need assistance or support around HIV, talk to a supervisor or call an AIDS hotline. Don't just start talking about it with friends or colleagues—remember, it's important that you protect any individual's confidentiality.

Support Materials

Resource Sheet: Infection Control

Staff in social service organizations and private sector businesses need to be aware that there is little risk of occupational HIV infection—even in settings where individuals come into contact with blood or other infectious bodily fluids. Even so, some precautions are desirable. In fact, good infection control would be wise even in the absence of HIV; it will help reduce common diseases and infections (colds, flus, and the like) that tend to spread rapidly through workplaces.

Obviously employees should consult organizational policy for details on the practice of infection control. But the basics of infection control can be summarized in a few key procedural points.

1. Always assume that everybody one works with is potentially infectious for HIV and hepatitis B. Because of the limits of testing technology, one can never know with absolute certainty who is infected and who is not. Infection control practices, therefore, should be implemented in every single case. This approach is termed universal precautions.

2. Of particular concern to all employees will be avoiding direct contact with blood, semen, and vaginal secretions (and in the case of hepatitis, saliva as well). The implication is, of course, that as a practical matter most employees will encounter risk only in the case of accidental injuries—cuts, for example, that produce bleeding.

3. If contact with potentially infectious bodily fluids is necessary, latex gloves will provide an impermeable barrier. It should be noted that even infected blood on unbroken skin cannot cause infection; HIV has to get inside *the body.*

4. Common household bleach kills HIV and will be an efficient disinfectant.

5. Good general hygiene and facility cleanliness are wise in any case. Regular handwashing will help reduce the number of common infections (colds, flus, and the like) that will tend to spread through the workplace. And it should be kept in mind that because of suppressed immunity, people without HIV infection pose a greater risk to people with HIV than vice versa. In the interests of continued good health for people with HIV and AIDS, the organization should be kept clean and free of all possible exposure to bacteria, fungi, and viruses.

In the end a rational, level-headed approach to infection control is best. There is no reason to overreact; HIV is difficult to transmit. Occupational transmission is rare, even among healthcare workers. But the presence of the HIV/AIDS epidemic provides organizations with the opportunity to reevaluate their approach to healthy workplaces in general.

WE ARE ALL LIVING WITH AIDS

Resource Sheet: Pre/Post-Test for HIV/AIDS Training

This is a "before" and "after" test that can be administered to staff undergoing any training about HIV and AIDS. The answers are given in italics.

HIV/AIDS Questionnaire

1. **Identify three major routes of HIV transmission.**

    Sexual intercourse (anal, vaginal, and oral).
    Sharing IV injection equipment.
    From mother to child through pregnancy/childbirth.
    Infected blood products (no longer a problem in the U.S.).

2. **What *specific* sexual behaviors (assuming one partner is HIV-infected) are risk behaviors for HIV infection? In each case, why?**

    Anal intercourse.
    Vaginal intercourse.
    Oral sex: fellatio.
    Oral sex: cunnilingus.

3. **Define the following terms as they relate to HIV infection.**

    ### Seropositive

    Positive for HIV antibody, usually after both ELISA and Western Blot tests.

    ### Opportunistic infection

    A secondary infection that "seizes the opportunity" of HIV-compromised immunity to take hold.

    ### Co-factors

    Refers to other events or conditions that activate HIV infection or the development of opportunistic infections after primary infection has taken place. It is on considerable evidence suggesting that the actions of HIV in the body are multiplied by other events or conditions. Commonly suggested co-factors include drug/alcohol abuse, the presence of other STDs, poor nutrition, stress, and others.

Seroconversion

Passing from HIV negative to HIV positive antibody status.

PCP

Pneumocystis Carnii Pneumonia, an opportunistic infection associated with AIDS.

Kaposi's sarcoma

A cancer or tumor of the blood and/or lymphatic vessel walls.

Vaginal secretions

The natural lubrication inside a woman's vagina. Not menstrual blood.

Universal precautions

Assuming that everybody is HIV positive and HBV positive, and taking infection control precautions accordingly.

AZT

Azidothymidine, known under the trade name Retrovir, is perhaps the best-known antiviral now in use against HIV.

Lymphadenopathy

A condition marked by chronic swelling of the lymph nodes.

4. **Name two tests used to detect the HIV antibody.**

   ELISA (Enzyme Linked Immunosorbent Assay or EIA).
   Western Blot.

5. **Speaking in general terms, what are some possible *benefits* of the HIV antibody test?**

   Possible notification of infected partners.

> May lead to lifestyle changes to promote general health.
> May encourage more consistent risk-reduction practices.
> Early detection of HIV antibody allows for early medical intervention.
> Others.

6. **Again speaking in general terms, what are some possible *disadvantages* of the HIV antibody test?**

   > Negative test may give false sense of security.
   > Negative test cannot account for window period.
   > Positive test result may be psychologically devastating.
   > Individual may not understand test fully and misinterpret test results.
   > Others.

7. **What does a positive test result mean? What does it *not* mean?**

   > Means that the person has the antibody to HIV in their body, thereby signifying the presence of HIV itself. It does not mean the person has AIDS, will get sick, or will develop AIDS. It does not mean the person will necessarily die in the near future.

8. **Other than AZT, what drugs or treatments are currently available to people with HIV infection?**

• ddI	[antiviral]
• ddC	[antiviral]
• pentamadine	[PCP prophylaxis]
• Acyclovir	[herpes]
• Bactrim	[PCP]
• Pyrimethamine	[toxoplasmosis]
• Humatin	[cryptosporidium]

   • Many others, including non-pharmaceutical approaches.

9. **If you had a client in need of services related to his or her HIV infection, to what agencies or programs might you refer that person? (List all that you can think of.)**

   > Many, particularly your local, state, or provincial HIV/AIDS service organizations.

Support Materials

10. **What are three things you, or any of your employees or clients, can do in your personal lives to reduce the risk of HIV infection?**

   If you are sexually active, use condoms.
   If you are sexually active, reduce your number of partners.
   Do not have (vaginal, anal, or oral) intercourse.
   Do not share injection equipment.

11. **What are two things you can do in the workplace to reduce your risk of inadvertent occupationally-related HIV infection?**

   Adhere to common infection control standards.
   Assume that everyone is positive for HIV/HBV.
   Be careful with sharp instruments.
   Use latex gloves when in contact with bodily fluids.
   Others.

12. **According to the research available, will everyone who is currently HIV-infected die of AIDS?**

   No.

353

Resource Sheet: Taking Care of Yourself in the Face of HIV/AIDS

Working with people with HIV or a diagnosis of AIDS can be painful. Sometimes it means watching helplessly as co-workers and friends get sicker and sicker, and then die. Sometimes the experience of advocating for services for clients can be frustrating, even maddening. Sometimes professionals have to look on while people with AIDS experience rejection, discrimination, isolation, or outright hostility.

Ultimately, confronting HIV and AIDS means that we must face our own beliefs and attitudes about mortality, sexuality, sickness, and diversity. Those are not easy confrontations, though in them lies incredible opportunities for growth, greater awareness, and a keener understanding.

And in all that we—professionals who come face-to-face with HIV and AIDS in our jobs, our lives—must learn to take care of ourselves. No amount of self-negation, no level of grim self-sacrifice, will ever help any person with AIDS get better. If anything, all it does is set a dubious example of self-care.

What can professionals do to take care of themselves when dealing with HIV/AIDS becomes difficult? Advice from people working in the field might be helpful:

- Talk to family, friends, or co-workers about your experience, protecting, of course, any confidentiality that might be required. No one should bear the burden of painful feelings alone.

- Examine your own attitudes about life, death, sexuality, and spirituality. Most of us live our lives blissfully pretending we won't die; it's one of the ways we cope. But AIDS makes it difficult to pretend.

- Feel free to ask for supervision if you need to talk about a particular client and her or his situation.

- Learn as much as you can about HIV disease. Listen to people living with HIV or AIDS who have come to some kind of terms with the disease. Remember that now, in the 1990s, HIV infection is no longer an automatic death sentence, and that there are valid reasons for hope.

- There are now a number of support groups for professionals working with HIV and AIDS. They are open to all comers. Find one through your local or regional AIDSline/helpline and attend.

- Volunteer for an AIDS organization. Contribute money, or time. Write a letter to the editor, or design a panel for the Names Quilt (The Names Project AIDS Memorial Quilt is a tapestry of 3 foot by 6 foot panels, each memorializing the life of someone who has died of AIDS. The Quilt travels from city to city for public viewing; over 2,000,000 people have seen the Quilt or part of it during one of its displays.) Whatever it is, do *something* to focus and channel feelings of anger, pain, or sadness.

Support Materials

Resource Sheet: When a Friend Has AIDS

AIDS is now a fact of life and poses new challenges for everyone—not only for people who are ill, but for their friends and loved ones as well. When someone you know is struggling with a serious illness like AIDS, you may feel helpless, useless, frustrated, or afraid. All of that is normal, natural; it doesn't mean you don't care. Just like your friend, you deserve support and a chance to talk through your experience.

But if you feel helpless, like there's nothing you can do, that's simply not the case. The following "tips" may be useful. (This material is adapted from *Saying Goodbye to Someone You Love*, by Dixie Beckham, CSW, ACSW; Luis Palacios-Jimenez, CSW, ACSW; Vincent John Patti, CSW, ACSW; and Michael Shernoff, CSW, ACSW; edited by Philip G. Ryan.)

- Don't avoid your friend. Be there. It gives hope. Be the loved one, the friend, you've always been, especially now when it is most important.

- Call before you visit. Your friend may not feel up to visitors that day. Don't be afraid to phone again and visit on another occasion.

- Weep and laugh with your friend. Don't shy away from such intimate experiences. They may enrich you both.

- Tell your friend what you'd like to do to help. If she or he agrees, do it. Keep any commitments you make.

- Call to say you are bringing her or his favorite food. Make sure it is something she or he can eat. Spend time together savoring the food.

- Call to find out if there's anything he or she needs from the store. Ask for a shopping list and make a "special delivery."

- Be creative. Bring books, magazines, a wall poster, home-baked goodies. Clip out funny cartoons and send them.

- Volunteer to take your friend for a walk or an outing, but ask about—and respect—any limitations.

- If your friend is a parent, ask about and offer to help care for any children. And pay attention to the child's needs and feelings.

- Celebrate holidays! Bring flowers or other special gifts. Include your friend in your (and her or his) holiday plans.

- Offer to do household chores. But don't take away chores your friend can still do; he or she has lost enough already. Ask first.

- Don't be reluctant to ask about HIV/AIDS. Your friend may need to talk. Find out by asking, "Do you feel like talking about it?"

- Discuss current events. Talk about mutual friends and other common interests. Your friend may be tired of

355

We Are All Living With AIDS

talking about AIDS.

- Everybody has good days, bad days. On good days, treat your friend the same as other friends. On bad days, be sensitive.

- Talk with your friend about the future; next week, next year. It is helpful to look toward the future, to have hope.

- You don't always have to talk. It's okay to sit together reading, watching television, or holding hands.

- Touch your friend. A simple squeeze of the hand can let her or him know you care. There's no reason to be afraid of infection.

- Crying can be healthy, cleansing. But not everyone is a crier, so don't try to force tears if it isn't a natural response.

- Grief has lots of physical symptoms: shortness of breath, sadness, fatigue, sleep difficulties. Respect these signs.

- If your loved one has died, check a local AIDS service organization to see if they have bereavement support groups. Attend one.

- Rest and take care of yourself, but be careful not to isolate yourself from friends and family. Reach out.

- The period of mourning immediately after a death is not a time to make major decisions. Put them on the back burner for a while.

- The death of a loved one may trigger memories of other losses. These memories may make this time even more painful.

- You may be very angry at the deceased for dying. This is normal. Forgiveness plays an important part in grief and recovery.

- Mourning is a way of saying good-bye. Don't avoid it. And take your time; you don't have to "get over it" on other's schedules.

- It is especially difficult for a parent to have a child die. It's not in the "natural order of things" for a parent to bury a child.

- Birthdays, anniversaries, and holidays following the death of a loved one may be especially painful. Go easy. Don't isolate yourself.

- After the initial shock, a period of feeling overwhelmed, confused, scattered, or numb may take place.

- You cannot continue to live your life as though the deceased were still alive. The task is to find ways to let that person live on in memory.

- Don't ignore any desires to exercise your faith, religion, and spirituality. It may provide some needed comfort and answers.

- The hardest time is usually after everyone has gone. Life returns to what it was before, except that your loved one is gone. It may feel empty.

- Take better care of yourself than ever before. And remember, it's okay to survive the death of a loved one.

Resource Sheet: Educational Materials

Newsletters and Periodicals

AIDS Alert: The Monthly Update for Health Professionals
American Health Consultants, Inc.
67 Peachtree Park Drive N.E.
Atlanta, GA 30309

AIDS: An International Bimonthy Journal
Gower Academic Journals
101 Fifth Avenue
New York, NY 10003

AIDS & Public Policy Journal
University Publishing Group
107 East Church Street
Frederick, MD 21701

AIDS Center News
World Hemophilia AIDS Center
2400 South Flower Street
Los Angeles, CA 90007

AIDS Clinical Care
Massachusetts Medical Society
1440 Main Street
Waltham, MA 02154-1649

AIDS Education and Prevention: An Interdisciplinary Journal
Guilford Publications, Inc.
72 Spring Street
New York, NY 10012

AIDS File
San Francisco General Hospital
Medical Center Ward 84
99 South Potero Avenue
San Francisco, CA 94110

AIDS Information Exchange
United States Conference of Mayors
1620 I Street N.W.
Washington, D.C. 20006

AIDS Law and Litigation
University Publishing Group
107 East Church Street
Frederick, MD 21701

AIDS Medical Update
UCLA AIDS Center, CIRID at UCLA
Division of Clinical Immunology and Allergy
UCLA School of Medicine
Los Angeles, CA 90024

AIDS Medicines in Development
Pharmaceutical Manufacturers Association
Communications Division
1100 15th Street N.W.
Washington, D.C. 20005

AIDS Nursing Update
UCLA AIDS Center, CIRID at UCLA
Division of Immunology and Allergy
UCLA School of Medicine
Los Angeles, CA 90024

AIDS Policy and Law
Buraff Publications, Inc.
1231 25th Street N.W.
Washington, D.C. 20037

AIDS Reference & Research Collection
University Publishing Group
107 East Church Street
Frederick, DE 21701

AIDS Targeted Information
428 Preston Street
Baltimore, MD 94141

Support Materials

AIDS Treatment News
P.O. Box 411256
San Francisco, CA 94141

Being Alive
4222 Santa Monica Boulevard
Los Angeles, CA 90029

BETA (Bulletin of Experimental Treatments for AIDS)
San Francisco AIDS Foundation
Box 6182
San Francisco, CA 94101

Body Positive
2095 Broadway
Suite 306
New York, NY 10023

CDC AIDS Weekly
P.O. Box 830409
Birmingham, AL 35283-0409

Critical Path AIDS Project
2062 Lombard Street
Philadelphia, PA 19146

Eclipse
Shanti Project Newsletter
890 Hayes Street
San Francisco, CA 94117

Focus
AIDS Health Project
333 Valencia Street, 4th Floor
San Francisco, CA 94103

Minnesota Department of Health Disease Control Newsletter
Minnesota Department of Health
717 Delaware Street S.E.
Minneapolis, MN 55440

Minnesota Positive
HIV Programs

640 Jackson Street, Suite 125
St. Paul, MN 55101

Morbidity and Mortality Weekly Report
Massachusetts Medical Society
C.S.P.O. Box 9120
Waltham, MA 02254

Notes from the Underground
PWA Health Group
31 West 26th Street, 4th Floor
New York, NY 10010

Optimist
AIDS Project Los Angeles
7362 Santa Monica Boulevard
West Hollywood, CA 90046

PWAlive
Sabathani Community Center
310 East 38th Street
Minneapolis, MN 55409

PWA Coalition Newsline
31 West 26th Street
New York, NY 10010

Treatment Issues
Gay Men's Health Crisis
Department of Medical Information
129 West 20 Street
New York, NY 10011

Books

Abt, C. C. and Hardy, K. M., eds. *AIDS and the Courts.* Cambridge: Abt Books, 1990.

Aggleton, P., Hart, G., and Davies, P., eds. *AIDS: Social Representations, Social Practices.* Philadelphia: Falmer Press, 1989.

Aggleton, P., Hart, G., and Davies, P., eds. *AIDS: Individual, Cultural, and Policy Dimensions.* Philadelphia: Falmer Press, 1990.

AIDS Health Project. *The San Francisco Protocol: Disclosing HIV Test Results.* San Francisco: AIDS Health Project, 1989.

Altman, D. *AIDS in the Mind of America.* Garden City, NY: Anchor Press/Doubleday, 1986.

Support Materials

Alyson, S. *You Can Do Something About AIDS*. Boston: The Stop AIDS Project, 1988.

American Foundation for AIDS Research. *Learning AIDS: An Information Resources Directory*. New Providence, NJ: AmFAR, 1989.

Andrulis, D. P. *Crisis at the Front Line: The Effects of AIDS on Public Hospitals*. New York: Priority Press, 1989.

Badgley, L. *Healing AIDS Naturally*. San Bruno, CA: Human Energy Press, 1987.

Baker, R. A., Moulton, J. M., and Tighe, J. *Early Care for HIV Disease*. Second edition. San Francisco: San Francisco AIDS Foundation, 1992.

Bateson, M., and Goldsby, R. *Thinking AIDS*. Reading, MA: Addison-Wesley, 1988.

Battjes, R. H., and Pickens, R. W., eds. *Needle Sharing Among Intravenous Drug Users: National and International Perspectives*. NIDA Research Monograph 80. Rockville, MD: National Institute on Drug Abuse, 1988.

Baumgartner, G. H. *AIDS: Psychosocial Factors in the acquired immune deficiency syndrome*. Springfield, IL: Charles C. Thomas, 1985.

Bayer, R. *Private Acts, Social Consequences: AIDS and the Politics of Public Health*. New York: The Free Press, 1989.

Blanchot, K., ed. *AIDS: A Health Care Management Response*. Rockville, MD: Aspen Publishers, 1988.

Brandt, A. M. *No Magic Bullet: A Social History of Venereal Disease in the United States Since 1880*. Cambridge: Harvard, 1985.

Breitman, P., Knutson, K., and Reed, P. *How to Persuade Your Lover to Use a Condom...And Why You Should*. Rocklin, CA: Prima Publications and Communications, 1987.

Bridge, T. P., et. al., eds. *Psychological, Neuropsychiatric, and Substance Abuse Aspects of AIDS*. New York: Raven Press, 1988.

Callen, M., ed. *Surviving and Thriving with AIDS*. New York: PWA Coalition, 1988.

Cass, V. *There's More to Sex Than AIDS: The A to Z Guide to Safe Sex*. Richmond Victoria, Australia, 1988.

Center for Women Policy Studies. *The Guide to Resources on Women and AIDS*. Washington, DC: Center for Women Policy Studies, 1991.

Centers for Disease Control. *Recommended Additional Guidelines for HIV Antibody Testing and Counseling in the Prevention of HIV Infection and AIDS*. Atlanta, GA: Centers for Disease Control, 1987.

Clarke, L. K., and Potts, M., eds. *The AIDS Reader: Documentary History of a Modern Epidemic*. Boston: Braden Publishing, 1988.

Cleveland, M. *The Twelve Step Response to Chronic Illness and Disability*. Center City, MN: Hazelden Educational Materials, 1988.

Cohen, P. T., et. al., eds. *The AIDS Knowledge Base*. Waltham, MA: Medical Publishing Group, 1990.

Colman, W. *Understanding and Preventing AIDS: A Guide for Young People*. Chicago: Children's Press, 1988.

Corless, I. B. and Pittman-Lindeman, M. N. *AIDS: Principles, Practices & Politics*. New York: Hemisphere Publishing Corp., 1988.

Crimp, D., ed. *AIDS: Cultural Analysis, Cultural Activism*. Cambridge: MIT Press, 1988.

Dalton, H. L. and Burris, S., eds. *AIDS and the Law: A Guide for the Public*. New Haven, CT: Yale Press, 1987.

DeVita, V., Jr., Hellman, S., and Rosenberg, S., eds. *AIDS: Etiology, Diagnosis, Treatment, and Prevention*. Second edition. Philadelphia: J. B. Lippincott, 1988.

Dilley, J.W., Pies, C., and Helquist, M. *Face to Face: A Guide to AIDS Counseling*. San Francisco: AIDS Health Project, 1989.

Everett, J. and Glanze, W. D. *The Condom Book*. New York: Signet, 1987.

Fisher, D. G., ed. *AIDS and Alcohol/Drug Abuse*. New York: Harrington Park Press, 1991.

Fleming, A. F., et. al., eds. *The Global Impact of AIDS*. New York: Alan R. Liss, Inc., 1988.

Fortunato, J. *AIDS: The Spiritual Dilemma*. San Francisco: Harper & Row, 1987.

Fraser, K., and Mitchell, P. *Effective AIDS Education: A Policymaker's Guide.* Alexandria, VA: National Association of State Boards of Education, 1988.

Frazer, K. *Someone at School Has AIDS: A Guide to Developing Policies for Students and School Staff Members who are Infected with HIV.* Alexandria, VA: National Association of State Boards of Education, 1989.

Galea, R., Lewis, B., and Baker, L. *AIDS and IV Drug Abusers: Current Perspectives.* Owings Mills, MD: National Health Publishing, 1988.

General Accounting Office. *AIDS Education: Reaching People at Higher Risk.* Washington, DC: U.S. General Accounting Office, 1989.

Gostin, L. *AIDS and the Health Care System.* New Haven: Yale University Press, 1990.

Hartsock, P., and Genser, S. G. *Longitudinal Studies of HIV Infection in Intravenous Drug Users.* Research Monograph 109. Rockville, MD: National Institute on Drug Abuse, 1991.

Hatcher, R. A., et. al. *Contraceptive Technology.* New York: Irvington Publishers. [A new edition is published every other year.]

Hay, L. *The AIDS Book: Creating a Positive Approach.* Santa Monica, CA: Hay House, 1988.

Hildalgo, H., Peterson, T. L., and Woodman, N. J., eds. *Lesbian and Gay Issues: A Resource Manual for Social Workers.* Silver Spring, MD: National Association of Social Workers, 1985.

Hochhauser, M. and Rothenberger, J. H. *AIDS Education.* Dubuque, IA: William C. Brown Publishers, 1992.

Infield, D., ed. *AIDS and Long-Term Care: A New Dimension.* Owings Mills, MD: National Health Publishing, 1989.

Institute of Medicine. *Confronting AIDS: Update 1988.* Washington, DC: National Academy Press, 1988.

Institute of Medicine. *HIV Screening of Pregnant Women and Newborns.* Washington, DC: National Academy Press, 1991.

Isay, R. A. *Being Homosexual: Gay Men and Their Development.* New York: Farrar, Straus, Giroux, 1989.

James, J. S. *AIDS Treatment News.* [Vols. One & Two.] Berkeley, CA: Celestial Arts, 1991.

Jones, J. H. *Bad Blood: The Tuskeegee Syphilis Experiment.* New York: The Free Press, 1981.

Joseph, S. C. *Dragon Within the Gates: The Once and Future AIDS Epidemic.* New York: Carroll & Graf, 1992.

Kain, C., ed. *No Longer Immune: A Counselor's Guide to AIDS.* Alexandria, VA: American Association for Counseling and Development, 1989.

Kaslow, R. A., and Francis, D. *Epidemiology of AIDS.* New York: Oxford University Press, 1989.

Kramer, L. *Reports from the Holocaust: The Making of an AIDS Activist.* New York: St. Martin's Press, 1989.

Kubler-Ross, E. *AIDS: The Ultimate Challenge.* New York: Macmillan, 1987.

Lambda Legal Defense and Education Fund. *Living with AIDS: A Guide to the Legal Problems of People with AIDS.* Washington, DC: Lambda, 1987.

Legal Action Center of the City of New York. *AIDS: A Guide to Legal and Policy Issues.* New York: Legal Action Center, 1988.

Leibowitch, J. *A Strange Virus of Unknown Origin.* New York: Ballentine Books, 1985.

Masters, W. H., Johnson, V. E., and Kolodny, R. C. *Sex and Human Loving.* Revised edition. Boston: Little, Brown and Company, 1988.

McNeill, W. H. *Plagues and People.* Magnolia, MA: Peter Smith, 1992.

Melroe, H., and Rothenberger, J., eds. *Living with HIV: Reaching Outward and Inward.* Minneapolis: Midwest AIDS Training and Education Center, 1990.

Mikluscak-Cooper and Miller, E. E. *Living in Hope: A 12-Step Approach for Persons at Risk or Infected with HIV.* Berkeley, CA: Celestial Arts, 1991.

Miller, H. G., Turner, C. F., and Moses, L. E., eds. *AIDS: The Second Decade.* Washington, DC: National Academy Press, 1990.

Minnesota Department of Health. *Meeting the Needs of Minnesotans with HIV Disease.* Minneapolis, MN: Minnesota Department of Health, 1991.

Moffatt, B., et. al. *AIDS: A Self-Care Manual.* Los Angeles: AIDS Project Los Angeles, 1987.

Support Materials

Monette, P. *Borrowed Time: An AIDS Memoir.* New York: Harcourt Brace Jovanovich, 1988.

National Association of People with AIDS. *HIV in America: A Profile of the Challenges Facing Americans Living with HIV.* Washington, DC: NAPWA, 1992.

National Guidelines Task Force. *Guidelines for Comprehensive Sexuality Education.* New York: Sex Information and Education Council of the U. S., 1991.

National Research Council. *Risking the Future: Adolescent Sexuality, Pregnancy, and Childbirth.* Washington, DC: National Academy Press, 1987.

National Safety Council. *An Educational Package on AIDS.* National Safety Council, 1988.

O'Connor, T., and Gonzalez-Nunez, A. *Living with AIDS.* San Francisco: Corwin Publishers, 1987.

O'Malley, P., ed. *The AIDS Epidemic: Private Rights and the Public Interest.* Boston: Beacon Press, 1988.

Patton, C. *Sex and Germs: The Politics of AIDS.* Boston: South End Press, 1985.

Patton, C., ßand Kelly, J. *Making It: A Woman's Guide to Sex in the Age of AIDS.* Ithaca: Firebrand Books, 1987.

Patton, C. *Inventing AIDS.* New York: Routledge, 1990.

Pohl, M., and Kay, D. *Sexuality and AIDS.* Center City, MN: Hazelden Educational Materials, 1991.

Pohl, M, Deniston, K., and Toft, D. *The Caregivers' Journey: When You Love Someone with AIDS.* Center City, MN: Hazelden Educational Materials, 1990.

Quackenbush, M., and Villarreal, S. *"Does AIDS Hurt?" Educating Young Children About AIDS: Suggestions for Parents, Teachers, and Other Care Providers of Children to Age 10.* Santa Cruz, CA: Network Publications, 1988.

Quackenbush, M., and Benson, J. D. *Risk and Recovery: AIDS, HIV and Alcohol.* San Francisco: The AIDS Health Project, 1992.

Reinisch, J. M. *The Kinsey Institute New Report on Sex.* New York: St. Martin's Press, 1990.

Richardson, D. *Women and AIDS.* New York: Metheun, 1988.

Rieder, I., and Ruppelt, P., eds. *AIDS: The Women.* San Francisco: Cleis Press, 1988.

Rowe, M., Ryan, C., Thomas, C., et. al. *AIDS: A Public Health Challenge. State Issues, Policies and Programs. Vols. 1 - 3.* Washington, DC: The George Washington University, 1987.

Rudd, A., and Taylor, D., eds. *Positive Women: Voices of Women Living with AIDS.* Toronto: Second Story Press, 1992.

Sabatier, R. *Blaming Others: Prejudice, Race, and Worldwide AIDS.* London: The Panos Institute, 1988.

Sande, M. A., and Volberding, P. A., eds. *The Medical Management of AIDS.* Philadelphia: W. B. Saunders Company, 1988.

Schinazi, R. F., and Nahmias, A. J., eds. *AIDS in Children, Adolescents, and Heterosexual Adults: An Interdisciplinary Approach to Prevention.* New York: Elsevier, 1988.

Schumacher, M. *The National Association of State Boards of Education HIV/AIDS Education Survey: Profiles of State Policy Actions.* Alexandria, VA: National Association of State Boards of Education, 1989.

Scientific American. *The Science of AIDS: Readings from the Scientific American.* New York: W. H. Freeman and Company, 1989.

Service Employees International Union, AFL-CIO, CLC. *The AIDS Book: Information for Workers.* Third revised edition. 1988.

Shilts, R. *And the Band Played On: Politics, People, and the AIDS Epidemic.* New York: St. Martin's Press, 1987.

Siegel, B. S. *Love, Medicine & Miracles.* New York: Harper & Row, 1986.

Siegel, L., M.D. and Korcok, M. *AIDS: The Drug and Alcohol Connection.* Center City, MN: Hazelden Educational Materials, 1987.

Siegel, L., and Korcok, M. *Preventing AIDS: Hope Through Awareness.* Center City, MN: Hazelden Educational Materials, 1991.

Sisk, J. *How Effective is AIDS Education?* Washington, DC: Office of Technology Assessment, Congress of the United States, 1988.

Sontag, S. *AIDS and Its Metaphors.* New York: Farrar, Straus, Giroux, 1989.

Sorensen, J. L., et. al. *Preventing AIDS in Drug Users and Their Sexual Partners.* New York: Guilford

Press, 1991.

    Stimmel, B., ed. *Cocaine, AIDS, and Intravenous Drug Use.* New York: Harrington Park Press, 1991.

    Tilleraas, P. *The Color of Light: Daily Meditations for All of Us Living with AIDS.* Center City, MN: Hazelden Educational Materials, 1988.

    Tilleraas, P. *Circle of Hope; Our Stories of AIDS, Addiction, and Recovery.* Center City, MN: Hazelden Educational Materials, 1990.

    Tilleraas, P. *A Spiritual Response to AIDS.* Center City, MN: Hazelden Educational Materials, 1990.

    Turner, C. F., Miller, H. G., and Moses, L. E., eds. *AIDS: Sexual Behavior and Intravenous Drug Use.* Washington, DC: National Academy Press, 1989.

    Valdisseri, R. O. *Preventing AIDS: The Design of Effective Programs.* New Brunswick, NJ: Rutgers University Press, 1989.

    Watney, S. *Policing Desire: Pornography, AIDS, and the Media.* Minneapolis: University of Minnesota Press, 1987.

    Weisfeld, V. D., ed. *AIDS Health Services at the Crossroads: Lessons for Community Care.* Princeton, NJ: Robert Wood Johnson Foundation, 1991.

    Whitmore, G. *Someone was Here: Profiles in the AIDS Epidemic.* New York: New American Library, 1988.

    Wood, G. J. and Marks, R. *AIDS Law for Mental Health Professionals.* San Francisco: The AIDS Health Project, 1990.

Articles

Rather than even attempting to list some of the many thousands of important newspaper and periodical articles that have been written about HIV/AIDS, the reader is advised to access any of a variety of databases when seeking information on specific topics. Medical schools are a good place to start, and if you are unfamiliar with database use, they will be able to help you.

A good all-purpose database is the **NAPWA-Link,** maintained by the National Association of People with AIDS. For $65 a year users have unlimited access to NAPWA-Link, which is a computerized database and bulletin board covering a broad range of information and concerns. Contact NAPWA at 1413 K Street NW, Washington, DC 20005-3405. Their phone number is (202) 898-0435.

Educational Materials: Videos and Other AV Resources, Brochures, Handouts

There have been hundreds of educational videotapes about HIV/AIDS marketed since the beginning of the epidemic, and there are probably thousands of different brochures, flyers, handouts, and pamphlets that address every aspect of HIV and which speak to nearly every prospective audience. In short, there are far too many to list here.

My experience tells me that for every good videotape about AIDS there are ten others that are somewhat to seriously flawed in some way. Common flaws include:

- *Presentation of outdated material,*

- *Use of incorrect or misleading terminology (e.g., "risk groups," "the AIDS test," "catching AIDS," and so on),*
- *Presentations that tend to make people afraid of persons with HIV, rather than the virus itself,*
- *Cultural or gender insensitivity,*
- *Unnecessary avoidance of "controversial" issues related to HIV (e.g., anal intercourse, the use of condoms, same-gender sexual orientation, and so on),*
- *Presentations that seem unnecessarily judgemental or provocative,*
- *Presentations that are too technical for the intended audience, and*
- *Presentations that perpetuate an "us vs. them" stance in relation to HIV.*

In other words, anyone considering the use of audiovisual or print resources for educational purposes should be a *critical consumer*. There is one good resource volume that can help. The American Foundation for AIDS Research published *Learning AIDS: An Information Resources Directory* (see under "Books" above), a comprehensive review of over 1,700 HIV/AIDS educational items, many of which have been reviewed by expert panels of people working in HIV service, education, and policy. For each listing the book discusses target audience, strength and weaknesses, cost, and ordering source. No one should order HIV/AIDS materials without first consulting this volume.

Resource Sheet: HIV/AIDS Terminology

AIDS: Acquired Immunodeficiency Syndrome is a weakness in immune system functioning which reduces the affected person's resistance to certain infections and cancers, which can, in turn, prove life-threatening. Diagnostic criteria for AIDS are fairly specific.

AIDS-Related Complex (ARC): ARC is a term that describes HIV-related health problems occurring before a person develops an AIDS-defining infection. Because it is an inaccurate term, "ARC" is used less and less often today. Instead physicians chart HIV as usually starting with no apparent symptoms and progressing to symptoms.

Anemia: A decrease in the number of a person's red blood cells or in the amount of hemoglobin carried by those cells.

Ano-genital Warts: Raised bumps or protruding pieces of skin in the anal or genital area. In people who are HIV-positive they are most often caused by human papillomavirus (HPV) and can spread quickly on the body or to another person through sexual contact.

Antibiotic: Any drug that slows the growth of or kills bacteria or other microorganisms. Examples include penicillin, sulfa drugs, and antifungal medications.

Antibodies: Proteins in the blood that are produced by the body to fend off foreign organisms or toxins. Antibodies are usually effective in suppressing the invaders. With infections such as HIV, however, the antibodies only "mark" its presence chemically.

Antibody Test: The testing process employed to determine whether one is carrying antibody to HIV.

Antigen: Any substance to which the body reacts by mounting an immune system response, including the formation of antibodies.

Antiviral: The term literally means "against the virus." It refers to any drug or treatment that can destroy or weaken a virus. Much of current research in HIV/AIDS is focused on the development of a safe, effective **antiretroviral** (since HIV is part of a subclass of viruses called "retroviruses"); though some show promise, none are completely without serious shortcomings.

Aphthous Ulcers: Also known as canker sores, they are small, painful white sores on the gums or elsewhere inside the mouth or esophagus. They may respond to steroid treatment.

Candidiasis: Also called "thrush," candidiasis is the third most frequent disease listed as evidence of an AIDS diagnosis. Candida is a yeast infection which normally lives in the intestines but can flourish in other parts of the body, such as the mouth, in cases of immunosuppression. Vaginal candidiasis is a serious health problem for immune-compromised women, and is often the first sign of HIV infection in women.

CD4 Cells: CD4 cells are a type of blood cell important to the body's immune system. HIV infection results in a loss of CD4 cells, reducing the immune system's ability to fight off infection. Also known as T4 cells and CD4+ lymphocytes.

CD4 Count: A measurement of CD4 cells (also known as a T4 cell count). Usually, as HIV infection progresses, the number of CD4 cells drops.

Chronic Herpes Simplex: In people with AIDS, CHS causes chronic mucocutaneous ulcers, especially in and around the anus. It is another frequent opportunistic infection in AIDS cases and sometimes progresses to encephalitis or pneumonia.

Co-factor: A situation or activity that may increase a person's susceptibility to HIV infection. Examples of co-factors include other sexually-transmitted diseases, drug or alcohol use, poor nutrition, genetic factors, and stress.

Cryptococcosis: A fungal infection that may cause meningitis or damage to the central nervous system; it can also produce pneumonia or pleurisy.

Cryptosporidiosis: A disease characterized by severe watery diarrhea that can last for months. Other symptoms can include weight loss, abdominal cramps, nausea, vomiting, fever, and headache. This illness usually affects people with fewer than 100 CD4 cells and is rarely the first AIDS-defining illness. Cryptosporidium, the intestinal parasite that causes the disease, is common among farm and domestic animals. Highly infectious, it can be transmitted through contaminated food or water.

Cytomegalovirus (CMV): An opportunistic infection associated with AIDS, CMV causes mononucleosis-like syndrome with infection of some internal organs. CMV may manifest as pneumonia or colitis; the most common manifestation is spots on the retina of the eye, which can lead to blindness.

Dementia: AIDS Dementia Complex (ADC) signifies HIV infection of the brain and Central Nervous System that evidences itself as failing memory, disconnected thought patterns, motor impairment, and a host of other symptoms.

Diarrhea: Diarrhea is one of the most common symptoms of HIV illness. Diarrhea in the HIV-infected person can be due to any number of causes, including secondary infections, stress, or diet.

DNA: Deoxyribonucleic acid (DNA) is a complex molecule that carries genetic information and controls cell function. HIV can insert itself into the DNA of a cell and use cell mechanisms to reproduce.

ELISA: The ELISA (Enzyme Linked Immunosorbent Assay) test indicates the presence of antibodies to HIV.

Encephalitis: Inflammation of the brain is called encephalitis. It is usually due to an infection, but can also result from drug interactions or other disorders.

Esophagitis: An inflammation of the esophagus, the tube that carries food to the stomach. Symptoms include painful or difficult swallowing and pain in the center of the chest. It is most commonly caused by stomach acid backing up into the esophagus; however, in the case of HIV, candida is the main source.

Gastroenteritis: Inflammation or infection of the lining of the stomach and intestines, often due to infection with bacteria or viruses.

Hemophilia: An inherited condition wherein normal blood clotting is impossible. Many people with hemophilia require a blood product called *Factor VIII* to aid clotting. Factor VIII is made from the pooled blood of many people. At one point Factor VIII was often contaminated with HIV; now, in the United States, it is treated to kill the virus.

Hepatitis: An inflammation or infection of the liver, usually caused by viruses. Symptoms may include fever, abdominal pain, and jaundice.

Histoplasmosis: A fungal infection caused by *Histoplasma capsulatum*, most often seen in the Midwestern part of the United States. Symptoms include fever, swollen glands, coughing, shortness of breath, weakness, and anemia. It is rarely fatal, but in persons with HIV it can become severe, affecting almost any organ of the body.

HIV (Human Immunodeficiency Virus): The name adopted by a subcommittee of the International Committee on the Taxonomy of Viruses. Previous names include ARV, HTLV-III, and LAV; "HIV" is now, and will be for the future, the accepted standard.

HIV seropositivity/HIV positive/HIV+: These are all terms signifying the presence of HIV antibody in an individual. Generally they refer to people who are otherwise free of the symptoms of infection or opportunistic disease, though (of course) people with AIDS are also HIV seropositive.

Homophobia: An unfounded fear of or hatred of gay men and lesbians, same-sex intimacy, and gayness in general.

Human Papillomavirus: Known by the initial HPV, this virus causes skin and venereal warts. The virus and warts may multiply faster in HIV-infected persons. HPV has been linked to certain tumors, including cancer of the cervix.

Immune System: A complex system of cells and organisms that enables the body to defend itself against infections and organisms such as bacteria, fungi, protozoa, and viruses.

Immunosuppression: A condition in which the immune system is weakened by a variety of factors, including HIV infection, drug and alcohol use, chemotherapy, or other illnesses.

Invasive Cervical Cancer: Although cervical cancer is a common form of cancer among women, the conditions that lead to it appear to be more common in HIV-positive women. When abnormal cells are present (detected through a Pap smear) they may indicate infection, cancer, or a pre-cancerous condition known as dysplasia. Dysplasia may progress to localized cancer. When cancer cells grow into other tissue, they are termed "invasive."

Isosporiasis: An opportunistic infection that results in chronic watery diarrhea. It is caused by the organism *Isospora belli*, most often carried in contaminated food or water.

Kaposi's Sarcoma (KS): A cancer or tumor of the blood and/or lymphatic vessel walls. It usually appears as pink to purple painless spots on the skin. Before the appearance of AIDS it was extremely rare; the type associated with AIDS is much more aggressive than the earlier form of the disease.

Lymphadenopathy: A condition marked by chronic swelling of the lymph nodes.

Lymphoid Interstitial Pneumonia (LIP): LIP imitates standard pneumonia but responds to different treatments. It is seen most often in HIV-infected children.

Lymphoma: A cancer that starts in the lymph nodes. The two major types of lymphoma are Hodgkin's disease and non-Hodgkin's lymphoma. Lymphoma of the brain is considered an AIDS-defining illness unless HIV infection is completely ruled out.

Macrophage: A type of white blood cell that destroys degenerated cells and blood tissue. Macrophages break down antigens, foreign particles such as bacteria that provoke an immune response. Macrophages appear to serve as a reservoir of HIV in the body, and have the potential to transmit HIV to all other cells with which they come into contact.

Meningitis: An infection of the meninges, the covering of the brain and spinal cord. In HIV-infected persons, meningitis is most often caused by cryptococcus.

Molluscum: A viral infection that causes small, white bumps on the skin, especially in the beard area of HIV-positive men.

MRI: Magnetic resonance imaging (MRI) produces three-dimensional images of the body similar to a CAT scan, but without using X-rays.

Mycobacterium avium Complex (MAC): MAC is the most common HIV-related disorder caused by mycobacteria, organisms found in soil, food, and water. In persons with AIDS, infection throughout the body is common, with disease often beginning in the gut. Common symptoms of MAC include night sweats, fever, weight loss, and diarrhea.

Myopathy: Any disease of the muscles is called myopathy. It can cause wasting of tissue, leaving muscles sore and weak. HIV and some medications can affect muscle tissue directly.

Neuropathy: A general term for any disease of the peripheral nerves, those that control muscles and sensation. Symptoms include burning pain (especially in the feet), loss of sensation, numbness, tingling, muscle weakness, or even paralysis.

Neutropenia: A shortage of neutrophils, the most common form of white blood cell. The condition may be caused by infections, medications, or disease of the bone marrow, the part of the body where neutrophils are produced.

Night sweats: Night sweats are episodes of heavy sweating during the night. They can be so severe that a person may need to change her or his sheets and nightclothes many times. In HIV-infected people night sweats, fever, and chills warn of HIV-related disease progression or other infection.

Opportunistic infections: Infections or diseases that "seize the opportunity" of weakened immunity to take hold in the body. Many are caused by agents that are commonly present in our bodies or environment but which do not generally cause disease in healthy persons because of intact immunity. PCP and KS are both opportunistic infections.

Oral Hairy Leukoplakia: This infection is distinguished by creamy white patches in the mouth and a striped pattern on the sides of the tongue that resembles small hairs. It is generally not painful and is not considered contagious.

Pneumocystis Carinii Pneumonia (PCP): Formerly the most common life-threatening opportunistic infection diagnosed in people with AIDS. It is caused by the parasite Pneumocystis carinii. Symptoms include shortness of breath, a dry and persistent cough, and unexplained fevers higher than 101 degrees that last more than 24 hours.

Progressive Multifocal Leukoencephalopathy (PML): A viral infection of the brain causing memory impairment, motor control loss, and diminished strength. It can lead to coma and even death.

Retrovirus: A specific type of virus unknown in humans until very recently. HIV is a retrovirus.

Shingles: A disease caused by one type of herpes virus called herpes zoster, it is the cause of chicken pox in children. In adults, it infects nerve cells and appears as small, painful white blisters.

Thrombocytopenia: A decrease in the number of platelets, cell fragments that help control bleeding. It may be caused by infections or drugs that combat HIV. When the number of platelets is low, bleeding can occur spontaneously, resulting in bleeding gums or bruise marks on the skin known as purpura.

Toxoplasmosis: Caused by parasites in undercooked meats, cat feces, and contaminated water, toxoplasmosis infects the brain and central nervous system, and is evidenced by memory loss, motor control dysfunction, and mood swings.

Tuberculosis: A highly contagious disease affecting the lungs. Symptoms may include fatigue, night sweats, weight loss, and a cough that produces mucus and sometimes blood.

Vaccine: A substance used to protect the body against a certain virus or germ. There is no available vaccine against HIV.

Virus: A microorganism causing infectious diseases. It can only survive in living cells, which it invades and destroys as it multiplies.

Wasting Syndrome: AIDS wasting syndrome is a loss of ten percent or more of body weight with no explanation other than HIV infection. Contributing factors include malabsorbtion due to opportunistic infections, diarrhea, lack of adequate food intake because of decreased appetite, or vomiting.

Western Blot: A highly accurate blood test which is able to identify HIV antibody in a blood sample. It is employed to confirm HIV seropositivity when the patient has already tested positive with the ELISA.

Commonly Used HIV (and General Medical) Terms

Acute infection: Any infection that begins suddenly, with intense or severe symptoms, is called acute.

Aerosolize: To change a liquid medicine, such as pentamadine, into a mist so it can be inhaled.

Antidepressants: Medications that help control depression, popularly (and inaccurately) known as "mood elevators."

Asypmtomatic: Having no symptoms; free of any sensation of poor health.

Bacteria: Single-cell organisms that lack any nucleus.

Biopsy: Any procedure in which a sample of tissue is removed from the body for examination in a laboratory.

Bronchoscopy: A procedure in which a tube-like instrument is inserted through the mouth or nose, enabling the physician to see inside the lungs and obtain tissue samples or smears.

Chemotherapy: The use of drugs to combat disease, especially cancer.

Chronic infection: An infection that persists for longer than a couple of weeks or tends to recur over time.

Culture: Any method used to grow microorganisms in the laboratory.

Cutaneous: Dealing with the skin.

Cytotoxic: Damaging to cells.

Disseminated: Scattered throughout the body.

Dormant: Inactive, as in a dormant infection.

Double-Blind: A way of investigating drugs or treatments in which neither patients or physicians know which treatment is given to the patient.

Edema: Accumulation of excess fluid in cells, tissues, or parts of the body.

Fungus: A general term used to describe a variety of yeasts and molds.

Incubation period: The time between exposure to an infection and the first signs of the body's response.

Infection: The invasion of the body by bacteria, fungi, viruses, or other organisms.

Inflammation: When tissue becomes swollen, red and heated, usually in response to an infection.

Intravenous: Within or into the veins.

Invasive: An invasive disease is one in which organisms or cancer cells are spreading throughout the body; an invasive medical procedure is one in which a device is inserted into the body.

Laboratory marker: Results of any test (most often a blood test) used to detect or monitor a disease process.

Malabsorbtion: Failure of the intestines to absorb food or nutrients properly.

Mucous membrane: The moist lining of the eyes, nose, mouth, rectum, and genitals.

Open-Label Trial: A study in which all participants know what drugs they are taking. The opposite of a blind or double-blind trial.

Organism: Any form of life, especially microscopic ones capable of causing disease.

Pap smear: Microscopic examination of cells obtained by scraping the lining of the vagina and the cervix.

Parasite: Any form of life that lives on another; usually refers to protozoans, tapeworms, amebas, and the like.

Prophylaxis: Prevention; a treatment intended to preserve health.

Protozoa: Simple animal-like organisms composed of only one or a few cells.

Spinal Tap/lumbar puncture: Insertion of a needle into the spine to obtain a sample of spinal fluid.

Steroids: Medications used to combat inflammation.

Stool culture: A way of finding the cause of diarrhea by taking a stool sample and growing the organisms contained in it.

Symptomatic: A person who doesn't feel well and has medical problems that can be observed or measured.

Thrush: Yeast infection occurring in the mouth.

Support Materials

Resource Sheet: Common HIV (and Medical) Abbreviations

Ab	Antibody.
ACTG	AIDS Clinical Trials Group.
ACTU	AIDS Clinical Trials Unit.
Ag	Antigen.
AIDS	Acquired Immune Deficiency Syndrome.
AP	Aerosol pentamadine.
ARC	AIDS-Related Complex.
ASO	AIDS Service Organization.
bid	Twice a day.
biw	Twice a week.
CBC	Complete blood count.
CBO	Community-based organization.
CD4	CD4 blood cells or T4 cells.
CDC	Centers for Disease Control.
CMV	Cytomegalovirus.
CNS	Central nervous system.
CSF	Cerebrospinal fluid.
DNA	Deoxyribonucleic acid.
dx	Diagnosis.
EBV	Epstein-Barr virus.
ELISA	Enzyme-Linked Immunosorbent Assay.
FDA	Food and Drug Administration.
GI	Gastrointestinal.
Hgb	Hemoglobin.
HIV	Human Immunodeficiency Virus.
HSV	Herpes simplex virus.
Hx	History.
IDU	Injecting drug user.
IFN	Interferon.
IND	Investigational new drug.
IV	Intravenous.
KS	Kaposi's sarcoma.
LIP	Lymphocytic interstitial pneumonitis.
MAI	*Mycobacterium avium-intracellulare.*
MAC	*Mycobacterium avium* complex.
mcg	Microgram.
mg	Milligram.

373

MTD	Maximum tolerated dose.
MU	Million units.
NCI	National Cancer Institute.
NDA	New Drug Application.
NHL	Non-Hodgkin's Lymphoma.
NIAID	National Institute of Allergy and Infectious Diseases.
NIH	National Institutes of Health.
OI	Opportunistic infection.
PCP	*Pneumocystis carnii* pneumonia.
PCR	Polymerase chain reaction.
PGL	Persistent generalized lymphadenopathy.
PHS	Public Health Service.
PLWA	Person living with AIDS.
PML	Progressive multifocal leukoencephalopathy.
PO	By mouth.
prn	As needed.
PWA	Person with AIDS.
PWHIV	Person with HIV.
q	Every.
qd	Once daily.
q4h	Every four hours.
RBC	Red blood cell.
RNA	Ribonucleic acid.
RT	Reverse transcriptase.
SC	Subcutaneous.
STD	Sexually-transmitted disease.
sx	Symptom.
TMP-SMX	Trimethoprim-sulfamethoxazole.
tx	Treatment.
WBC	White blood cell.

Resource Sheet: Common HIV Medications in Use

Antiretrovirals

HIV is a retrovirus, and drugs which attack HIV are termed antiretrovirals. No antiretroviral actually kills HIV or completely stops it from weakening the immune system or CD4 cells, but antiretrovirals can slow down replication of HIV in the body, and therefore the course of HIV-related disease. The antiretrovirals we have today are expensive and can cause serious side effects.

But with all their flaws, antiretrovirals have had a considerable impact on the longevity and well-being of people living with HIV-related illness. In trials involving thousands of HIV-infected people, antiretrovirals have been shown to extend the period of time in which people are asymptomatic, reduce the frequency and severity of HIV-related illnesses, and increase the length of life for persons with AIDS. The benefits and harmful effects of long-term treatment are still relatively unknown.

Antiretrovirals have been shown to increase CD4 counts or slow their decline, increase body weight, improve other laboratory indicators of HIV disease, and delay or reduce mental or neurological impairments. Not everyone experiences these benefits.

Almost all side effects of antiretrovirals occur more often and with greater severity in people who have advanced HIV disease, or in people who start retroviral therapy late in the course of their infection.

The leading retrovirals in use today are **AZT, ddI, ddC,** and **d4T.**

AZT—also called azidothymidine, zidovudine and Retrovir, AZT was the first drug licensed for treating HIV. It is approved by the FDA for HIV-positive people with CD4 counts below 500.

Many large studies have established that AZT increases survival among people with AIDS and delays the onset of AIDS in HIV-positive people who have no symptoms.

Some users of AZT may experience drug-related fatigue, rash, nausea, headache, and muscle pain during their first month of treatment; these side effects often resolve during the first few weeks. Myopathy may occur after long-term use. Many patients have been using AZT therapy for more than five years.

AZT is not without controversy, however. Some people consider it unacceptably toxic, and have avoided its use. As with all antiretrovirals, patients must weigh all possible benefits and undesirable effects before beginning therapy.

ddI—also called didooxyinosine and Videx, this antiretroviral is licensed for use by people who cannot tolerate AZT or who have taken AZT for a long time and developed a resistance.

The most common side effect of ddI is pancreatitis and inflammation of the pancreas. Symptoms include abdominal pain, nausea and vomiting—and pancreatitis can be fatal. ddI may also cause peripheral neuropathy. Pancreatitis and peripheral neuropathy are usually reversible when detected early and if use of ddI is halted.

ddC—also called dideoxycytidine, zalcitabine and Hivid, this antiretroviral is licensed for use only in combination with AZT; it cannot be employed as a single therapy.

ddC has received mixed results in clinical trials, sometimes performing as effectively as AZT, sometimes less so. A primary problem with ddC has been peripheral neuropathy, which, in a number of studies, occurs in 16% of patients. Pancreatitis is another reported side effect.

And a fourth antiretroviral, **d4T,** is still in clinical trials, but shows promise. It is also called Stavudine, and is a close cousin of AZT and ddI. It has been recommended for people who cannot tolerate AZT or ddI or who show no improvement after therapy with AZT or ddI.

Non-antiretrovirals

There are a large number of drugs now in use to treat many opportunistic infections associated with HIV disease. Their effectiveness, cost, and side effects vary considerably, and a detailed discussion of such is not possible here. But a brief survey of common drugs and their intended purpose would include:

acyclovir (Zovirax)—used to control herpes simplex.
amikacin—one of the drugs used to control MAC.
amitriptyline (Elavil)—used to treat depression.
amphotericin B—an antibiotic for severe fungal infections.
amoxicillin—a form of penicillin commonly used for sinus and respiratory infections.
ampicillin—another common form of penicillin.
azithromycin (Zithromax)—an antibiotic used to treat sinus and lung infections.
ciprofloxacin (Cipro)—an antibiotic commonly used for lung and urinary infections.
clarithromycin—one of the newer drugs used to treat MAC.
clindamycin—an antibiotic commonly used for PCP and toxoplasmosis.
clotrimazole (Lotrimin, Mycelex)—used for fungal infections of the skin and vagina.
dapsone—one form of prophylaxis for PCP.
erythromycin—an antibiotic commonly used for respiratory infections.
erythropoietin—a substance which stimulates red blood cell production.
fluconazole (Diflucan)—used for control or prevention of thrush.
foscarnet (Foscavir)—one of two drugs available to treat CMV.
ganciclovir—the first drug approved for treatment of CMV.
Heptavax—a vaccine for hepatitis B.
interferon—used for control of Kaposi's sarcoma.
isoniazid (INH)—one of the most commonly used anti-TB drugs.
ketoconazole (Nizoral)—a medication for fungal infections.
megestrol (Megace)—used to stimulate appetite and weight gain.
nystatin (Mycostatin)—a drug used for control of fungal infections.
pentamadine—used for prevention or treatment of PCP.
Pneumovax—a vaccine to prevent pneumococcal pneumonia.
prednisone—used to fight inflammation.
pyrazinamide—one of the anti-TB agents.
pyrimethamine (Fansidar)—used for treatment of toxoplasmosis.
rifabutin—commonly-used drug for TB.
TMP/SMX (Bactrim, Septra)—used for prevention or treatment of PCP.

Section Five:
APPENDICES

Appendices

In the public health management of HIV disease, one dilemma that has consistently surfaced has to do with HIV-infected persons who cannot or will not change their behavior, according to public health guidelines, to reduce the risk of infecting others through sexual intercourse or needle-sharing. What should society do, for example, if an HIV-positive person, who is aware of their HIV serostatus, continues to engage in unsafe sex with others? The question is problematic because the answer requires a sensitive balance between individual liberty and the "public good," however that may be defined.

There are few effective answers, and where there are, one can always find exceptions that do not fit the rule. Some very draconian legislation has been proposed in the name of "protecting the public," and on the other hand, some jurisdictions have chosen to avoid the dilemmas altogether.

Minnesota's response is one example of a fairly balanced approach, though it is still far from perfect. It is outlined, in the form of a bulletin issued by the Minnesota Department of Human Services, below.

INFORMATIONAL BULLETIN NO. 89-53A   January 17, 1989

TO: Chairperson, Board of County Commissioners
Attention: Director
Chairperson, Human Services Board
Attention: Director
Chairperson, Community Health Board
Attention: Director
Chairperson, Mental Health Centers
Attention: Director
Attention: Directors, Rule 12/36 Providers
Attention: Directors, Rule 14 Providers
Attention: Directors, Rule 5 Providers

SUBJECT: 1) Procedures for notifying the Commissioner of Health of persons with communicable diseases who pose a health threat to others; and
2) Authorized actions the Commissioner of Health may take to alleviate health threats posed by others.

I. PURPOSE

The purpose of this bulletin is to provide information to mental health providers to facilitate serving persons infected with a communicable disease, including human immunodeficiency virus (HIV, the causative agent of AIDS), hepatitis B virus (HBV), or *Mycobacterium tuberculosis* (*M. tuberculosis*). As additional information, a recent article from *Minnesota Medicine* on the confidentiality of medical records is attached.

II. BACKGROUND

The Health Threat Procedures Act (Minnesota Statutes, sections 144.4171 to 144.4186) grants authority to the Commissioner of Health, or a local board of health with delegated authority from the Commissioner, to deal with communicable disease carriers who pose a health threat to others. The Act outlines the procedures the Commissioner of

Health and the courts must follow when intervening against such a carrier and takes into account the full due process rights of the individual.

Under the Act, communicable disease means:

"a disease or condition that causes serious illness, serious disability, or death, the infectious agent of which may pass or be carried, directly or indirectly, from the body of one person to the body of another" (Minnesota Statutes, section 144.4172, subdivision 2).

Directly transmitted means predominantly:

"(1) sexually transmitted;

(2) blood-borne; or

(3) transmitted through direct or intimate skin contact"

(Minnesota Statutes, section 144.4172, subdivision 5).

(e.g., HIV, HBV)

Indirectly transmitted means:

"any transmission not defined by" the above *(Minnesota Statutes, section 144.4172, subdivision 9)*

(e.g., M. Tuberculosis)

Carrier means:

"a person who serves as a potential source of infection and who harbors or who the commissioner reasonably believes to be harboring a specific infectious agent whether or not there is present discernible clinical disease. In the absence of a medically accepted test, the commissioner may reasonably believe an individual to be a carrier only when a determination based upon specific facts justifies an inference that the individual harbors a specific infectious agent" (Minnesota Statutes, section 144.4172, subdivision 1).

Health threat to others means that:

"a carrier demonstrates an inability or unwillingness to act in such a manner as to not place others at risk of exposure to infection that causes serious illness, serious disability, or death." It includes one or more of the following:

(1) With respect to an indirectly transmitted communicable disease:
    (a) behavior by a carrier which has been demonstrated epidemiologically to transmit or which evidences a careless disregard for the transmission of the disease to others; or
    (b) a substantial likelihood that a carrier will transmit a communicable disease to others as is evidenced by a carrier's past behavior, or by statements of a carrier that are credible

indicators of a carrier's intention.
(2) With respect to a directly transmitted communicable disease:
- (a) repeated behavior by a carrier which has been demonstrated epidemiologically to transmit or which evidences a careless disregard for the transmission of the disease to others;
- (b) a substantial likelihood that a carrier will repeatedly transmit a communicable disease to others as evidenced by a carrier's past behavior, or by statements of a carrier that are credible indicators of a carrier's intention;
- (c) affirmative misrepresentation by a carrier of the carrier's status prior to engaging in any behavior which has been demonstrated epidemiologically to transmit the disease; or
- (d) the activities referenced in clause (1) if the person whom the carrier places at risk is: (i) a minor, (ii) of diminished capacity by reason of mood-altering chemicals, including alcohol, (iii) has been diagnosed as having significantly subaverage intellectual functioning, (iv) has an organic disorder of the brain or a psychiatric disorder of thought, mood, perception, orientation, or memory which substantially impairs judgment, behavior, reasoning, or understanding, (v) adjudicated incompetent, or (vi) a vulnerable adult as defined in Minnesota Statutes, section 626.557.

(3) "Violation by a carrier of any part of a court order issued pursuant to this chapter" (Minnesota Statutes, section 144.4172, subdivision 8).

III. COMMUNICATING TO THE COMMISSIONER OF HEALTH REGARDING PERSONS BELIEVED TO POSE A HEALTH THREAT TO OTHERS

Minnesota Statutes, section 144.4175, subdivision 1 states that "any licensed health professional or other human services professional regulated by the state who has knowledge or reasonable cause to believe that a person is a health threat to others or has engaged in noncompliant behavior...may report that information to the commissioner."

The statute also states that a professional "who has knowledge or reasonable cause to believe that a person is a health threat to others or has engaged in noncompliant behavior, and who makes a report in good faith under subdivision 1, is not subject to liability for reporting in any civil, administrative, disciplinary, or criminal action" (Minnesota Statutes, section 144.4175, subdivision 2).

To facilitate effective and efficient reporting of carriers who are health threats to others or noncompliant, the Act provides for a waiver of privilege which may otherwise prohibit certain health and human services professionals from disclosing pertinent information and opinions about patients and clients. These professionals include licensed physicians or surgeons, dentists, chiropractors, public health officers, registered nurses, psychologists, consulting psychologists, and sexual assault counselors. Minnesota Statutes, section 144.4175 states that "any privilege otherwise created in (Minnesota Statutes) section 595.02, clauses (d), (e), (g), and (j), with respect to persons who make a report under subdivision 1, is waived regarding any information about a carrier as a health threat to others or about a carrier's non-compliant behavior in any investigation or action."

Mental health providers should note that Minnesota Statutes, section 144.4186 classifies all data on individuals contained in a health directive as private. Such data is thus not available to the public but is accessible to the individual subject of the data.

IV. AUTHORIZED ACTION BY THE COMMISSIONER OF HEALTH

When a report of a suspected carrier who poses a health threat is received at the Minnesota Department of Health, an investigation is conducted to confirm that the person is, in fact, both a carrier and a health threat to others, as defined by the Act. Efforts are then made to alleviate the carrier's health threat behavior through education and counseling. If the carrier continues to demonstrate an inability or unwillingness to conduct himself or herself in such a manner as to not place others at risk despite education and counseling, then the Commissioner of Health may issue a directive to the carrier. The directive, a written statement, or, in urgent circumstances, an oral statement, may require a carrier to cooperate with health authorities in efforts to prevent or control transmission of communicable disease and must be individual, specific, and cannot be issued to a class of persons (Minnesota Statutes, section 4172, subdivision 6).

If a carrier fails or refuses to comply with the commissioner's directive, then the carrier is considered "noncompliant" and the commissioner may petition the court for relief. Upon a finding by the court that the commissioner has proven the allegations set forth in the petition, the court may order one of several remedies available, with the least restrictive alternative used.

For procedural and informational questions, and to make a report of a person who may be a health threat to others, contact:

>AIDS Prevention Services Section
>Minnesota Department of Health
>717 Delaware St. S.E.
>Minneapolis, MN 55440
>(612) 623-5698

Daycare centers, schools, families, and others who may have contact with children with HIV or HBV will find the following outline of daily care concerns useful. Much of it will also prove valuable to any setting—workplaces, service sites, homes—where individials are living or working alongside individuals with HIV disease.

Daily Care of the Child with Acquired Immunodeficiency Syndrome (AIDS), Human Immunodeficiency Virus (HIV) Infection, and Related Conditions

The child with Acquired Immunodeficiency Syndrome (AIDS) is unable to defend himself or herself from a variety of infections. This condition usually becomes apparent early in life.

These guidelines were developed in order to protect the child from infections and protect anyone caring for the child from the possibility, however remote, of acquiring HIV infection from the child. There have been *no* documented cases of persons acquiring HIV infection from routine care of infected children.

The person caring for a child infected with HIV should avoid contact with the child's bodily fluids. The bodily fluids of all persons should be considered to contain potentially infectious agents such as bacteria and viruses. The term "bodily fluids" includes blood, drainage from cuts and scrapes, feces, urine, vomitus, respiratory secretions (e.g., nasal discharge), semen, cervical secretions, and saliva. Contact with bodily fluids presents a risk of infection with a variety of bacteria and viruses, including HIV. In general, however, the risk is very low and dependent on a variety of factors, including the type of fluid with which contact is made and the type of contact made with it.

The following guidelines are consistent with good child care, even in the absence of known HIV, and will assist persons caring for HIV-infected children by encouraging good health practice.

Handwashing

Routine handwashing is one of the best ways to prevent infections. Proper handwashing requires the use of soap and water and vigorous washing. Hands should be lathered well and scrubbed for 15–30 seconds, paying attention to the backs of hands, wrists, and fingernails, then rinsed under running water for approximately 10 seconds. Soap suspends easily removeable soil, bacteria and viruses, allowing them to be washed away. Make sure to dry hands thoroughly with a clean towel after washing. Always wash hands in this manner after using gloves.

Feeding

Bacteria can get into formula bottles in several ways: (1) from the hands, nose, or throat of the person preparing the bottle; (2) from an unsanitary counter area; (3) through an inadequately cleaned bottle; (4) through unsanitary water used to prepare the formula; and (5) through formula held too long in storage. For these reasons formula must be carefully prepared.

It is not necessary to wear gloves unless you have a skin rash or an open break in the skin.

Putting an infant to bed with a bottle of milk or juice is not recommended, since bacteria grow quickly in both of those fluids; if it is necessary, the bottle should be removed after the child is asleep. It is best to hold the baby during feedings.

Unpasteurized milk and milk products have been linked to intestinal infections such as salmonellosis; they should not be included in the child's diet.

Feeding of Solid Foods

Bacteria from the mouth, if left in a partially empty jar of food, can cause spoilage. To avoid contaminating an entire jar of food, do not feed directly from the jar. Use a clean spoon to remove the amount you think the baby will eat and place it in a bowl or cup. If the baby wants more, use a new clean utensil to spoon additional food from the jar. Never put food back in the jar and always use the contents of opened baby food jars within 24 hours.

Fruits and vegetables should be peeled or cooked before serving to the child. Meats should always be thoroughly cooked.

Do not feed the child with your fingers or hands; use utensils. Wash all utensils with hot sudsy water followed by thorough rinsing and drying. Dishwashers are fine.

Diapering

Prompt diaper changing and cleansing the soiled area can prevent diaper rash and promote the comfort of the child. Always wash your hands before and after changing diapers. A sink with hot and cold running water should be readily available. The diaper-changing area must be physically separate from food preparation and serving areas.

Any skin-care products should be labeled for the child's sole use, in order to prevent cross-contamination of ointments, since they are applied by direct hand contact.

Sponges and cloth towels used in the diaper-changing area should be restricted for that use only. They should be laundered daily in hot soapy water.

Disposable diapers are recommended because they require less handling than cloth diapers. If you are using cloth diapers, clean ones should be carefully stored to prevent accidental contact with soiled ones. Solid matter should be removed from cloth diapers in the toilet. Place soiled cloth diapers in a sturdy plastic bag until laundered, on a daily basis, in hot soapy water. A separate container, also lined with a plastic bag, should be available in the changing area for soiled disposable diapers. This bag should be removed daily, sealed, and discarded with other household garbage.

If contact with feces cannot be avoided, latex gloves should be used while diapering. This precaution is necessary only in the presence of loose, watery stools. Dispose of gloves after each use, and wash hands after removing gloves.

After each diapering, the changing area should be cleaned with a sanitizing solution. A mixture composed of 1 part common household bleach to ten parts water is more than adequate. Gloves should be worn when using a bleach solution of that concentration. The solution should be labeled and stored away from children. A plastic spray bottle of water can be employed to rinse off surfaces after sanitizing with a bleach solution.

Use of Potty Chairs and Toilets

Potty chair frames should be smooth and easy to clean. The waste receptacle should be removeable. Sanitize the chair and frame with a bleach solution after each use. Wash your hands—and the child's—after use of potty chair or toilet.

Skin Care

Since the body of a child with HIV infection or AIDS is not as able to defend against common bacteria and viruses, it is important to keep her or his skin clean and intact (free of cuts or openings). Regular baths, proper drying, and use of lotions to prevent dryness or irritations (as recommended by the child's physician) is critical.

Keep the bathtub free of detergents which may cause dermatitis or other skin irritations. You should shield the child from both sunburns and windburns, being careful in both very hot and very cold weather.

If the child has a cold, wash his or her face and hands more frequently.

For all infants—especially those with HIV infection—fingernails and toenails should be cut straight across and kept trim, to avoid infection or ingrowing and to minimize scratching. Always dry feet after bathing to prevent fungal infections. Observe feet for irritations from shoes and possible allergic reactions to shoes or socks.

Cleaning and Laundering

In general, clothing and linens may be laundered with those of other household members. However, laundry visibly soiled with blood, stool, vomit, or urine should be wiped clean with a disposable towel, placed in a plastic bag, and laundered separately in hot soapy water. Disposable gloves should be worn when wiping soiled areas, and wash hands after removing gloves.

Household bleach is a very effective disinfectant. Bleach may be added to the wash according to manufacturer's instructions, but clothing should be completely rinsed of bleach residue, since it may cause skin irritations and subsequent infections. For noncolorfast materials, a phenolic disinfectant (such as Lysol) can be added to the wash load.

Cloth toys may be laundered in the washing machine.

If dry cleaning is necessary, any visibly soiled areas should be wiped clean with a damp paper towel (which should be discarded with other waste from the child).

Housekeeping Chores

In general, housekeeping chores can be performed in a routine manner. However, surfaces of equipment or furniture contaminated with blood, urine or feces should be cleaned thoroughly and disinfected. A 1:10 dilution of bleach or other disinfectant should be applied and left on surfaces for several minutes, and then rinsed completely. Wear gloves when cleaning soiled areas, and wash hands after removing gloves. Mops and brooms should be disinfected after use by soaking in a 1:10 dilution of bleach for five minutes (longer soaking may disintegrate them). *Caution:* Do not mix cleaning solutions, such as bleach and ammonia. Doing so will release harmful fumes.

Rugs and cloth furniture which have become contaminated with bodily fluids may be cleaned with a rug shampoo containing a germicidal detergent, then vacuumed as usual. Any solid material should be removed first.

Trash can be disposed as in any household. Body wastes can be flushed down the toilet. Other trash may be handled by normal means (weekly trash pick-ups from cans lined with sturdy plastic bags).

Normal kitchen cleaning can help prevent the spread of bacteria and other organisms. Keep the refrigerator clean to prevent mold formation. Be sure counter tops are cleaned before and after food preparation.

Play

Do not allow the child's toys to be shared or borrowed. Toys should be kept as clean as possible. Dishwasher-safe toys may be disinfected by running them through a complete cycle. Other toys can be disinfected by dipping or spraying with a 1:10 solution of household bleach, then rinsed off with water.

Children can go on swings and play in parks, but do not take them out if they are feeling sick. Contact between children playing together will *not* transmit HIV. The parents or guardians of any child living with HIV infection will need to decide who does and does not need to know about the child's HIV status.

Keeping pets can be problematic. While pets offer much-needed companionship and affection, they may also harbor bacteria and parasites that could infect the child. If you do have a pet, it is essential that the child not have contact with its feces, urine, or vomitus. In addition, you should avoid animals that bite or scratch. Maintain the health of the pet and make sure it receives up-to-date immunizations. Pets that are exclusively indoor animals and isolated from other animals pose the least risk.

Health Care

Though parents are generally encouraged to handle minor illnesses at home, the child's physician should be contacted at the beginning of even minor problems. Since children with HIV infection may not handle other infections as well as healthy children do, it's important to be able to recognize signs and symptoms of common illnesses. They include red watery eyes, sticky eyelids, red or scaly skin, yellowish skin or eyes, rashes, runny nose, sores around the mouth, fever, sore throat, coughing, increased tiredness, muscle aches, crankiness, change in appetite, vomiting, diarrhea, or changes in the color of urine or stool.

To help you monitor the child's health you will need a thermometer. After each use it should be cleaned with soap and water, soaked in alcohol for ten minutes, dried, and stored in its container.

If the child becomes ill with diarrhea or vomiting, you should use gloves if cleaning or changing diapers. Gloves should also be worn for treating any bleeding cuts, bites, nosebleeds or burns, and you should wash hands after removing gloves. Any dressing or bandages used to clean and protect the child should be discarded in a sealed plastic bag.

The usual immunization schedule for HIV-infected children may be altered; your physician will advise you. Certain immunizations may not be given and substitutions may be required. Some additional vaccinations against influenza or pneumonia may be advised.

Medical examinations and checkups may be scheduled more frequently than usual. You may be asked to monitor the growth of the child more closely.

Try to prevent children from visiting others who are sick from acute infections such as tonsillitis or bronchitis. Common colds among family members and friends will occur and transmission to the child with HIV cannot always be avoided; however, if you or others around the child develop contagious diseases, the child's physician should be contacted. You should make arrangements, in advance, for an alternate caregiver should the primary caregiver become ill.

Summary

At first glance these procedures may seem difficult and overwhelming. However, many of them represent good health care for *all* infants and children. The special precautions for infants with HIV and AIDS have been described in detail to protect the child from additional infections and to minimize the already-remote possibility of HIV transmission from child to caregiver.

RESOURCES

National HIV/AIDS Referral Lines and Hotlines

American Civil Liberties Union
AIDS and Civil Liberties Project
(215) 592-1513

American National Red Cross
(800) 26-BLOOD

National AIDS Hotline
(800) 342-AIDS (English)
(800) 344-SIDA (Spanish)
(800) 243-243-7889 (TTY/TDD)

National Institute of Allergy and Infectious Diseases (NIAID)
(800) TRIALS-A

Project INFORM
Treatments and Experimental Drugs
(800) 822-7422

National Organizations, Foundations, and Coalitions

AIDS Action Council
2033 M Street, N.W., Suite 801
Washington, DC 20036
(202) 293-2886

AIDS Project Los Angeles
6721 Romain Street

Los Angeles, CA 90038
(213) 962-1600

American Association of Physicians for Human Rights
P. O. Box 14366
San Francisco, CA 94114
(415) 255-4547

American Association of School Administrators
Office of Minority Affairs-AIDS
1801 N. Moore Street
Arlington, VA 22209
(703) 528-0700

American College Health Association
1300 Piccard Drive, Suite 200
Rockville, MD 20850
(301) 963-1100

American Dental Association
211 E. Chicago Avenue
Chicago, IL 60611
(312) 440-2543

American Federation of Teachers
555 New Jersey Avenue, N.W.
Washington, DC 20001
(202) 879-4400

American Foundation for AIDS Research
1515 Broadway, Suite 3601
New York, NY 10036
(212) 719-0033

American Hospital Association
Special Committee on AIDS/HIV Infections Policy
840 N. Lake Shore Drive
Chicago, IL 60611
(312) 280-6511

American Institute for Teen AIDS Prevention
P.O. Box 136116
Fort Worth, TX 76136   (817) 237-0230

American Medical Association Office of HIV
515 N. State Street
Chicago, IL 60610
(312) 464-4566

American Nurses Association
2420 Pershing Road
Kansas City, MO 64108
(816) 474-5720

American Psychiatric Association AIDS Project
1400 K Street, N.W.
Washington, DC 20005
(202) 682-6104

American Psychological Association Task Force on AIDS
1200 17th Street, N.W.
Washington, DC 20036
(202) 955-7727

American Public Health Association
1015 15th Street, N.W.
Washington, DC 20005

American Red Cross AIDS Education Office
American Red Cross
17th and D Streets, N.W.
Washington, DC 20006
(202) 662-1584

Associated Catholic Charities
Emergency Assistance
Catholic AIDS Network
1618 Monroe Street, N.W.
Washington, DC 20010
(202) 332-8666

Association of State and Territorial Health Officials
AIDS Committee
6728 Old McLean Village Drive
McLean, VA 22101
(703) 556-9222

Appendices

Gay Men's Health Crisis
129 West 20th Street
New York, NY 10011
(202) 807-6664

Hispanic AIDS Forum
Room 505
121 Avenue of the Americas
New York, NY 10013
(212) 966-6336

Human Rights Campaign Fund
1012 14th Street, N.W., Suite 607
Washington, DC 20005
(202) 628-4160

Insurance Industry AIDS Initiative
1001 Pennsylvania Avenue, N.W., Suite 500
Washington, DC 20004-2599
(202) 624-2424

Lambda Legal Defense Fund
666 Broadway
New York, NY 10012
(212) 995-8585

National AIDS Clearinghouse
P.O. Box 6003
Rockville, MN 20850
(800) 458-5231

National Association of Community Health Centers, Inc.
1330 New Hampshire Avenue, N.W., Suite 122
Washington, DC 20036
(202) 659-8008

National Association of People with AIDS
P.O. Box 18345
Washington, DC 20036
(202) 429-2856

National Association of Public Hospitals AIDS Committee
Suite 800

1212 New York Avenue, N.W.
Washington, DC 20005
(202) 408-0223

National Association of State Boards of Education
1012 Cameron Street
Alexandria, VA 22314
(703) 684-4000

National Community AIDS Partnership
1726 M Street, N.W.
Suite 501
Washington, DC 20036
(202) 429-2820

National Council of Churches
Minority Task Force on AIDS
92 St. Nicholas Avenue, Room 1B
New York, NY 10026
(212) 749-2816

National Conference of State Legislatures
1050 17th Street, Suite 2100
Denver, CO 80265
(303) 623-7800

National Gay and Lesbian Task Force
1517 U Street. N. W.
Washington, DC 20009
(202) 332-6483

National Hemophilia Foundation
104 East 40th Street, Suite 506
New York, NY 10016
(212) 682-5510

National Lawyers Guild AIDS Network
558 Capp Street
San Francisco, CA 94110
(415) 824-8884

National Leadership Coalition on AIDS
1150 17th Street, N.W., Suite 202

Washington, DC 20036
(202) 429-0930

National Minority AIDS Council
300 Eye Street, N.W., Suite 400
Washington, DC 20002
(202) 544-1076

National Native American AIDS Prevention Center
6239 College Avenue, Suite 201
Oakland, CA 94618
(415) 658-2051

National PTA
700 N. Rush Street
Chicago, IL 60611
(312) 787-0977

National Parents Resource Institute
50 Hurt Plaza
Hurt Building, Suite 210
Atlanta, GA 30303
(404) 577-4500

National Sherrifs' Association AIDS Project
1450 Duke Street
Alexandria, VA 22314
(703) 836-7827

People of Color Against AIDS Network
1200 South Jackson, Suite 25
Seattle, WA 98144
(206) 322-7061

Planned Parenthood Federation of America
P.O. Box 6182
San Francisco, CA 94101
(415) 864-5855

Sex Information and Education Council of the United States (SIECUS)
130 West 42nd Street, 25th Floor
New York, NY 10036
(212) 819-9770

The Names Project
2362 Market
San Francisco, CA 94114
(415) 863-5511

WHO Global Program on AIDS
1121 Geneva 27
Switzerland

Federal Government Agencies

Centers for Disease Control (Atlanta)
1600 Clifton Road
Atlanta, GA 30333
(404) 639-0975

Centers for Disease Control (Washington, DC)
Hubert H. Humphrey Building, Room 714B
200 Independence Avenue, S.W.
Washington, DC 20201
(202) 245-8598

Department of Education
Office of the Secretary
400 Maryland Avenue, S.W. FOB-6
Washington, DC 20202
(202) 732-3630

Department of Health and Human Services
Assistant Secretary for Health
Hubert H. Humphrey Building, Room 716 G
200 Independence Avenue, S.W.
Washington, DC 20201
(202) 619-0257

Food and Drug Administration
5600 Fishers Lane
Parklawn Building, Room 1471

Rockville, MD 20857
(301) 443-1544

National Cancer Institute
National Institutes of Health
Building 31, Room 11 A-48
9000 Rockville Pike
Bethesda, MD 20892
(301) 496-4000

National Institute of Allergy and Infectious Diseases
National Institute of Health
Building 31, Room 7 A-03
9000 Rockville Pike
Bethesda, MD 20982
(301) 496-4000

National Institute on Drug Abuse
5600 Fishers Lane, Room 10-05
Rockville, MD 20857
(301) 443-6480

National Institutes of Health
Building 1
9000 Rockville Pike, Room 6
Bethesda, MD 20892
(301) 496-2433

National Institute of Justice/AIDS Clearinghouse
P.O. Box 6000
Rockville, MD 20850
(301) 251-5500

Public Health Service AIDS Coordinator
Hubert H. Humphrey Building, Room 729 H
200 Independence Avenue, S.W.
Washington, DC 20201
(202) 245-0471

Surgeon General of the United States
Public Health Service
5600 Fishers Lane, Room 18-67
Rockville, MD 20857   (301) 443-4000

Policy Research Groups and Clearinghouses

CDC AIDS Clearinghouse
(301) 251-5641

Computerized AIDS Information Network (CAIN)
1213 N. Highland Avenue
Hollywood, CA 90038
(213) 464-7400

Institute for Health Policy Studies
University of California, San Francisco
1326 Third Avenue
San Francisco, CA 94143
(415) 476-8266

National AIDS Information Clearinghouse
P.O. Box 6003
Rockville, MD 20850
(800) 458-5231